Laboring for Rights

**Unions and Sexual Diversity
Across Nations**

In the series

Queer Politics, Queer Theories

edited by Shane Phelan

Laboring for Rights

Unions and Sexual Diversity Across Nations

EDITED BY

Gerald Hunt

TEMPLE UNIVERSITY PRESS

PHILADELPHIA

Temple University Press, Philadelphia 19122
Copyright © 1999 by Temple University,
except for Chapter 4 copyright © 1999
by Christian Arthur Bain.
Published 1999
Printed in the United States of America

♾ The paper used in this publication meets the requirements of the American
National Standard for Information Sciences—Permanence of Paper for Printed
Library Materials, ANSI Z39.48-1984

Library of Congress Cataloging-in-Publication Data

Laboring for rights: unions and sexual diversity across nations / edited by
Gerald Hunt.
      p.   cm.   —   (Queer politics, queer theories)
   Includes bibliographical references.
   ISBN 1-56639-717-0 (alk. paper)
   ISBN 1-56639-718-9 (pbk.: alk. paper)
     1. Gays—Employment—Case studies. 2. Lesbians—Employment—
Case studies. 3. Trade-union democracy—Case studies. 4. Sexual
orientation. 5. Gay rights. I. Hunt, Gerald, 1948– . II. Series.
   HD6285.L33 1999
   331.5'3–dc21   99-14081
                                                                CIP

Dedicated
with enduring love
to
Grace (Rumney) Hunt
1918–1997

Contents

Acknowledgments

This book examines organized labor's response to inequity concerns raised by gays, lesbians, and other sexual minorities with a collection of original scholarship covering the United States, Canada, Australia, Germany, Britain, France, the Netherlands, South Africa, and parts of the South Pacific. Contributors to this volume include men and women from different racial backgrounds, sexual orientations, and political dispositions. I am deeply indebted to each and every one of them, and I thank them for their outstanding work. A lack of suitable authors and space limitations meant that some potentially interesting countries, such as those in Scandinavia and South America, could not be included, but the door is now open for others to take up the challenge and report on these areas of the world.

I wish to thank a number of research assistants who helped over the course of the project: Michael Johnson and Karen Murray in Toronto, Brent Bauer at the University of Montreal, Angela Desliva in Germany, and Vanessa Farr in South Africa. I am also indebted to Nipissing University, which provided several research grants (funded by the Social Sciences and Humanities Research Council) and granted me a sabbatical leave to complete this project. Various colleagues from Nipissing, in particular Deborah Flynn, provided moral support along the way. I thank Doris Braendel, my editor at Temple, for her no-nonsense approach and wise advise about how to deal with contributors. I also thank Shane Phelan, series editor for Temple, who believed in the project from the beginning and provided many helpful comments along the way. The final product was enormously assisted by the never tiring assistance and counsel of my domestic partner, David Rayside, and the extraordinary editing help of Judi Stevenson.

Finally, I would like to dedicate this book to my mother, Grace (Rumney) Hunt, who died in July 1997. How I wish she could be here to help me celebrate the completion of this book. I am comforted somewhat by knowing exactly what she would say if she could be here: "Where on earth did everyone find all those words!"

Gerald Hunt

| I | **What Can Be Done?**
| | **Sexual Diversity and**
| | **Labor Unions in Perspective**

This book examines organized labor's response to inequity concerns raised by sexual minorities.[1] Although organized labor has often been preoccupied with wage and benefit issues—its policies shaped by traditional conceptions of social class and gender—a number of trade unions and labor federations have expanded their mandate to include equity issues. This is an important development because organized labor remains one of the largest and most powerful of social and political movements. As such, it has the potential to force equity issues onto the agendas of public and private corporations that might otherwise be unreceptive to such concerns. In countries where the percentage of unionized workers is high, labor's influence is readily apparent; in settings where the percentage of unionized workers is relatively small (such as the United States), organized labor remains an important player.

Although labor's response to the equity issues raised by women and racial minorities is well established in the literature, little documentation exists of labor's engagement with those issues raised by gays and lesbians. Lack of attention may reflect the fact that these developments are fairly recent, or it may speak to reluctance on the part of scholars of industrial relations to be associated with issues involving sexuality. In any event, because gay and lesbian activism is increasingly focused on the workplace, and trade unions continue to be an important component in any effort to reshape the experience of work, the topic invites exploration. This book represents the first systematic attempt to document and compare, across nations, the actions taken by organized labor in relation to sexual diversity issues.

The chapters that follow offer considerable evidence of a prospering gay/lesbian/labor alliance in many parts of the world. In 1974, for example, the San Francisco gay and lesbian activist community joined the trade unions in a massive boycott against the products of the Coors Brewing Company in the United States. The unions appealed to this rather unusual (for them) constituency on grounds that the company was extremely anti-union and anti-gay and as part of their hiring practices had been administering lie detector tests during which candidates were asked about such things as their sexual orientation and their attitudes to unions. In return for the gay community's support, the unions involved in the boycott promised among other things that they would help openly gay and lesbian people get jobs in the organizations they represented and that they would publicly support openly gay candidate Harvey Milk's bid for a seat on the city's Board of Supervisors.[2] The boycott proved enormously successful, resulting in a drop in Coors's share of the California beer market from 43 percent to 14 percent. A similar alliance occurred in Britain during the height of Thatcherism: gays and lesbians formed a very influential support group for the coal miners during the strikes of 1984–1985. Subsequently, the National Union of Mine Workers became a vigorous initiator of pro-gay resolutions within the Trade Unions Congress. In South Africa, during the apartheid period of the 1980s, the mine workers' union proved to be an important early venue for openly gay camaraderie. A more recent example can be seen in Germany in 1994, during the reconciliation of legal systems after reunification: unions provided support in striking down the notoriously anti-gay "Paragraph 175" in force in West Germany, enabling the adoption of the more liberal East German law. Another recent example is the Canadian Union of Public Employees' successful 1998 legal challenge to the heterosexual bias in the Income Tax Act. Noteworthy as well is the August 1997 recognition by the American Federation of Labor–Congress of Industrial Organizations (AFL-CIO) of the gay/lesbian/bisexual caucus, "Pride at Work," as a formal constituency group.[3]

These chapters also indicate that attempts at gay/lesbian/union alliances have had their share of disappointments—labor unions' passive stance in the marriage debate in Hawai'i is an example. Overall, however, throughout the 1990s such alliances have become more common and have achieved many of their objectives. For sexual diversity activists, union support holds forth the promise of more rapid reduction in discriminatory practices in the workplace. For labor, these alliances create new constituencies and advocates for a trade union movement now beleaguered by declining membership.

What Can Labor Do?

The workplace has become an important site of activism for gays and lesbians in the 1980s and 1990s because of the centrality of work in most people's lives and because of the blatantly discriminatory policies and practices encountered on the job. Not only is the workplace where most gay and lesbian people spend a great deal of their time and make their livelihood, it is also where they gain or lose a large measure of their self-worth and status. Being devalued and discriminated against at work can lead to serious psychological problems as well as to economic discrepancies. Employment-related issues such as hiring, firing, promotions, benefits, perks, leaves of absence, pensions, allowances, harassment, violence, and education initiatives, all can be shaped to discriminate against sexual minorities in ways that can be economically and psychologically harmful. In recent years, winning full access to employment benefits for those involved in same-sex relationships has become an important focus of lesbian and gay activist energy. Whether or not gaining such benefits is a high personal priority being denied them is now considered a slap in the face to gays and lesbians.[4]

To address employment and workplace discrimination, activists have challenged employers directly, fought for change in relevant legislation, initiated legal challenges, and undertaken extensive educational efforts to highlight the problem of homophobia at work. In tandem with these efforts, some activists have also attempted to forge alliances with the labor movement, seeking its leadership and assistance in confronting injustices perpetuated by governments, employers, or by unions themselves.

In most countries, organized labor has the kind of political, financial, legal, and human resources that make it a powerful and attractive potential partner to activists. Trade unions have the capacity to address inequalities by ensuring that sexual orientation is included as a protected category in nondiscrimination clauses and using this provision to support grievances and arbitration proceedings based on such discrimination. Furthermore, unions can bargain collectively to ensure that same-sex partners are covered in all available benefit provisions. Couching these protections in the appropriate language in union manifestoes, policy statements, and collective agreements is important even in jurisdictions where these rights are included in legislative statutes and constitutions since it provides workers with a local grievance mechanism and makes these injustices more visible to the wider community of workers. Localizing the struggle in this way makes the redress process quicker and less intimidating than appealing to courts and human rights tribunals. Enshrining these rights within union agreements has the added bonus of circumventing a political system that in many settings has proved to be slow, reluctant, fickle, and all too often downright resistant to such changes.

Connections with the trade union movement are especially appealing to gay and lesbian activists because organized labor plays an important role beyond the boundaries of a given workplace. Unions can lend vital support for court and tribunal cases either by direct sponsorship or by the offer of financial support. They can pressure governments for legislative change in discriminatory policies and practices. Where unions are associated with particular political parties, they can use their leverage to help shape party policies on sexual diversity matters. In tripartite systems, such as are found in parts of Europe, unions have access to government policy-making forums that in principle can provide openings to push for progressive policies on sexual orientation.[5]

Partnerships between gay/lesbian/labor activists also have the potential to enhance the goals of organized labor. When issues concerning inequity in benefits and opportunities, harassment, disrespect, and violence within the workplace are raised by gays and lesbians, unions are given a powerful opportunity to affirm their core values of fair representation and equal treatment for all members. They can demonstrate clearly that union membership is of benefit to all workers, including minorities. Nevertheless, it can sometimes be difficult for unions to address the issues raised by gays and lesbians; such issues may involve member-on-member discrimination or they may antagonize members who disagree with them. Issues raised by sexual minorities may require a realignment in bargaining strategies and priorities, not to mention changes in organizational cultures, both of which may be resisted by some union members. Still, successful responses can enhance the loyalty and commitment of members, and unleash new activist energies. Engaging with sexual diversity issues also has the potential to raise labor's profile within a wide range of progressive social-movement networks, potentially opening doors to coalitional opportunities and enhancing the profile, goals, and influence of the labor movement. These kinds of outcomes have become more and more urgent for labor in recent years because union membership worldwide has been in a period of decline, and the potential for bargaining on economic issues has been constrained.

Alliances between equality-seeking groups and organized labor are relatively new in most parts of the world. They have been prompted by the increasing participation of women in the workforce since the 1960s and by the increasing activism of women, cultural minorities, and others calling for changes in union policies and organizational practices. As one commentator noted, "The growth of large, independent social movements focused on, for instance, gender relations, racism, and the environment has encouraged groups that have long experienced subordination within the working class and the labor movement to turn their concerns into serious union issues."[6] In most countries, feminists appear to have been the first to break the mold of traditional labor issues, subsequently opening the door to a broader range of equity issues.[7]

An established literature assesses labor's engagement with issues raised by women and visible minorities. Research highlights the fact that gender-related issues, and to a lesser extent race-related issues, are now on the agenda of many labor organizations around the world. Many federations and unions now have policies on workplace equality for women, and some have taken steps on affirmative action, maternity leave, sexual harassment, and violence.[8] A growing number pursue these equity objectives through lobbying governments, building coalitions with social-movement activists, encouraging increased diversity in decision-making forums, and negotiating for more change at the bargaining table. As one example of change, women now hold some of the top labor positions in Canada, Australia, and Britain, and many organizations have designated seats on their executive boards for women. Similarly, visible minorities have made gains by allying with labor, and one measure of this is the increased number of visible minorities that are unionized.[9] In the United States, for example, unions representing workers in teaching, health care, food and processing, garment making, and catering have all had a significant rise in membership from Asian Pacific Americans during the last two decades, even though unionization overall has declined. These sorts of developments led to the creation of the Asian American Federation of Union Members, an organization with an increasingly strong voice in national and local labor circles, including formal representation in the AFL-CIO.[10] Similar developments have occurred in other settings. Around the world, labor has sponsored a growing number of programs designed to enhance occupation mobility and fight racial discrimination.

Nevertheless, activist groups taking up gender, race, and ethnicity issues within labor organizations have not seen the degree of gains they would like. Women and visible minorities continue to dominate in lower-paying occupations and jobs, even though many unions have anti-racist and affirmative action policies. Most of the progressive change has been made in larger nonindustrial unions and in the public sector.

Toward a Gay/Lesbian/Labor Alliance

Despite the high profile of examples such as the Coors boycott and gay/lesbian activity in the British miners' unions, there has been little scholarly examination of labor's response to sexual orientation issues.[11] As a start toward closing this gap, this book provides a collection of original scholarship describing labor's engagement with equity issues raised by gays and lesbians in Canada, the United States, Australia, South Africa, the South Pacific, and several European countries. The chapters explore the motivations toward, impediments to, and outcomes of alliances between organized labor and sexual diversity activists. All of the chapters speak to relationships that have been difficult, some much more than others, and several deal with settings where coalitions have failed or remain tenuous, but most describe settings where considerable progress has taken place.

Chapters 2 through 7 cover primarily North America. The first two chapters look at Canada, where labor's engagement with sexual orientation issues is now firmly established. Chapter 2 summarizes my own research, providing an overview of the largely positive developments in Canada since the early 1990s, and offers case studies of a number of unions that have assumed a leadership role. The Canadian situation illustrates the fact that connections have been uneven across regions and between unions, a characteristic that emerges as a theme in later cases. Chapter 3 undertakes a detailed analysis of the role played by labor in the many precedent-setting legal challenges to sexual orientation discrimination that have taken place in Canada since the 1970s. Cynthia Petersen, a lawyer who has been active in these battles, enlivens her article with an insider's perspective.

Chapter 4 undertakes a chronology-based account of the rise of labor and gay/ lesbian connections in the United States. Here we see a relationship present from a surprisingly early date, but highly fragmented and regionalized, and until recently without a national focus. Christian Bain finds many signs of a growing bond between labor and gay/lesbian activism, not the least the recent establishment of a "Pride at Work" committee within the AFL-CIO. He suggests that labor is beginning to play a more assertive role in confronting sexual orientation discrimination throughout the United States and predicts that the next five years will see the solidification of a very strong and powerful alliance. The following three chapters cover specific developments in the United States. Miriam Frank, in Chapter 5, discusses the very important activist role played by lesbian and gay caucuses within unions. Desma Holcomb, in Chapter 6, covers the rise and development of nondiscriminatory, domestic-partner benefits as a core issue within some American unions, and Jonathan Goldberg-Hiller, in Chapter 7, assesses the reasons for the lack of labor support in the Hawai'i-based same-sex marriage battles. Frank's and Holcomb's contributions are mostly optimistic about the extent of gains achieved through progressive alliances with unions in gay/lesbian rights battles, noting the particular importance of broad-based coalitions in the United States, where anti-gay opposition is perhaps better organized and more assertive than in any other democratic country. Goldberg-Hiller, on the other hand, is much more pessimistic. He finds a labor movement extremely reluctant to engage when the issue is framed as the right to marry rather than as equity in benefit coverage. Support for same-sex marriage, at least in the Hawaiian context, appears to be a significantly more demanding test of the depth of labor's support. Notably, in comparison to developments in Canada, labor's engagement with sexuality issues in the United States has been more cautious, slower, and less complete.

Chapters 8 through 10 look at developments in the Southern Hemisphere. Jacqueline Leckie, an anthropologist based in New Zealand, looks at the South Pacific region, where labor and gay/lesbian activists have established almost no relationship, and where the prognoses for change remain uncertain. She finds that contradictory ideologies in Pacific Island societies in relation to gender, sexuality, and worker identity are at the root of the apparent silence. Nevertheless, she sees some precursors to change, such as increasing pressure from international aid agencies to incorporate diversity issues into funded programs. Shane Ostenfeld, in Chapter 9, chronicles the long and sometimes tempestuous history of labor and sexual diversity activism in Australia, a journey that has led to what is arguably among the best developed relationship of this type in the world. In contrast, Chapter 10 on South Africa, by Mazibuko K. Jara, Naomi Webster, and Gerald Hunt, portrays a country where coalitions between labor and sexual diversity activists are in their infancy, but where the need for such relationships is particularly important and appealing because the country has the fastest growing union membership in the world and a labor movement with very strong ties to the new, post-apartheid government.

Chapters 11 through 14 cover Europe. Chapter 11 assumes a broad mandate, covering sexual diversity activism in relation to the labor movement in Europe as a whole, drawing particularly on Britain, Germany, France, and the Netherlands for representative examples. David Rayside finds that progress has been mixed. Although little in the way of a labor/gay/lesbian alliance appears to have developed in France, such alliances are well developed in Britain and increasingly in Germany and the Netherlands. Some labor organizations, especially those in Britain, have been active on gay and lesbian issues at the level of the European courts, but without much success. Rayside concludes that sexual diversity issues remain on the margins of the new European confederation, in spite of a recent flurry of activity in this area. This overview of the situation in Europe is followed by three chapters assessing in more depth the experience in Germany and the United Kingdom. Looking at Germany, Ronald Holzhacker, in Chapter 12, finds that partnerships between labor and sexual-minority activists in the post World War II period have been slow to coalesce but now appear poised to grow and prosper. Chapter 13, on Britain, summarizes the results of several surveys that have been conducted since 1980 about labor's record on sexual diversity issues, noting considerable evidence of a strong and growing connection between labor and gay/lesbian activists. Phil Greasley notes "the fact that Britain as a whole, and the labor movement itself, were so long in thrall of traditional views of gender and sexuality makes such developments even more striking." Fiona Colgan, in Chapter 14, summarizes the contemporary social, economic, and political context in which British activists and unions have forged alliances. She presents a detailed case study of UNISON, a union that has attempted with considerable success to ensure the participation and representation of all sections of its membership, including lesbians and gays. Through the use of extensive interview material, Colgan is able to offer an insider's portrait of the challenge of harmonizing sexuality issues with other union concerns.

Chapter 15, the concluding chapter, provides a global perspective for the scholarship presented here. This book represents the first systematic attempt to examine the recent intersection of lesbian and gay rights activism and labor movements around the world, and there are lessons for activists, union organizers, social movement specialists, and other educators. These cases suggest that the readiness of at least some unions to take up issues of concern to sexual minorities has been largely a product of the work of activists operating within the union movement itself. However, the increasing visibility of gays and lesbians in the workforce has also helped to convince labor organizations that this is a constituency in need of support, and the issue of same-sex benefit coverage has provided a rallying point.

These cases dramatically illustrate the range of responses within and between countries. Although such variation clearly reflects differences in the social and political context, it is also a function of the relative strength of organized labor in a given country or region, along with the extent of historical commitment to "social unionism." Another factor explaining variation is the character and intensity of opposition to sexual diversity inclusiveness. Countries such as the United States and Australia demonstrate that the force of the religious opposition in the overall political environment and within the union movement itself can have a profound impact on progressive development. The Hawai'i case highlights how much the specific sexual orientation issue being debated may matter. Here we see that appeals from activists for union endorsement and support for same-sex marriage garner a very different reaction than does an appeal for equitable distribution of employment-related benefits for those in same-sex relationships. The decline in union strength that has occurred in most parts of the world is also an important factor in shaping union engagement with sexual orientation issues, though one that can operate in contradictory ways. In some contexts it seems to narrow union agendas; in others, it provides a vehicle for labor movement re-energizing and reinvention.

As the reader will see in these chapters, authors working in different national and regional contexts emerge with contradictory degrees of optimism about the potential for bridge-building between labor movements and lesbian/gay activists. Variations in optimism also depend, of course, on the analytical framework of the authors themselves.

The alliances between the lesbian and gay rights movement and the labor movement documented here provide new evidence for the debate in social theory around so-called "old" and "new" social movements.[12] The labor movement has been seen to typify old social movements largely concerned with "materialist" goals, whereas the gay and lesbian rights movement is often put forward as a model of new formations, focused on cultural change, and suspicious of more traditional, institutionalized movements such as labor. These cases draw attention to the artificiality of such distinctions. Here we see examples of labor movements assertively pursuing not only materialistic goals, but also social and cultural ones. Likewise, we see gay and lesbian movements increasingly focused on workplace issues, including the distribution of social goods and benefits, alongside issues and objectives related to cultural change. These cases provide dramatic examples of the way in which more established and more recently spawned movements may be interlinked, often involving many of the same participants. In Chapter 15, I explore these analytical issues in more depth.

Much of the scholarship gathered here explores the growing momentum for coalitions between labor and sexual diversity activists. This book documents what already has been achieved by these alliances, hints at what is possible, and provides a map for what still remains to be done.

Notes

1. Throughout this book a number of terms will be used to refer to differences in sexuality. *Homosexuality, sexual orientation, sexual diversity,* and *sexual minority,* all are intended to evoke people who identify as gay, lesbian, bisexual, and transgendered and the issues that affect them within and because of their identity. Because issues of particular concern to bisexuals and the transgendered have been rarely addressed by organized labor, however, there is less to report in those areas.

2. Harvey Milk was the first openly gay candidate to run and win in elections for the San Francisco Board of Supervisors. Subsequently, he and the mayor were assassinated by an anti-gay supervisor. He has become an icon for the gay community, symbolizing not only the potential of gay political activism but also its risks.

3. These cases and many others are discussed at length in the book. I raise them here as examples of the activity that has taken place.

4. Activists who are disinclined to model traditional, marriage-like relationships and family structures, and who reject initiatives designed to perpetuate these arrangements for gays and lesbians within collective agreements, also look to unions for assistance because it is often within the unions' mandate to fight for social and benefit coverage for people in a variety of domestic and social partnerships.

5. Tripartite systems such as found in Sweden undertake social and economic planning in a way that formally aligns labor, management, and the government.

6. See C. Heron, *The Canadian Labour Movement: A Brief History,* 2nd ed. (Toronto: James Lorimer and Company, 1996), p. 143.

7. These developments are discussed briefly here and will be dealt with in more depth in the concluding chapter.

8. A sizable literature now exists documenting and assessing labor's engagement with feminist issues. See, for example, A. Cook et al., eds., *Women and Trade Unions in Eleven Industrialized Countries* (Philadelphia: Temple University Press, 1984); S. Ledwith et al., "The Making of Women Trade Union Leaders," *Industrial Relations Journal* 21, no. 2 (1990): 112–125; P. Kumar and L. Acri, "Unions' Collective Bargaining Agenda on Women's Issues: The Ontario Experience," *Relations industrielles/Industrial Relations* 47, no. 4 (1992): 623–653; L. Briskin and P. McDermott, eds., *Women Challenging Unions: Feminism, Democracy, and Militancy* (Toronto: University of Toronto Press, 1993); D. Cobble, ed., *Women and Unions: Forging a Partnership* (Ithaca: Cornell University Press, 1993); N. Gabin, *Feminism in the Labor Movement: Women and the United Auto Workers, 1935–1975* (Ithaca: Cornell University Press, 1990); J. Lovenduski and V. Randall, *Contemporary Feminist Politics: Women and Power in Britain* (Oxford: Oxford University Press, 1993); J. White, *Sisters and Solidarity: Women and Unions in Canada* (Toronto: Thompson Educational Publishing, 1993); M. Trelfall, ed., *Mapping the Women's Movement* (London: Verso, 1996); B. Pocock, ed., *Strife: Sex and Politics in Labour Unions* (St. Leonards, Australia: Allen and Unwin, 1997).

9. Compared to gender, a less substantial literature assesses the response of organized labor to racial and ethnic minorities. Some examples of what is available include K. Aguilar-San Juan, ed., *The State of Asian America: Activism and Resistance in the 1990s* (Boston: South End Press, 1994); G. Defreitas, "Unionization Among Racial and Ethnic Minorities," *Industrial and Labor Relations Review* 46, no. 2 (1993): 284–301; R. Leah, "Black Women Speak Out: Racism and Unions," in *Women Challenging Unions,* ed. Briskin and McDermott; R. Horowitz, *Negro and White Unite and Fight* (Urbana: University of Illinois Press, 1997).

10. These developments were reported in Aguilar-San Juan, *The State of Asian America.*

11. One important exception is A. Gluckman and B. Reed, eds., *Homo Economics: Capitalism, Community and Lesbian and Gay Life* (New York: Routledge, 1977), which has two short chapters considering labor issues.

12. I am indebted to correspondence from Barry Adam for helping to shape this argument. See B. Adam, "Post-Marxism and the New Social Movements," in *Organizing Dissent: Contemporary Social Movements in Theory and Practice*, ed. W. Carroll (Toronto: Garamond, 1992).

Gerald Hunt

2   No Longer Outsiders: Labor's Response to Sexual Diversity in Canada

Dateline Ottawa: Clearly, the organizers of the first Canadian Labour Congress (CLC) conference on sexual orientation held in October 1997 were a bit surprised at their own success. In opening the conference, a spokesperson said they had imagined a hundred or so people would attend, but 350 people registered. Her announcement was followed by much applause; some conference participants hooted and hollered with excitement. When a semblance of silence returned (this was a very excited crowd!), the spokesperson said in a beautifully restrained voice: "I guess it's our time, and it's about time." Five minutes of craziness followed: People hugged strangers, someone turned the lights off and on, everyone clapped, and you couldn't hear a thing. Then the conference began.

Organized labor in Canada has shown an increasing commitment to equity issues raised by gays and lesbians; the CLC conference mentioned above offered a powerful and affirming indicator of these developments. Since the late 1980s, a growing number of unions and labor federations have taken a leadership role in this area and now have anti-discriminatory policies and same-sex benefit provisions firmly in place. Many have also been active in developing and delivering educational programs on issues related to homosexuality, lobbying government to make legislative changes, and committing financial and human resources to assist litigants in relevant court challenges. As one measure of labor's involvement, the Canadian Union of Public Employees (CUPE)—the largest union in the country—undertook a legal challenge to the Income Tax Act because the act prevented the union from offering identical benefits and pensions to different and same-sex couples. Undeterred by losing the case in a trial court decision in 1995, CUPE took the case to the Ontario Court of Appeal and won by unanimous decision in April 1998.

Parts of this chapter have been drawn from "Sexual Orientation and the Canadian Labour Movement," *Relations industrielle/Industrial Relations* 52, no. 4 (1997): 787–811 (used with permission).

Despite the positive turns of events cited above, the overall performance of labor has been somewhat cautious and uneven. Although some unions and federations have been very actively engaged with sexual diversity issues since the 1980s, others have done very little or nothing at all. This chapter examines and assesses these developments. It includes a consideration of sexual orientation issues in the Canadian context, with particular reference to changes in the social, political, and legal environment.

Sexual Orientation in the Canadian Context

In 1967, not long after Prime Minister Pierre Trudeau's famous speech declaring that the government had no place in the bedrooms of the nation, the Canadian government legalized homosexual behavior between consenting adults. Since then, a continuing series of social and legislative changes have positioned Canada as one of the more progressive and liberal jurisdictions in the world in relation to homosexuality. As early as 1990, legal experts were commenting on the fundamental changes occurring in Canadian law on the issue of sexual orientation.[1] By 1998, the Supreme Court had ruled that the Canadian Charter of Rights and Freedoms was to be interpreted to include sexual orientation in its nondiscrimination provisions, and there were formal equality provisions in all federal and provincial jurisdictions except the Northwest Territories.

Of the political parties in Canada, the New Democrats have been the most supportive of initiatives in gay and lesbian rights. The federal New Democratic Party (NDP) and its provincial counterparts are officially supportive, and most have a wide range of policy positions aimed at equality on the basis of sexual orientation. Their record when in power has sometimes been mixed. For example, Saskatchewan has never been a leader in the area of gay rights, even though the NDP has been in power for most of the past twenty years. In 1994, when the NDP was in power in Ontario, it introduced Bill 167, designed to enact sweeping changes in same-sex relationship recognition, but divisions within its own caucus contributed to the eventual defeat of the measure.

Federal and provincial NDP structures have been sites of substantial lesbian and gay activism. They are also important locations for labor activists. This has contributed to the process by which union representatives have become familiar with sexual diversity issues. That some unions have been willing to support sexual orientation initiatives speaks to the importance of these relationships.

In most of the country, the most contentious legal issue remaining has to do with same-sex relationship recognition for such things as equal access to benefit and pension plans, adoption of children, estates, immigration, and marriage. This remains a highly contested arena in which the law is contradictory and where federal and provincial governments have been reluctant to take action. In recent years, however, there have been definite signs of progress even in this area. For example, the NDP government in British Columbia recently has been willing to pursue and enact some of the most progressive relationship recognition legislation in the country. The Canadian government and the armed forces now make extended health care benefits available to same-sex couples, as do a growing number of provincial governments, most universities, and many other private and public sector employers. Although not formally legislated, same-sex

partner immigration has begun to become a reality after a number of favorable interpretations of family reunification provisions in the Immigration Act. Legal marriage for
same-sex couples is still not possible, but a case currently before the Supreme Court is
forcing the judges to grapple with the right of a lesbian to petition her ex-partner for
support payments.

In spite of a legal, political, and organizational climate that is in general more favor-
ably disposed to lesbian and gay rights, the reality of discrimination continues. In addition to formal inequity in family, inheritance, immigration, and taxation laws, many
other provisions governing such things as education, affirmative action programs, and
health care embody anti-gay assumptions.

Throughout the 1980s and 1990s, more and more gay and lesbian activism in Canada
has focused on the workplace. This reflects the presence of stronger allies within some
political parties and the now positive legal apparatus available to challenge discrimination that continues to occur in such areas as hiring, firing, promotions, benefits, and
pensions. In order to confront discrimination in the workplace, activists have undertaken educational programs, fought for changes in discriminatory legislation, and
challenged employers directly. Additionally, some activists have turned to the labor
movement for help; Canadian unions tend to have jurisdiction in many of the areas
where discrimination exists, as well as considerable financial clout with which to attack
it. Among other things, they have the capacity to include sexual orientation in their nondiscrimination policies, bargain collectively for inclusive benefits, educate their members about discrimination against homosexuals, confront workplace homophobia and
related violence, undertake and fund legal challenges, and lobby governments for
changes in discriminatory legislation. Challenging discrimination at the level of the
firm, with union support, can present a much less intimidating field of battle than
human rights tribunals or courtrooms, even though these avenues are available. Linkage with organized labor is especially appealing for Canadian activists because unions
continue to be a relatively powerful social and political force.

Organized Labor and Equality Issues

In recent years, organized labor's power and influence in Canada have been threatened
by free-trading agreements with the United States and Mexico, increasing globalization
of production, persistently high unemployment, the growth of a large, mainly nonunionized service sector, decreasing public support, especially among younger people entering the workforce, and a political shift toward the conservative right. In spite of these
challenges, unions and labor federations continue to be a dynamic force and important
players on the Canadian social, economic, and political landscape. The labor movement
in Canada, unlike that in many other western democracies, has enjoyed relatively stable union density of about 37 percent throughout the 1990s, in spite of a rapidly
increasing population. The largest unionized workforces are found in construction,
transportation, manufacturing, and the public sector. The largest area of growth since
the 1960s has been in the public sector, where nearly everyone who can legally belong
to a union does (members of the armed forces and Royal Canadian Mounted Police
are not allowed to join unions). There are more than 250 unions in Canada, ranging

in membership from twenty to more than 400,000. Most of these unions are affiliated with central labor organizations at the provincial and federal level.

A feature somewhat unique to the Canadian labor movement is the presence of national and internationally based unions. Reflecting Canada's close proximity to the United States and historical links to Britain, most of the first unions to develop in Canada were subsidiaries of unions based in either of those countries. Although the number of so-called "international unions" has fallen over the years, many of the most powerful unions in Canada continue to be of this type. In the modern period, the unions that speak for steelworkers, carpenters, electrical workers, and aerospace workers, among others, are branches of American unions. Thus, many policy directives and priorities for these unions emanate from head offices in Washington, D.C., or from the American Federation of Labor–Congress of Industrial Organizations (AFL-CIO), to which most belong. On the other hand, all public sector unions and many of the industrial, manufacturing, and service sector unions are Canadian based; currently, about 70 percent of unionized workers belong to exclusively Canadian trade unions.

Historically, organized labor in Canada has generally adhered to the conservative philosophy of "business unionism," emphasizing wages and working conditions.[2] However, beginning in the 1970s, there was a shift toward increased "social unionism" in some parts of the labor movement, especially in the rapidly growing public sector unions and in the Canadian Auto Workers (CAW) after it broke away from the United Auto Workers of America. As a result, by the mid-1980s, the leadership in at least a few unions was paying increasing attention to issues raised by women and other minority members. Today, most federal and provincial labor federations, as well as many unions, have progressive policies on workplace equality for women and visible minorities in areas such as pay equity, employment equity, affirmative action, sexual harassment, and violence. A growing number go so far as to pursue their equity objectives by lobbying governments, building coalitions, encouraging increased diversity in decision-making forums, and negotiating at the bargaining table.[3]

Labor's engagement with sexual orientation issues has come later, although the first of such developments were taking place by the 1980s.[4] One labor activist, for example, noted that by the early 1980s, "a few" union collective agreements included sexual orientation in their no discrimination clauses, but only one union had attempted to force an employer to provide same-sex benefits.[5] By the late 1980s, a study by White found that three of the thirteen large unions she was looking at were dealing with gay and lesbian rights (Canadian Auto Workers, Public Service Alliance, Canadian Union of Public Employees), and noted that others appeared poised to become more active.[6] By 1994, a reporter for a gay newspaper had identified four large, Ontario-based unions somewhat involved in gay rights.[7]

Following on from these reports, in 1995 I undertook to survey twenty-nine of the largest unions in Canada, along with fourteen of the most important union federations, to assess their responses to sexual diversity issues.[8] I found that there had indeed been momentum throughout the late 1980s and early 1990s, but that it had been mixed and uneven, with stark differences among unions and labor federations. Six of the federations specifically included sexual orientation in their no discrimination policies, and seven included it in their harassment policies. Four had a caucus or committee focused on these issues, and seven were in the process of debating initiatives related to discrimination in this area. In other words, four labor federations were quite active, three were somewhat active, and seven were inactive.

Similarly, I found some of the unions I surveyed to be very actively engaged and others to be completely inactive. Of the unions I polled, seven, based mostly in the public sector, had assumed a leadership role by adopting anti-discrimination policies, fighting for same-sex benefit coverage in collective agreements as well as offering them to their own employees, and authorizing a caucus to address sexual diversity issues. Twelve other unions had undertaken at least one type of initiative, in four cases limited to discussion and debate, and ten unions had taken no action whatsoever.

For this chapter, I undertook to update my earlier survey. The results, summarized in Tables 2.1 and 2.2, demonstrate that there has indeed been progress over the three years. Progress was especially notable among federations. As Table 2.1 indicates, by 1998, nine of them had taken at least three major initiatives, and seven (compared to four in 1995) had a caucus or committee in place or in the works to deal specifically with gay and lesbian issues. Similarly, as shown in Table 2.2, more unions had become engaged with sexual diversity issues, although still only seven unions had taken all five of the initiatives I assessed. Twenty-two had taken at least one initiative, compared to nineteen in the earlier survey. Two particularly illustrative examples of change were the Alberta Teachers' Federation and the United Steelworkers, which had both shifted from no initiatives to three.

In my 1995 survey, private sector unions had lagged very much behind public sector unions, as had international versus Canadian unions. Table 2.2 shows that even though this trend continued in 1998, it was less stark, with signs of growing momentum among more and more private sector and at least a couple of international unions. Another observation I made in 1995 was that unions with higher proportions of women were more likely to be active around gay and lesbian issues. Although this observation held true in 1998 and was reinforced by progress in the Alberta Teachers' Federation, several heavily male-dominated unions, such as the Steelworkers (85 percent male) and Postal Workers (78 percent male), were beginning to change. Also of note, in 1995, a number of organizations declined the opportunity to participate in my survey, some expressing the view that sexual orientation was a "marginal union issue." In the 1998 survey, however, nearly everyone I contacted was happy to volunteer information. Those reporting little or no activity seemed anxious to tell me that it was an area of growing concern and one that would be receiving more attention in the future.

The results of the 1998 survey are discussed below in more detail, along with abbreviated case studies of a number of labor organizations that are particularly active around sexual diversity issues.

The Response of the Labor Federations

Most of the labor federations in Canada are now in some way engaged with sexual orientation issues. As Table 2.1 indicates, eleven have taken at least one initiative, albeit three of them are only at the discussion stage. For some, their activism has been limited to a couple of policy initiatives, but some have become major players in this area. All of the larger federations now include sexual orientation in their nondiscrimination

TABLE 2.1. Ranking of Canadian Labor Federations on Sexual Orientation Initiatives

Labor Federation:	Gay/Lesbian Initiatives[1]			
	Ongoing Debate	SO in Disc. Policy	SO in Harassment Policy	G/L Caucus
Canadian Labour Congress	Yes	Yes	Yes	Yes
Ontario Federation of Labour	Yes	Yes	Yes	Yes
Confédération des syndicats nationaux (CSN)	Yes	Yes	Yes	Yes
British Columbia Federation of Labour	Yes	Yes	Yes	Yes
Manitoba Federation of Labour	Yes	Yes	Yes	Yes[2]
Saskatchewan Federation of Labour	Yes	Yes	Yes	No[3]
New Brunswick Federation of Labour	Yes	Yes	Yes	No[3]
Nova Scotia Federation of Labour	Yes	Yes	Yes	No
Alberta Federation of Labour	Yes	Yes	Yes	No
Fédération des travailleurs et travailleuses du Québec	Yes	No	No	No[4]
Newfoundland Federation of Labour	Yes	No	No	No
Northwest Territories Federation of Labour[5]	No	No	No	No
Prince Edward Island Federation of Labour[5]	No	No	No	No
Yukon Federation of Labour	No	No	No	No

Notes:
1. Initiatives:
   a) Active, ongoing debate on issue of sexual orientation and same-sex benefit coverage?
   b) Sexual orientation specifically included in no discrimination policy?
   c) Sexual orientation specifically included in anti-harassment policy?
   d) Gay/lesbian caucus present that is supported by federation?
2. Gay/lesbian caucus is a subgroup of human rights committee
3. In the process of forming a gay/lesbian caucus/committee
4. An informal committee is discussing sexual orientation issues
5. Indicated the federation supports CLC policies

and anti-harassment policies; seven have a formal caucus to deal with concerns in this area (two not quite yet established); and several have been involved in path-breaking legal challenges. Of those that have no initiatives, one indicated they had "adopted Canadian Labour Congress policies."

Taking a clear leadership role is the Canadian Labour Congress (CLC), the largest and most influential national confederation of trade unions in Canada. Based in Ottawa with regional offices throughout the country, its membership includes all provincial federations, local labor councils, and most trade unions in the country, for a total membership of more than 2 million people. Although its mandate includes the establishment of policy and ethical standards for the trade union movement, and it does get involved in jurisdictional disputes, its primary role is political, acting to influence governments, business, and society in ways that accord with the principles of the labor movement.

In October 1997, the CLC organized a meeting called "Pride and Solidarity: A Conference for Lesbian, Gay, and Bisexual Trade Unionists and Our Allies." The conference was the first of its kind in Canada and represented another important milestone in the

TABLE 2-2. Ranking of Canadian Unions by Initiatives on Sexual Orientation

Union and Membership (in thousands)	% Female[1]	Union Type[2]	Gay/Lesbian Initiatives[3]				
			On-going Debate	SO in Disc. Policy	SSB for Staff	SSB in One Coll. Agree.	G/L Caucus
Five Initiatives:							
Canadian Union of Public Employees (410)	55	c/p	Y	Y	Y	Y	Y
Public Service Alliance (168)	47	c/p	Y	Y	Y	Y	Y
Canadian Auto Workers (170)	20	c/pr	Y	Y	Y	Y	Y
Communication, Energy, & Paper Workers (149)	17	c/pr	Y	Y	Y	Y	Y
Ontario Public Service Employees (105)	57	c/p	Y	Y	Y	Y	Y
BC Govt. Service Employees (49)	55	c/p	Y	Y	Y	Y	Y
BC Hospital Employees[4] (39)	85	c/p	Y	Y	Y	Y	Y
Four Initiatives:							
Postal Workers (51)	22	c/p	Y	Y	Y	Y	N[5]
United Steelworkers (161)	15	i/pr	Y	Y	Y	Y	N
Three Initiatives:							
Ontario Secondary Teachers' Assoc. (49)	41	c/p	Y	Y	Y	N[6]	N[5/7]
Federation of Quebec Nurses (45)	92	c/p	Y	Y	Y	N	N
BC Teachers' Federation (41)	67	c/p	Y	Y	Y	N	N[7]
Alberta Teachers' Assoc. (45)	(a)	c/p	Y	Y	N	Y	N
Two Initiatives:							
Santé et services sociaux (95)	68	c/p	N	Y	N	N	Y
Service Employees International (80)	72	i/pr	Y	Y	N	N	N
Ontario Nurses Association (50)	97	c/p	Y	Y	N	N	N
Employés du secteur publique (46)	55	c/p	Y	N	N	N	Y
One Initiative:							
Alberta Provincial Employees (52)	64	c/p	Y	N	N	N	N
IWA Canada (40)	8	c/pr	N	Y	N	N	N
Quebec School Board Federation (75)	67	c/p	Y	N	N	N	N
Hotel/Restaurant Workers (36)	58	i/pr	N	N	N	Y	N
Brotherhood of Electrical Workers (67)	11	i/pr	Y	N	N	N	N

(continued)

organization's ongoing commitment to sexual diversity issues. As far back as 1980, the CLC had passed a resolution calling for the inclusion of sexual orientation in the Canadian Human Rights Act, Canadian Charter of Rights and Freedoms, and provincial human rights codes (at that time only the province of Quebec had taken this step). The 1980 resolution also encouraged its members and affiliates to bargain for the inclusion of sexual orientation in the nondiscrimination clauses of their collective agreements. Then, at its 1986 convention, a resolution was passed instructing the leadership of the CLC to cooperate with other organizations seeking human rights amendments on sexual orientation, and to begin the process of preparing a policy statement on lesbian and

TABLE 2-2.   Continued

Union and Membership (in thousands)	% Female[1]	Union Type[2]	Gay/Lesbian Initiatives[3]				
			On-going Debate	SO in Disc. Policy	SSB for Staff	SSB in One Coll. Agree.	G/L Caucus
Zero Initiatives:							
Operating Engineers (36)	14	i/pr	N	N	N	N	N
Food & Commercial Workers (176)	45	i/pr	N	N	N	N	N
Teamsters (95)	13	i/pr	N	N	N	N	N
Brotherhood of Carpenters & Joiners (56)	3	i/pr	N	N	N	N	N
Machinists & Aerospace Workers	13	i/pr	N	N	N	N	N
Brotherhood of Rail/Transport Workers[8]	30	c/pr	N	N	N	N	N
Plumbers & Pipe Fitters (38)	(b)	i/pr	N	N	N	N	N

Notes:
1. Sources: Bureau of Labour Information (1995); CALURA (1993); White (1993); personal interviews
2. c = Canadian-based union; i = international-based union; p = mainly public sector; pr = mainly private sector;
3. Initiatives (y = yes; n = no)
   a) Active, ongoing debate on issue of sexual orientation and same-sex benefit coverage?
   b) Sexual orientation specifically included in no discrimination policy?
   c) Same-sex benefits for staff employed by union?
   d) Same-sex benefits available in at least one local collective agreement?
   e) Gay/lesbian caucus present that is supported by the union?
4. Affiliated with CUPE
5. Gay/lesbian issues are included in mandate of human rights committee for union
6. Same-sex benefit coverage is covered by school boards outside of collective agreement
7. Gay/lesbian educator groups exist but operate outside of the union
8. Now merged with CAW; data reflect 1995 period
   (a) Union will not release this information
   (b) Union does not compile this information

gay rights. During its 1990 convention, a resolution calling for same-sex benefit coverage as a collective bargaining priority was passed, as were resolutions calling for lobbying to pressure the government to include sexual orientation in the Canadian Human Rights Act and for the creation of materials to educate affiliates about issues of concern to gays and lesbians.

At the 1994 convention, the CLC overwhelmingly approved a policy that "the labor movement can and should play a key role in the achievement of lesbian, gay and bisexual rights. This is an integral part of the new approach to unionism which is essential if we are to survive as a vital force in society."[9] A position paper accompanying the policy directive called for workplace education about homophobic harassment, political action, public campaigning, legal action, gay and lesbian participation in union management, union participation in nonunion forums dealing with homophobia, and negotiation of inclusive collective agreement language. Specific recommendations included establishing a lesbian, gay, and bisexual working group with caucus status, encouraging provincial federations of labor and labor councils to include sexual orientation in anti-harassment policies, participating "visibly" in gay pride parades across the country, preparing and distributing educational materials, and offering educational workshops to CLC officers and affiliates. Moreover, affiliates were encouraged to recognize same-sex spousal relationships and make benefit coverage a priority at the bargaining table. The CLC also committed itself to a future evaluation of how well it had been able to implement its policies and directives.

By most measures, the CLC has met its goals. A lesbian, gay, and bisexual caucus with official status and support now meets regularly; sexual diversity issues are now part of a senior officer's portfolio; a successful two-day seminar on "Fighting Heterosexism" was tested on the east coast and will be taken across the country; CLC representatives visibly participate in gay and lesbian pride festivals around the country; and many of the affiliate federations now have pro-gay policies. In 1996, when the federal government was debating amendments to the Human Rights Code, the CLC lobbied very assertively to add sexual orientation as a protected area. Additionally, the CLC intervened in a successful Supreme Court case that forced the Alberta government to include sexual orientation as a protected area in its human rights legislation. In 1997, as already mentioned, the CLC organized a very successful gay/lesbian conference. Current plans are to organize events of this type on a regional basis, with a focus on smaller, rural communities. The next conference is scheduled to be held in October 1999.

Despite oversights and opposition, the CLC is clearly committed to overturning inequity based on sexual orientation. What accounts for the CLC's extraordinary support? Much of the CLC's progress is a result of support from the leadership of the organization, by a few committed individuals in particular, and by committees concerned with women's issues who laid the groundwork for a broader range of diversity issues to come forward. One insider suggested that CLC's success was the product of "networks, networks, networks," explaining that as early as the 1970s the foundations had been secured bit by bit in committee meetings, caucuses, and coffee conversations, sometimes involving acrimonious debate. When the time came to formalize policy and practice, dissent had already been worked through. Many people also cite the strong advocacy of Bob White (former head of the Canadian Auto Workers and current president of the CLC) for social justice issues in language unequivocally supportive of gay and lesbian rights.

At the same time, activists caution against complacency and continue to see the need to prod the CLC. At the CLC conference held in Toronto in May 1999, for example, activists from a number of unions were surprised to read several new position papers that made reference to equity groups and human rights initiatives but failed to mention sexual orientation. At the same conference, activists questioned the wisdom of electing Ken Georgetti as the new CLC president (Bob White had decided to retire). According to some activists, Georgetti's response to sexual diversity issues while head of the British Columbia Fereration of Labour had been lackluster, and they wondered if he could be counted on to show leadership in this area at the CLC.

Clearly, the CLC has positioned itself as a leader in the international labor movement in tackling sexual diversity discrimination. As a CLC officer put it at the 1997 conference, "there's no looking back now—we're there." She went on to suggest the organization was determined to see the issue acquire more prominence not only in the provinces of Canada, but at the level of international labor organizations.

As shown in Table 2.1, many of the provincial labor federations in Canada have also been active around sexual diversity issues. Eight of them include sexual orientation in formal nondiscrimination and harassment policies, and six of them have a formal gay/lesbian/bisexual caucus. Only the three smallest federations indicated sexual diversity was not a topic of debate or concern.

Besides these formal developments, some of the provincial federations have been active in other ways. The Nova Scotia Federation of Labour has lobbied for legal equality and recently passed resolutions calling for the preparation of education resources to combat heterosexism, the inclusion of sexual orientation issues in all events dealing with human rights, and the support of unions fighting for same-sex benefits in their collective agreements. The Saskatchewan Federation of Labour rewrote its constitution in 1997 in order to make specific reference to nondiscrimination on the basis of sexual orientation and recently approved the establishment of a gay/lesbian/bisexual caucus. A spokesperson for the Manitoba Federation of Labour indicated that it prided itself on having made issues related to sexual orientation a feature of debates for many years, and that it required a statement regarding homophobia to be read at all MFL functions. The MFL has presented briefs to provincial and federal governments in favor of extending rights to gays and lesbians and passed a resolution declaring the Manitoba Human Rights Code, which includes sexual orientation, to be deemed part of all collective agreements and therefore grievable at the local level. The British Columbia Federation of Labour has taken initiatives similar to those in Manitoba, developing educational materials, organizing workshops, and lobbying the government around discrimination issues related to sexual orientation. On the other hand, activists wonder if the level of commitment is as strong as it could be, citing the number of British Columbia affiliates that have been relatively inactive on sexuality issues.

Standing out as the earliest leader in promoting equality for gays and lesbians is the Ontario Federation of Labour. Since the early 1980s, the OFL has steadfastly prepared educational materials, delivered workshops, lobbied governments, held press conferences, and built coalitions with other groups as part of its efforts to reduce sexual orientation discrimination. Apparently, the rise of a feminist agenda within the OFL in the 1970s paved the way for issues brought forward by visible minorities and disabled people and opened the door politically for gay and lesbian unionists. In 1991, the OFL's efforts increased even further with the formation of a gay and lesbian issues committee, charged with the task of bringing together people from unions across the province for discussion, pressuring union locals to recognize gay and lesbian issues (especially same-sex spouse rights) as a bargaining priority, allocating funds to support activist community groups, organizing educational sessions, and integrating gay and lesbian rights issues into all human rights and collective bargaining courses offered by the OFL. These efforts and organizational changes have had a powerful effect at the personal level. One example cited is a speech given at a convention by the head of the United Steelworkers, who confessed that he "beat up fags" in the past, acknowledged such violence as a common response to homosexuals in his union, and then talked of his realization that such behavior is intolerable.

Of the two principal labor federations in Quebec, the Confédération des syndicats nationaux (CSN) has been more active in dealing with sexual orientation than has the Fédération des travailleurs et travailleuses du Québec (FTQ). In part this is explained by a longer tradition of social unionism within the CSN. The CSN established a gay and lesbian committee in 1988 with the goal not of focusing on formal policy change, but rather on educational programming within the federation itself, followed by initiatives designed to convince its member unions of the need to eliminate discriminatory policies in the area of same-sex partner benefits in their collective agreements. As part of its efforts, the CSN prepared guidelines for collective bargaining on issues related to relationship recognition and encouraged insurance companies to provide benefits for same-sex couples. By 1998, a substantial number of CSN's affiliated unions, particularly in the hotel, day care, and restaurant sectors, had bargained for same-sex benefits. Many of the activities undertaken by the CSN have been coordinated by Le Comité des Gais et Lesbiennes du Conseil Central du Montréal Metropolitain du la CSN, perhaps reflecting a lack of activity in other regions of Quebec.

In contrast, the FTQ was later on the scene. Not until its December 1995 congress did it pass a resolution calling for educational programming and policy changes to challenge discrimination and promote recognition of same-sex relationships. The informal Comité de Triangle Rose operates without the FTQ's official sanction. A spokesperson for the group indicated it had made a presentation at the federation's congress in late 1998. Gay and lesbian activists in Quebec generally agree that neither of the Quebec federations was in the vanguard on sexuality issues until recently, but that the CSN has now positioned itself among the most progressive in the country.

Some of the most encouraging recent events within federations have been at the Alberta Federation of Labour (AFL). Based in one of the most populous but more conservative regions of Canada, the AFL had as recently as 1995 avoided discussion about sexual diversity issues. However, by 1998, the AFL had not only brought the topic onto the discussion docket, but it had included sexual discrimination in its no discrimination and sexual harassment policies (albeit after considerable disagreement and conflict within its membership). Also as a measure of change, the AFL supported a recent, successful Supreme Court challenge to the province's human rights legislation exclusion of sexual orientation.

Even among those federations that have been most inactive, there are signs of movement. The executive director of the Newfoundland Federation of Labour (NFL), for example, had walked in the local gay pride march the day before I talked to her in 1998 and indicated she was determined to elevate sexual diversity issues within the organization, in spite of what she described as "Newfoundland's traditional labor environment." She told me proudly that the NFL had unanimously passed a resolution in support of recent amendments to the provincial human rights code to include sexual orientation, and she talked about moves to organize an inclusive human rights committee.

Overall, the response of Canadian labor federations to sexual orientation issues has been quite positive. That said, response has varied between regions of the country, most of it has been quite recent, and much of it remains at the level of policy. The response among federations in the smaller, less urbanized provinces and territories remains weakest, leaving gay and lesbian unionists in the more rural and isolated areas—where the need for support may be the greatest—to face the impact of homophobia without as much support from labor. Even on this front, however, there is momentum. For example, the CLC has earmarked smaller communities as its next target for action, and there are signs of growing support in jurisdictions such as Newfoundland. It will be a few years yet before the impact of these recent developments is clear.

The Response of Trade Unions

As indicated in Table 2.2, Canada's trade unions show considerable variation in their response to issues of sexual diversity. Some have been extraordinarily active on many fronts; others have yet to articulate the problem. Seven unions have taken all five initiatives I measured, and fifteen others have undertaken at least one type of action. Six unions have taken no action at all (excluding the Carpenters Union, which is now part of the CAW). All of the inactive groups are international unions, operating primarily in the private sector. In contrast, the seven most active unions are Canadian-based unions, operating mostly in the public sector. Two other patterns become readily apparent from looking at Table 2.2. First, most of the more progressive unions are large— five of the six largest unions in the country. Second, most have higher than average female membership. The average female membership for all unions in Canada is 41 percent, and five of the top unions exceed this average. All but one of the inactive unions are male-dominated.

To understand why there has been mixed progress on sexual orientation as an issue within Canadian trade unions, it is necessary to probe deeper into the history of debate and decision-making, especially among progressive unions. The abbreviated case studies that follow tell the stories of a number of unions at the forefront of change.

The Canadian Union of Public Employees (CUPE)

CUPE, the largest trade union in Canada, stands out for its approach to equity issues, including sexual orientation. Gays and lesbians in CUPE began to organize as early as 1980. One union member indicated that lesbian and gay members "found" each other at conferences and other meetings, initially for social support, but gradually they became more and more political. The first to become outspoken and vocal on gay/lesbian issues were library workers from across the country. They produced a fact sheet on homosexuality and worked to build support within influential circles, not least of which was the powerful women's committee. Formalization of lesbian and gay activism within CUPE began at a 1989 women's conference when a small group of lesbians formed a caucus to pressure the union to take on gay and lesbian issues. Helping tremendously to position these issues on the union's agenda was the presence of a very supportive senior official in the head office, who stated: "I could have assigned one of my staff to work with them, but I wanted to give the committee the profile of having a director as a resource. I saw it as my role to show them the political channels, and how to move those channels. They politicized very quickly, and brought political skills from having worked in the gay/lesbian community." The group's first major undertaking was to prepare an information kit on sexual orientation, the first of its kind in Canada. It appeared in February 1990 and covered such general topics as homophobia, discrimination in benefit coverage, contract language, insurance, legal decisions, and current legislation. It also provided specific information about the way in which CUPE locals might negotiate to end discrimination. The packet (updated in 1996 and 1998) received wide distribution to locals across the country.

The union's increasingly public and positive engagement with sexual orientation aroused some opposition, especially at the local level. As one person put it, CUPE had its share of "old liners" for whom homosexuality represented a category for contempt rather than celebration. Another person described a large metropolitan local this way as an example of the educational work that lay before gay and lesbian activists: "Very old line. The local executive (all male) goes to conventions, gets 300 bucks a day (in expenses), brings in some dancing girls, pays for prostitutes, has a hospitality room with 5,000 bucks' worth of booze for four days. That sort of thing. These are the sorts that go into the bar at convention and crack homophobic jokes."

Nevertheless, and in spite of fears on the part of some organizers, a resolution to create a national gay and lesbian committee presented at the 1991 convention passed unanimously, thanks to extensive lobbying and education at the national and local levels. National directors had been coached by head office staff to understand and argue in favor of the issue. What was perhaps more important, a number of grass roots activists were willing to speak publicly from their hearts about the sort of discrimination they had experienced within their workplace and union. One union member from Newfoundland, who had never stood in front of a microphone before in his life, described a local union meeting in which he was told that there was no place for queers in the union movement, that he was probably dripping with AIDS, and that he was probably going to kill his coworkers. As one observer described the moment, "At the end, his voice trailed away and he said, 'I just want to belong, that's all,' and he got really choked up. The room went up. There were convention brochures flying in the air. There were people on chairs screaming, hollering. Jeff (the president) called the vote—all those in favor of the Pink Triangle Committee?—and the whole room just went up again. And he said, 'I am going to take that as a unanimous vote; I am not even going to call for dissent.' And that was it. We had an official committee." The Pink Triangle Committee was put on a par with other committees within the union, and so was eligible to receive funding and have access to national office support staff. The group held a first meeting in early 1992 and set out a number of goals: to prepare a policy on homophobia in unions, prepare educational materials, look into ways to undertake wider political action, and monitor the union's commitment to gay and lesbian equality.

Since then, CUPE has undertaken a number of important initiatives. The union helped to finance community groups and undertook educational programs on a number of topics, including AIDS, homophobia, and bargaining strategies for negotiating same-sex benefits. It continued to exert pressure, with considerable success, on employers (such as the airlines) who had remained intransigent on sexual diversity issues. Nevertheless, oversights still happen. As one example, a Regina nursing home worker told participants at the CLC gay/lesbian conference in 1997 that she had attended the CUPE Saskatchewan Summer School on human rights training only to discover that anti-homophobia was not going to be covered. Others identified with her frustration and spoke of the need for CUPE to remain attentive to the creation of a safe and welcoming environment throughout its vast constituency, especially in more rural settings. Others spoke of the need for CUPE to become more attentive to the needs of bisexuals and the transgendered.

By 1998, CUPE's record was impressive by any standard. Perhaps the best example of CUPE's impressive financial and legal support for gay and lesbian rights is a recent court case instigated on behalf of two head office employees that challenged the exclusively heterosexual definition of spouse in the Income Tax Act. The case began with an attempt by CUPE to amend its registered pension plan to provide survivor benefits to same-sex spouses of plan members. Revenue Canada refused to allow the amendment to the union's plan on the grounds that the definition of spouse in the act only allowed for heterosexual partners. CUPE then took the case to court. Although the case was lost in the lower courts, the Ontario Court of Appeal unanimously agreed that the exclusion of same-sex partners was unconstitutional under the Charter of Rights and Freedoms. As a result, the court rewrote the definition of "spouse" to mean "a person of the opposite sex or the same sex," thus removing one of the major impediments gays and lesbians had faced in acquiring equal pension coverage from their employers.[10]

The Canadian Auto Workers(CAW)

The Canadian Auto Workers (CAW) has been described as "aggressive and innovative, with a strong and well-articulated social unionism orientation."[11] Even though feminist researchers have been quick to point out that its record is not without flaws, it has clearly led the pack on many women's issues.[12] It was among the first labor unions in the world to hold a woman's conference (as early as 1964), to establish a Women's Bureau, and to push provincial governments to include gender in their human rights codes, long before such activities were commonplace. Now the CAW holds an annual women's and human rights conference and sponsors an extensive training program for women and visible minority members. It stands out, too, as the private sector union most active in the area of equal rights for gays and lesbians. As a spokesperson put it, "we had the ground fertile with the human rights work that we've done; this is one more thing that you can't leave out when you're doing the fight." This commitment dates back to the time of the UAW's first president, Walter Reuther, who believed strongly in social justice and human rights. One informant explained how his ideas left an imprint on subsequent leadership by describing Pat Clancy, a former president of the huge local 707, who easily fit the stereotype of the "white, male, trade unionist bread-and-butter kind of guy." He moved up through the Ford system—"not exactly a hot bed of radicalism"—but took on equity issues in the early 1980s and was not shy about defending lesbians and gays when this was unfashionable.

Along the way, there have been policy disagreements between rank and file and head office. Buzz Hargrove, the national president, estimates he has received more mail from members on the CAW's stand on gay and lesbian issues than any other policy area—most of it negative. In another situation, John Kovacs, president of a large bargaining unit at General Motors, made the national news when he indicated that his membership supported a local member of parliament's stand *against* the Ontario same-sex benefits bill, at precisely the same time Hargrove was leading a news conference in support of the bill. At an April 1994 council meeting, a member from Kitchener felt free to stand up and say, "The human rights issue stops at same-sex benefits . . . my conscience is my guide and I feel in no way obligated to blindly follow the pursuit of this issue just because it has been adopted by this council."[13]

By 1999, in spite of some internal opposition, CAW's achievements are impressive. Most collective agreements now include sexual orientation in a general anti-discrimination statement, sometimes after very hard-fought battles. For example, in 1996, during one of the the most tense and conflicted downsizing exercises in Canadian history, CAW held firm on the issue of same-sex benefits during multi-union negotiations with Canadian Airlines. Even when the other unions were ready to settle without this clause, the CAW remained steadfast, refusing to sign until this goal was achieved. As a measure of the union's ongoing support, it is now mandatory that same-sex benefits be on the table during collective bargaining negotiations in any setting where these benefits are not already available, with a proviso that the National President be informed before they can be taken off the table.

On other fronts, gays and lesbians are now specifically covered in most anti-harassment policies, and a staff lawyer has been assigned gay and lesbian issues as one of the main components of her job. The union actively lobbies provincial and federal governments to enact equality provisions, and makes significant donations to gay and lesbian community organizations. The CAW very actively urged the federal government to add sexual oientation to the Canadian Human Rights Code (which it finally did in 1996). Another mark of support is a CAW teaching video called "Working It Out" in which a lesbian is depicted in a harassment situation because of her sexuality.

Activists inside the union note with pride the achievements at the CAW but acknowledge that there is still much to be done, citing the fact that many people still fear being open about their sexuality while on the job. A a result, education efforts are the current priority, and activists hope to offer workshops on homophobia throughout the country. The first of these seminars is scheduled to be held with senior officers at Northern Telecom in late 1999, and a national conference on sexual orientation issues is scheduled for early 2000. In an effort to raise their political profile even further, activists have adopted the logo "Pride At Work" and have organized three gay/lesbian/bisexual support groups (in Vancouver, London, and Windsor).

By any standard, and especially among unions operating primarily within the private sector where there are few exemplary models, the CAW stands out as a leader. Overall, the reasons for its success can be traced to three key factors: first, the social unionism orientation of the union itself; second, the preparedness of gay and lesbian people to be "out" in CAW circles and make the issue personal and visible; and third, the creation of space within the union for activists to maneuver and to challenge the status quo.

The Public Service Alliance of Canada (PSAC)

PSAC, founded in 1966, grew quickly to become the fifth largest union in Canada, with more than 167,800 members, nearly half of whom are women. It has a reputation of being somewhat traditional, and its organizational structure is complex and cumbersome by design, with each of its eighteen component unions having their own elected officials, policies, and priorities. Nevertheless, PSAC has established some noteworthy benchmarks for human rights issues. By 1973, it was one of the few unions to have negotiated maternity leave benefits; by 1976, it had an Equal Opportunities Committee at the national level and stood out among Canadian unions by having a woman as one of its top five officers; by 1985, it had held a women's issues conference; by the early 1990s, it had circulated position papers on aboriginal workers' rights, human rights, technological change, equal opportunity, and AIDS/HIV.

However, the union was slower in taking up sexual diversity issues. A little burst of activity occurred in 1985. When the federal government tabled its "Equality for All" report, which suggested that sexual orientation be included in the Canadian Human Rights Act, some of the component unions wrote to the prime minister in support of the amendment. Although PSAC had an Equal Opportunities Committee as early as 1976, sexual orientation issues were not part of its mandate. Women's issues seemed the committee's main concern. As one historian noted: "Although responsible for equity issues in general, its focus has been primarily upon women's issues, and it has been primarily white, able-bodied and straight women who have sat on the committee, with sometimes a few white, able-bodied straight men."[14] The Equal Opportunities Committee did draft a human rights policy statement in 1988 that mentioned sexual orientation as a category in need of special attention, but no strategies were outlined, and the issue stayed on the back burner.

Two events in the early 1990s helped to position gay and lesbian equality on PSAC's agenda. First, a steward from Vancouver submitted an article for the union's magazine, *Alliance,* describing a grievance over same-sex partner dental benefits for a member she was representing, but the article was rejected by the editorial board, which included the president of the union, on the grounds that it did not have broad enough interest for the membership. The second incident occurred when the union's national office agreed to investigate complaints that lesbian issues had been covered "too sympathetically" at a women's conference. Both events enraged the few openly gay and lesbian members who had been active on these issues within the union and provided the motivation for them to begin mobilizing on a much larger scale. Among other things, they organized a meeting attended by the country's only (at that time) openly gay member of parliament, placed ads in the gay press across the country asking people, especially PSAC members, to make their displeasure known, met with executives of the union expressing their anger, and undertook a series of mail-outs (using their own money). Their campaign was immediately successful in raising the visibility of gay and lesbian issues within the union. According to one activist, "it was pivotal because it did a lot to mobilize people around the issue, including those who were not lesbian or gay, and we quickly became a very organized and effective lobbying group." Ultimately, an article on heterosexism was approved for publication in *Alliance.*[15]

The Human Rights Committee was restructured at the 1991 convention to include gay and lesbian issues, but not without some dissent. As an activist recalled:

> With the exception of one man who went a little apey and, after the elections, started throwing around chairs and saying it was "the fucking women and dykes" who were taking over the union, there wasn't a lot of openly hostile stuff—but you knew it was there. You could see the eyes rolling. . . .
>
> After that convention they (the executive) decided to add equity seats to the Committee. So they decided they would come up with seven seats: two for racial minorities, two for aboriginals, two for people with disabilities, one for lesbians and gays. So it became our next cause (only one seat versus two for everyone else). We were successful in that little organizing fight, but again we had to react, we had to organize around it nationally in order to have a change. But we had it changed and they added an extra seat for us.

At the 1994 convention, more resolutions were debated and approved. The gay and lesbian organizing group had prepared a position paper on sexual orientation, which proposed official sanction for a gay and lesbian caucus. The proposal passed without incident. Since then, developments have been quite positive. The union included lesbians and gays in its employment equity goals, funded a number of grievances over same-sex benefits, offered a couple of workshops on homophobia, helped to set up a number of regional groups, and lobbied for legislative changes. On the other hand, PSAC had little success in negotiating same-sex partner benefits in most of its collective agreements, especially for government workers. Ironically, the treasury board volunteered to include same-sex benefit coverage for government workers shortly after amending the Human Rights Code in 1996, even though they had stridently resisted such proposals at the bargaining table. However, PSAC's role in bringing such inequities to the government's attention and fighting early battles during negotiations no doubt played an important role in these developments.

After a somewhat checkered history, PSAC appears now to be fully committed to combating sexual orientation discrimination. It should be noted, however, that many PSAC members still feel it is unsafe to be open at work, typified by the fact that the caucus has two mailing lists; the private one is three times the size of the public one.

British Columbia Government and Service Employees Union (BCGEU)

BCGEU is the largest trade union in the province of British Columbia, with a membership of close to 50,000 government employees and others in the broader public sector. During the 1980s, it went on strike four times, during every round of bargaining, a record which reflects its preoccupation with job survival in the face of an assertively anti-union government. In 1991, a government more sympathetic to organized labor was elected. This ushered in a more stable phase for the union, allowing it to turn some of its attention and resources away from job security toward matters such as environmental causes and diversity initiatives. Now the union has developed policies and practices to equalize opportunities for women and minorities such as the disabled and aboriginals, and its record on sexual diversity issues is impressive.

Although same-sex partner benefits are part of the master agreement and appear in most local agreements, the union's main focus has been on educational initiatives for its employers and general membership, within a program that emphasizes valuing diversity generally. The union's efforts to expand and emphasize its commitment to fair treatment and equal opportunity took shape in 1991 with its adoption of a position paper called "Valuing Our Diversity." In addition to the formalization of an anti-discriminatory philosophy and set of policies, the document laid out terms of reference for the establishment of a Diversity Coordinating Committee and proposed that the 1995 42nd Constitutional Convention have the theme "Unity in Diversity—Strength in Solidarity." The Diversity Committee was created officially in 1994 and quickly mapped out a strategy for change that included community forums around the province to collect and disseminate information regarding diversity issues, a set of action plans for union officials including training initiatives for stewards and union leaders, and the organization of a diversity conference.

The committee has been able to meet most of its goals and has become one of the highest profile groups in the union. Its very successful 1997 conference called "Building on Diversity" opened with a keynote address by the chief of the BC Human Rights Commission, attracted eighty-five stewards, officers, and other members, and included workshops on such things as aboriginal awareness and confronting homophobia. The committee also has broadened its mandate to include the preparation of resource materials for bargaining units and cross-component committees, as well as intervention in legislation and political incidents involving diversity issues.[16] Still, the union recognizes there is work to be done. A recent set of goals and action plans directs the organization to work toward the elimination of the occupational ghettos dominated by women and minorities in low-paying job categories, and to confront its lack of proportional representation in shop stewards, executive members, leaders, and activists.

The growing prominence of sexual diversity issues within BCGEU's mandate is the result of a particular confluence of events in British Columbia politics. The center-left New Democratic government elected in 1991 quickly moved on a slate of human rights amendments, including protection for sexual minorities and same-sex relationship recognition. The government's leadership on gay and lesbian rights meant there was less need for unions such as the BCGEU to fight for these provisions at the bargaining table. Instead, the thrust of union leadership was to take up diversity issues for a broad range of minorities, including gays and lesbians, by confronting its own internal culture and acting as a catalyst for social change.

Ontario Public Service Employees Union (OPSEU)

OPSEU has more than 100,000 members, representing employees of the provincial government of Ontario, the faculty and support staff in twenty-five Ontario community colleges, and hundreds of agencies in the broader public sector. Since the early 1980s, OPSEU has had an active Women's Committee, and in 1986 it established a Race Relations and Minority Rights Committee. OPSEU had been active in fighting for same-sex benefits in its collective agreements since the late 1980s but had little success until a 1992 court decision said that a crown attorney had been discriminated against when the province denied benefit coverage to his male partner. Following on this decision, in 1993, a number of activists formed a province-wide network called the Gay and Lesbian Action Group to force the union to tackle sexual-minority discrimination more assertively. The action group started out without money or formal union support but with a list of names of people prepared to take on this issue. This created a semblance of organization and led to the establishment of contacts in each of OPSEU's seven regions. In 1994, a brainstorming session was organized among seven regional "representatives" who were able to obtain transportation and accommodation expenses from the union. After this meeting, the group decided to become more formally constituted in order to act as a pressure group within the union.

At about the same time, the province of Ontario began an unprecedented program of restructuring and downsizing that shifted diversity issues off to one side of the union's agenda. A particularly difficult and prolonged strike during 1996 absorbed the lion's share of the union's energy and resources. Nevertheless, during the course of the 1990s, OPSEU managed to achieve a commendable record in addressing sexual orientation discrimination.

Although not all local collective agreements contain the same provisions, the master agreement covering most government employees and the agreement covering the community colleges contain some of the best coverage for gays and lesbians found anywhere in the world. For example, a 1992 amendment to the agreement covering academic employees of community colleges states: "The parties agree that the Life Insurance, Extended Health, Dental, Spousal and Dependent Insurance, Vision Care, Hearing Care Benefit Plans and survivor benefits shall be amended to include coverage for same-sex spouses." Then, in 1994, OPSEU was able to negotiate a new pension plan, separate from the Public Service Pension Plan, for most government workers as well as Liquor Control Board Employees and other smaller groups. This new plan specifically defined a spouse as either a man or a woman, married or not, who was living in a conjugal relationship for a period of not less than three years. In order to circumvent the Income Tax Act's restriction of "spouse" to mean a person of the opposite sex, OPSEU set up a separate "same-sex benefits plan." This new pension plan, among the first of its kind in the world, ensured that same- and opposite-sex spouses had the same benefits and pension options.

Furthermore, OPSEU has created one of the most comprehensive harassment and discrimination policies in Canada. The policy applies to all members, retirees, staff, and guests of the union when in the workplace and at all union-sponsored functions, within sixteen prohibited grounds, including sexual orientation. In addition, the union has made efforts to support the wider gay and lesbian community by doing such things as providing funding to the Gay Youth Hotline over the past five years, and being a visible presence at the Pride festival in Toronto.

Activists inside OPSEU note that support for sexual diversity initiatives has not been universal. One activist says she continues to hear arguments from some people in leadership positions within the union, as well as on the shop floor, that sexuality issues are "private issues" and not union issues, even though they have been on the union's agenda for years. Another activist talks of the differences in acceptance between urban and rural settings and calls for increased educational programs (rather than more policies or partner benefits) to combat homophobia. Both of these activists point out that many gays and lesbians do not feel it is safe to be on the confidential mailing list. Informants also point to the tenuous nature of the Gay and Lesbian Action Group, which still does not have its own budget line, continues to be financially supported by the Women's and Human Rights Committee, and often seems close to collapse. When one member of the group went on a leave and another was "downsized" recently, the group nearly folded, suggesting that the loss of just two active members was sufficient to hamper the group's entire existence.

Overall, OPSEU has achieved a great deal since beginning to tackle sexual orientation discrimination in the late 1980s, and its record in regard to the equalization of benefits for homosexuals and heterosexuals is impressive. At the same time, support for an independent gay and lesbian caucus and educational initiatives to fight homophobia seem to lack secure footing within the union. Developments at OPSEU have been driven largely by activists within the union who found a receptive union leadership, but one preoccupied by government restructuring. Although the union leadership fought hard for policy and benefit changes, perhaps too little attention has been paid to head office structures and programs that would address gay and lesbian issues on an ongoing basis.

Other Unions

Other Canadian trade unions have been active on issues related to sexual orientation, some in extraordinary ways. The Hospital Employees Union in British Columbia (HEUBC) has a membership of around 38,000 but is strengthened through its amalgamation with CUPE.[17] Pushed by a group of gay and lesbian members, the union sent out a notice in September 1991 announcing a conference on gays and lesbians in the law. According to reports, many of the notices did not even make it to union bulletin boards, and some were defaced. Nevertheless, a few people indicated their willingness to attend, marking the beginning of a gay and lesbian visibility in the union. Then, in October 1992, a motion calling for the formation of a gay and lesbian caucus was put forward and approved at the union's biannual convention, apparently to the accompaniment of some laughter and sarcasm. Subsequently, in 1996, HEUBC amended its constitution to establish four new equity-oriented committees, including one for gays and lesbians. As an official body, the Gay and Lesbian Standing Committee was given the right to send resolutions and one delegate to wage-policy conventions and have representation on the executive's Equal Opportunities Committee. Since these events, it has contributed to a number of workshops (including a shop steward course), initiated a quarterly newsletter, and arranged to have one of its members sit on CUPE's national Pink Triangle Committee. As with CUPE, initiatives at HEUBC began at the grass roots level, but once issues were articulated and pushed by activists, they found a receptive audience in the union's hierarchy and ultimately in its larger membership—so much so that now it stands as a startling example of the rapid progress than can be made by a relatively small union in a short period of time.

The Canadian Union of Postal Workers (CUPW) was among the first to negotiate inclusive harassment and discrimination language in the early 1980s, and shortly thereafter initiated what is probably the first arbitration case involving same-sex benefits in Canada.[18] The case involved a lesbian wishing leave in order to care for her partner of sixteen years who was ill, a provision available to heterosexual couples. Even though her collective agreement contained a clause prohibiting discrimination on the basis of sexual orientation, the person pursuing it was unsuccessful. It was, however, the first time a union had supported a challenge over same-sex benefits all the way to arbitration. After this, progress at CUPW seems to have stalled, perhaps because of an increasingly harsh negotiating environment dominated by downsizing and restructuring battles. At present, the union gives the appearance of being poised to re-engage. The Pacific branch recently negotiated one of the few collective agreements that includes "marriage" leave for up to five days for same-sex couples, and its harassment policy allows the removal of homophobic harassers to other work sites, including other cities. An informal gay/lesbian organizing group does exist but is not yet an official CUPW caucus or committee.

Even within the private sector and international unions, where progress has tended to be slowest, there are recent noteworthy developments. The Communication, Energy, and Paper Workers Union was one of the first in Canada to establish a gay and lesbian caucus, prompted in part by pressure from a gay and lesbian employee group at Bell Canada, who were at loggerheads with their employer over same-sex benefit coverage. The union now has inclusive discriminatory language, with same-sex benefit coverage in many agreements. The very large United Steelworkers (USW) has also taken a number of important initiatives, especially in the Atlantic and Ontario regions. In addition to nondiscrimination language, some local agreements specifically provide for same-sex benefit coverage, and an informal lesbian/gay caucus called "Steel Pride" has achieved formal endorsement from headquarters. As a measure of improved tolerance, one person cited the willingness of more gays and lesbians to be visible at work, even in traditional settings such as northern Ontario mines, and described same-sex partners dancing at shop steward social events. Although pressure from activists would appear to account for most of these developments, recent moves by the USW to strengthen its presence in the service and public sectors—they now represent secretarial and support workers at the University of Toronto, for example—may also help to explain shifting policies.

Within the construction and craft-based unions, evidence of progress is harder to find, although not impossible. The International Brotherhood of Electrical Workers, for example, sent a letter to the premier of Alberta in support of changes to the human rights legislation, and it has recently appointed an openly lesbian member as one of its representatives to the AFL-CIO in Washington, D.C.

Even in Alberta, where movement has been sluggish, unions representing government workers, nurses, and teachers now talk of growing momentum, the way facilitated by the 1998 changes to human rights legislation. A spokesperson for the Alberta Teachers' Association (ATA) claims that these legislative changes have helped to make gay/lesbian rights more of an issue within the organization. He indicated that ATA would now assist any teacher facing discrimination on the basis of sexual orientation. Nevertheless, he suggested the organization's approach would remain "low key and administrative in style," rather than activist, apparently in recognition that members of the Catholic school boards and those in rural areas are opposed to change. Similarly, even though the Alberta Union of Provincial Employees (AUPE) faces one of the most hostile employers on this issue in the country, and has no members prepared to be openly active on gay/lesbian rights, one informant suggested the majority sentiment in the union favors change. Although the past three conventions have included discussion of same-sex benefits, nothing tangible has emerged so far.

Developments in Quebec

Although Quebec led other provinces in adding sexual orientation to its human rights legislation in 1977, it has not been in the lead of other jurisdictions since then.[19] On some fronts, it has lagged behind other provinces.[20] Progress within the labor movement has also been slower, although a number of recent developments are suggestive of change. From a general gathering of unionized gays and lesbians held in 1996, a call went out to unions to enter into the struggle. Recommendations were made by the group to hold a forum so that different union organizations could exchange ideas, and a first meeting with nearly seventy representatives from several different unions was held in

April 1997. A permanent structure was put into place at this forum, and in May 1998, an administrative council was elected.[21] The objectives of the forum are to coordinate the lobbying of different unions, distribute information on the conditions of gay and lesbian workers, and intervene in government policy-making. So far, the forum has published a booklet for wide distribution and held a news conference urging the Quebec government to institute a wider and more comprehensive set of policies regarding equality for people in same-sex relationships. On another front, the collective agreements between the Quebec government and its public service union has expired, which activists see as an opportunity to push for change. In this regard, the forum has issued a call for gays and lesbians within the public service union to press their representatives to review the definition of spouse.

These developments have in part been motivated by Quebec's private sector outpacing the public sector in the extension of same-sex benefits. On this issue in particular, a new group has been formed—the Coalition pour la reconnaissance des conjoints et conjointes de même sexe—an alliance of lobbying groups that includes the forum. In July 1998, they held a press conference and issued a letter to Premier Bouchard urging the elimination of discrimination against same-sex couples in all Quebec laws. The Quebec government pledged to take these matters in hand, but did not take any actiom, and the group held a second press conference in April 1999 to voice their discontent. Finally, in May 1999, the Quebec government introduced legislation to overhaul twenty provincial laws and eleven regulations so that all common-law couples, whether heterosexual or homosexual, would have the same rights. These changes affect many different areas including pension and taxation benefits, automobile insurance coverage, and prescription drug coverage.

Progress to Date

Despite the array of positive developments cited here, many unions remain uninvolved with these issues and seem puzzled by all the fuss. Spokespersons from several of the craft-based unions suggested that homosexual relationship coverage was not available to their members because no one had ever asked, thus denying the need for principled action at the top. Equally perplexing, the spokesperson for one craft-based union talked about the lack of difficulty in offering relationship-based benefit coverage to people with multiple partners and dependents if they were *all* heterosexual, even though there were no provisions at all for same-sex relationships (for example, a heterosexual ex-spouse, a heterosexual common-law partner, and children from either relationship could *all* get benefits, but a same-sex partner would not be eligible for benefits).

Although many Canadian labor federations and unions have supported gay and lesbian rights in many ways, perhaps nothing can match the drama and impact of their support for litigation and legal challenges. In grievance protocols, arbitration hearings, legal challenges, and direct litigation, labor has often been a key player, sometimes in the foreground, sometimes in the background. Where it has not been a player, it often provided legal, financial, and institutional support. Although I have made reference here to several of these engagements, the scope of this activity is broad and highly significant and will be covered in depth in the next chapter.

Conclusion

Parts of the Canadian labor movement have been actively supporting gay and lesbian rights since the early 1980s, with growing momentum and success throughout the 1990s. Many of these gains have depended on the institutional, financial, and political support of the trade union movement. Labor/lesbian/gay partnerships are relatively recent, and while many federations and a growing number of trade unions have taken a leadership role in promoting equal rights for sexual minorities, others have not been active. Important differences in response occur between federations, within and between various types and sectors of unions, and in different regions of the country. Public sector and Canadian-based unions have tended to be more active, but there are important exceptions to these trends. These variables have created a situation whereby it is possible for homosexuals to have radically different union experiences, not only from heterosexuals, but from each other as well. Nonetheless, the Canadian labor movement, as a whole, stands out as progressive and committed in relation to these issues, especially when compared to some of the other countries profiled in this volume.

What accounts for these developments and trends? The evidence I have collected leads me to conclude that five factors largely explain the evolution and character of the gay/lesbian/labor alliance found in Canada: political and regional dynamics, union demographics, levels of activism, the support and presence of women's committees, and the nature of union leadership.

That labor has often fought against sexual orientation discrimination certainly reflects the particular political, legal, and social context of the country. In Canada, a gay and lesbian rights movement has been very politically active for more than twenty years, and demands for equity in the workplace are now among its best articulated and most emphatic demands for change. This has helped to foster a gay and lesbian community, especially in urban centers, where more and more people are prepared to be open at work and make demands on their unions and employers to provide equal treatment. Another explanatory factor is that Canada now has a legal climate supportive of gay and lesbian rights, and a growing number of court challenges have established that workplace discrimination is less and less permissible. That labor organizations based in regions such as Alberta and the smaller east coast provinces have tended to be slower to respond to the issues is not surprising, given that these locations are more conservative and tend to have less developed gay and lesbian rights movements. On the other hand, the unions and federations where there has been the most progress are based in the capital (Ottawa) and the larger, arguably more liberal, urban centers such as Toronto, Montreal, and Vancouver. In addition, Canada is less troubled by organized opposition to gay and lesbian rights, especially from the religious right wing, than seems to be the case elsewhere, most notably in the United States. This factor may also help to explain the weak response of Canada's American-based unions, which continue to frame much of their policy within a foreign mind set. But even here, there are significant signs of change, including gay-positive activity in the Steelworkers Union and encouraging signals from the American Federation of Labor.

The role of the New Democratic Party as a force connecting labor and gay/lesbian activists and providing a forum for mutual education and policy development is critical.[22] The development of gay and lesbian representation in unions finds a parallel in the development of activist groups within the party.

Union demographics also influence the level of activity on this issue. The average female membership in Canadian unions is 41 percent, and those unions with a higher than average proportion of women tend to have taken more initiatives on sexual orientation. This is a trend and not a rule. The Food and Commercial Workers, for example, have higher than average numbers of women but have taken few initiatives, whereas the CAW and the Communications Workers, with significantly fewer women than average, are among the most active. Nevertheless, those unions with a predominately male membership, such as the Teamsters and most of the craft-based unions, have clearly been the least involved. Besides gender composition, other demographic factors have a role. CUPE, one of the most responsive unions, for example, covers many workplaces and occupations (such as libraries and librarians, hospitals and nurses, schools and teachers) that have traditionally attracted gays and lesbians, making the issue of more immediate relevance than might be the case in other settings. These workers also tend to be in domains where discrimination against gays and lesbians is more visible. Teachers are more likely to see teasing and bullying in the schoolyard and to be more aware of measures to discourage positive teaching around diverse sexuality; nurses would be more likely to see the consequences of long-standing, same-sex partners being denied the right to make important medical decisions for one another. Part of the unevenness in labor's response may be explained by the fact that public sector unions, where there has been the most change, tend to have a more highly educated membership and to be located in government settings where equity issues have been on the agenda for a number of years. The evidence here suggests that there has been a somewhat natural progression in these unions from early preoccupation with women's issues and racial discrimination to a more recent concern for a broader set of diversity issues, including sexuality.

The readiness of at least some of the country's unions to take up these issues and to pursue them forcibly owes much to the visibility and work of activists operating within the union movement, often in considerable isolation. That activism gained momentum in part as a response to greater sexual-minority visibility in Canadian society and a rise in progressive-movement activism generally. We see no situations in which unions have spontaneously taken on sexual diversity; in all situations, the catalyst has been activist pressure and, in many cases, the insistence of a small group of courageous people committed to the cause of equity. At the CLC and the more progressive provincial federations and unions, progress on lesbian/gay rights can be traced directly to the efforts of activists working within the institution. Positioning sexual orientation on the agenda at CUPE, for instance, came about initially through the actions of a few who were prepared to stand up, tell their personal stories of discrimination, and put a face on the problem. A similar situation took place at the CSN in Quebec, where hotel and restaurant workers were the first to press for change within their federation. At the CAW on the other hand, activism emerged at the top within the central office, perhaps reflecting the union leadership's sense of itself as an advocate of social change, even in the face of rank and file opposition.

Unions at the forefront of the movement toward greater recognition of sexual diversity are often those in which feminists have made the greatest inroads in securing institutionalized support against discrimination related to gender. In many of the unions described here, activists found their voices and their courage and built their strongest alliances within women's caucuses, rather than from a broader-based diversity group. That women have been at the forefront is perhaps not very surprising, given the common roots of discrimination in traditional constructs of gender.

Executive leadership has also had a role, not only in the degree to which labor organizations have become engaged with sexual orientation issues, but also in the pace of change. At most of the labor organizations dealt with here, senior executives appear to have been largely supportive, although sometimes only after initial resistance or apathy, once issues and recommendations were brought forward by activists and women's committees. At CUPE, getting the issue on the national agenda was greatly facilitated by the presence of a head office champion and union directors prepared to support the drive. In unions such as BCGEU, where the executive and membership were totally preoccupied with survival and strikes throughout the 1980s, progress on equity issues has been a little slower in coming, although the catch-up has been swift. Male executives have often been just as ready as females with a show of support: Bob White, president of the CLC, and Buzz Hargrove, president of the CAW, stand out as two exemplars. By contrast, the disappointing record of Canada's American-based unions must partly be a reflection of the lack of leadership and momentum on equity issues at their headquarters, or inertia on the part of the leadership at Canadian branches.

Large Canadian-based labor organizations in the public sector, especially those with a strong activist presence, higher than average female membership, supportive leadership, and women's committees, are the most likely to have made significant progress on sexual diversity issues, even though one factor may be more pivotal in a given setting. CUPE is a prototypical union: It is Canadian-based, has above average female membership (55 percent), a very strong and well-established women's caucus assertively endorsing equity initiatives, and a high proportion of assertively sympathetic senior executives, including the president.

One might ask whether it makes a difference that the Canadian labor movement is beginning to address inequities to do with sexual orientation. It surely must make a difference for the thousands of gay/lesbian union members who now have formal redress within their unions when experiencing discrimination, and for the growing numbers that have equal access to benefit and pension schemes. Not only that, but when federations and unions as large as OFL, CSN, BCFL, CUPE, CAW, PSAC, and BCGEU take this issue on, the potential for education and political action on gay/lesbian rights is dramatically expanded within and far beyond the labor movement. These developments mean that many people, inside and outside of unions, are much more likely to be exposed to opinions, speeches, and educational programs debunking myths and stereotypes about homosexuality. Further, as more and more labor organizations become active agents of change, peer pressure may prod lagging colleagues to do the same.

Will the momentum continue? If the enthusiasm expressed at the CLC conference on sexual orientation held in October 1997 is an example, the answer must be a resounding yes. Another measure of ongoing developments is my own research: I found considerable progress had been made in just three years. Nevertheless, much remains to be done. Progressive policies and access to benefits are important first steps toward equity but do not necessarily change heterosexist attitudes and behavior. Organized labor has already proven it can make a huge difference in the area of lesbian and gay rights. If it now rallies its considerable resources toward educational programming designed to change negative attitudes and stereotypes about homosexuals and other minority groups, we will all be the better for it.

Notes

Acknowledgments: I would like to thank David Rayside, Michael Johnson, and Brent Bauer for their assistance in preparing this chapter. I would also like to express my gratitude to the Nipissing University Research Grants Committee for its financial support.

1. B. Ryder, "Equal Rights and Sexual Orientation: Confronting Heterosexual Family Privilege," *Canadian Journal of Family Law* 9 (1990): 39–97; D. Sanders, "Constructing Lesbian and Gay Rights," *Canadian Journal of Law and Society* 9, no. 2 (1994): 99–143.

2. M. Gunderson and A. Ponak, "Future Directions for Canadian Industrial Relations," in *Union-Management Relations in Canada,* 3rd ed., ed. M. Gunderson and A. Ponak (Toronto: Addison-Wesley, 1995).

3. A sizable literature now exists documenting and assessing labor's engagement with feminist issues. See, for example, P. Kumar and L. Acri, "Unions' Collective Bargaining Agenda on Women's Issues: The Ontario Experience," *Relations industrielles/Industrial Relations* 47, no. 4 (1992): 623–653; L. Briskin and P. McDermott, eds., *Women Challenging Unions: Feminism, Democracy, and Militancy* (Toronto: University of Toronto Press, 1993); D. Cobble, ed., *Women and Unions: Forging a Partnership* (Ithaca: Cornell University Press, 1993); N. Gabin, *Feminism in the Labor Movement: Women and the United Auto Workers, 1935–1975* (Ithaca: Cornell University Press, 1990); J. Lovenduski and V. Randall, *Contemporary Feminist Politics: Women and Power in Britain* (Oxford: Oxford University Press, 1993); J. White, *Sisters and Solidarity: Women and Unions in Canada* (Toronto: Thompson Educational Publishing, 1993); B. Pocock, ed., *Strife: Sex and Politics in Labour Unions* (St. Leonards, Australia: Allen and Unwin, 1997). There is a less substantial literature assessing the response of organized labor to visible minorities than in relation to gender. Some examples of what is available include: R. Leah, "Black Women Speak Out: Racism and Unions," in *Women Challenging Unions,* ed. Briskin and McDermott; Aguilar-San Juan, ed., *The State of Asian America: Activism and Resistance in the 1990s* (Boston: South End Press, 1994); G. Defreitas, "Unionization Among Racial and Ethnic Minorities," *Industrial and Labor Relations Review* 46, no. 2 (1993): 284–301; R. Horowitz, *Negro and White Unite and Fight* (Urbana: University of Illinois Press, 1997).

4. S. Genge, "Lesbians and Gays in the Union Movement," in *Union Sisters: Women in the Labour Movement,* ed. L. Briskin and L. Yanz (Toronto: The Women's Press, 1983); J. Bailey, "On Our Own Terms: Same Sex Spousal Benefits," *Our Times* 8, no. 4 (1989): 16–17; P. Wagner, "Coming Out: Homophobia as a Union Issue," *Our Times* 12, no. 1 (1993): 26–30.

5. S. Genge, "Lesbians and Gays in the Union Movement."

6. J. White, *Sisters and Solidarity.*

7. M. Battista, "Planes, Trains and Automobiles: The Labour Movement Is Taking Up the Same-Sex Benefits Battle," *Xtra,* no. 251 (10 June 1994): 15.

8. G. Hunt, "Sexual Orientation and the Canadian Labour Movement," *Relations industrielle/Industrial Relations* 52, no. 4 (1997): 787–811. The information to follow is based on data

collected by telephone and fax from union federations and union headquarters, personal interviews with union leaders, personal interviews with labor activists (who operate both inside and
outside of unions), union newsletters and other documents, collective agreements, interviews
with lesbian and gay activists, and newspapers (local and national newspapers as well as the gay-
and labor-oriented press).

9. Canadian Labour Congress, "Policy Statement: Sexual Orientation" (Ottawa: Canadian
Labour Congress, 1994), p. 5.

10. My report of this case was helped by a fact sheet prepared by William Mercer Limited
based in Toronto and reproduced with permission.

11. P. Kumar and N. Meltz, "Industrial Relations in the Automobile Industry," in *Industrial
Relations in Canada,* ed. R. Chaykowski and A. Verma (Toronto: Holt, Rinehart and Winston,
1992).

12. A number of feminists have studied the auto workers. See, for example, P. Sugiman,
Labour's Dilemma: The Gender Politics of Auto Workers in Canada, 1937–1979 (Toronto: University of Toronto Press, 1994).

13. Canadian Auto Workers, "Council Minutes, 8–9 April 1994."

14. J. White, *Sisters and Solidarity,* p. 227.

15. D. Kilby, "Heterosexism: Challenging the Norm." *Alliance* 6, no. 4 (1992): 21–23.

16. For example, the committee formally contested an incident in the BC legislature when a
Dutch-Canadian MLA made offensive remarks about the use of Cantonese in the legislature by
a Chinese Canadian who argued that it was important for her constituents to hear her argument
on a particular point.

17. Some of the information reported here is contained in a backgrounder that appeared in
*Out and About: Newsletter of the Lesbian, Gay and Bisexual Committee of the New Democ-
ratic Party of Canada* 1, no. 3 (1998).

18. CUPW information is partially based on a report in S. Gordon, "Inside Out Inside," *Our
Times* 17 (1998): 18–22.

19. I am particularly indebted to Brent Bauer at the University of Montreal for help in completing this section.

20. David Rayside's *On the Fringe: Gays and Lesbians in Politics* (Ithaca: Cornell University
Press, 1998) makes the argument that, on a number of sexual orientation policy issues, Quebec
has lagged behind larger provinces.

21. In addition to the CSN and the FTQ, the participating unions in this new Forum des gais
et lesbiennes syndiques du Québec include CDQ, SFPQ, SPGQ, SCFP, FIIQ, and TCA.

22. I am indebted to Barry Adam for this observation.

Cynthia Petersen

---

3 Fighting It Out in Canadian Courts

In the previous chapter, Gerald Hunt summarized the kinds of discrimination that lesbians and gay men face in Canada and highlighted the role that organized labor has played in addressing these problems. As he pointed out, employment discrimination based on sexual orientation has become less common over the past two decades, but it persists in many sectors and continues to affect the lives of countless workers. Certainly, unions bear some responsibility for human rights violations against lesbian and gay employees. Some unions, for example, have negotiated collective agreement clauses that benefit heterosexual employees exclusively. Some have failed in other ways to provide representation to lesbian and gay members. A number of unions, however, have been increasingly supportive of lesbian and gay equality rights in the workplace. Many unions have bargained for contract language to protect their members from discrimination based on sexual orientation, fought discriminatory employment practices through their grievance procedures, supported human rights complaints filed by individual workers, and devoted considerable resources to challenging discriminatory laws in the courts.

This chapter focuses primarily on the participation of unions in same-sex spousal benefits litigation. Litigation is, of course, only one small avenue in the queer liberation movement, and access to spousal benefits constitutes only one of the issues involved in the struggle for full equality. Court battles arise in a broader context of increased political activism and changed social climate. The willingness of union members to challenge discriminatory workplace practices is a byproduct of the growing visibility of lesbian/gay/bisexual/transgendered movements, and the readiness of tribunals to side with them is attributable to the advances made by overall movement activism.

The focus on spousal benefits litigation is not intended to suggest that it is the only area in which unions have been instrumental in advancing lesbian and gay equality claims. Even in the area of same-sex relationship recognition, many claims and grievances supported by unions never make it to arbitration boards and courts, simply because they are not firmly resisted by management. Much of the day-to-day support by unions is therefore invisible to the legal system. Unions have, however, been particularly active in litigation efforts to assert and enforce spousal claims on behalf of employees in same-sex relationships. Although many unions have remained outside the struggle for equality, those that have participated have had a significant impact. Several of the landmark rulings by courts and tribunals on the recognition of same-sex relationships have been supported by labor.

The Early Human Rights Cases, Mid-1970s to Mid-1980s

In 1977, Quebec became the first province to amend its human rights legislation to prohibit discrimination based on sexual orientation. At that time, human rights statutes existed in all ten provinces and the two territories, as well as in the federal jurisdiction, but outside Quebec they did not include sexual orientation as a prohibited ground of discrimination. Consequently, with the exception of provincially regulated employees in Quebec, individuals who suffered anti-gay discrimination in the workplace had no recourse to human rights commissions for redress. Some employees made creative attempts to file human rights complaints about anti-gay discrimination on grounds other than sexual orientation, but those attempts consistently failed.

For example, in the first reported human rights case involving employment discrimination against a gay man, the complainant alleged that his employer had discriminated against him on the basis of sex. Douglas Wilson was a graduate student employed as a sessional lecturer in the College of Education at the University of Saskatchewan. In 1975, he was suspended from supervising the practice teaching of his students in public schools because the university discovered that he was gay. When the Saskatchewan Human Rights Commission notified the university of its intention to investigate Wilson's complaint, the university applied to the Court of Queen's Bench for an order prohibiting the commission from conducting a formal inquiry. The university's application was granted by Judge Johnson, who ruled that the Saskatchewan human rights legislation outlawed discrimination based on sex, which meant gender, not sexual orientation, sexual proclivity, or sexual activity.[1]

A similar case arose in Ontario in 1975, when John Damien attempted to file a human rights complaint alleging that the Ontario Racing Commission (ORC) had fired him because he was gay. The Ontario Human Rights Commission refused to investigate Damien's complaint of sex discrimination, so he applied to the High Court of Justice for an order requiring the commission to receive and deal with his complaint. He also initiated a wrongful dismissal lawsuit against the ORC. The merits of his legal arguments were never determined by a court because Damien died before his cases proceeded to a hearing.[2]

A somewhat different sex discrimination argument was made by another gay man in a 1982 case. Chris Vogel, an employee of the Manitoba government, filed a human rights complaint against his employer because he was denied dental benefits for his same-sex partner, Richard North. Vogel complained that the opposite-sex restriction on eligibility for spousal benefits constituted discrimination based on marital status and sex, both of which were forbidden by the Manitoba Human Rights Act. A Board of Adjudication rejected his sex discrimination argument, ruling that the denial of benefits arose "not because Mr. Vogel is a male but because he chooses to live with another male."[3] His complaint of marital status discrimination was also rejected by the board, which concluded that same-sex partners have no marital status and consequently cannot claim discrimination on that ground.[4]

The Lobby for Human Rights Protection

As a result of these decisions, lesbian and gay activists became involved in a concerted lobby for legislative amendments to add sexual orientation as a prohibited ground of discrimination in provincial and federal human rights codes. Ontario, Manitoba, and the Yukon finally outlawed discrimination based on sexual orientation in 1986 and 1987. The federal government and most other provinces have since followed suit, but only after years of sustained lobbying and repeated resort to courts. Labor organizations have supported lesbian and gay communities in these efforts.

The *Canadian Charter of Rights and Freedoms* played a significant role in shifting the balance in favor of lesbian and gay activists. The *Charter* was proclaimed as part of the Canadian Constitution in 1982, and its equality rights provision came into effect in 1985. The *Charter* applies to all acts of government, federal and provincial. Its primary purpose is to restrain the state from enacting laws or engaging in conduct that infringes upon the fundamental rights and freedoms of individuals. Human rights codes also restrain discriminatory state action, but they do not enjoy the same legal status as the *Charter*. As a constitutional document, the *Charter* takes precedence over all Canadian statutes, including human rights codes.

Lesbian and gay activists have used the *Charter* to obtain human rights protection in several jurisdictions. After years of trying in vain to persuade the federal government to add sexual orientation to the *Canadian Human Rights Act,* a *Charter* challenge was initiated by Joshua Birch and Graham Haig, two gay men living in Ottawa. The case resulted in a 1992 declaration by the Ontario Court of Appeal that the federal government is required to protect individuals from discrimination based on sexual orientation.[5] Three years later, the Newfoundland Supreme Court ruled that the *Human Rights Code* in that province violated the *Charter* because it did not include sexual orientation as a prohibited ground of discrimination.[6] More recently, in April 1998, the Supreme Court of Canada held that the Alberta government's refusal to prohibit discrimination based on sexual orientation in its human rights code was unconstitutional.

The Alberta case involved Delwin Vriend, a laboratory coordinator at King's College in Edmonton, who had been fired from his job because he is gay. He tried to file a complaint against his employer, but the Alberta Human Rights Commission explained that he could not do so because discrimination based on sexual orientation was not prohibited by the provincial human rights statute. He reacted by initiating a court case against the Alberta government. When the case reached the Supreme Court of Canada, the Canadian Labour Congress was among the many organizations that intervened in support of Vriend, continuing its long-standing commitment to the advancement of lesbian and gay rights and to the elimination of employment discrimination generally.

The decision of the Supreme Court in the *Vriend* case was an important victory, not only because it gave human rights protection to lesbians and gay men in Alberta, but also because it set an important precedent for the governments of Prince Edward Island, the Northwest Territories, and Nunavut, which have not yet amended their human rights legislation to include sexual orientation.

Collective Bargaining and Grievance Arbitration Cases, 1975–1992

In addition to supporting litigation and lobbying efforts for greater human rights protection, the organized labor movement in Canada has been instrumental in advancing lesbian and gay equality rights through the collective bargaining process. Since the 1970s, and throughout the last two decades, unions have been negotiating comprehensive "no discrimination" clauses that cover sexual orientation. In many instances, this has provided unionized employees with contractual protection from discrimination even before applicable human rights statutes were amended. In Alberta, for example, the University of Lethbridge Faculty Association negotiated a collective agreement in 1992 that prohibited discrimination against any member of the academic staff by reason of their sexual orientation. Subsequently, when the university refused to allow a gay professor to enroll for family coverage under the employee health care and dental care plans, the Faculty Association filed a grievance pursuant to the collective agreement. A labor arbitrator ruled that the university had violated the no discrimination provision in the agreement by restricting eligibility for spousal benefits to heterosexual partners.[7] As a result of this decision, all lesbian and gay members of the academic staff at the University of Lethbridge became eligible to receive spousal benefits for their same-sex partners, notwithstanding that their equality rights were not protected by the province's human rights legislation at that time.

Collective agreement protection continues to be vitally important to lesbian and gay employees, even in jurisdictions where human rights statutes have been amended to add sexual orientation. In the event that lesbians and gay men suffer discrimination at work, they have access to a grievance procedure, which is often preferable to the human rights complaints process. Moreover, contractual protection frequently exceeds the limited scope of protection afforded by human rights statutes. The significance of collective agreement protection is evident from the fact that grievance arbitration has become the most fruitful avenue for advancing lesbian and gay equality claims in the employment context, though for a time it was not as effective as it is now in securing same-sex spousal benefits for lesbian and gay workers.

The initial phase of same-sex spousal benefits arbitrations occurred in the late 1980s and early 1990s. In virtually all of the early grievances, the union relied on a collective agreement clause that protected workers from discrimination based on sexual orientation. Although the facts in each case clearly demonstrated that employees in lesbian and gay relationships were denied benefits available to employees in heterosexual relationships, the grievances consistently failed.

The first such arbitration case appears to have arisen from a grievance filed by a Quebec local of the Canadian Union of Postal Workers (CUPW).[8] The grievor was a lesbian who was denied leave to care for her ailing same-sex partner of sixteen years. The collective agreement between CUPW and the Canada Post Corporation allowed employees to take leave in the event of illness of an "immediate family member," including a "common-law spouse," the latter term not being defined in the agreement. The union argued that the expression should be interpreted broadly to include the grievor and her same-sex partner, particularly since the agreement contained a clause prohibiting discrimination based on sexual orientation. The arbitrator rejected CUPW's argument and ruled that the "universally recognized meaning" of a common-law relationship excludes "homosexual partners." He also stated that "it is not because the Grievor is a homosexual that the Employer refused to grant her a benefit under the collective agreement, but instead because her friend [*sic*] did not fit into the specific context of members of the immediate family."

Two similar cases were decided in Ontario during this initial phase of arbitrations. The first involved a grievance filed by Local 2424 of the Canadian Union of Public Employees (CUPE) in 1985. Jim Carleton was an employee of Carleton University who sought a tuition waiver and health insurance coverage for his partner, Bob Krawczyk. The university denied him the benefits, arguing that its collective agreement with CUPE defined "spouse" as a "husband or wife in law or in common law."

Carleton grieved the university's decision, alleging that it amounted to discrimination based on sexual orientation, which was specifically prohibited by the collective agreement. At the arbitration hearing, CUPE argued that the definition of spouse in the collective agreement should be interpreted in light of the no discrimination provision in the agreement, as well as the Ontario *Human Rights Code,* which had just recently been amended to forbid discrimination based on sexual orientation. Ironically, it was the *Human Rights Code* that ultimately defeated the union's argument. The arbitration board dismissed the grievance because the definition of spouse in the collective agreement was consistent with the heterosexual definition of spouse contained in the *Code.*[9] Consequently, the board held that the definition of spouse in the agreement did not discriminate based on sexual orientation. CUPE applied for judicial review of the board's decision, but its application was dismissed by Judge Reid, who issued an endorsement stating that "the law [as reflected in the *Human Rights Code*] does not recognize homosexual partners as spouses."[10] CUPE attempted to appeal Judge Reid's decision to the Ontario Court of Appeal, but its motion for leave to appeal was denied.[11]

The second Ontario grievance involved Steven Chalkley, a gay man employed by Parkwood Hospital in London. When he requested health benefits coverage for his same-sex partner, his employer advised that the coverage would not be provided because of the cost and because "homosexuals are at risk from AIDS." The London and District Service Workers' Union filed a grievance, arguing that the employer's refusal to grant spousal coverage to Chalkley's partner was arbitrary and discriminatory. Although the collective agreement did not include a clause to prohibit discrimination based on sexual orientation, the union argued that the employer was required to manage its enterprise in accordance with the Ontario *Human Rights Code,* which had been amended to prohibit discrimination based on sexual orientation. An arbitrator denied the grievance, ruling that the case could not be meaningfully distinguished from the earlier *Carleton* decision.[12]

Two other unsuccessful grievances during this initial phase of arbitrations involved federal public servants. The first was initiated by James Watson, an employee in the Department of Indian and Northern Affairs in Vancouver, who grieved the denial of bereavement leave following the death of his same-sex partner's sister. According to the Master Agreement between the Public Service Alliance of Canada (PSAC) and Treasury Board, employees were eligible for bereavement leave upon the death of certain family members, including a sister-in-law. ("Sister-in-law" was not defined in the agreement, but "common-law spouse" was defined in exclusively heterosexual terms.) At the arbitration hearing, PSAC argued that the government's refusal to grant Watson's request for bereavement leave violated the Master Agreement, which specifically prohibited discrimination based on sexual orientation. The Public Service Staff Relations Board rejected the union's argument and ruled that it did not have the power to amend the collective agreement by disregarding the words "of the opposite sex" in the definition of "common law spouse."[13]

The second federal public service case involved the grievance of David Hewens, a gay man employed in the Department of Public Works in Ottawa. In July 1992, Hewens participated in a marriage ceremony with his same-sex partner, Marc Laflamme. The ceremony had the traditional rituals of a Christian wedding, including the exchange of vows and rings before friends and family, and was performed by an ordained minister of the Independent Anglican Church. According to the Master Agreement between the Treasury Board and PSAC, employees were entitled to "five days' marriage leave with pay for the purpose of getting married," but Hewens's application for leave was denied by the government on the basis that "the arrangement . . . with his male partner did not constitute a marriage."

The word "married" was not defined in the Master Agreement. PSAC argued that an expansive interpretation of the word should be applied in light of the agreement's specific prohibition against discrimination based on sexual orientation. The Public Service Staff Relations Board rejected the union's argument, ruling that the term must be given "its ordinary meaning as understood both in law and in common parlance," namely that marriage is a "union between a man and a woman."[14] The board also held that it was "doubtful whether . . . the grievor was discriminated against on the ground of sexual orientation" because he was treated no differently than a heterosexual employee would be if she or he sought marriage leave for the purpose of participating in a ceremony that was not legally recognized as a valid marriage.

Union Involvement in Court Cases, 1988–1993

The early grievance arbitration decisions were not anomalous. They mirrored the early decisions rendered by courts in a variety of lesbian and gay equality rights cases. For example, the first *Charter of Rights and Freedoms* case involving a claim of spousal status by a same-sex couple was initiated in 1987 by CUPE Local 1996 and one of its members, Karen Andrews, who was an employee of the Toronto Public Library Board. Andrews had lived with her same-sex partner, Karen Trenholm, and her partner's two children for approximately nine years. Under CUPE's collective agreement, the Library

Board was required to pay Ontario Health Insurance Plan (OHIP) coverage for employees and their dependants. The Library Board was willing to pay dependant coverage for Trenholm and her children, but the Ontario Hospital Insurance Commission refused to recognize Trenholm as Andrews's spouse for the purposes of insurance coverage under the provincial *Health Insurance Act.*

In the court application, CUPE asserted that Andrews and Trenholm were spouses, but Judge McRae of the Ontario High Court of Justice disagreed. Although there was no definition of the word spouse in the *Health Insurance Act,* he relied on dictionary definitions and other Ontario statutes that define a spouse as a person of the opposite sex. CUPE then argued that, if cohabiting lesbian partners were precluded from obtaining dependant coverage under the *Health Insurance Act,* then the *Act* violated equality rights guaranteed by the *Charter.* Judge McRae rejected that argument as well, ruling that the *Act* was not discriminatory because "heterosexual couples of the same sex" were treated the same as lesbian couples.[15] In other words, heterosexual "brothers and brothers, sisters and sisters, . . . cousins, parents and adult children and any combination of them may be living together under similar circumstances to [Andrews and Trenholm] but would in each case pay OHIP premiums as 'single persons.'"

This type of reasoning was frequently adopted by courts in other early *Charter* cases involving claims for same-sex spousal recognition.[16] It also prevailed in human rights cases at that time, engendering disappointment and frustration for lesbian and gay litigants. Perhaps the best example is the decision of the Manitoba Court of Queen's Bench in the case involving Chris Vogel and Richard North's 1988 human rights complaint. Vogel had made his earlier unsuccessful complaint in 1982, arguing that his employer was discriminating against him based on sex and marital status by refusing to provide him with dental benefits for his same-sex partner. After the Manitoba *Human Rights Act* was amended to add sexual orientation as a prohibited ground of discrimination, Vogel and North filed a new complaint against both the Manitoba government and the Manitoba Government Employees' Association (MGEA). Although the MGEA was named as a respondent because of its role in negotiating a collective agreement that denied spousal benefits to same-sex partners, it supported the arguments presented by the complainants.

When Vogel's first complaint of sex discrimination was dismissed in 1983, the Board of Adjudication ruled that the "denial of benefits to Mr. North arises because of Mr. Vogel's sexual preference and not his gender."[17] The 1988 complaint therefore should have been successful because it was framed as discrimination based on sexual orientation. The complaint was, however, dismissed by the Board of Adjudication, and the dismissal was subsequently upheld by the Manitoba Court of Queen's Bench. Judge Hirschfield found that the denial of same-sex spousal benefits did not constitute discrimination based on sexual orientation, since "homosexual" employees were eligible to receive spousal benefits, provided that they had an opposite-sex spouse.[18]

At this stage, then, arbitrators, adjudicators, and judges all adhered to the circular reasoning that the refusal to grant spousal benefits to same-sex partners was not discriminatory because same-sex partners simply were not spouses. The absurdity of this reasoning was most apparent when tribunals concluded that "homosexuals" were treated equally because they were entitled to precisely the same benefits as heterosexuals, namely spousal benefits for a conjugal partner of the opposite sex.

Lesbian and gay rights litigation might have been abandoned in despair had it not been for a few lower court and tribunal decisions that signaled the jurisprudential tide could be changing in favor of same-sex spousal recognition. First, in 1991, the British Columbia Supreme Court ruled that the exclusion of cohabiting same-sex partners from the definition of spouse in the provincial health insurance regulations violated the *Charter* equality rights of lesbians and gay men.[19] This landmark ruling was made in a case that involved precisely the same issue as the 1988 *Andrews* case in Ontario.

The applicant was Timothy Knodel, a nurse employed by Vancouver's Shaughnessy University Hospital. His employment was governed by a collective agreement that required the hospital to pay Medical Services Plan premiums for employees and their dependants. When his same-sex partner became ill, however, the Medical Services Commission (which administers the provincial Medical Services Plan) refused to register his partner as his spouse. The commission based its refusal on regulations under the *Medical Services Act,* which contained a heterosexual definition of the word spouse. With the support of both the Hospital Employees' Union and his employer, Knodel successfully challenged the regulations' definition of spouse as an unconstitutional infringement of his *Charter* equality rights.

The next important victory came in 1992, when a Board of Inquiry ruled that the Ontario government had violated the provincial *Human Rights Code* by denying public servants coverage for their same-sex partners under various employment benefits plans.[20] The case began in 1988 when Michael Leshner, a lawyer employed by the Ministry of the Attorney General, complained that his employment benefits were discriminatory. The Ontario government argued that the benefit programs were lawful because the *Code* included heterosexual definitions of the terms spouse and marital status. The *Code* also included a section that specifically allowed discrimination based on marital status within insured benefits plans and pension plans. A Board of Inquiry ruled that, by providing the government with a defense against Leshner's complaint, the *Code* was itself discriminatory based on sexual orientation and was therefore unconstitutional. As a result of this ruling, employees represented by the Ontario Public Service Employees' Union became entitled to same-sex spousal benefits, including survivor pension benefits.

The third important victory occurred in 1992, when the British Columbia Workers' Compensation Board (WCB) awarded Shirley Petten a monthly pension as the surviving spouse of Beverly Holmwood, a nurse who died as a result of a work-related injury. Petten's application for the pension was initially rejected by a WCB adjudicator, who held that a same-sex partner could not qualify as a spouse. The British Columbia Nurses' Union assisted Petten in challenging the adjudicator's decision. She successfully argued that the workers' compensation legislation should be interpreted in accordance with the provincial human rights statute, which had just been amended to prohibit discrimination based on sexual orientation.[21]

These three decisions in 1991–1992 offered hope to lesbians and gay men that the earlier trend of negative rulings in same-sex spousal benefits cases might be reversed. However, they also created significant confusion for employees and employers alike, who were unclear as to their respective rights and obligations. Thus, employers, unions, and lesbian and gay workers eagerly awaited a pronouncement from the Supreme Court of Canada to resolve the inconsistencies that had emerged in the jurisprudence.

The *Mossop* Case (1993)

The first same-sex spousal benefits case to reach the Supreme Court was decided in February 1993. It was initiated by Brian Mossop, a translator employed by the Department of the Secretary of State, after he was denied bereavement leave to attend the funeral of his male partner's father. His employment was governed by a collective agreement between the Treasury Board and the Canadian Union of Professional and Technical Employees (CUPTE). The agreement provided employees with up to four days' leave upon the death of an "immediate family member," which was defined to include a father-in-law. "Father-in-law" was not defined in the agreement, but "common-law spouse" was defined in a manner that restricted its application to the opposite-sex partners of employees.

Mossop's request for bereavement leave was rejected. A subsequent grievance, launched with the support of CUPTE, was denied. Rather than proceeding to arbitration, Mossop chose to submit a complaint to the Canadian Human Rights Commission, alleging that both his employer and his union had violated his rights by negotiating a collective agreement that discriminated against him on the basis of family status. When he filed the complaint in 1985, sexual orientation was not a prohibited ground of discrimination under the *Canadian Human Rights Act* (CHRA).

Mossop's complaint eventually reached the Supreme Court of Canada, which ruled that the denial of bereavement leave did not constitute discrimination based on family status. The legislative history of the CHRA revealed that Parliament had deliberately decided not to add sexual orientation to the statute when it added family status to the list of prohibited grounds of discrimination in 1983. The Supreme Court ruled that the reason for the denial of bereavement leave was so closely related to Mossop's sexual orientation that to allow his complaint on the basis of family status would effectively introduce into the CHRA a prohibition that Parliament had specifically decided to exclude.[22]

It is important to note that, approximately six months prior to the release of the *Mossop* decision, the Ontario Court of Appeal had declared (in the *Haig* case) that the CHRA was unconstitutional because it did not prohibit discrimination based on sexual orientation. The Court of Appeal also ordered that the CHRA be interpreted and applied as though it included sexual orientation. After the release of the *Haig* decision, the Supreme Court of Canada invited the parties in *Mossop* to submit new arguments with respect to the constitutionality of the CHRA, but the parties declined, insisting that the court dispose of the *Mossop* appeal based on an interpretation of the meaning of family status. Significantly, Chief Justice Lamer suggested in *Mossop* that the Supreme Court might have decided the case differently if the parties had accepted the invitation to submit *Charter* arguments. Without a *Charter* challenge to the constitutional validity of the CHRA, the Supreme Court was powerless to interfere with Parliament's intent to exclude lesbians and gay men from the protection afforded by that statute.

Union Supported Grievances in the Wake of the *Mossop* Decision

Although Mossop lost his legal battle for bereavement leave, his case established a positive precedent for same-sex spousal rights litigation. Prior to the *Mossop* decision, arbitrators and most tribunals and courts had ruled that the failure to treat same-sex and opposite-sex partners equally did not constitute discrimination based on sexual orientation. It was therefore significant that the Supreme Court of Canada effectively told Mossop that the real reason he was denied bereavement leave was not because of his family status, but rather because he was gay. The reasoning that had characterized previous negative decisions in same-sex spousal benefits cases was clearly inconsistent with the Supreme Court's decision in *Mossop*.

The impact of the *Mossop* case was apparent almost immediately in the labor arbitration field. In workplaces where a collective agreement or the governing human rights statute prohibited discrimination based on sexual orientation, unions began to win same-sex spousal benefits grievances. The first successful grievance was decided in September 1993. The Public Service Staff Relations Board ruled that the Treasury Board had violated its Master Agreement with PSAC by refusing to recognize a gay employee's same-sex partner as his common-law spouse for the purpose of certain leave provisions in the collective agreement. The grievance was filed by David Lorenzen after he was denied family-related leave to care for his injured partner, Steven Pauls, and denied bereavement leave to attend the funeral of Pauls's father. The Public Service Staff Relations Board, citing the *Mossop* decision, found that the government had discriminated against the grievor on the basis of his sexual orientation.

The *Mossop* decision was also cited by arbitrators in three successful grievances in 1994. The University of Lethbridge Faculty Association won a grievance (cited earlier) that resulted in same-sex spousal coverage for academic staff enrolled in the university's life insurance, dental care, extended health care, and vision care plans. The Canadian Telephone Employees' Association won a similar grievance on behalf of Michael Lee and Ritchie Waller, two gay employees who wanted to register their respective same-sex partners for spousal coverage under Bell Canada's comprehensive benefits program (which included pension, extended health care, dental care, and vision care benefits).[23] Finally, PSAC won a grievance against Canada Post Corporation on behalf of Luc Guevremont, a payroll clerk who was denied reimbursement of vision care expenses incurred by his same-sex partner, Raymond Milne.[24] The latter case involved the second grievance filed by Guevremont in an effort to obtain same-sex spousal benefits. His first grievance had been dismissed by an arbitrator only six months earlier.[25]

The arbitrator who heard Guevremont's first grievance appears to have misinterpreted the *Mossop* decision. He treated *Mossop* as a precedent for the broad principle that a denial of same-sex spousal benefits is not discriminatory, rather than for the narrower principle that it does not constitute *discrimination based on family status*. A similar error was made by a different arbitrator in another 1994 grievance against the Canada Post Corporation, which was filed by a Winnipeg local of CUPW. The latter case involved a lesbian employee's request for same-sex spousal coverage under the corporation's dental plan.[26] The union argued that the corporation's refusal to provide the benefits violated the collective agreement, which specifically prohibited discrimination based on sexual orientation. The arbitrator dismissed the grievance, ruling that the grievor had not suffered discrimination based on her sexual orientation, because her request for spousal benefits would have been granted—despite her sexual orientation—if only her partner had been of the opposite-sex.

Fortunately, these two cases did not represent a renewed trend in same-sex spousal benefits litigation. They did contribute, however, to ongoing confusion about the respective rights and obligations of lesbian and gay workers and employers, and the uncertainty in the law generated further litigation. For example, in 1995, the Canadian Media Guild filed a grievance on behalf of Denis-Martin Chabot, a legislative reporter employed by the Canadian Broadcasting Corporation (CBC) in Edmonton. Chabot had been denied spousal benefits for his same-sex partner, Dwayne Zoeteman, under the CBC's health care, dental care, and employee pension plans. The union argued that the denial of benefits violated the collective agreement, which specifically prohibited discrimination based on sexual orientation. The arbitrator agreed, quoting extensively from the *Mossop* case, which he regarded "as providing authoritative guidance." He found that the corporation's refusal to grant same-sex spousal benefits "must be construed as discrimination on the basis of sexual orientation."[27] The CBC was ordered to rid its employee benefit plans of discrimination.

The Supreme Court's Decision in *Egan* and Its Impact on Grievance Arbitrations

In May 1995, the Supreme Court of Canada released its decision in the *Egan*[28] case and thereby eliminated whatever doubt remained after *Mossop* about whether the denial of same-sex spousal benefits constitutes discrimination based on sexual orientation. James Egan and John Nesbit challenged the opposite-sex definition of spouse in the *Old Age Security Act* (OASA), arguing that it constituted a violation of their *Charter* equality rights. Under the OASA, a spouse of a pensioner is entitled to receive an allowance from the ages of 60 to 65, provided that the couple's joint income falls below a particular amount. Egan was a pensioner whose partner of forty years was denied a spousal allowance even though their joint income was lower than the requisite threshold. The denial of Nesbit's request for a spousal allowance was upheld by both the trial division and the appellate division of the Federal Court. The case was appealed to the Supreme Court of Canada, where the Canadian Labour Congress intervened with other organizations in support of the appellants.

The outcome of the *Egan* case was complex. First, the Supreme Court ruled that the *Charter* prohibits discrimination based on sexual orientation, although it does not do so explicitly. The court also concluded that the opposite-sex definition of spouse in the OASA discriminates based on sexual orientation, thereby eliminating any uncertainty that existed about the import of the earlier *Mossop* decision. Egan and Nesbit's appeal, however, was dismissed by a majority of the court on the basis that the discrimination in the OASA was justifiable pursuant to section 1 of the *Charter,* which permits governments to impose reasonable limits on constitutional rights. The precise reasons for the court's ruling under section 1 were somewhat difficult to decipher, since four out of the five judges who held that the discrimination was justifiable expressed their reasons for doing so in a single sentence. The fifth judge, Justice Sopinka, wrote separate reasons for his decision. He outlined several factors, including the cost of extending the spousal allowance to same-sex partners, the ostensible "novelty" of the claim for spousal recognition, and the fact that Parliament requires time to move "incrementally" in developing social policy initiatives.

In the *Egan* case, the Supreme Court unequivocally affirmed that a denial of spousal benefits to same-sex partners constitutes discrimination based on sexual orientation. The ultimate rejection of Egan and Nesbit's claim, based on section 1 of the *Charter,* did not detract from the significance of the court's ruling in the labor arbitration field, since collective agreements do not contain clauses similar to section 1 of the *Charter.* The *Egan* case consequently did not assist employers who were seeking to deny lesbian and gay workers access to same-sex spousal benefits.

For example, shortly after the decision in *Egan* was released, the Canadian Broadcasting Corporation returned before the arbitrator who had ruled in February 1995 that it must rid its employee benefits plans of discrimination based on sexual orientation. The CBC argued that, with respect to pension benefits, the earlier arbitration award had been superceded by the Supreme Court's ruling in *Egan.* The arbitrator rejected the CBC's argument, stating that *Egan* did not create "any sort of legal impediment" to the establishment of a pension plan that provides spousal survivor benefits to employees in same-sex relationships.[29] The issue of pension benefit was especially significant because the *Income Tax Act* provided preferential tax treatment to registered pension plans that restricted spousal survivor benefits to opposite-sex partners. The *Income Tax Act*'s definition of spouse would later become the subject of separate litigation in the *Rosenberg* case, which is discussed below.

In the past three years, numerous other successful arbitration cases have involved claims for same-sex spousal benefits. Many of the grievances have raised issues identical to those that were litigated and lost prior to the *Mossop* and *Egan* decisions. For example, in December 1995, CUPW won a grievance on behalf of Archie Aebly, a longstanding employee of the Canada Post Corporation, who was denied bereavement leave to attend the funeral of his same-sex partner's father. The corporation argued that Aebly's request was denied not because of his sexual orientation, but rather because no member of his immediate family had died. According to the corporation, the deceased was not Aebly's father-in-law because Aebly and his same-sex partner were not (and could not be) legally married. The arbitrator ruled in favor of the union, declaring that Aebly's same-sex partner qualified as his common-law spouse, and that the deceased consequently qualified as his father-in-law within the meaning of the bereavement leave provisions in the collective agreement.[30]

CUPE Local 1582 also won an arbitration case late in 1995. The grievance was filed against the Metro Toronto Reference Library, which had denied a gay employee bereavement leave upon the death of his same-sex partner.[31] In 1996, two successful grievances were decided by the Public Service Staff Relations Board against the Treasury Board of Canada. One was filed by PSAC on behalf of Lahl Barbara Sarson, an employee of the Canadian Grain Commission in Winnipeg, who was denied relocation leave to accompany her partner, Rebecca Van Sciver, when she moved to British Columbia.[32] The other was filed by the Professional Institute of the Public Service of Canada (PIPSC) on behalf of Stephen Yarrow, an employee of Agriculture and Agri-Food Canada, who was denied bereavement leave when his partner, Joseph Adam Murray, died.[33] In the latter case, PSAC intervened in support of Yarrow's grievance.

In June 1997, the Public Service Staff Relations Board revisited the issue of marriage leave for public service employees who have a commitment ceremony with their same-sex partner. As discussed above, PSAC had lost a grievance on this very issue in 1992. This time, PIPSC was filing a grievance on behalf of Ross Boutilier, an employee in the Department of Natural Resources in Halifax, Nova Scotia, who had requested leave to participate in a church wedding ceremony with his partner, Brian Mombourquette. His request was denied on the basis that his holy union with Mombourquette was not legally recognized as a valid marriage. At the arbitration hearing, the government argued that the board would be required to "do violence to the ordinary meaning" of the word marriage in order to allow Boutilier's grievance. The union argued that the board should interpret the word marriage to include a same-sex commitment ceremony because the collective agreement must be interpreted in a manner consistent with the *Canadian Human Rights Act,* which had been amended to prohibit discrimination based on sexual orientation. The board accepted the union's argument and upheld Boutilier's grievance.[34] The government, however, applied for judicial review of this decision. (The Federal Court has not yet ruled on the government's application.)

Another important arbitration case decided in 1997 involved a grievance filed by the British Columbia Government and Service Employees' Union (BCGSEU). The grievor was Liav Gold, an employee in the provincial Ministry of Women's Equality, who was in a long-term same-sex relationship with Rhys Liat del Valle. The case began shortly after del Valle gave birth to their son, Elias, in 1995. Gold applied for parental leave benefits under the *Unemployment Insurance Act* (now the *Employment Insurance Act*). She also applied for parental leave and for an additional allowance to "top up" her unemployment benefits, as provided by the Master Agreement negotiated by the BCGSEU. (The "top up" provision in the agreement ensured that employees on parental leave received 75 percent of their regular wages.)

Gold's requests were denied. The employer asserted that Gold was neither the biological nor the adoptive mother of Elias and consequently was not a parent of the child with respect to whom she had made her application for parental leave. The employer also asserted that Gold's sexual orientation was irrelevant because all applicants, regardless of their sexual orientation, must meet the criteria for being a parent before they qualify for parental leave and the leave allowance under the collective agreement. The union filed a grievance on Gold's behalf, alleging that the employer's decision violated the collective agreement, which prohibited discrimination based on sexual orientation.

The grievance was referred to arbitration, where the union's position prevailed.[35] The arbitrator ruled that the "form of parenthood selected by the grievor and Ms. del Valle was one dictated by their sexual orientation" and that to require Gold to bring herself within the definition of a parent urged by the employer would amount to discrimination based on sexual orientation. (It should be noted that this grievance arose before it became legal in British Columbia for a woman to adopt her same-sex partner's biological child. It was therefore not possible for Gold to adopt her son Elias unless del Valle relinquished her rights as his mother.)

Following the arbitration decision, an issue arose with respect to the appropriate remedy in the case. The federal government had also denied Gold's request for unemployment benefits, and the arbitrator did not have the jurisdiction to order Employment Canada to reverse its decision. The collective agreement required the employer to "top up" unemployment benefits received from Employment Canada, but in Gold's case, there were no benefits to top up. The union argued that the employer should fund the entire leave allowance (i.e., 75 percent of the grievor's regular wages); the employer argued that such a remedy would be unfair. The arbitrator ruled that the "Employer cannot avoid the obligation to pay leave allowance on the basis that Employment Canada does not recognize the grievor's status as a parent and thus refuses to fund its portion of the benefit." Since the loss to the grievor of denying the benefit outweighed the cost to the employer of funding the benefit, the arbitrator ordered that the full allowance be paid by the employer.

Cases Brought Before Human Rights Tribunals After *Egan*

Same-sex spousal benefits cases continue to be litigated before human rights tribunals, although not as often as labor arbitration boards. Unions have often been directly involved in these cases, in some instances supporting complainants even when the unions have been named as respondents. The case of Chris Vogel provides a useful illustration. His 1982 and 1988 attempts to secure same-sex benefits from the Manitoba government have already been discussed. His second human rights complaint eventually reached the Manitoba Court of Appeal, which ruled in June 1995 that, as a result of the *Egan* decision, it was "bound to conclude that the denial of spousal benefits [to Vogel's] same-sex partner is the result of their sexual orientation, and is, therefore, discriminatory treatment" under the Manitoba Human Rights Code.[36] The court referred the complaint back to the Board of Adjudication for a hearing as to whether there was a *bona fide* and reasonable cause for the discrimination.

When the case was subsequently heard by the Board of Adjudication, the Manitoba government attempted to defend its position by relying on Justice Sopinka's reasoning in *Egan*. In particular, the government argued that the board should adopt an "incremental approach to expanding the protection against discrimination" and should "take into account the additional costs and administrative burden" of extending spousal benefits to the same-sex partners of employees.[37] Although the Manitoba Government Employees' Union (MGEU) was named as a respondent in the complaint, it supported the position of Vogel and North, arguing that the reasons of Justice Sopinka in the *Egan* case do not apply to situations in which a government acts as an employer. Evidence was adduced with respect to the MGEU's unsuccessful attempts to obtain same-sex spousal benefits through collective bargaining. The Board of Adjudication ruled against the Manitoba government with respect to the dental, health care, and group life insurance plans. On the other hand, it ruled that the government's refusal to provide survivor pension benefits to same-sex spouses was reasonable, in light of the applicable income tax regulations (which are discussed below).

Another significant human rights case involved the complaints of Dale Akerstrom and Stanley Moore, two federal public servants who were denied spousal benefits for their respective same-sex partners. Akerstrom, an employee of Citizenship and Immigration Canada, was seeking health care and dental care coverage for his partner, Alexander Dias. Moore, a Foreign Service Officer employed by the Department of External Affairs, was seeking a variety of insured and uninsured spousal benefits. He had been denied a spousal relocation allowance when his partner, Pierre Soucy, had accompanied him on a posting to Indonesia. They had been assigned housing in Jakarta as though Moore was single, and while in Jakarta, Soucy had been denied access to the recreational hardship support program offered to opposite-sex spouses. Soucy had also been denied spousal coverage under Moore's extended health care and dental care plans.

Akerstrom was a member of a bargaining unit represented by PSAC. Moore's bargaining agent was the Professional Association of Foreign Service Officers (PAFSO). Both men named their unions and the federal government as respondents in their respective complaints, alleging that the unions were partially responsible for the discrimination because they had negotiated the benefits contained in the collective agreements. However, at the hearing before the Canadian Human Rights Tribunal, both PSAC and PAFSO supported the complainants' positions. In addition, PIPSC intervened in the case in support of the complainants. There was evidence during the hearing that all three unions had made repeated efforts to acquire same-sex spousal benefits for employees through collective bargaining.

After reviewing the decisions in *Egan* and *Vogel,* the tribunal held that the law "is now crystal clear" that "denial of the extension of employment benefits to a same-sex partner which would otherwise be extended to opposite-sex common-law partners is discriminatory on the prohibited ground of sexual orientation."[38] The government relied on the reasoning of Justice Sopinka in *Egan,* arguing that the denial of spousal benefits constitutes a reasonable limit on human rights, in light of the government's limited resources and the need for flexibility in making decisions about eligibility for benefits. The tribunal rejected that argument, noting that it is important to make a distinction between the role of government as the developer and implementer of social policy initiatives and the role of government as employer. In this case, the government was an employer who could "no more rely upon s.1 of the *Charter* to justify discrimination on a ground prohibited under [the *Canadian Human Rights Act*] than can a private employer who is federally regulated." The tribunal also described the benefits at issue in the complaints as "earned benefits" that were "part of the remunerative package of employees," distinguishing them from the "discretionary social benefits" at issue in the *Egan* case.

As a result of this case, the federal government was ordered to extend spousal benefits to the same-sex partners of all public service employees. The government attempted to implement the tribunal's order by granting lesbian and gay employees the same benefits as heterosexual employees without actually recognizing that cohabiting same-sex partners are spouses within the meaning of the PSAC, PIPSC, and PAFSO Master Agreements. The unions rejected that proposal, and the matter was referred back to the tribunal, which ordered the government to treat cohabiting same-sex partners as spouses. The government was advised that it cannot segregate employees with same-sex partners as a separate category of benefits recipients.[39]

The Special Case of Pension Benefits

Until very recently, lesbian and gay workers' claims for spousal pension benefits faced unique hurdles due to complications created by the *Income Tax Act*. The outcome of Chris Vogel and Richard North's human rights complaint illustrates this point. As mentioned above, in 1997 the Manitoba Board of Adjudication ruled in their favor with respect to all employment benefits except the spousal survivor pension. A similar result was reached in March 1998 in an arbitration case involving several grievances filed by two locals of the Canadian Auto Workers (CAW) against Chrysler Canada Ltd. The CAW was successful in winning an array of same-sex spousal benefits for its lesbian and gay members (including health and dental care, legal services, and various forms of leave) but lost its claim for survivor pension benefits for same-sex spouses.[40] In both of these cases, the pension benefits were denied due to the impact of income tax regulations.

Prior to the April 1998 court ruling in the *Rosenberg* case, which is discussed below, the *Income Tax Act* created a strong disincentive, if not an outright barrier, to the provision of same-sex spousal pension benefits. The *Act* required that certain conditions be satisfied in order for a pension plan to be registered. One of the criteria for registration was that a plan had to provide survivor benefits for the spouses of deceased plan members, but only for opposite-sex spouses. Consequently, Revenue Canada would revoke the registered status of any pension plan that purported to pay survivor benefits to same-sex widows or widowers. Since deregistration of a pension plan had severe negative tax consequences, virtually all employers refused to provide same-sex spousal pension benefits in order to preserve the registered status of their plans.

Despite these tax rules, in the early 1990s, lesbian and gay employees began to challenge their employers' refusal to provide survivor pension benefits for same-sex partners. Unions played an active role in supporting many of these challenges. Arbitrators and adjudicators were, however, understandably reluctant to order employers to take any action that could result in the deregistration of a pension plan, because that would have adverse financial implications that could jeopardize the very existence of the plan. Most pension benefits cases were therefore unsuccessful.

One notable exception was the *Leshner* case, which was decided by the Ontario Board of Inquiry in 1992.[41] As discussed above, Michael Leshner was a lawyer employed by the Ministry of the Attorney General who filed a human rights complaint against the provincial government because it refused to extend spousal benefits to his same-sex partner. Leshner succeeded in obtaining not only health care and dental care benefits, but also survivor pension benefits for all same-sex spouses of public service employees. The Board of Inquiry ordered the Ontario government to create a separate unregistered pension plan for lesbian and gay employees. The creation of such an "off-side" plan enabled the government to provide same-sex spousal pension benefits to its employees without jeopardizing the registered status of its regular pension plan.

In subsequent grievances and human rights cases, unions and employees sought similar orders for the creation of off-side pension plans, but their efforts were often unsuccessful. Once again, the impact of income tax regulations presented a barrier to lesbian and gay equality claims. Since off-side pension arrangements do not receive preferential tax treatment, they are considerably more expensive to administer than registered pension plans. Many tribunals were therefore reluctant to impose off-side plans upon employers.[42] The *Leshner* case was unique because the employer in that case, a provincial government, was not subject to the same tax liability as private sector employers.

Despite the difficulties created by the *Income Tax Act,* unions obtained survivor pension benefits for lesbian and gay workers in a few grievances. For example, the 1994 arbitration case that the Canadian Telephone Employees' Association won on behalf of Michael Lee and Ritchie Waller against Bell Canada resulted in the creation of an off-side pension plan including same-sex spousal survivor benefits. Similarly, in the 1995 case initiated by the Canadian Media Guild on behalf of Denis-Martin Chabot, an arbitrator ordered the Canadian Broadcasting Corporation to implement an off-side pension plan that included same-sex spousal benefits. (Both of these cases have already been discussed.)

Even these successful cases, however, did not achieve equal benefits for lesbian and gay workers. The pension benefits provided by off-side arrangements were not as secure as the benefits provided by registered plans. Moreover, the implementation of off-side pension plans did not alter the heterosexist income tax regulations that were the real source of the problem.

The *Income Tax Act* was eventually challenged directly in a *Charter* application initiated by CUPE and two of its employees, Nancy Rosenberg and Margaret Evans. The *Rosenberg* case involved CUPE's own employee pension plan. All CUPE employees, including Rosenberg and Evans, were required to make regular contributions to the plan, but they were denied survivor pension benefits for their same-sex partners. CUPE wanted to eliminate the discriminatory exclusion of same-sex partners, but Revenue Canada threatened to deregister CUPE's pension plan if same-sex spousal survivor benefits were offered. CUPE responded by challenging the heterosexual definition of spouse in the *Income Tax Act.*

After an initial defeat in August 1995, CUPE won its case in April 1998.[43] The Ontario Court of Appeal ruled that the income tax regulations violated the *Charter* equality rights of lesbians and gay men. The court declared that same-sex partners must be treated the same as opposite-sex partners for the purposes of survivor benefits and pension plan registration under the *Income Tax Act.*

The *Rosenberg* case was an important victory for lesbian and gay workers across the country because it eliminated the excuse most commonly cited by employers for refusing to provide same-sex spousal pension benefits. The federal government chose not to appeal the court decision. Almost immediately, the government of Nova Scotia settled an employee's human rights complaint by agreeing to extend same-sex spousal pension benefits to teachers and public servants in that province. The government of British Columbia then introduced legislation to provide same-sex spousal pension benefits to its public service employees, and the government of New Brunswick followed suit. The government of Quebec has announced that it will examine its own provincial laws with a view to taking similar action.

In Ontario, the government initially refused to extend survivor pension benefits to the same-sex partners of public service employees. Although the *Rosenberg* case made it clear that Revenue Canada could no longer refuse to register a pension plan simply because the plan offered survivor benefits to same-sex partners, the case did not address the issue of whether the Financial Services Commission of Ontario (FSCO) could or should refuse to register such a plan provincially. The Ontario government took the position that the provincial *Pension Benefits Act,* which contains an opposite-sex definition of "spouse," precludes the registration by FSCO of pension plans that offer same-sex survivor benefits. The Ontario Public Service Employees' Union (OPSEU) disagreed and argued that the heterosexual definition of "spouse" in the OPSEU Pension Plan should be amended to provide survivor benefits to the same-sex partners of public service employees.

In December 1998, the Trustees of the OPSEU Pension Fund applied to an Ontario court for directions as to whether the OPSEU Pension Plan had to be amended in light of the *Rosenberg* decision and whether the Plan could be registered by FSCO if it were amended. OPSEU, the government, and FSCO were all named as Respondents in the case. OPSEU argued in favor of the proposed amendment. The Court interpreted the *Pension Benefits Act* as requiring that survivor pension benefits be provided to opposite-sex spouses, but not forbidding the provision of similar benefits to same-sex spouses.[44] The Trustees were directed to amend their plan and, as a result, same-sex survivor benefits are now provided by the registered OPSEU plan, instead of through an off-side arrangement.

There were three intervenors in the *OPSEU Pension Plan* case: CUPE, the Trustees of the CUPE Pension Fund (which was at issue in the *Rosenberg* case), and the Ontario Teachers' Federation (which is jointly responsible with the Ontario government for the administration of the largest pension plan in the province). The intervenors argued that the *Pension Benefits Act* is discriminatory and unconstitutional, even tough it *permits* the registration of pension plans offering same-sex survivor benefits, because the *Act* does not *require* that survivor benefits be provided to same-sex spouses in every pension plan. OPSEU supported these arguments.

The Court was persuaded that the provincial legislation violates the *Charter* equality rights of lesbian and gay workers. It declared the heterosexual definition of "spouse" in the *Pension Benefits Act* to be unconstitutional and ordered that it be interpreted to include same-sex partners. The Ontario government has appealed this aspect of the ruling. If the lower court decision is upheld on appeal, every pension plan in the province (including private sector plans) will be required to offer survivor benefits to same-sex partners.

The Supreme Court's Decision in M. v. H.

The movement of Canadian courts and tribunals toward greater recognition of same-sex relationships was solidified in May 1999, when the Supreme Court of Canada issued its decision in the M. v. H. case. The case involved a lesbian couple who had separated after more than ten years of cohabitation. One of the women wanted to sue the other for spousal support, but she did not have the right to do so because the applicable definition of "spouse" in Ontario's *Family Law Act* is restricted to opposite-sex partners. She challenged the constitutional validity of that definition, relying on the equality rights section of the *Charter*. The Supreme Court ruled that the heterosexual definition of "spouse" in the statute is invalid because it discriminates on the basis of sexual orientation. The Court also ruled that there is no acceptable justification for the discrimination. The Ontario government was given six months from the date of the Court's judgment to amend its family law regime by granting cohabiting same-sex partners the same support rights and obligations as opposite-sex partners. Although the decision in M. v. H. only directly affects the right of lesbians and gay men in Ontario to sue their ex-partners for spousal support, it has broad implications. It sends a clear message to federal and provincial governments that the discriminatory exclusion of same-sex partners from eligibility for all kinds of spousal benefits will no longer be tolerated by the courts.

Conclusion

Unions and labor organizations have been at the forefront of lesbian and gay rights litigation for many years. Their prominent role in the struggle for same-sex spousal benefits is probably due, at least in part, to the centrality of employment benefits as an issue in collective bargaining. Employment benefits are an integral part of every employee's compensation package. Many trade unionists, who might not otherwise be vocal supporters of the queer liberation movement, are quick to object to an employer's attempt to provide lesser compensation (e.g., fewer benefits) to an employee simply because that employee is in a same-sex relationship. The fundamental principle of "equal pay for work of equal value" is one of the keystones of the organized labor movement. The denial of same-sex spousal benefits constitutes a flagrant breach of that principle because it effectively denies some employees equal compensation based solely on their sexual orientation.

Evidently, unions have played a particularly active and critical role in cases that involved same-sex spousal benefits claims. The record of unions in addressing sexual orientation issues more generally has been uneven, although in the 1990s, the number of unions and labor organizations speaking out in favor of respect for sexual diversity has significantly increased. Many unions have deepened their commitment over the course of the decade and demonstrated a willingness to apply considerable resources to assisting lesbian and gay workers in achieving equality through grievance procedures, human rights tribunals, and court actions. Labor involvement in all of these cases has been important, not only in helping to establish useful legal precedents, but also in forging space for lesbian and gay workers to become visible in the workplace.

Notes

Acknowledgments: I would like to thank Gerald Hunt and David Rayside for their comments and suggestions on earlier drafts of this chapter. I also want to acknowledge that the work of Janice Cheney has influenced my thinking on the issues addressed.

1. *Re Board of Governors of the University of Saskatchewan and the Saskatchewan Human Rights Commission* (1976), 66 D.L.R. (3d) 561 (Sask. Q.B.).

2. *Re Damien and Ontario Human Rights Commission* (1976), 12 O.R. (2d) 262 (H.C.J.), and *Damien v. Ontario Racing Commission* (1975), 11 O.R. (2d) 489 (H.C.J.).

3. *Vogel v. Government of Manitoba (no. 1)* (1983), C.H.R.R. D/1654 (Man. Bd. Adj.).

4. Vogel and North had participated in a wedding ceremony in 1974 and had failed in an attempt to compel the province to register their union as a marriage. See *North v. Matheson* (1974), 20 R.F.L. 112 (Man. Co. Ct.).

5. *Haig v. Canada* (1992), 9 O.R. (3d) 495 (C.A.).

6. *Newfoundland and Labrador (Human Rights Commission) v. Newfoundland and Labrador (Minister of Employment and Labour Relations)*, [1995] N.J. No.283 (Nfld. S.C.) (QL).

7. *Re University of Lethbridge and University of Lethbridge Faculty Association* (1994), 48 L.A.C. (4th) 172.

8. *Re Canada Post Corporation and CUPW*, unreported decision of arbitrator Pierre Jasmin dated 27 March 1986. If any readers are aware of an earlier arbitration award involving same-sex spousal benefits, I would greatly appreciate receiving information about the case.

9. *Re Carleton University and CUPE, Local 2424* (1988), 35 L.A.C. (3d) 96.

10. Endorsement of Judge Reid, Ontario Divisional Court, dated 8 June 1990. It should be noted that, in more recent cases, arbitrators and Boards of Inquiry have ruled that the opposite-sex definition of spouse in the Ontario *Human Rights Code* is itself discriminatory and is unconstitutional because it violates equality rights guaranteed by the *Canadian Charter of Rights and Freedoms*. See, for example, *Leshner v. Ontario* (1992), 16 C.H.R.R. D/184 (Ont. Bd. Inq.); *Re Metro Toronto Reference Library and CUPE, Local 1582* (1995), 51 L.A.C. (4th) 69 (Ontario); *Dwyer and Sims v. Metro Toronto (no. 3)* (1996), 27 C.H.R.R. D/108 (Ont. Bd. Inq.); *McCallum v. Toronto Transit Commission*, [1997] O.H.R.B.I.D. No. 19 (QL) and [1996] O.H.R.B.I.D. No. 8 (QL); and *Re Chrysler Canada Ltd. and C.A.W., Locals 1498 and 444*, unreported decision of Ross Kennedy dated 6 March 1998.

11. *CUPE, Local 2424 v. Carleton University*, [1990] O.J. No.1890 (C.A.) (QL).

12. *Re Parkwood Hospital and McCormick Home* (1992), 24 L.A.C. (4th) 149.

13. *Re Canada (Indian and Northern Affairs) and Watson (PSAC)* (1990), 11 L.A.C. (4th) 129 (PSSRB).

14. *Re Canada and Hewens (PSAC)*, decision of the Public Service Staff Relations Board dated 25 November 1992 (file no. 166-2-22732).

15. *Andrews v. Ontario (Minister of Health)* (1988), 49 D.L.R. (4th) 584 (Ont. H.C.).

16. See, for example, *Egan v. Canada*, [1993] 3 F.C. 401 (C.A.) and *Layland v. Ontario (Minister of Consumer and Commercial Relations)* (1993), 14 O.R. (3d) 658 (Gen. Div.).

17. *Vogel v. Government of Manitoba (no. 1)* (1983), C.H.R.R. D/1657 (Man. Bd. Adj.).

18. *Vogel v. Manitoba (no. 2)* (1992), 90 D.L.R. (4th) 84 (Man. Q.B.). The decision was eventually reversed on appeal (see notes 36 and 37 below).

19. *Knodel v. British Columbia (Medical Services Commission)* (1991), 58 B.C.L.R. (2d) 356 (S.C.). In a 1989 case, a gay prison inmate won the right to have visits with his same-sex partner; however, the case did not involve a declaration that the two men were spouses. See *Vesey v. Correctional Services Canada* (1990), 109 N.R. 300 (F.C.A.).

20. *Leshner v. Ontario (no. 2)* (1992), 16 C.H.R.R. D/184 (Ont. Bd. Inq.).

21. This case is summarized in CUPE, *Winning Out at Work* (Ottawa: 1993 edition) at C-11, and in Donald Casswell, *Lesbians, Gay Men and Canadian Law* (Toronto, Emond Montgomery Publications, 1996), p. 425.

22. *Mossop v. Canada,* [1993] 1 S.C.R. 554.

23. *Re Bell Canada and Canadian Telephone Employees' Association* (1994), 43 L.A.C. (4th) 172.

24. *Re Canada Post Corporation and PSAC (Guevremont no. 3),* unreported decision of Stephen Kelleher dated 8 March 1994.

25. *Re Canada Post Corporation and PSAC (Guevremont no. 1),* unreported decision of Robert Blasina dated 5 October 1993. See also *Re Canada Post Corporation and PSAC (Guevremont no. 2)* (1993), 38 L.A.C. (4th) 332.

26. *Re Canada Post Corporation and CUPW (Evinger),* [1994] D.A.T.C. No. 1164 (QL) (judgment written in French).

27. *Re Canadian Broadcasting Corporation and Canadian Media Guild* (1995), 45 L.A.C. (4th) 353.

28. *Egan v. Canada,* [1995] 2 S.C.R. 513.

29. *Re Canadian Broadcasting Corporation and Canadian Media Guild* (1996), 52 L.A.C. (4th) 350.

30. *Re Canada Post Corporation and CUPW (Aebly),* [1995] C.L.A.D. No. 1134 (QL).

31. *Re Metro Toronto Reference Library and CUPE, Local 1582* (1995), 51 L.A.C. (4th) 69.

32. *Re Treasury Board and PSAC (Sarson),* decision of the Public Service Staff Relations Board dated 1 March 1996 (file no. 166-2-25312).

33. *Re Treasury Board and PIPSC (Yarrow),* decision of the Public Service Staff Relations Board dated 5 February 1996 (file no. 166-2-25034).

34. *Re Treasury Board and Boutilier* (1997), 65 L.A.C. (4th) 102 (PSSRB).

35. *Re British Columbia and B.C.G.S.E.U.,* [1997] B.C.C.A.A.A. No.514 (QL).

36. *Vogel v. Manitoba* (1995), 23 C.H.R.R. D/173 (Man. C.A.) at D/175.

37. *Vogel v. Manitoba (no. 3),* decision of the Manitoba Board of Adjudication dated 21 November 1997.

38. *Moore v. Canada* (1996), 25 C.H.R.R. D/352 (C.H.R.T.).

39. *Canada Attorney General v. Moore,* [1998] F.C.J. No. 1128 (T.D.) (QL).

40. *Re Chrysler Canada Ltd. and CAW, Locals 1498 and 444,* unreported decision of Ross Kennedy dated 6 March 1998.

41. *Leshner v. Ontario (no. 2)* (1992), 16 C.H.R.R. D/184 (Ont. Bd. Inq.).

42. See, for example, *Laessoe v. Air Canada* (1996), 27 C.H.R.R. D/1 (C.H.R.T.) and *Dwyer v. Toronto (Metro) (no. 3)* (1996), 27 C.H.R.R. D/108 (Ont. Bd. Inq.).

43. *Rosenberg v. Canada,* decision of the Ontario Court of Appeal dated 23 April 1998.

44. *Trustees of the OPSEU Pension Plan Trust Fund v. Ontario, FSCO, and OPSEU,* unreported decision of Judge Rivard, dated 4 December 1998.

Christian Arthur Bain

4 A Short History of Lesbian and Gay Labor Activism in the United States

The union movement is our [the lesbian and gay rights movement's] biggest ally. There is no other progressive force in America that has the numbers, the money, and the clout to match the labor movement— they can reach into areas we can't reach. Even before Stonewall, unions held that private behavior was not the employer's business. . . . Labor is the major buffer between us and the extreme right. We face the same opponents—the political reactionaries want to destroy anyone who's different—gay, women, minorities, and labor. . . . We need each other more than ever.

Howard Wallace, veteran gay union activist[1]

Like Howard Wallace, lesbian and gay labor activists across the country have long seen themselves as a bridge between two natural allies. On the labor side, they have brought the concerns of lesbian and gay union members to a movement that has traditionally protected the right of workers to live their personal lives freely, without fear of discrimination or dismissal by their employers.

In the lesbian and gay rights movement, these activists have worked to raise awareness of a generally middle-class leadership to the issues of working-class lesbians and gay men and to the critical role that unions have played in supporting gay rights. Their efforts have received sparse attention.[2] Outside of the San Francisco Bay area, where a lively alternative press has often covered gay union news, little coverage has been given to lesbian and gay labor activism. Private-sector mainstream media (which rely heavily on corporate advertising) have generally neglected both union and lesbian and gay issues. With occasional exceptions, the established lesbian and gay press has systematically avoided labor-related stories.

Much of the information in this chapter comes from interviews with key participants, some of whom have farsightedly maintained personal archives of flyers, brochures, and notes going back to the early 1970s to share with future historians. The process has more closely resembled creating a map than following one; different areas have been filled in (or added to the map) at varying levels of detail in each successive interview. In most cases, participants in these interviews have provided referrals to other people who have in turn provided additional information and referrals, sometimes leading to surprising revelations. I am truly grateful to the many people who agreed to talk to me about their experiences.[3]

This chapter represents a preliminary attempt to chronicle the largely unwritten history of lesbians and gay men in the U.S. union movement over a seventy-year period spanning the 1920s through the 1990s. It is a history that sometimes mirrored national trends and sometimes led the way, when unions supported gay rights well ahead of many other sectors of American society. It is a history exceptionally rich in the courage, determination, and resourcefulness of dedicated lesbian and gay union activists (and their heterosexual allies) whose names and achievements remain unknown even to many other lesbian and gay labor activists around the country. Moreover, it is a history that will take on growing significance as lesbian, gay, bisexual, and transgender trade unionists, and their issues, become a visible, recognized, *and valued* part of the larger union movement.

Before Stonewall: Points of Light on a Dark Background

As with much gay history, information about early lesbian and gay union activity is only beginning to emerge. One striking revelation comes from the pioneering research of Allan Berube on the Marine Cooks and Stewards Union (MCS) during the 1930s through the early 1950s.[4] The union organized the waiters, cooks, mess men, laundrymen, and other service workers—a group that included a large percentage of gay men— on the luxury liners and freighters that sailed the Pacific Ocean. Noted for being one of the most left-wing and racially integrated labor unions of the period and boasting up to 20,000 members at its high point during World War II, the MCS was also unusually supportive and accepting of its gay members, including gay seamen kicked out of the U.S. Navy.

Although the MCS never specifically addressed homosexuality in its written policies, the union routinely defended its members against gay baiting and violent harassment and elected gay men to leadership positions. The union's leaders made explicit connections between politics, race, and homosexuality. As Revels Cayton, a black heterosexual leader of the MCS put it: "If you let them red bait, they'll race bait. If you let them race bait, they'll queen bait. These are connected—that's why we have to stick together."

One indication of an even wider acceptance of gay men, at least within the Congress of Industrial Organizations (CIO) to which the MSC belonged, was the election of Frank McCormick, an openly gay man, as vice president of the California CIO, a position he held for several years in the late 1930s.

This acceptance, and the Marine Cooks and Stewards Union itself, came to an abrupt end in the McCarthy era of the late 1940s and early 1950s when the Coast Guard was ordered to screen out left-wing, black, and gay men from their jobs aboard ship. The MCS's reputation as being "red, black, and gay" made it a particular target for anti-union attacks.

A wave of anti-communism in the early 1950s led to expulsion of left-wing unions (including the MCS) from the CIO. Propaganda directed at these unions during the period often explicitly linked homosexuals, and those who favored racial integration, with Communism. During the 1950s, many left-wing union leaders and activists, among them McCormick and other MCS members, were blacklisted and harassed by the FBI, which actively intimidated employers into firing them from even the most menial jobs.

By the mid-1950s, right-wing unions had replaced the MCS in the Pacific. At about the same time, shipping firms began registering their ships under foreign flags, and what may have been the most gay-friendly union of the period ceased to exist. Later, in the 1960s, many of the buildings formerly used by the now defunct shipping industry, which had moved offshore, became gay bars—often opened by former members of the MCS.

According to pioneering gay rights activist Harry Hay,[5] coastal marine unions organized by The International Workers of the World (IWW) were thoroughly homophobic in the latter half of the 1920s. "The IWW was 'All for one and one for All'—except for queers," reports Hay, who fled his middle-class family at age 14 to work on Pacific Coast freighters.

Later, in New York as an organizer for the Department Store Workers Union in the 1930s and early 1940s, Hay found the atmosphere little better. "I was an organizer for the Department Store Workers Union in New York, working at Macy's and organizing [underground since union activity was both illegal and cause for immediate dismissal] at Gimbel's. If it had been known I was gay I wouldn't have been a union member. They would have [expelled me from the union]. Macy's would have fired me in a moment if they knew [and the union would have backed them up].

Skills learned in underground union organizing would be crucial to the success of the Mattachine Society, the first ongoing gay rights organization in the U.S., which Hay founded in 1950. It had taken him two years of searching to find a small group of men willing to join an enterprise that could have led to their arrest simply because it was gay. "The first five members of the Mattachine Society were all union members experienced in working in underground unions," says Hay. "We took an oath that we would plead the Fifth Amendment before we divulged information of any sort about the group."

"If we hadn't had the discipline of being underground union members we wouldn't have known how to do it," Hay believes. "We knew how to work without leaving any telephone numbers written down—they were in our heads." Each group of nine men was called a guild. Meetings were attended by a tenth man, who served as a contact with another guild and whose identity was known by only two members.

"You only knew the names the other eight gave themselves, not their real names," says Hay. "It was a politically radical underground experience." Hay believes that it was a shift away from its underground working-class union roots into an open and more middle-class organization that led to the Mattachine Society's demise in 1953.

The history of the 1950s and 1960s is still mostly blank as it relates to gay unionists. In addition to Harry Hay, three notable exceptions were Bayard Rustin, organizer of the 1963 March on Washington for Jobs and Civil Rights; Tom Kahn, speechwriter and close assistant to George Meany, national president of the AFL-CIO; and Bill Olwell, an official of a Retail Clerk's Union local in Seattle who subsequently rose to become a vice president of the United Food and Commercial Workers (UFCW).

Following the success of the March on Washington for Jobs and Civil Rights in 1963, Rustin, who was not publicly out but was known to be gay by Martin Luther King and other leaders of the civil rights movement, moved from his former job as executive secretary of the War Resisters League to become head of the A. Philip Randolph Institute. The new organization, created and funded in response to the march by the AFL-CIO with the strong support of its president George Meany, was designed around Rustin's talents and focused on job creation for minorities.

Rustin and Kahn—who while serving as Meany's speech writer also had responsibilities involving foreign policy issues—became lovers for a time and friends for years thereafter.[6] Although it is not publicly known whether Rustin, Kahn, or Olwell made any private efforts in support of gay rights during this period, none of them felt sufficiently secure in the pre-Stonewall years to be publicly identified with homosexual issues. Even Hay did not feel comfortable being publicly out until the mid-1960s.

A few (often heterosexual) union leaders, however, were willing to defend the rights of their gay and lesbian members, years before the advent of the modern gay rights movement. One such leader, Walter Johnson, became head of Department Store Employees Union Local 1100 (part of the Retail Clerks International Association)in 1965. He soon began to encounter the issues of gay members of his local who were working at Macy's San Francisco store[7] : "We had a young man who wanted to transfer from the stock department to the Tiger Shop, which was young men's clothing," reports Johnson, who is now secretary-treasurer of San Francisco's AFL-CIO Labor Council. "They refused to transfer him and he brought his complaint to us. The personnel manager, Mrs. T., was an arsenic and old lace type, right out of the old movies. When I asked her about it, she said: 'Mr. Johnson, we're not going to transfer him; he's a queer. We only have one in the store and that's a man selling shirts. We even have a man interviewing [job applicants] so we don't get any of them.' I said: 'Mrs. T., you'd better check the man doing the interviewing, because *I know* you have more than one here.' I went up the [management] ladder and finally got him into sales, but they put him into unfinished furniture and later he went into selling women's shoes. What I said then was that it was discrimination in terms of sex. We didn't have the terminology [for sexual orientation] in those days. We had language in the contract dating back to the 1930s that any act by the employer or union which interferes with their harmonious relationship was a violation of the agreement. It had a very broad connotation and I used it in a lot of different situations."

This case was but one of several involving gay and lesbian employees in which Johnson intervened. Another particularly striking case involved a man who, after women gained the right to wear pants, first wanted to wear lipstick and then dresses at Macy's. Johnson succeeded in asserting his right to do both, but he failed in a subsequent effort to get a sex change operation covered by the union's health plan.

1970 to 1979: The Dawning of Gay Labor Activism

What may have been the first explicit union endorsement of gay rights came in 1970, only a year after Stonewall, when the executive council of the American Federation of Teachers (AFT) endorsed a resolution "that the American Federation of Teachers protest any personnel actions taken against any teacher solely because he or she practices homosexual behavior in private life."[8] What precipitated this resolution is unclear, but it is known that Bayard Rustin was a close friend and political ally of Albert Shanker, a council delegate and president of the AFT's largest local, the United Federation of Teachers (UFT) Local 2 in New York.[9]

In 1973, the AFT's national convention backed up the executive council's policy statement with a more general resolution "that the American Federation of Teachers work for repeal of state laws and local school district regulations which attempt to punish acts committed by teachers in the course of their private lives unless such acts can be shown to affect fitness to teach."[10] It was also in 1973 that the National Education Association (NEA) added sexual orientation to its nondiscrimination policy, something that the AFT would not do until 1990. This change came as a direct result of grass roots networking in NEA's Resolutions Committee and on the floor of their annual Representative Assembly.[11]

The following year, members of the UFT in New York organized what may have been the first gay union caucus, the Gay Teachers Alliance (GTA). Starting with a June 1974 meeting with Sandra Feldman, then the UFT's representative responsible for minority issues and subsequently national president of the AFT, they urged the UFT to acknowledge and support its thousands of gay teachers and support passage of a gay rights resolution in New York's City Council.

The nascent group also met with UFT president Albert Shanker in September. As reported by Mark Rubin, a GTA founder, "he told us that he had no objection to our forming a group although he was opposed to the UFT's taking a public stand on the issue of gay rights because it would be divisive."[12] That same week the group also placed a classified ad in the *Village Voice*. Much to their surprise, fifty teachers showed up at their first meeting. "The vast majority were less interested in lobbying the UFT and City Council than with basic concerns of loneliness, alienation and fear felt [as] gay teachers," Rubin states. According to Rubin, most of the gay teachers they met were afraid that they would lose their jobs if anyone found out their sexual orientation.

One early success for the GTA was in establishing a direct working relationship with Frank Arricale II, executive director of the personnel division for the Board of Education. In a letter to the new group, he stated: "Homosexual teachers have exactly the same rights and protections as any other teachers in the system. Not only are we not involved in any process of ferreting out homosexual teachers, frankly we are not particularly interested in whether teachers are homosexual or not."

Arricale subsequently qualified his statement when he told the group that anything a teacher did outside the classroom was okay, but "advocacy" had to be avoided in the classroom. Rubin called the question of "advocacy" merely the latest code word in an unending stream of quasi-theological discussions and obfuscations.

Despite these frustrations, the GTA scored another success with passage of what may have been the first union resolution calling for legislation to prohibit discrimination based on sexual preference. Reflecting the language and understanding of the time, the AFT's resolution stated: "Whereas, a person's lifestyle, sexual preference, and political association are an individual's choice, with freedom of choice being an integral part of the democratic process. . . . Resolved, that the 1977 Convention go on record supporting legislation and other reforms which prohibit discrimination in employment and the abrogation of individual liberties based on an individual's personal and political preferences."[13] Convoluted discussions with and resistance from the New York City Board of Education and the UFT have continued throughout the more than two decades of existence of the Gay and Lesbian Teachers Association (as the GTA was subsequently renamed), which currently has several hundred members.[14]

At about the same time that gay teachers were organizing in New York in 1974, the independent Transportation Employees Union, representing about 200 employees in Michigan's Ann Arbor Transportation Authority, was negotiating what may have been the first contract including a clause banning discrimination based on sexual preference: "I was a bus driver from 1977 to 1981 and eventually became a vice president and chief steward," remembers Shelley Ettinger. "It was a very progressive, very militant union, committed to being anti-racist. There were a lot of out-of-the-closet bus drivers and dispatchers. From the mid-70s on, a lot of the union's officers were out lesbians and gay men—it was very noteworthy for the lesbian and gay presence in the union. It was known among lesbians especially that if you didn't want to be in the closet, this was a good place to work. It didn't pay that great, but the benefits were decent, and there were a lot of lesbians (and a few gay men)—and if you were into driving a bus, it was cool."[15]

Sue Schurman, an out lesbian who is now the executive director of the George Meany Center, the national AFL-CIO's education center/labor college, was one of the union's executive board members who negotiated the contract. "From the start, possibly as early as 1974, we asked for full benefits for the 'mates' (we didn't have the term domestic partner then) of all unmarried employees, including heterosexual couples; there were plenty of them as well," Schurman reports.[16]

"My lover was a diabetic and we had a lot of trouble paying for her insulin and medical care," says Ettinger. "Management said it just couldn't be done—almost as if it was a natural law." Although the union continued to demand full domestic partner benefits each year through the 1970s and early 1980s, it achieved only limited success in such areas as bereavement leave.

"We had links to almost all activist groups in the area," says Schurman. "There was a vision there about how trade unionism can be used to achieve civil rights—which is the same approach as John Sweeney is now following. A majority of the members were middle-aged heterosexual guys, but there was never any division within the union."

Much of the earliest gay union activity was occurring in Northern California, where a political alliance between labor and San Francisco's growing gay community was emerging. The Coors boycott helped catalyze the relationship. The first initiative for a gay/labor alliance came from the unions in 1974 when Allan Baird and Andy Ciraellis—heterosexual representatives of the Teamsters Newspaper Drivers Union—approached

Harvey Milk, the unofficial "Mayor" of San Francisco's rapidly growing gay Castro Street neighborhood, and Howard Wallace, an out gay union and anti-war activist, to enlist their support in convincing the city's numerous gay bars to stop serving Coors beer. Unlike previous leaders of the local, who had asked for and received support from both Milk and Wallace but were unwilling to publicize this homosexual support, Baird, a Castro resident and coordinator of the Coors boycott in San Francisco, had no qualms about publicly embracing the gay community in exchange for its backing.[17]

Baird, who had already won the support of the city's Chinese and Arab communities, believed that a gay boycott could tip the scales. As part of its anti-union practices, Coors had been routinely administering lie detector tests to prospective employees, including questions about their sexual orientation. Milk and Wallace enthusiastically embraced the boycott—insisting that the union hire openly gay truck drivers in return for their support—and a new alliance between San Francisco unions and the gay community was born. "Allan and Harvey and I had a series of meetings to organize the boycott," reports Wallace. "There were one hundred gay and lesbian bars in San Francisco—it did damage to the whole [Coors] market in the city. We reached people as consumers in the supermarkets and groceries, not just in the bars, and explained that the company was a major funder of the ultra-right in the U.S." Wallace notes that although the boycott was less successful elsewhere, it had a tremendous impact within the gay community. According to Wallace, it showed "that we were a considerable force to be reckoned with."

The boycott—which caused Coors' share of the California beer market (easily the company's largest) to drop from 43 percent to 14 percent—helped strengthen an often uneasy political alliance between San Francisco's gay community and organized labor. Several major unions and their members subsequently supported Milk's campaigns for a seat on San Francisco's Board of Supervisors, spurred by the gay community's support for the Coors boycott as well as their mutual dislike for the then conservative board. (Wallace would later be a candidate to fill the seat after Milk's assassination.) Another early result of the budding gay/labor alliance was that Wallace was able to enlist labor support for community picketing of ABC-TV, protesting a homophobic episode of *Marcus Welby, M.D.*

Almost from its founding in January 1975, Bay Area Gay Liberation (BAGL) made its presence felt at the focal point between gay rights and labor issues. Within six months of its founding, the new activist group had scored a major success with the June 17th reversal by the San Francisco Board of Education of its stand against including sexual orientation in its nondiscrimination policies. In an analysis shortly after the victory, the *San Francisco Bay Guardian* described a sea change in the city's gay political climate

> Spearheaded by Bay Area Gay Liberation (BAGL), gays used mass organizing tactics, leaflets, picket lines and demonstrations to pressure the school board into forbidding discrimination against gay teachers. BAGL's success in mass organizing signals a major change in gay politics in San Francisco.
>
> In the past, gay political power was exercised quietly through traditional political channels. Power brokers lobbied with local politicians, promising to deliver gay campaign contributors, precinct workers and votes. . . . There were no street demonstrations and little grass

roots organizing.... This style of relative quietude changed drastically after SF police randomly arrested 13 gay men on Castro Street after closing time on Labor Day 1974. For months after the incident, gays packed the Eureka Valley Police Community Relations meetings. Frustration grew. When BAGL founders Howard Wallace and Jane Sica tacked up flyers announcing BAGL's first meeting January 22, there was a vacuum to be filled....

BAGL has also allied itself with other activist groups like the United Farm Workers ... and the Coors beer boycott sponsored by Union Local 888 [Baird had asked for and enthusiastically received the group's support at its second meeting]. In return, Local 888 helped get Howard Wallace a beer truck driving job.[18]

Tom Ammiano, then a member of the Gay Teachers Caucus (and later a member of the San Francisco Board of Supervisors), described the effort as "a terrific blend of confrontational politics and lobbying." Even Dr. Eugene Hopp, president of the school board, was relatively happy with the result. "I haven't had a single adverse letter or phone call," he said. "I'm amazed. I thought the parents would be up in arms."

When the AFL-CIO held its national convention in San Francisco in October 1975, BAGL seized the opportunity for national visibility. Wallace and several other members of the group's labor committee passed out leaflets on the convention floor, handing copies directly to Bayard Rustin and Albert Shanker. Under the title "A Call for Labor Leadership and Action on Human Rights," the leaflet said: "The labor movement needs allies ... [such as] minorities including gay people in California. Thus far only a small number of labor leaders have spoken out on our behalf.... It's time to end the discrimination against gay people and support the recently introduced extension of the federal civil rights law to cover sexual orientation."[19] The leaflet also urged labor support for inclusion of sexual orientation in negotiated nondiscrimination clauses. It was almost certainly the first time that grass roots gay union activists had canvassed the floor of a national AFL-CIO convention.

By October 1976, the stage was set for a joint news conference between BAGL's labor committee and twenty-two San Francisco union leaders, which received prominent coverage in the city's leading newspapers and on local TV news broadcasts. In what the *Advocate* called "a new breakthrough" and "a somewhat unusual alliance ... between two of the city's most potent power blocks," the union leaders promised support for inclusion of gay rights clauses in future contracts, while BAGL promised to work against eight anti-labor ballot measures before San Francisco voters the following month.[20] It was the strongest support that organized labor had ever offered for lesbian and gay civil rights.

Support came from unions as diverse as the Building and Construction Trades Council, the Teamsters, the International Longshoreman and Warehousemen's Union, the United Farm Workers, the Communications Workers of America, the National Association of Broadcast Employees and Technicians, the Retail Store Employees, the Civil Service Association, and the International Ladies Garment Workers Union. Among those present were Allan Baird; Joan Dillon, president of the Civil Service Association; and Stanley Smith of the Building and Construction Trades Council, who said that his union already had a sexual preference protection clause in its contracts.

"The press conference had a tremendous impact in terms of the climate of labor," says Wallace, who organized the conference along with Pat Jackson, the heterosexual leader of the City Employees Union Local 400, who would later play a major role in the campaign against the anti-gay Briggs ballot initiative. "After the agreement with labor, we got a lot of invitations [to speak to local unions], but we had only the little labor committee. Later I heard that Tim Twomey, secretary-treasurer of Hospital and Health Care Workers Local 250 SEIU, put out word to all of his staff that people needed education on lesbian and gay issues and should not use derogatory language [in reference to gay people]."

Two years later, in 1978, when the Briggs initiative (Proposition 6) sought to ban gay teachers from public schools, the value of the gay/labor alliance became abundantly clear. The California Teachers Association (an affiliate of the NEA), California Federation of Teachers (an affiliate of AFT), and the California AFL-CIO—which sent 2.3 million slate cards to voters—all took firm "No-on-6" positions. The alliance was a natural one because the proposition would have resulted in the firing of union members and because unions had long insisted that employees' personal lives should not be a factor in employment.

"When we started fighting Briggs, all the early polls showed us losing by a landslide," Wallace remembers. "Even up to the last minute a lot of people thought we were going to lose. Some of us went out there and got a host of endorsements, and we also got the whole State Federation of Labor and the United Farm Workers at a very early stage. They started urging people to get out and vote, and that played a major role. Labor came on early in a big way and contributed a lot of money and sent out several million pieces of literature. It was their support that made it safe and popular to condemn the initiative—it was only when it began to look like we were going to win that establishment groups like the Catholic Church came out against the amendment."[21]

1980 to 1986: Visibility and Recognition

In Chicago, Tom Stabnicki and Barry Friedman, two union leaders who were also lovers, were working to increase lesbian and gay visibility at both the local and national levels. Stabnicki and Friedman were officials of the American Federation of State, County, and Municipal Employees (AFSCME) Local 2081, representing social workers, support workers, and clerical workers for the Illinois Department of Children and Family Services. "We were successful in our union because we had credibility," says Stabnicki. "I was always out, as was Barry. He was first elected to the board of Local 2081 in 1976, and my first term as an officer of the union was in 1978, and I served for the next sixteen years until I retired in 1994. He was in the field as a child welfare worker, and then a full time trade unionist, and I was a social worker."

Stabnicki and Friedman were surprised by the lack of a gay community in AFSCME. "That just didn't seem right for an institution that called everybody brother and sister," Stabnicki states, adding, "What we were about was making the union more comfortable for lesbian and gay people." According to Stabnicki, when he and Friedman first became involved in union activism, only the airline unions such as the flight attendants and Teamsters for a Democratic Trade Union seemed to be doing anything on gay rights.[22]

The two men, who alternated in the positions of steward and president of the local, decided to host a gay hospitality suite at the 1979 AFSCME leadership conference in Washington, D.C. "We announced it and nobody attended," says Stabnicki, "and there were some 1,000 local union leaders there from around the country. We did get some phone calls—some harassing and some supportive from people who were presidents of their locals but where afraid to come out. Since Barry and I were out and were secure in our jobs, we felt we could take some leadership on this issue."

Friedman and Stabnicki decided to work toward getting the 1.2 million-member AFSCME international union to amend its constitution to prohibit discrimination in membership based on sexual orientation, which they hoped to achieve at the 1980 convention. "Prior to going to the national level, we were able to gain support first of Council 31, the statewide organization of AFSCME in Illinois," Stabnicki recalls. "The union relies very much on the recommendations of leadership. We learned very fast that the way to accomplish something in the union is to work through the leadership. By the time we went to the convention, we had the endorsement of Local 2081 as well as the leadership of Council 31." The amendment passed by voice vote without opposition.[23]

At the end of 1981, a complementary approach was being pursued by the newly formed Human Rights Campaign Fund (HRCF). This gay rights lobbying group based in Washington, D.C., would subsequently become the nation's largest lesbian and gay organization. An important part of the HRCF strategy was to work with labor, building on its strong support for other forms of civil rights. AFSCME, one of the most progressive unions in the country with long and deep roots in the civil rights movement, was a natural place to start.

Vic Basile, president of a Washington, D.C., AFSCME local and a member of one of the union's councils (and later the HRCF's first executive director), was hired on a part-time basis by Steven Endean, the founder of the HRCF, to work on getting a gay rights resolution passed at the 1982 AFSCME convention. According to Basile, "AFSCME was ripe for doing it now. It was the union Martin Luther King was supporting when he was shot in Memphis, the garbage union workers. It's always prided itself on supporting those who were the most oppressed in the workforce. They've always been very supportive on civil rights issues. It was also way out in front in opposing the war in Vietnam." Basile also notes that AFSCME was "the polar opposite of the conservative, cigar-chomping, George Meany types."

"In a union, the best way to get things done is from the inside and hopefully to get the leadership to take credit for it," Basile states. His goal was to convince people at the top like Bill Lucy, AFSCME's young secretary-treasurer and the highest ranking African American labor leader in the United States, that this was the right thing to do. "Lucy's backing was essential. It wouldn't have happened without his support. We worked with Lucy and people close to him on the language of the resolution. We also started to try to gather support in the union from elected officials of the locals and build support along the way."[24]

Sometime during the spring of 1982, Basile called Friedman and Stabnicki. "It was [already] our intention to bring a resolution," says Stabnicki, "and when we heard from Vic, we decided the best idea was to work with him and coordinate our effort. We had the backing of our international vice president, Steve Culen from our council,

Paul Booth, head of organizing in Illinois, and others from outside of Illinois were also supportive."

"My sense was that by the time it got to the convention, it was a done deal," says Basile. Still the three activists took no chances, spending most of their time lobbying delegates both on and off the convention floor. "No opposition ever surfaced anywhere. There was no big fight. Whatever he [Lucy] did was enough that by the time he rose to speak, no one spoke against it and it just passed by a voice vote and it was over with."

Under the title "Civil Rights for Gay and Lesbian Citizens," the Atlantic City convention's 4,000 delegates resolved that "AFSCME endorse the passage of federal, state and local legislation that extends basic civil rights in the areas of employment, housing and public accommodations to lesbian and gay citizens." "Without leadership support it would have had a very hard time passing," Basile believes. "There really had not been a strong grass roots gay force . . . in the union. Part of the effort was trying to find gay members of AFSCME around the country, and it wasn't easy." Basile regularly discussed strategy with Bill Olwell, vice president of the United Food and Commercial Workers, who was then the top out gay labor leader in the United States. "He was someone who had access to a lot of important people," Basile states.

One result of the 1980 and 1982 conventions was the emergence of more gay caucuses, particularly in AFSCME, but elsewhere as well. After that, "lesbian and gay activists had a license to be out in the union," says Stabnicki. "Because it was in the constitution, it was much harder for union leaders to exercise homophobia. It became much easier to see a lesbian and gay presence in the next two to four years."

Basile states, however, that by 1984, "people were aware that there was a health crisis, and we turned our attention to helping the union to deal with the AIDS crisis. So we never got to be really effective in those years. We got concerned about looking after those with AIDS and dealing with it ourselves and never got to the place where we would find out what a gay-and-lesbian-friendly union might look like. The 80s might have been a really incredible age had it not been for AIDS."[25]

Nevertheless, the AFSCME resolutions helped trigger a chain reaction. "Lucy went from doing this at AFSCME to the building trades department of the AFL-CIO and had it passed there and then did it at the national AFL-CIO," Basile reports. "It was coming from the top."

In October 1982, the 6 million-member Industrial Unions Department (IUD) of the AFL-CIO—composed of thirty-four unions, including the United Steelworkers, United Auto Workers (UAW), Communication Workers of America (CWA), International Association of Machinists, Service Employees International Union (SEIU), and AFSCME—passed its own gay rights resolution. It was introduced by Bill Lucy and, as with the AFSCME resolution, passed by voice vote without opposition.[26]

By the end of 1982, gay union activism was reaching a new level in San Francisco with the formation of a citywide lesbian and gay labor organization by representatives of a dozen San Francisco unions. The new group—which became the Lesbian/Gay Labor Alliance in 1983—committed itself to helping lesbians and gay men to organize their workplaces, secure gay rights clauses in union contracts, monitor compliance with San Francisco's gay rights law, and help form gay caucuses in every union. Another goal was to break down anti-union bias in the gay community and anti-gay bias in unions.[27]

One of the alliance's first actions was to picket two gay-oriented restaurants, joining workers who were striking for affiliation with the Hotel and Restaurants Employees and Bartenders Union.[28]

At the national level, an informal coalition of powerful labor leaders—including Bill Lucy, Bill Olwell, and John Sweeney, who had been elected president of the huge Service Employees International Union (SEIU) in 1980—was smoothing the way for an important breakthrough at the AFL-CIO. In October 1983, the national convention of the AFL-CIO unanimously adopted two resolutions relating to lesbian and gay rights and AIDS. The first resolution urged enactment of legislation banning discrimination based on sexual orientation in jobs, housing, credit, public accommodations, and government services and stated that workers should not be subject to discrimination in any form because of their sexual orientation. A second resolution called for the federal government to "increase funds for research to determine the cause of AIDS," attributing the government's slow response to the AIDS crisis to "a history of discrimination against the people in the high-risk groups."[29]

The following year, SEIU, which holds its conventions every four years, joined the AFL-CIO and AFSCME in incorporating sexual orientation into its definition of diversity. By 1984, a prohibition against discrimination based on sexual orientation had been added to the nondiscrimination portion of the constitutional oaths required for both members and officers.[30] "That was a direct result of Sweeney's election [as SEIU president] and the group of young Turks he brought with him," says Oakland-based John Mehring, an AIDS activist and health and safety officer for the SEIU's Western Conference. "They combed through the constitution, dropped outdated clauses like the prohibition on Communist members, and generally brought it into line with their more progressive vision of the union."[31]

The SEIU's 1984 convention also passed two significant gay rights resolutions. One, closely paralleling the 1982 AFSCME resolution and the 1983 resolution of the AFL-CIO, stated: "We support and urge the enactment of legislation at the federal, state and local levels that would guarantee the civil rights of all persons without regard to sexual orientation in employment, housing, credit, public accommodations and public housing." A second resolution broke important new ground by addressing domestic partner benefits, stating: "The union recognizes the concern of those who are discriminated against for spousal benefits because of sexual orientation and/or non-marital relationships and supports means to correct these situations."[32] Mehring was also responsible for organizing support for passage of a third resolution, on AIDS-related issues.

In New York and Boston, with the notable exception of the United Federation of Teacher's Lesbian and Gay Teacher's Association, most lesbian and gay union activism did not begin until the 1980s. A major breakthrough came in 1982 when a lesbian and gay caucus at New York's *Village Voice* persuaded their union (District 65, UAW) to negotiate the first domestic partnership benefits in their new contract that year. Still, it would not be until four years later, and a year after the addition of sexual orientation in New York City's civil rights ordinance, that a regional New York labor organization, the Lesbian and Gay Labor Network (LGLN) was formed in April 1986. A July 1986 flyer succinctly captured the combination of informality and purposefulness that characterized the new group: "Come and talk about what it's like to be out on the job, or not out on the job. We are a handful of lesbian and gay activists, hoping to become an armful. Our goals are to educate union members on issues of relevance to their gay brothers and sisters, [such as] equal spousal benefits, nondiscrimination contract clauses, mandatory employee blood testing, and to encourage trade union principals in the lesbian and gay community." Across the bottom of the flyer were the words: "A worker is a worker is a worker."[33]

LGLN cofounder Shelley Ettinger, then a clerical worker and member of AFT 3882, New York University Staff Association, remembers that "One of the first things we did was to participate in a major anti-apartheid campaign. We also said we would have a contingent in Gay Pride that year.... We issued a news release announcing formation of our group and invited people to join us. There were a dozen or so of us in the parade under the banner 'Lesbian and Gay Labor Network: Gay Pride at Work.' Within the next few months we put together a brochure describing our goals and what we had done. It included logos for boycotting grapes and Coors." Coors had recently begun to expand into the New York market, and the Coors boycott provided LGLN with opportunities for coalition building with labor and a common cause with gay activists outside of the labor movement.[34]

The Coors boycott also provided the opportunity for a dramatic excursion into political theater. According to LGLN cofounder Vivienne Freund, someone (possibly Peter Tenney, a recent arrival from San Francisco who had played a key role in founding LGLN) discovered that Googies, a bar in Greenwich Village near NYU, was serving Coors. "We told the bar owner that if he didn't stop doing it, we were going to boycott and picket his bar. The owner said he wanted to return the beer but still had a half keg."[35] So LGLN decided to organize a Coors Beer Dump. Freund reports: "Chanting 'Out of the bars and into the sewers,' hundreds of people standing shoulder to shoulder passed pitchers of the remaining Coors beer hand by hand from the bar all the way down the block to the sewer on the corner," where it was dumped.[36]

Meanwhile, during the early 1980s, Boston School Drivers Local 8751 of the United Steelworkers of America negotiated inclusion of sexual orientation in their nondiscrimination clause. In 1984, Boston's first gay and lesbian union caucus was organized by Harneen Chernow at Boston University. Chernow recalls: "I organized the Gay and Lesbian Workers Caucus at the university in UAW District 65 to work on getting sexual orientation into the nondiscrimination clause in the union contract. John Silber, a notorious homophobe, was president of Boston University, and there was no way Silber was going to allow the words. We built a lot of support and got a compromise that they would abide by all federal, state, and city ordinances—and Boston had added sexual orientation to its nondiscrimination law." According to Chernow, there was a significant number of lesbian leaders and staff members in Boston unions "who were out there dealing with other issues, but not gay issues, and we wanted gay issues to get on the agenda. People were alienated—they wanted to meet other gay unionists and deal with gay issues." In 1986, several lesbian union officials from around Boston met to organize a group for the region. "We called it the Gay and Lesbian Labor Activists' Network (GALLAN)," Chernow states. "We had seen what was going on with the Coors boycott and building of a gay/union coalition in New York, and we wanted to educate gay people about unions and working-class issues, and to educate the unions about gay issues and gay rights as a social justice issue."[37]

1987 to 1998: Going National

Development of a national gay and lesbian labor group, a gradual process spanning more than a decade, began at the March on Washington for Lesbian and Gay Rights in October 1987. Working from both coasts, Howard Wallace in San Francisco and Shelley Ettinger in New York collaborated on the daunting task of remotely organizing and coordinating a reception in Washington for lesbian and gay labor activists on the day before the march, as well as a national labor contingent in the march itself. Prior to the March on Washington, LGLN was invited by United Auto Workers (UAW) District 65 in New York to join their annual Labor Day parade in early September. LGLN was the first openly gay group to participate in the city's most public labor event. They carried a Lesbian and Gay Labor Network banner while UAW marchers held up placards calling for equal rights for gay workers.

"I also went to the September monthly meeting of the New York AFL-CIO's Central Labor Council and got up and spoke about the march, and it was big deal," says Ettinger, a council delegate. "This was like breaking a big taboo. The leadership of the council was conservative, from the construction trades, and no one had brought up gay rights before, and I was shaking. I was told later that the president of the council made faces behind me while I was speaking. I [explained] that there was going to be a march and why we should support it. When I finished, there was a pause and then applause, and afterward people came up and thanked me for bringing it up—and I met a number of people on the council who had been closeted until then. It broke the ice for gay issues in the council."[38]

On October 10th, months of preparation came to dramatic fruition when the reception in the lobby of the AFL-CIO's national headquarters in Washington drew over 500 people, despite the refusal of the editor of the *AFL-CIO News* to carry an announcement of the event.[39] Overcoming a terrible sound system, the last-minute cancellation of SEIU's John Sweeney, and a virtual blackout of news coverage by the mainstream and gay media, this first national gathering of gay union activists was a resounding success. Officials of the national AFL-CIO and seven AFL-CIO affiliates, the Coalition of Labor Union Women (CLUW), the Coalition of Black Trade Unionists, and the District of Columbia Metro Labor Council addressed the gathering, along with U.S. Representative Barney Frank of Massachusetts and Bill Olwell, who was now a vice president of the 1.3 million-member United Food and Commercial Workers Union. For many of those present—often after many years of separating their "gayness" from their dedication to the union cause—it was a liberating and unifying coming out as lesbian and gay union activists.[40]

"The labor contingent [in the march] was one of the smaller groups," reports Ettinger, "but it was also very diverse, [with workers from] the AFT, the Postal Workers, Farm Workers, AFSCME, and a lot of other unions, including straight union members."[41] Among the featured speakers at the march was Cesar Chavez, president of the United

Farm Workers (UFW), who subsequently appointed Howard Wallace to be a full-time national field representative for the union to promote the boycott in the lesbian and gay community and to speak out as a UFW representative in support of lesbian and gay issues.[42]

The period following the march saw a notable upsurge in gay and lesbian union activism, including the formation of national gay and lesbian caucuses at the NEA in 1987 and at the AFT the following year. In Boston and New York, GALLAN and LGLN separately turned their focus to supporting the start up of gay and lesbian caucuses in their city's largest unions. In July 1988, Ginny Cutting, a GALLAN cofounder, started the Lavender Caucus in SEIU Local 509, covering social workers, teachers, rehabilitation workers, and municipal and state workers in the Boston area.

The following year, in March 1989, ten activists from New York's AFSCME District Council 37 (comprising fifty-seven locals representing 135,000 city and state employees) met at New York's Lesbian and Gay Community Services Center to discuss the need for domestic partner benefits. The group founded the Lesbian and Gay Issues Committee (LAGIC) and received organizing help from LGLN, but it would not be until April 1990 that Council 37, which already had African American and women's caucuses, granted it official recognition.

During the same time, Boston's GALLAN was engaged in a reexamination of its identity and role in the larger community beyond labor. Chernow recalls the internal discussion about what GALLAN's role should be, whether they mainly should support each other to be out in their unions, or if they should be more of an activist organization. "At some point we decided to become a more activist and visible force," Chernow states. "Our big premiere event was in 1989, Allies in the '90s United for Health, a joint fund raiser for the Fenway Health Center and the United Farm Workers, uniting gay health issues with workers' health around the grape boycott." The fund raiser, with Cesar Chavez as the featured speaker, drew over 600 people from the gay community and labor unions, the first time the two groups had joined together in a shared event. According to Chernow, the fund raiser "put us on the map as a progressive group that was really out there, that could organize and get union support. Having Cesar Chavez helped tremendously to get unions to sign on. The event created an [opportunity] . . . for us to do a lot of educating of union leadership."[43]

The 1990 Massachusetts election of Republican Governor Weld led to a less hospitable climate for both labor and gay rights. The 1989 gay civil rights law faced a repeal effort in 1990. Moreover, a proposed tax rollback threatened to cut many state services and cost many unionized state workers their jobs. GALLAN helped mobilize the half-million-strong Massachusetts labor movement against repeal of the gay rights law; within the gay community, they supported the labor-organized opposition to the tax rollback. The "No" vote won on both counts. Chernow remembers, "We accomplished both of our goals, raising visibility of gay people and combating anti-union feeling in the gay community. After the campaign we had a different level of access to labor leaders within the unions. I think that we made it possible for some of the union leaders to come out, and for gay union members to have a way of being gay and bringing those issues back to their unions. Within the gay community, GALLAN and labor were now seen as a group that had to be included."

During 1990 and 1991, GALLAN and New York's LGLN each initiated projects that would have significant national impact. In New York in 1990 the writing, publication, and distribution of an organizing manual, *Pride at Work: Organizing for Lesbian and Gay Rights in Unions,* became a major LGLN project. By 1997, all 7,000 copies of the manual had been distributed. "The book has really put the issue out there," says Miriam Frank, who co-authored the manual with Desma Holcomb, a LGLN founder and UNITE staff member. "At the peak of interest in 1992-93, it was being distributed by Coalition of Labor Union Women and was being reviewed and distributed at labor union conferences. It was also used in some labor studies courses. It was really a break-through piece of organizing. The first few copies sold quickly, but bookstores weren't keen on it because it was staple bound." The manual was financed through several sources. "We had a writing grant from the Chicago Resource Center, which paid me to do the bulk of the research and writing," says Frank. "We also got a loan [from the People's Life Fund], and LGLN had some money of its own. We made money on it and we used it to pay for conferences."[44]

In Boston, Harneen Chernow and GALLAN were also working to increase lesbian and gay visibility and communication at the national level. Chernow recalls that meeting Desma Holcomb at the March on Washington helped the Boston activists to connect. "We were starting to build a national network," Chernow states. Between 1987 and 1991, Chernow, Holcomb, Howard Wallace, and others including Vivienne Freund were speaking at conferences like NGLTF and gatherings like the Michigan's Womyn's Music Festival, where Chernow held a workshop on lesbians in unions.

The 1991 Labor Notes Conference in Detroit would be the scene of the next important national advance for lesbian and gay labor activists. Sponsored every two years by *Labor Notes,* a progressive monthly labor publication, and attended by over 1,000 trade unionists from around the country and abroad, the conference regularly assembles many of the most progressive elements of the labor movement. "When I called in '89 to ask about a gay caucus, they said there wasn't any interest," says GALLAN's Chernow.

> So I volunteered to chair one, and we had a meeting and people were *very* interested in hearing each other's experiences. We had always hoped there would be a national gay labor organization, so a number of us from Boston decided to use the next conference in April of 1991 to help build a national connection with other gay unionists. I called around the country to find people who were going, to encourage people to come and get together to talk about what was happening and build a national network. About ten people from GALLAN went. We organized a panel on domestic partnership and then had a meeting of the gay caucus attended by forty or fifty people.
>
> In 1989, a caucus of Asian workers had formed and had made a presentation to the entire conference at the big plenary benefit. We decided we wanted an opportunity to do the same thing, to address the entire conference and announce the formation of the International Network of Lesbian and Gay Labor Activists and make people realize they had gay members in their groups.
>
> It became a major incident. The conference organizers were not happy—they didn't want us to do this in any way, shape, or form. We felt it was an issue of homophobia, of them being worried about alienating the majority of participants who weren't necessarily open to a bunch of gay people being up in front. We did a whole organizing effort—we had all

kinds of people we knew talk to the leadership of *Labor Notes*. They really had to pressure them into it. Since then we've had a good relationship with *Labor Notes*, and they've done education on gay concerns and broadened their perspective to deal with gay issues as union issues. But at the conference it was very tense.

[When our time came] . . . about forty of us stood up and marched to the front and made our announcement. It was a big deal at the time to be so public and so out at a union event. We had some silence and some cheers. We had 1,100 people there from all over the world. When it was over we were high as a kite; we felt exhilarated and proud of what we were building. People were excited for us. We had a lot of straight allies there. It was a major civil rights victory event; for a lot of people it may have been the first time that they had thought about gay workers being in their shop.[45,46]

In January 1992, the loosely organized national network of lesbian and gay activists published the first issue of *Lavender Labor*, with news from the Bay Area, Boston, and New York. The next issue, published in December 1992, featured stories about a burst of organizing in SEIU, particularly in its Western regional conference, which in February had formed a Lesbian and Gay Labor Association (later renamed the Lavender Caucus).

New York's LGLN hosted its first Pride at Work regional conference in June 1992, bringing together the growing number of lesbian and gay caucuses in New York unions, ranging from firefighters and communications workers to writers and legal aid lawyers. Held at AFSCME District Council 37 headquarters in New York, the conference drew roughly 250 people, mostly from the New York metropolitan area. Several representatives of Boston's GALLAN participated in a number of the panels.

The Pride at Work conference also accelerated efforts to create a national organization. Boston followed New York with the first Northeastern regional meeting on 24 October 1992, which drew twenty-one rank and file union members, staff, and leadership from Boston, Western Massachusetts, New York, and New Jersey. "We came together as a planning meeting for what we hoped would be the Stonewall Lesbian and Gay Labor Conference," Chernow reports. "Those of us in Boston were hoping to organize a national conference to found a national organization—that was our vision." After a day-long meeting, they decided to have a reception at the Lesbian and Gay March in Washington, D.C., in 1993 that would help build toward a 1994 conference at Stonewall 25 in New York City.

Other meetings followed over the next year. Calling themselves the Organizing Committee for a National Lesbian and Gay Labor Coalition, the networking activists were starting a national group virtually from scratch. "None of us were working at the national level," says Chernow. "We were working in our own cities, in our own locals." Differences in organizational structures further complicated matters. New York's LGLN had evolved into an umbrella group of gay union caucuses, whereas in Boston's GALLAN, most members participated as individuals.

None of the planners lived in Washington, D.C., and there was no money for paid staff. Despite these obstacles, the planning group decided to organize a reception at AFL-CIO headquarters, similar to that in 1987. They also decided to hold a one-day planning meeting to prepare for the national conference at Stonewall 25. The planning meeting was scheduled for the day after the 1993 Lesbian and Gay March in Washington, D.C.

To build labor visibility and presence, the group got labor delegates appointed to the national organizing committee for the march and sent letters to national unions to try to get funding. They also decided to give awards to the presidents of the two most supportive unions, Sweeney of SEIU and Gerald McEntee of AFSCME, and to honor the three founding gay labor organizations: San Francisco's Lesbian/Gay Labor Alliance (LGLA), LGLN, and GALLAN. Howard Wallace now also became involved, giving the group a West Coast presence and a broader sense of national ownership and representation.

"We received funds from a number of international unions," Chernow recalls. "Sweeney sent a letter to the local union presidents of SEIU encouraging each local to send two representatives to join the labor contingent of the march and attend the reception on Saturday. He also sent a letter to the presidents of the other internationals asking them to support the event."

Efforts to get march organizers to schedule a labor speaker at the march's main rally proved problematic. Eventually, Regina Shavers of AFSCME New York spoke, but at a pre-march rally instead of the big stage. "It may have been that things were disorganized," Chernow theorizes. "There were lots of speakers and it may have been too close to the march date to schedule her on the big stage. Or it may have represented the political consciousness of the march."[47]

Nevertheless, the reception was very successful, with as many as a thousand people attending. Unlike the 1987 reception, the sound system worked, Sweeney and McEntee were both there to receive their awards, and announcements for the reception had been carried in march publications across the country. Still, as with the 1987 reception, media coverage of the event itself was negligible.

Following the march, the group held a one-day conference at SEIU headquarters that was attended by over one hundred people from more than a dozen unions in fifteen states. They agreed to hold a national conference at Stonewall 25, and a structure was set up with regional conveners across the United States.

"As we had hoped, we ended with a broader group than just the Northeast people," says Chernow. "There was a lot of really good local organizing around the country." One of the more important additions was Van Alan Sheets, a political action coordinator for AFSCME. Sheets was also building a new Washington, D.C., gay labor umbrella group, Lambda Labor, largely made up of staff from the international offices of AFSCME, SEIU, the Teamsters, other major unions, and the AFL-CIO itself. Based in AFSCME's Washington headquarters since 1982, he brought with him the experience, contacts, and political savvy of a Beltway insider—all of which were invaluable for an embryonic national organization. At the other end of the country, in Washington State, Seattle's lesbian and gay caucuses were forming their own regional group, the Out Front Labor Coalition, which joined in planning the conference.

The regional conveners were encouraged to meet on 1 October 1993, in Oakland, California, at a meeting designed to coincide with the first SEIU Western Conference's Lavender Caucus Leadership Conference, which was in turn timed to coincide with the AFL-CIO's 20th Constitutional Convention across the Bay in San Francisco. The Oakland gatherings brought together a thousand representatives of SEIU Lavender Labor groups from California, Oregon, Washington State, Colorado, and Utah; representatives of GALLAN, LGLN, San Francisco's LGLA, and Washington's Lambda Labor; and official delegates from AFSCME and SEIU. UNISON, Britain's largest union, also sent its National Lesbian and Gay Officer. The combined meeting helped solidify national involvement and support for the Stonewall 25 labor conference.

There was a second and perhaps equally important result. "We had invited John Sweeney [SEIU president] to come to Oakland to speak to the Lavender Caucus," says SEIU conference organizer Bob Lewis, "and instead they arranged for us to go over to San Francisco to make our presentation to them [the international leadership of the SEIU]." The caucus presentation, which included a discussion of domestic partner benefits, was a unique opportunity to reach, educate, and influence the man who would succeed Lane Kirkland as president of the national AFL-CIO two years later.[48]

In a year colored by the furor over "gays in the military" and the worrying precedent set by Colorado's passage of its anti-gay constitutional amendment the previous November, there was no backing down from gay rights by organized labor. During its convention, the national AFL-CIO reiterated its support for "enactment of legislation at all levels of government to guarantee the civil rights of all persons without regard to sexual orientation." The AFL-CIO further urged affiliated groups to "take an active role in opposing measures which reduce the rights of people based on sexual orientation" and to "participate in appropriate coalitions to defeat such measures."[49]

In a speech earlier in the year, Jim Baker, executive assistant to AFL-CIO president Kirkland, had stated the message even more starkly: "in this critical period, as in the past, . . . we must not shrink from defending the rights of groups which may be unpopular or under attack. Just as, for example, no union would allow an employer to dismiss or harass a trade unionist for being gay or lesbian, we must be ready to carry that fight publicly, so that those who consider God's message to be one of hatred and intolerance cannot intimidate the rest of the community."[50]

Events in Oakland and San Francisco gave significant new momentum to the planned Stonewall 25 labor conference. It was a huge effort. For the nascent group's regional conveners, the months leading up to the conference were a marathon of organizing, coordinated largely through long-distance conference calls. At various times, conference-call participants would include Teresa Conrow, Vivienne Mendoza, Mark Friedman, Tom Barbara, Howard Wallace, Cal Noyce, Nancy Wohlforth, Vince Quackenbush, Larry Kelly, Ed Hunt, Jeff Bigelow, Linda Romero, Regina Shavers, Glen Francis, Van Alan Sheets, Chernow, and others. Many would not meet in person until the conference itself. A few, like Cal Noyce, a Communications Workers of America (CWA) lineman and founder of the Utah Coalition of Gay, Lesbian, and Bi Union Activists and Supporters in Salt Lake City, had been totally isolated from the national gay labor movement only a few months earlier.[51]

"We came up with a group of committees which were needed to put on the conference: fund raising, outreach, by-laws, logistics, etc.," Chernow reports. "Howard [Wallace] did a lot of the fund raising from the internationals," including $5,000 grants from SEIU and AFSCME, and smaller amounts from the CWA and eleven other unions.

When the Stonewall 25 labor conference finally convened at AFSCME District Council 37 headquarters in New York in June 1994, it brought together more than 300 labor activists representing twenty-five private and public sector unions as well as local and regional gay and lesbian labor groups across the United States. Participants came from diverse occupations ranging from factory, office, restaurant, and health care workers to journalists and lawyers.

The goals, and needs, of those attending were as diverse as their backgrounds. Those who came from unions with a gay caucus saw a national group as a supplement. Isolated gay unionists, however, like those in rural areas, were looking for more support from a national organization. There were also major differences in political vision, Chernow recalls. "Did we want to focus on building caucuses in locals and [developing] good contract language on domestic partner benefits and nondiscrimination, or did we want to build coalitions within the gay communities on issues which are not directly labor issues but affect lesbian, gay, bisexual, and transgender people, such as immigration?" The latter approach would follow a core precept of the U.S. labor movement: "An injury to one is an injury to all."[52]

Overcoming their differences, the activists adopted provisional by-laws broad enough to encompass their diverse objectives and a structure loosely modeled on that of the AFL-CIO. The new group, which would seek to be a nationwide organization working under the aegis of the AFL-CIO, would be known as Pride at Work: The National Association for Lesbian, Gay, Bisexual, and Transgender Labor. Tom Barbera, a founder and steering-committee member of Pride at Work, recalls that the response to the new national group was phenomenal. "We got calls from everywhere... Hawaii, Alaska, Wyoming... everything from atomic engineers, mechanics, police officers, carpenters... every type of union imaginable including the giants like the CWA, the UAW, and even the Teamsters."[53] At the same time, the official launch of Pride at Work was accompanied by a nearly total turnover in the movement's leadership. "When the organization was formed," says Chernow, "there was very little overlap between the original leadership of the Stonewall founding conference and the new leadership—mostly because of burnout. It was a lot of work with minimal resources. We spent a lot of our own money. It was an incredible thing to be part of.... [but] I knew that there would never be a national organization unless we did the work to make it happen."

"Our ability to replace almost the entire leadership in 1994 showed the strength of our movement," agrees Desma Holcomb, who had not been involved in organizing the New York conference. "There are enough experienced people so that they can alternate in and out of leadership."[54] One reason is the very nature of the movement; most Pride at Work activists were already seasoned union organizers.

Holcomb and Howard Wallace were elected the first national co-chairs of Pride at Work at a meeting of the thirty-member Executive Committee the following November. They took on a challenging assignment. "When the group started, there were all kinds of political differences and different union styles," says Holcomb. "There were some funds left over to pay for the very expensive conference calls," Holcomb recalls, and to help pay for part of people's travel expenses, "but there was no budget for paid staff. Trying to run a national organization without it was really hard."[55]

Lack of resources and staff would continue to be the major impediment for Pride at Work, severely limiting the group's ability to reach out and support its far-flung constituency. "If it weren't for the donation of time and in-kind services, we probably wouldn't be around now," says Cal Noyce, a steering-committee member who had recently been elected president of the Central Utah Labor Council. Printing was donated by locals of both the Office and Professional Employees International Union (OPEIU) and SEIU. Postage to mail 1,500 copies of the Pride at Work newsletter was donated by a local of the International Brotherhood of Electrical Workers (IBEW). Although some steering-committee members received help from their unions, others, including Noyce, paid their own considerable travel and telephone expenses.[56]

Because it had always been a grass roots movement, financial stringency could slow but not stop the national growth of gay labor union activism. "There's been a major upsurge in [lesbian and gay] organizing at all levels: local, state, and regional," reports Tom Barbera. "My union alone has thousands of members in over twenty Lavender Caucuses across the U.S., and gay and lesbian issues such as domestic partner benefits are always represented in our contract negotiations." New Pride at Work chapters were formed in Philadelphia (which paid dues for 300 members), Connecticut, Rhode Island, and Detroit. A chapter in Los Angeles that fell apart after the 1994 conference was reestablished a few months later by Kipukai Kuali'i, an AFSCME activist.[57]

The Detroit chapter was founded by Ron Woods, a UAW worker and steering-committee member of Pride at Work, who experienced how traumatic being openly gay can be when he organized protests against a new Cracker Barrel restaurant because of its policy of firing gay workers. After a photograph of Woods's picketing appeared on the front page of the *Detroit Free Press* in September 1991, he immediately became the object of intense harassment at Chrysler's Trenton, Michigan, plant, where he worked as an electrician maintaining and programming robotic production equipment. Previously highly regarded by his management and coworkers (he had been profiled in a company magazine), he was subjected to a wide range of harassment, including three incidents of physical assault over the next eleven months. "I felt totally abandoned—by the union, by Chrysler, and by the Detroit gay community—but I'm glad I didn't give up a good job because of those bigots," says Woods, who eventually transferred to Chrysler's technology center after filing a fifty-five-page grievance through his union local. His vindication came in January 1993 when the UAW's *Solidarity* magazine featured him in a highly supportive feature article documenting his experience, with directions on how to use the union's grievance process and civil rights committees. It was the magazine's first feature article on gay issues. In a remarkable turnaround from his former position of plant pariah, Woods was elected a delegate to the UAW's constitutional convention and to a special bargaining convention the following year which would determine proposed contract provisions.[58]

"It was truly a testament to Ron's political organizing that twenty-three cities participated in the first demonstrations against Chrysler," says Tom Barbera. Woods also proved astonishingly effective at getting media coverage, including a feature article in the *New Yorker* in 1997, which may have motivated Chrysler's almost surreptitious addition of sexual orientation to its Standards of Conduct and its Code of Ethical Behavior. But in early 1998, sexual orientation was still not part of either Chrysler's or the UAW's nondiscrimination clauses, although Ford and GM had made this addition. The UAW, however, had added sexual orientation to its "statement of inclusion" for membership. These partial victories came at enormous personal and professional cost for Woods, who eventually took an extended medical leave from his job at Chrysler.

For the steering committee of Pride at Work, whose members were dispersed across the United States, much of the focus shifted to preparing for the next national conference to be held in San Francisco in 1996. There was little progress on a second objective, exploring possible affiliation with the AFL-CIO as a constituency group.

The San Francisco conference, timed to coincide with the twenty-fifth anniversary of the city's Gay Pride celebration, would be Pride at Work's first weekend-long event, requiring substantially more organizational efforts than the group's 1994 founding conference. The program would address the varied needs of the group's increasingly diverse membership, with workshops ranging from organizing caucuses, political activism, homophobia on the job, and domestic partner benefits to the specific issues affecting transgender people and people of color.

With Jack Henning, president of the California AFL-CIO, as a featured speaker, the San Francisco conference also had heightened visibility. The 270 activists who came to the meeting from across the country approved a constitution providing for member chapters and a representation and dues structure based on the number of dues-paying members in each chapter.

A new slate of officers was elected at the conference, including co-chairs Nancy Wohlforth and Cal Noyce. Wohlforth, business manager and secretary-treasurer of Office and Professional Employees Local 3, would also be elected vice president of the California Labor Federation in July, the first out lesbian in that position. Noyce had just been appointed as the only openly gay member of the national AFL-CIO's new Labor Council Advisory Committee, assigned by Sweeney to develop a strategy to reactivate and energize regional labor councils throughout the country. AFSCME's Van Alan Sheets was elected Pride at Work's treasurer.

Perhaps the most important decision at the conference was adoption of a resolution supporting affiliation with the AFL-CIO as a constituency group on par with the Coalition of Union Women (CLUW), the Coalition of Black Trade Unionists (CBTU), the Labor Council of Latin American Advancement (LACLAA), and Asian Pacific Labor Alliance (APALA). "There was a groundswell for a resolution to seek dialog with the end goal of affiliation," Tom Barbera reports. "We wanted to negotiate it on terms that would maintain our integrity as gay and lesbian activists without compromising . . . our ability to criticize unions and the AFL-CIO when we needed to on gay and lesbian issues."

"I thought national AFL-CIO recognition was worth taking the risk," says Noyce. "We hoped that perhaps by our next conference in '98 we'd be voting to become a constituency group or not." Events would outpace these expectations. Over the next year, Wohlforth, Noyce, and particularly Sheets, strategically located in Washington, would play key roles in negotiating the protracted process of becoming an official AFL-CIO constituency group. Van Sheets comments that when Sweeney was elected AFL-CIO president in 1995, "with his long history of putting the resources there, not just saying the right things, many of us were very happy about it. My own union [AFSCME] was one of the prime sponsors of his candidacy. Another key person in the election was the new executive VP Linda Chavez-Thompson, who came out of AFSCME in Texas, because it is under Linda that all of the constituency groups fall." Sheets says that Pride at Work apparently had the support of Chavez-Thompson, Sweeney, and

Richard Trumka, the AFL-CIO's secretary-treasurer, "but we needed two other areas of support: their staff people and members of the executive council."[59]

Pride at Work leaders went to the AFL-CIO executive council meeting in Los Angeles to present their case for becoming a constituency group. While there, they also talked with as many people as they could to build support, focusing on people they thought would be supportive to make sure they understood the need for recognition.

John Sweeney had created the Full Participation Committee, chaired by Linda Chavez-Thompson. Recognition of Pride at Work was discussed by this group, and a subcommittee was appointed by President Sweeney to make a recommendation to the executive committee. "We were very pleased with those who were appointed to the subcommittee," says Sheets. "It didn't have anyone that we thought we might have to work on." Based on the understanding that there would be a vote on their constituency status at the AFL-CIO Pittsburgh convention in September, Pride at Work went into high gear.

"We got the SEIU executive board to pass a resolution during their convention in June/July supporting Pride at Work becoming a constituency group of the AFL-CIO," says Sheets. "We continued to talk with leaders in our own unions. In addition, Cal Noyce, as president of Central Utah Labor Council, was key in getting contacts through the national Labor Council Advisory Committee on mobilizing labor councils and gathering that support. In California, similar things were done with the secretary-treasurer of the state federation and many of their leadership people."[60]

Less than a week before the August executive council meeting, Sheets got a call asking for letters of endorsement for Pride at Work. Working on a very short deadline, Sheets and other Pride at Work leaders got endorsements from AFCSME, the Union of Needletrades, Industrial and Textile Employees (UNITE), the International Union of Electrical Workers (IUE), the SEIU, and other unions and faxed them to Chicago where they were presented to the subcommittee. Sheets recalls:

> Monday afternoon, Arlene Holt [executive assistant to Linda Chavez-Thompson] told me that everyone appeared to be in agreement, and that the full executive council might go ahead and officially recognize us that week. Then on Thursday, Arlene called my office to say that the vote had taken place and that Pride at Work was official. Up until this time, we've been a struggling organization relying on volunteer time and donations. You make every penny count, and that's good because it builds activism, but it also makes it very difficult to grow in size. Becoming a constituency group will give us a budget from the AFL-CIO, which will mean we have more resources to do things. Equally significant is that within the House of Labor we're an official organization, so when one of our members goes to a local union or local labor council or state federation of labor, we're an official part of labor already. It will also make it much easier to get coverage or stories in a whole slew of union publications.[61]

Pride at Work felt an immediate impact after the vote in August 1997. "I was contacted by different departments of the AFL-CIO for more information about Pride at Work to be included in their publications," says Noyce. "There was immediate recognition—we were included in the constituency group brochure prepared for the September convention. We also received half a dozen non-voting badges for the convention floor, and we have a representative on the planning committee for the full convention conference next year. Other unions also contacted us for a paragraph or membership form for Pride at Work to put into their newsletters."

The September 1997 AFL-CIO convention in Pittsburgh was like a giant coming out party for Pride at Work. As long-standing activist Shelley Ettinger recalls:

> What I saw there was such a sea change. Two nights before the convention opened, Pride at Work held a reception, and most of the national union leaders and all of the leaders of the other constituency groups came—and that would have been unheard of a short time before. There were booths for Pride at Work and the other constituency groups. President Sweeney announced the recognition of Pride at Work, and there was widespread applause from the union leaders. The official speech about the constituency groups was by Ken Wong of APALA, who gave a stirring welcome to Pride at Work. In their speeches, Jesse Jackson and Kweisi Mfume of the NAACP both mentioned gay rights.
>
> We're at a point now where what we envisioned in the first few years after Stonewall of the gay/lesbian/bi/trans movement uniting with the labor movement is coming to pass. Joining all of the movements—the gay movement, the struggle against racism, the labor movement—strengthens them all. I don't think it's a coincidence that this is coming at the time of a new more militant leadership [under John Sweeney] fighting for workers' rights. It's a very exciting time.[62]

Unhappily, expectations that Pride at Work, like other official constituency groups, would receive substantial financial support from the national AFL-CIO did not come to pass. Although APALA, the Asian Pacific constituency group, had received $250,000 funding in its first year after official recognition, Pride at Work received no funding whatsoever. Combined with the failure of the AFL-CIO to issue a press release to the mainstream media, as it had for all previous constituency groups, this lack of funding places Pride at Work in the anomalous position of an unwanted stepchild.[63]

The national AFL-CIO's unprecedented lack of financial support for a newly recognized constituency group points to a continuing, widespread ambivalence among unions and their highest national leadership toward their lesbian and gay members. Despite extensive negative publicity and pressure on Chrysler from the socially responsible investment movement, labor never organized a Coors-style boycott against Chrysler to induce the auto maker to implement a nondiscrimination policy including sexual orientation. In fact, labor made no significant effort at all. "The Coors boycott got off the ground because it already had strong union support," Tom Barbera explains, "but we don't have institutional support from the unions because this is a *gay* labor issue."[64]

Another difference is that union jobs were not at stake at Coors, which wasn't unionized, whereas thousands of UAW workers could have been adversely impacted by an action against Chrysler. Combined with the homophobia of many union leaders and members at the local level, this helps explain why labor has often failed to protect the rights of gay and lesbian union members in their workplaces. In fact, with many notable exceptions, labor's record on gay issues improves as the theater of activity becomes more removed from its rank and file members. One factor here may be the relatively liberal views, when compared with those of the often socially conservative rank and file, of state and national union leaders who have played critical roles in adopting gay-supportive positions and policies.

On a more positive note, union support for gay rights in the mid to late 1990s has generally been at its best in the political arena. From its inception, Pride at Work sought passage of the federal Employment Non-Discrimination Act (ENDA), which would prohibit discrimination based on sexual orientation. On 23 June 1994, a few days before the new group was formed in New York, and two years after the California Labor Federation supported similar state legislation, the national AFL-CIO declared its support for ENDA. In a statement issued at its national headquarters in Washington, D.C., the national AFL-CIO said:

> Employment decisions should be made on the basis of an individual's ability to perform the job. . . . Dismissal, harassment and intimidation of workers for reasons unrelated to job performance is an employer tactic well known in the labor movement. Trade unions have long fought for the right of workers to be judged on their work and not irrelevant criteria that address their private lives.
>
> This bill extends the legal protections from employment discrimination provided to those who historically have been denied equal opportunity in the workplace. It is a step in the right direction of providing equal opportunity for all Americans.[65]

During the 1990s, as with California's Briggs initiative in 1978, union backing at the national, state, and local levels was critical in defeating anti-gay initiatives and amendments in Oregon, Washington, and Idaho. It is particularly notable that in Colorado, where anti-gay Amendment 2 passed in 1992, and in Washington State, where an ENDA-like employment rights initiative failed in 1997, labor was late in actively supporting the gay rights side of the campaigns.

In Colorado in 1992, the new state AFL-CIO president, who had recently become a "born-again" Christian, initially took a neutral stance on Amendment 2. It was only after national AFL-CIO president Lane Kirkland sent a letter to him and AFL-CIO affiliates throughout the state reminding them of the union's 1983 resolution supporting gay rights that the state AFL-CIO publicly opposed the anti-gay amendment. Kirkland also sent a similar letter to AFL-CIO affiliates in Oregon the following year during that state's anti-gay initiative.[66]

In Washington State, labor support for the 1997 employment rights initiative came relatively late, at least partly because Hands Off Washington, the gay rights coalition behind the initiative, had been ineffective in soliciting union support. As with other statewide initiatives going back to Briggs in California, however, gay labor activists bridged the gap. Seattle's Out Front Labor Coalition, now a chapter of Pride at Work, were crucial in engaging labor.

"Hands Off hadn't consulted us, and we had to do a lot of work to get labor on board toward the middle, when it could have been done at the beginning," says Marcy Johnsen, an Out Front Labor Coalition member and co-chair of SEIU's Western Conference Lavender Caucus. "We were key in mobilizing labor," Johnsen states. Once engaged, unions provided critically needed funding as well as organizational and logistical support. Moreover, prominent labor leaders spoke at Hands Off rallies. "It could have been horrid without labor," Johnsen concludes.[67] Nevertheless, the vote went against the initiative. The election returns were 60 percent versus 40 percent, in a year in which all statewide initiatives were voted down.

Conclusion

At a critical turning point in the history of the American union movement, lesbian and gay union members can point to several encouraging signposts to the future. Their regional groups in areas such as New York, Boston, San Francisco, and Seattle provide an increasingly strong foundation. Their caucuses in major unions such as SEIU are ever more visible. Furthermore, Pride at Work has received official recognition, albeit incomplete and equivocal. With access to top leadership in the AFL-CIO, lesbian and gay labor activists seem poised and eager to bring their energy and enthusiasm into the mainstream of the American trade union movement—even as the larger labor movement seeks to reinvent itself to survive in a service-oriented economy.

In this rapidly changing environment, a national union strategy based on organizing women and minorities could come to rely on the activism of lesbian and gay members as a core component in a reinvigorated labor coalition. Still, the AFL-CIO's apparent discrimination against its officially recognized Pride at Work constituency group— a group devoted to fighting just such discrimination—is disconcerting and disturbing at best. Full and equal participation in the House of Labor, it would appear, remains more hope than reality for America's gay, lesbian, bisexual, and transgender union members.

Certainly the campaign for equality will continue. Like many lesbian and gay labor activists, Cal Noyce, national co-chair of Pride at Work, is able to take a pragmatic, long-term view. "We win friends by building coalitions with other groups and working together for common goals—that's what trade unionism is all about," Noyce says. Pride at Work's progress from its founding in June 1994 to its recognition as a constituency group by the AFL-CIO in August 1997 is "pretty amazing," according to Noyce. "When you compare us with other groups, we've accomplished a lot." He attributes this largely to "individual people who have been willing to take the risk and say: 'I'm going to get into this.' . . . You don't get the whole elephant at once—you've got to get your foot in the door first—and if you don't take 'No' for an answer, sooner or later you're going to get what you want."[68]

Indeed, the future of the lesbian and gay labor movement will depend, at least in part, on the success of the AFL-CIO in reversing the ebbing tide of labor unionism in the United States, which is still far from certain. And while lesbian and gay labor activists have come a very long way since the mid-1970s, there remains a very long way to go.

Notes

1. Interviews with Howard Wallace, summer 1995 and fall 1997. Wallace's newspaper clippings, documenting over twenty years of California gay labor history, can be found in *Solidarity in Action: An Historical Scrapbook* (published by Local 250, Hospital and Health Care Workers Union, 1994), which contains many of the articles from California publications cited elsewhere in this chapter.

2. One exception is D. Osborne, "Lavender Labor: A Brief History," in *Homo Economics: Capitalism, Community, and Lesbian and Gay Life,* ed. A. Gluckman and B. Reed (New York: Routledge, 1997).

3. Because no single person was aware of all of the events related in this chapter, it seems likely that important events were unknown to those interviewed for this project and unmentioned in the limited written sources available to this writer. Also, space limitations have forced deletion of some interesting and even titillating details (e.g., hotel workers in high drag on the picket line during hotel strikes in Boston in the 1960s and lesbians making out in the ladies room during union meetings at a Seattle bus company in the 1970s). Much remains to be discovered by historians who delve into this "virgin" territory.

4. Allan Berube, lecture and slide show, "The Marine Cooks and Stewards Union From the Depression to the Cold War," presented at the Wagner Labor Archives, New York University, 31 May 1995.

5. Interview with Harry Hay, September 1998.

6. Interview with David McReynolds, November 1997. McReynolds was a long-time friend and close political colleague of Rustin's at the War Resisters League.

7. Interview with Walter Johnson, December 1997.

8. Library of the American Federation of Teachers, Washington, D.C. This information was supplied by phone by their research librarian from a compilation of AFT resolutions in November 1997.

9. McReynolds, cited above, doubts that Rustin would have tried to influence UFT president Shanker to support the resolution. Rustin was not publicly out and, according to McReynolds, "wasn't very gay friendly" after he took over leadership of the A. Philip Randolph Institute in 1964. The possibility remains, however, that the resolution might have been an unsolicited "thank you" for Rustin's public support during the racially charged 1969 dispute between the UFT and the predominantly African American Brownsville local school board.

10. Library of the American Federation of Teachers, Washington, D.C. This information was supplied by phone by their research librarian from a compilation of AFT resolutions in November 1997.

11. E-mail interview with Jim Testerman, national co-chair of the NEA's gay and lesbian caucus, December 1997.

12. Mark Rubin, "History of the Gay Teachers Association," *Gay Teachers Association Newsletter* 1, no. 1 (July 1978). Curiously, in a telephone interview in December 1997, Rubin said that his group was unaware of the two earlier AFT resolutions on sexual orientation, and that Shanker made no mention of them during their meeting.

13. American Federation of Teachers, "Keeping Informed: AFT's Position on Sexual Orientation," undated.

14. Interview with Ron Madson, Gay Teachers Association, October 1997.

15. Interview with Shelley Ettinger, November 1997.

16. Interview with Sue Schurman, November 1997.

17. Interviews with Howard Wallace, summer 1995 and fall 1997.

18. The quotes and information to follow have been culled from the *San Francisco Bay Guardian* article, "Behind the School Board Fight," issue dated 28 June through 11 July 1975.

19. Interviews with Howard Wallace, summer 1995 and fall 1997.

20. "A New Breakthrough," *Advocate*, 17 November 1996, p. 6.

21. Interviews with Howard Wallace, summer 1995 and fall 1997.

22. Interview with Tom Stabnicki, December 1997.

23. Proceedings of the 1982 Convention of American Federation of State, County, and Municipal Employees.

24. Interview with Vic Basile, November 1997.

25. Interview with Vic Basile, November 1997.

26. George Mendenall, "AFL-CIO Unions Back Gay Rights," *Bay Area Reporter,* 4 November 1982.

27. Margaret Frost, "Locals Form Gay Union Caucus", *Bay Area Reporter,* 27 January 1983.

28. Sal Roselli, "Economic Rights for Gay Workers Sought by IGLA," *Alice Reports* (April 1983).

29. Howard Wallace, "AFL-CIO Takes Strong Stand for Gay Rights," *San Francisco Vector,* 13 October 1983.

30. Constitution and Proceedings of the 1980 and 1984 Service Employees International Union conventions.

31. Interview with John Mehring, November 1997.

32. Constitution and Proceedings of the 1980 and 1984 Service Employees International Union conventions.

33. For an in depth discussion of the founding of LGLN and other lesbian/gay/labor caucuses see Miriam Frank's chapter in this volume.

34. Interview with Shelley Ettinger, November 1997.

35. Interviews with Vivienne Freund, October and November 1997.

36. It is not clear whether LGLN invented the Coors Beer Dump. Several LGLN members think they did, but Dave Sickler, who was national coordinator for the boycott, says that the tactic had been used in 1985 in Detroit and other locations. Sickler also reports that although "the gay community played a key role in New York and Boston," he also received "wonderful" support from the local labor councils and state AFL-CIOs in New York, Massachusetts, and Rhode Island in 1984–1985 and afterward. By contrast, Vivienne Freund and other LGLN founders remember only tepid support for the boycott from these same unions.

37. Interviews with Harneen Chernow, November and December 1997.

38. Interview with Shelley Ettinger, November 1997.

39. Interview with Shelley Ettinger, November 1997. Ettinger also stated that the editor made openly homophobic remarks when refusing to run the announcement.

40. See Jean Bowdish, "Historic Labor Reception Draws 500," *United Labor Action,* vol. 14, no. 7, October 1987.

41. Interview with Shelley Ettinger, November 1997.

42. "Labor Pledges Solidarity," *Northern California Labor,* vol. 40, no. 7 (1997), and David Lamble, "Union Names Gay to National Office: Labor Activist Wallace Now Union Rep," *Bay Area Reporter,* 28 April 1988, p. 17.

43. Interviews with Harneen Chernow, November and December 1997.

44. Interview with Miriam Frank, September 1997.

45. Interviews with Harneen Chernow, November and December 1997.

46. Vivienne Freund reports that the group was determined to address the conference, even if the organizers refused to allow it.

47. Interviews with Harneen Chernow, November and December 1997.

48. Interview with Bob Lewis, December 1997.

49. See *Solidarity in Action: An Historical Scrapbook.*

50. From a speech given by James Baker at the Jewish Labor Committee, 18 June 1993.

51. Interviews with Cal Noyce, November and December 1997.

52. Interviews with Harneen Chernow, November and December 1997.

53. Interviews with Tom Barbera, November and December 1997.

54. Interview with Desma Holcomb, September 1997.

55. Interview with Desma Holcomb, September 1997.

56. Interviews with Cal Noyce, November and December 1997.

57. Interviews with Tom Barbera, November and December 1997.
58. Interviews with Ron Woods, 1995 and 1997.
59. Interview with Van Alan Sheets, November 1997.
60. Interview with Van Alan Sheets, November 1997.
61. Interview with Van Alan Sheets, November 1997.
62. Interview with Shelley Ettinger, November 1997.
63. E-mail interview with Van Alan Sheets, August 1998.
64. Interviews with Tom Barbera, November and December 1997.
65. *California AFL-CIO News,* vol. 37, no. 34 (1994).
66. Interviews with Howard Wallace, summer 1995 and fall 1997.
67. Interview with Marcy Johnsen, January 1998.
68. Interviews with Cal Noyce, November and December 1997.

Miriam Frank

5   Lesbian and Gay Caucuses in the U.S. Labor Movement

I was just gay. I don't put my lifestyle on you; I just don't deny it. There's a lot of prejudice out there. With me being black, you got to figure, is it your color, is it your gayness, and I do care inside.

They had a conference in Baltimore, a huge conference. Local 509 sent us. That was the first time in any union you knew you belonged. And when we got back here, we met and we wanted to have an East Coast Lesbian, Gay, Bisexual, and Transgendered group to get us closer together. . . . It all has to do with how the world is finally turning, that we are recognized in a different way.

(Shirley Clarke, Boston, 1995)

Shirley Clarke runs a community residence house for the mentally handicapped for the State of Massachusetts. She had been a union activist and officer and an ardent fighter for the rights of sexual minorities well before a job upgrade transferred her union membership from American Federation of State, County, and Municipal Employees (AFSCME) Local 402 to Service Employees International Union (SEIU) Local 509. As a Local 402 vice president, chief steward, newsletter staffer, and strike leader, Clarke had never been shy about her lesbian identity and had pushed the local to participate in Boston gay pride events.

When Clarke became a Local 509 member in the early 1990s, she was at first less involved in local leadership. At the same time, she found a thriving local lesbian and gay caucus already in place. The growth of Lavender Caucuses throughout SEIU created structures and strategies that have had a powerful impact on members like Clarke. She and many others have become newly empowered to find levels of union commitment that speak to their personal sense of community and solidarity.

Clarke's story of integrating her lesbian identity with her commitment to the union is becoming less and less unusual in the U.S. labor movement. At the heart of recent labor activism around sexual orientation issues are individual activists as well as rank and file interest committees that have operated to join sexual minority concerns to labor's wider cause of fairness and justice. There have been gay alliances in established unions since the 1970s; since the mid-1980s, gay and lesbian caucus organizations have grown more powerful, more widespread, and more connected to central power structures of local unions. Since 1990, as the labor atmosphere in the United States has become more liberal, sexual minorities have organized in coalitions reaching beyond their local unions to conference or district councils, national conventions, and the headquarters of international organizations.

This chapter examines the growth of local union lesbian and gay committees and caucuses in the 1970s and 1980s among teachers, restaurant workers, the *Village Voice*, hospital workers, and public sector workers. It also describes how regional or national union infrastructures have been developing in the 1990s. We shall see that these union-wide policy bodies have empowered local sexual minority activism with the resources of the union as a whole.

Gay Teachers: An Injury to One Is an Injury to All

Teachers were the first unionized gay and lesbian workers to formally organize, but their groups were not intended to function primarily as union pressure blocs. In New York, the Gay Teachers Association (GTA) started meeting in 1974. In San Francisco, a Gay Teachers Coalition (affiliated with Bay Area Gay Liberation, not with the teachers' union) got started in 1975. By 1978 groups in San Francisco, Boston, New York City, and Los Angeles were meeting once or twice monthly, publishing newsletters, and advocating gay teachers' rights. These teachers' groups reached out to school workers (often not only teachers) in public and private education.

In the 1970s, local teacher unions were less than supportive of gay rights. In 1975, the Bay Area group spearheaded a boisterous battle with the San Francisco School Board to include sexual orientation in its anti-discrimination policy. Even though the AFT had been on record since 1970 with a policy resolution denouncing discrimination, its San Francisco Local 61 avoided endorsement of the sexual orientation proposal before the local school board.[1] In New York City, members of the United Federation of Teachers (UFT) or AFT Local 2 who were active in the GTA experienced a similarly cool reception. More than three years of strenuous lobbying finally got the GTA's advertisements listed in the New York State United Teachers (NYSUT) monthly statewide newsletter, the *New York Teacher,* in 1978. A protracted campaign was also necessary to secure UFT support for sexual orientation language in the contract, as well as union support of the long-contested City Council gay rights bill.[2]

Leaders of New York's GTA reported on their occasional meetings with UFT officials in the GTA newsletter and made protection of gay and lesbian teachers in school workplaces an important organizing issue. However, the union's sanction of their cause was only one of many routes that gay and lesbian teacher activists explored. The caucus members could not and did not rely on their AFT locals as necessarily available resources. The Bay Area and New York City organizations were much more focused on securing autonomous, safe forums for gay and lesbian teachers. Gay and lesbian teacher groups would gather at community centers or in private homes—never in union meeting halls. The GTA newsletter was devoted to professional, rather than workplace, rights matters. It published curriculum discussions, book and media reviews, and reports on gay-themed classroom discussions, both formal and informal. In San Francisco and New York City, speakers' bureaus were formed, and volunteers reached out to community groups and offered time to in-service classes and Parent Teacher Associations.

With the 1978 threat of California Referendum Proposition 6, known as the Briggs initiative, the labor landscape changed radically. Briggs menaced the rights of all teachers and many public employees. A coalition of civil rights groups, unions, and gay organizations throughout the state campaigned vigorously to defeat this "injury to all." AFT rallied national labor support, and the statewide NYSUT newsletter ran an extensive interview with five GTA leaders under the headline "California's Proposition 6 Aims at Homosexual Teachers but Is Threat to All."[3]

In the early 1980s, GTA maintained its autonomous status while developing its power as a legitimate constituency in the 125,000-member UFT.[4] A core of activists organized popular monthly forums and kept up the lively newsletter. They attended biennial AFT conventions and networked with gay teachers' groups in other cities. They initiated a gay pride essay contest for students. There were dances, even a few romantic moments. Celebrating a first year's anniversary, Helayne Seidman reminisces in the GTA newsletter how she met her lover at a caucus function: "I wanted to get clearer on my rights as a gay teacher. Since that meeting things have never been the same."[5]

Dishrag: "Something of an Outside Agitator Kind of Group"

San Francisco's thriving restaurant industry has long been an employment haven for young gays who come to the city from somewhere else in the United States and need to make a living while pursuing their artistic dreams. Peter Tenney, who cooked and waited tables all over the Bay Area in the late 1970s, remembers the workplace arguments: "These gay/waiter/artist/dancer types would insist they were not a waiter but an artist or a dancer. Well then, what are those two plates in your hand and get them out quick before they get cold. It's understood that art is the passion, but here we are in a gay context saying 'I'm not really here,' which is not so different from being closeted."[6]

In early 1978, a rank and file opposition group in Local 2 of the Hotel and Restaurant Employees union (HERE) upset the entrenched leadership of the local. The new guard captured a few executive board seats as well as the presidency and vice presidency. Gay and lesbian restaurant workers had worked in the rank and file campaign, and at the election-night party, Tenney and his friends decided to form a gay caucus in the union. It was "somewhat affiliated" with the rank and file caucus, though never officially sanctioned by the union. According to Tenney, "It was always something of an outside agitator kind of group."[7]

Nevertheless, in that same year, with the Briggs initiative awaiting a November referendum, this gay caucus within a successful rank and file reform campaign added substantial clout to the Labor Committee of the Bay Area Committee Against the Briggs

Initiative (BACABI). The majority of local officials who signed onto the BACABI Labor Committee represented workers in the human services occupations (such as teachers and social workers) who would be directly affected by the repressive measure. Only a handful of liberal officials from private sector unions joined the committee,[8] and Dave McDonald, Local 2's newly elected insurgent president, took a real risk with his divided membership when he got involved. Tenney called on McDonald to take a stand at a Speakout rally:

> We asked him if he would deliver a speech. He said, "I don't have time to write it." We said, "We'll write it for you." He said okay—we wrote it. He read it and said, "I can't read this!" But he had made an agreement. [The speech] talked about things like coalition work, about being at the table and who was Briggs at the table with—where did his support come from, what were they dining on, at whose expense. It kept on using that metaphor of being at the dining table....
>
> I think Dave was learning. He was under a great deal of pressure in the union. There was a lot of inner conflict within the union—old guard, new guard.... We held him to his commitment to give a speech. He wasn't thrilled about what we wrote.... We were young; it was strident.[9]

In late 1979, the gay and lesbian caucus of Local 2 ("about a dozen people") designed and sold T-shirts, held a fund raising party, and collected $325 to finance the publication of "America's Leading Journal for Lesbian and Gay Hotel Restaurant and Bar Employees," *Dishrag*. To launch the project, the caucus met in the offices of Union Women's Alliance to Gain Equality (Union WAGE), an independent women's labor support organization. The paper had only one issue of less than 1,000 copies and was distributed haphazardly over the next six months.[10] The caucus wanted it to be an organizing tool and an educational vehicle, and the front-page essay clearly claimed an autonomous ground: "We are NOT gay mascots of the present union administration, easing the way for a union drive that builds the union treasury while disrespecting individuals and institutions within the gay community. NEITHER are we in cahoots with bar owners represented by the Tavern Guild who promote a false 'Gay Unity' that secures profits but not wages, benefits or decent working conditions for gay employees.... we won't choose any longer between job security and simple respect and support around being gay—we want it all."[11]

Dishrag featured testimony from the shop floor. A waiter who had been harassed by a chef in the kitchen of the upper-class, all-male Bohemian Club gives a graphic interview about the food-and-fist fight that ensued. The union suspended the harasser but did little else to improve the climate of fear that an entire gay kitchen crew lived within that exclusive workplace.

Dishrag also reported on a Local 2 drive at the Bakery/Patio Café. This popular spot was right on Castro Street at the center of San Francisco's gay neighborhood, a prime location for bars and restaurants. Patio workers picketed for six months, seeking union recognition and a contract, and local merchants and realtors felt the pressure. The owners fought the union full force. "It was the first strike in the gay Castro," Tenney recalls. "It didn't go down easily. It left a kind of bitterness in a lot of people's craw for a while."[12] In *Dishrag*, Patio striker Lisa Lawes reflects on the hard work of picket duty and strike leadership: "Had I really known the frustration

I would feel when occasionally lost in the bureaucratic maze of Local 2, I might have succumbed to easy arguments against union leaders. Had someone told me about the 12-hour days I might have thought twice about organizing. But . . . I still believe that all of us in the industry, whether in gay or straight businesses, would be better off in the union."[13]

The *Village Voice*: Caucus Work and the Bargaining Table

Some gay and lesbian union groups that met informally in the early 1980s sustained organization through the broad goal of mutual support. They successfully persuaded their local leadership and bargaining committees to include sexual orientation language in the standing nondiscrimination clause of local agreements, or like AFT Local 3882, the United Staff Association of New York University, to initiate the provision in early contracts.

Expanding language on bereavement leave to include the deaths of partners' family members or of partners themselves was also an important negotiating step that legitimized gay and lesbian households and lives in the mid-1980s. With the onset of the AIDS epidemic, the urgency of these bereavement leaves for partners became especially poignant. Like the addition of sexual orientation language to standard contract discrimination clauses, bereavement provisions were important changes. They unequivocally affirmed gay and lesbian workers' lives in the contract. Nevertheless, the direct economic impact of these reforms was minimal.[14]

However, an important turning point came in 1982 when gay and lesbian members of the *Village Voice* shop of District 65–United Auto Workers (UAW) won spouse-equivalent benefits. The conjunction of lesbian and gay and labor issues found an economic focus in that most important of union functions—collective bargaining for wages and benefits.

Voice workers' self-insured health coverage, funded by the District 65-UAW Security Plan, had covered unmarried cohabiting heterosexual couples well before gay union members made claims on the benefits. The *Voice,* a small and lively workplace of less than 200 writers, editors, and production workers, was already known in District 65-UAW for its creative alternatives within the security plan. "The gay caucus was an interest group and also helped coworkers come out at the *Village Voice.* But there was no homophobia to speak of here," editor Jeff Weinstein recalls. "We began talking about including gay couples in the health benefits in 1981, but we hadn't thought it through." By 1982, however, when Weinstein was joined on the negotiating team by sympathetic heterosexual coworkers, "the membership started to understand it as an issue of progressive labor relations, that having it would be good for nongay couples too—it would put into words what had been past practice."[15]

The phrase "spouse equivalent" used in the *Voice*'s 1982 memorandum of understanding (it was not originally written into the contract) was coined by management lawyer Bert Pogrebin, and it appealed to the broad membership as including all unmarried family arrangements. But the *Voice*'s example of full-fledged health insurance coverage for gay couples was not widely copied in other workplaces until the mid-1980s, when a wave of California municipal unions modeled the practice throughout the public sector.[16]

Union Reform and AIDS Work: SEIU Local 250

SEIU Local 250 represents 33,000 Bay Area hospital workers. In the early 1980s, rank and file reformers of the militant Committee for a Democratic Union (CDU) began organizing to oust the local's entrenched leadership. The CDU, a group committed to ethnic diversity, enlisted many gay and lesbian hospital workers in their fight for rank and file leadership and a more democratic constitution. "A gay man recruited me to the CDU," remembers John Mehring, a psychiatric technician. "There was heavy gay involvement. The CDU was supportive of gay people in general. People felt a need to put a lot of emphasis on that."[17] Bob Lewis, a psychiatric technician and shop steward at St. Mary's, remembers Mehring's involvement. As Lewis recalls, "after the union meeting, we'd go to a bar and talk about how to overthrow the union. The leadership wasn't doing what they were supposed to. It was Washington oriented. In a 1982 election we upset the place, yet they kept bluffing."[18]

The turmoil lasted for several years, during which Local 250 was involved in two major hospital strikes and a two-year trusteeship imposed by the international. The constitution had to be rewritten, and new leadership had to be elected. As Local 250 emerged from its trusteeship in 1988 and prepared for its local election, out gay and lesbian union activists were leading each of two vying factions; Mehring and Lewis, for example, were in opposing camps. The contest was passionate. "There were a lot of different positions to take. It was not an issue of gayness; it was a struggle for power," says Mehring. "It was one against another and angry and hurtful."[19]

At the same time that the reformers were plotting the transformation of Local 250, the AIDS crisis was gathering momentum. San Francisco General Hospital, a Local 250 shop, was the site of some of the first widely reported cases of AIDS in 1981. Mehring recalls the synergy of his union work and AIDS activism. "AIDS was an emergency we had to do something about," he states. "In 1982, I had been involved in the Harvey Milk Democratic Club, publishing *Can We Talk,* an explicit brochure about safer sex, specific to AIDS. I knew then that AIDS was going to have problems for health care workers." In July 1983, Mehring became active in organizing a Local 250 AIDS Committee. "CDU people put me in touch with other union members who were doing AIDS work, and there were staff people assigned right away to the AIDS Committee. Working with the Bay Area Physicians for Human Rights, we put together the brochure *AIDS and the Health Care Worker.*" SEIU published the brochure in 1984. "San Francisco hospital workers essentially weren't homophobic," says Mehring. "I wanted to work on AIDS because we as hospital workers had something to say about our humanity. If workers knew more about AIDS, there would be less discrimination. I was very much into the educational model. The union was so diverse, from so many racial and ethnic backgrounds. . . . I had to trust that health care workers because of what they do would be more progressive and liberal."[20]

The Local 250 AIDS Committee became a model for union education on AIDS. In the mid-1980s, it was a stronghold for CDU activity as well as gay and lesbian union consciousness. SEIU had *AIDS and the Health Care Worker* translated into Spanish; it was nationally distributed through five editions. The Local 250 AIDS Committee continued its work throughout the 1980s, and in 1989 the local served as a pilot for a "Train the Trainer" program led by the AIDS Labor Education Project at the University of California's Labor Institute. Eighty "indirect" hospital workers (from housekeeping and dietary departments) got training about AIDS through their educational leave, then went back and led lunch and after-work meetings, ultimately disseminating AIDS information to over 4,000 other union members.

Sustaining Local Caucus Work:
SEIU Networks West and East

When SEIU held its international convention in Dearborn, Michigan, in 1984, a similar and national coalition of progressive reformers and AIDS activists pushed the union to adopt strong resolutions on AIDS and on gay and lesbian rights. Pat Hendricks, a Licensed Vocational Nurse and CDU leader who by that time was on Local 250's executive board, remembers, "There was a loose affiliation at the convention, a progressive caucus that was well known to the leadership. We met in hotel rooms, and John Mehring and I were involved in it. At the convention, he stood up on the convention floor, with a thousand people there, and declared himself as a gay man, and you could have heard a pin drop. He said why this big health care workers union must address gay issues. They took a very progressive stand with that."[21]

The resolutions won by these convention delegates set the pace for gay and lesbian work in the local unions of SEIU; local work in turn strengthened developing union-wide networks. Local 503, representing State of Oregon public employees, had a successful record of feminist organizing around pay equity, and leadership was eager to develop further progressive policies. In 1986, an informal statewide network of lesbian and gay members responded to the local's bargaining survey with the demand that sexual orientation be included as a protected class in the 1987 contract's nondiscrimination Article 22. That demand, the most popular noneconomic item on the survey, was successfully negotiated. This in turn helped strengthen the contacts lesbian and gay leaders were developing in the statewide local. Becky Capoferri, a mental health worker and later a Local 503 staffer, noted how "a caucus started to evolve which had existed before, but it was not broad based."[22]

Ann Montague, a clerical worker at Oregon State University, wanted to push the issue. She reached out at SEIU conferences. "Eventually I realized that we needed a caucus." Montague went to an SEIU women's conference in Chicago in 1987 where "we got the word around, and there were probably about twenty people who came to that first meeting, many of them from the union's staff." Montague says that domestic partner benefits were discussed at that meeting. Subsequently, she recalls, "the union's director of civil and human rights was very supportive, and she put together a mailing list to keep us all connected and to keep the information flowing at the national level."[23]

A 1989 biennial civil and human rights conference for SEIU's Western states gathered fifty lesbian and gay activists. Here Montague met Mary Kay Henry, a staff trainer and veteran of the Local 250 battles. With the endorsement of Local 503 president Alice Dale, Henry and Montague were soon collaborating on scenarios and text for the local's groundbreaking Lesbian/Gay Member Discrimination Training for Stewards. The training, launched in 1992, had political consequences beyond the local. "The training centered on equipping stewards with the skills to *recognize* the existence of lesbian/gay discrimination in the workplace, *define* homophobia and heterosexism, and *defend* lesbian/gay rights on the job by enforcing Article 22 and *confronting* discrimination in the workplace," writes Montague, adding, "Our timing on the stewards training proved to be just right." As Montague relates, a ballot referendum known as Measure 9 "would have changed the Oregon Constitution to mandate discrimination against lesbians and gays. If passed, it also would nullify the no discrimination article in our contract. Had the educational work not been done over the previous year, I doubt that our union would have been ready to oppose Measure 9 as aggressively as we did." SEIU Local 503 spearheaded the "No on 9 Labor Coalition," and as Montague states, "In addition to defeating the ballot measure, an incredible amount of coalition building resulted from our work on the campaign."[24]

Massachusetts was also a major hotbed of lesbian and gay SEIU organizing. In Boston, the Gay and Lesbian Labor Activist Network (GALLAN) had been accomplishing successful coalition work since 1986. Activists from the Massachusetts State Workers Local 509 and Boston health care workers Local 285 were enthusiastic participants in GALLAN's efforts, confident that building a citywide organization would be the best way to accomplish their goals. As two of the organizers described the work of the coalition: "GALLAN has seen itself as having a dual mission: One, to bring union and class politics into the lesbian and gay movement; and two, to fight homophobia and bring lesbian and gay issues into the workplace and into the labor movement."[25]

Ginny Cutting, an AIDS claims examiner and Local 509 leader, helped found the local's Gay and Lesbian Concerns Committee (GLCC) in 1987; her experience in GALLAN and the support of her friends citywide empowered her local work.[26] By 1988, with the support of the local president, GLCC had become an official union committee with its own budget and had begun pressing for nondiscrimination contract language and domestic partner bereavement leave. GLCC's work with Local 509's legislative lobbyist helped other public employee unions to lobby more vigorously for statewide domestic partnership bills. The Massachusetts Committee on Occupational Safety and Health collaborated with the GLCC to develop employment guidelines for state workers with HIV/AIDS.

Cutting recruited lesbian and gay coworkers to the Local 509 GLCC who were not as seasoned in union work as the GALLAN veterans. Social service worker Michael Dias's introduction to lesbian and gay workplace organizing certainly fulfilled the GALLAN ideal. "At first I was not even aware of the grievance process," says Dias. "The GLCC pretty much pulled me into the union concerns. At the time, there weren't very many men in GLCC, maybe one or two men out of twenty, and I definitely felt out of place. Ginny was trying to mobilize whatever men she could get hold of. She tried to put together trainings and made me aware of how the union connected with politics."

Dias became chief steward for his office, working with eighty workers. "Prior to being chief steward, I wasn't really out in the workplace," Dias recalls, but after two lesbians were fired "it became clear that the membership in my office needed to know that they had a gay member, because the people in my office who aren't out need to know where to go to find a gay member." According to Dias, "other stewards were uncomfortable. Some people don't talk to me, but I feel more in control of the situation, and I see myself as getting stronger in the union and stronger about gay rights."[27]

SEIU's Lavender Caucus: Changing the Union

The call for SEIU's unionwide Lavender Caucus came from its 1991 women's conference. A call from SEIU's February 1992 Biennial Western Conference on Civil and Human Rights initiated the October 1993 "Coming Out, Coming Together" Lavender Caucus Leadership Conference in Oakland. Hosted by Local 250, the leadership conference coincided with the AFL-CIO's annual convention in San Francisco as well as with the National Lesbian and Gay Labor Coalition's planning meeting for a 1994 New York City Stonewall Pride at Work labor conference.

Panels on SEIU lesbian and gay history, discussions of organizing victories (e.g., the "No on 9" campaign in Oregon), and strategies for community building were the focus of the Oakland leadership conference. There were Lavender Caucus T-shirts and union buttons. SEIU backed the event heartily, featuring vignettes and interviews with gay and lesbian labor activists in the *SEIU Union* magazine.[28]

The Lavender Caucus effort widened as a national movement. In 1994, an Eastern Regional Civil and Human Rights meeting in Baltimore highlighted the importance of gay and lesbian civil rights in SEIU. Tom Barbera, a Massachusetts mental health worker and activist in Local 509's GLCC (renamed the Lavender Caucus) recalls: "There were about 400 people there, and every time President John Sweeney spoke about racial discrimination, he emphasized lesbian and gay workers fighting discrimination too. The members really supported that theme, and in each workshop there was a section about gay and lesbian issues."[29]

Barbera was elected and appointed to co-chair the Lavender Caucus for the SEIU Eastern Region, with the mission of assisting SEIU locals from Canada to Florida to form their own Lavender Caucuses. In 1997 there were nine active East Coast caucuses. The East/West Lavender Caucus organizations stay in touch by telephone. They support the development of local caucuses, they press SEIU leadership to advocate lesbian and gay rights throughout the labor movement, and they maintain a watch over sexual minority issues as they develop throughout the union. When SEIU asked Lavender Caucus leaders to attend a 1996 "Creating Change" convention of the National Gay and Lesbian Task Force to identify candidates for recruitment to the SEIU organizing staff, their efforts resulted in forty interviews.[30]

Gay Life in the World of the Union:
AFSCME DC 37's LAGIC

The 110,000 New York City employees represented by AFSCME's District Council 37 (DC 37) are members of fifty-six separate local unions. They work in a myriad of occupations—from zookeepers and school cafeteria cooks to secretaries at police stations, hospital technicians, and road repair crew workers. When gay and lesbian activists working for the city decided to organize a union caucus, they could count on their union's liberal record. AFSCME had unanimously adopted a constitutional sexual orientation clause at its 1982 convention, and later conventions included events with gay and lesbian themes. Similarly, DC 37 leaders spoke at hearing after hearing in support of the New York City civil rights bill, which City Council finally made law in 1986. Though not a high priority, domestic partner benefits were on the list of the union's demands package when DC 37 went to the table with the city.

The union's monthly *Public Employee Press* was the first public venue of agitation for lesbian and gay rights. "The outreach was through the union, not through personal friendships," recalls public health adviser Julie Schwartzberg of Local 768.[31] Angela Christofides, a Local 154 member and Human Rights Commission worker, wrote to the paper about benefit equity and bereavement leave. "I would like to see the union allow its lesbian and gay workers to organize across local lines so that we may work together and with the union in finding a solution," she stated in her letter.[32] Christofides then wrote to local presidents, requesting that they announce meetings that were taking place at the city's Lesbian and Gay Community Services Center (the district council wouldn't allow an unofficial group to use its rooms). When the *Public Employee Press* published a letter announcing the meetings, the turnouts jumped from ten to fifty; by the end of 1989, 200 DC 37 members were attending organizing sessions at the center, "representing over a dozen locals and a healthy mix of lesbians and gay men and blacks, whites and Latinos."[33] Subcommittees developed programs for unionwide outreach, HIV/AIDS issues, legislative tasks, and domestic partner benefits.

Schwartzberg recalls the fervor to form the Lesbian and Gay Issues Committee (LAGIC). "We spent the next year lobbying DC 37 and organizing them to create a standing official committee. I think we did very good organizing, and the leadership knew we had a lot of members and a lot of support. There were lots of petitions and grass roots organizing and getting local presidents to support the formation and lobby the executive board, and in April 1990 it was approved—so it only took a year." Schwartzberg reports that "All the energy had gone into establishing a committee, so then we decided to have a dinner dance, because that's what unions do, and we raised money and it was a great party! There was a lot of food and a good DJ, and local presidents came and we had same-sex dancing. We had it at the center, in June for gay pride. It was a big thing in terms of positive feeling about being lesbian/gay in the union."[34]

LAGIC's sophisticated program of integration into the life of the union took several directions. With the material support of an office, a budget, and a telephone, LAGIC members continued to lobby for domestic partnership benefits.[35] They also participated in DC 37's legislative conferences, educating other union members on the state's gay civil rights bill, anti-bias crime legislation, and AIDS issues. Monthly forums with speakers such as Marjorie Hill, Mayor Dinkins's liaison to the lesbian and gay community, helped draw in more members. Gay and lesbian committees formed in Public Library Guild Local 1930, Clerical Local 1549, and Public Health Local 768. These groups advocated the unionwide work of LAGIC while strengthening local support for gay and lesbian coworkers.

LAGIC's participation in the cultural world of DC 37 enriched the union's diverse communities. In February 1991, LAGIC invited Lavender Light, a popular New York City gay and lesbian gospel choir, to perform for the union's annual Black History month. Schwartzberg states, "We wanted to participate as a gay group in union events. It would give us more visibility, and our people would feel like we were in the union. DC 37 really loves gospel, and the people enjoyed it so much—it wasn't mainly a gay audience. We were overwhelmed at how many people came—it really put us on the map! A lot of gay people who are active in the committee today came into LAGIC as a result of attending that event. It had recruiting power."[36]

When LAGIC extended its power to the wider world of New York City's lesbian and gay union activism, the contributions were substantial. With sponsorships and endorsements by ten council affiliates, a regional "Pride at Work" conference in June 1992 attracted 200 trade unionists to DC 37 headquarters. Two years later at DC 37 headquarters, the national "Pride at Work—Stonewall 25" conference laid the groundwork for Pride at Work as a national organization, and in September 1997 the AFL-CIO recognized Pride at Work as an official constituency group of the AFL-CIO.

At its best, LAGIC, like many sexual minority caucuses thriving in unions today, breaks down isolation and gives people a cause worth working for. Caucuses like LAGIC can push the gay rights agenda in the labor community while strengthening union activism in the lives of lesbian, gay, and other sexual minority workers, thus challenging individual fears and enriching the spirit of labor solidarity. In the June 1997 *Public Employee Press*, Cheryl Minor, a Local 1549 secretary in New York City's Department of Transportation, grins proudly in a photograph as she reflects on five years with LAGIC: "I didn't know the union had a lesbian and gay committee. I didn't even know where the union building was. I didn't go to meetings, didn't read the paper— nothing. I was on another planet." Minor recalls the successful gay pride parade, noting, "When we marched behind the union banner, people on the sidelines held up their union cards and yelled 'Hey I'm DC 37 too.'" Because of LAGIC, Minor became more involved in the union, serves as a shop steward for her local, and has attended a summer school for union women.[37]

Conclusion

Gay, lesbian, and other sexual minority organizing in unions was rare in the 1970s and usually took the form of union officials joining with community activists around mutually important issues, for example, the Briggs initiative. The union philosophy of social justice and mutual defense—an injury to one is an injury to all—pushed these disparate groups toward successful coalition work.[38]

Social justice was also at stake when international unions at their conventions began promulgating a series of statements of solidarity, condemnations of discrimination, and resolutions of nondiscrimination focusing on members' sexual orientation. Progress began with the AFT in 1970 and increased especially after the 1978 Briggs initiative. At the 1982 national meetings of AFSCME and the International Ladies Garment Workers Union (ILGWU), justice for gay and lesbian union members found its place on the convention agenda. Moreover, nondiscrimination for sexual orientation clauses have been written as a principle into many union constitutions. Some of these national resolutions were proposed by ad hoc groups of gay and lesbian delegates who met at conventions and decided the time was right to pressure the union; they worked with righteous heterosexual allies who recognized the timeliness of the issue. However, lesbian, gay, and other sexual minority constituencies in local unions were not organized to articulate an agenda specific to those workplace issues that affected them as rank and file members.

When gay and lesbian groups began forming in local unions, they often came out of those international unions that had already laid the constitutional groundwork for defense of sexual orientation. They also emerged in cities with large, thriving gay communities—for example, the pioneering AFT-based gay teachers' groups in San Francisco and New York City. Workplaces in cities with more gays and lesbians than the one-in-ten average saw early caucus formations—for example the San Francisco caucus of restaurant workers (1978–1980) and the District 65-UAW *Village Voice* caucus in New York (1982).

Workers who have organized lesbian and gay caucuses in local unions have enjoyed victories in contract negotiations, from achieving bereavement leaves for domestic partners to winning full domestic partner health coverage. The District 65-UAW *Village Voice* contract was the first of many successful domestic partner benefit plans won through union negotiations. Caucus members have supported sexual minority workers in hostile work environments, encouraging all union members to appreciate diversity, and mobilizing union resources to defeat anti-gay political campaigns. SEIU Local 503's public campaign against Oregon Measure 9 was paralleled by the locals' anti-homophobia stewards' training that gay and lesbian caucus members initiated.

Caucuses are excellent training environments for union members who have not yet felt an activist commitment. Mutual support in the caucus can help talented members participate as shop stewards or local delegates, thus contributing to the wider programs of the union. SEIU Local 509 steward Michael Dias might never have known how to support his coworkers in the State of Massachusetts Department of Social Services were it not for the training he received from Local 509's GLCC.

Like most union interest groups, these caucuses have had to adapt to the local union's organizational structures and culture. AFSCME DC 37's LAGIC used the councilwide *Public Employee Press* to initiate organization, actively participated in legislative conferences, and hosted popular cultural events. When caucuses have stabilized in local unions, they have reached out to the wider community of gays, lesbians, and other sexual minorities to accent the union's role in community issues. SEIU's Local 250 AIDS Committee cooperated with other San Francisco AIDS organizations to educate hospital workers about AIDS, and thereby created a remarkable model for AIDS education that was influential throughout the labor movement.[39]

While lesbian, gay, and other sexual minority union caucuses can emerge anywhere, local unions with a lively history of democratic participation are better environments than unions where members have little access to the governing structures. The San Francisco restaurant workers' caucus and the Local 250 AIDS Committee both emerged during periods of insurgent organizing in the local. The *Village Voice* shop was well known in District 65-UAW for its independent criticisms of union policy. The founding activists of DC 37's LAGIC claimed entitlement and equity with other issues committees when they attended council meetings, made use of the monthly newsletter, met at the union hall, and accessed other resources and programs.

Strong lesbian and gay committees have changed the way the labor movement understands itself and operates. SEIU Lavender Caucuses' visibility at educational conferences and national conventions, and underscored by vigorous networking, has influenced hiring practices, education programs, and political lobbying by the international. Certainly, the 1997 resolution of the AFL-CIO to recognize Pride At Work (PAW), the national lesbian and gay labor organization, as an official constituency group could not have come about without the strong advocacy of labor leaders from unions that had successful experience with lesbian and gay caucus formations.

None of this activity has come easily. Success around sexual orientation issues has a longer history in the public sector unions with large female and white collar memberships like AFT, SEIU, and AFSCME. Even here, however, it has taken many years to develop local caucuses strong enough to activate the considerable energies of rank and file sexual minority members. In a national workforce with varying degrees of sensitivity to sexual orientation issues, the goal of influencing unionwide infrastructures and international policy is not only organizationally complicated but also politically difficult. In New York City, Retail Employees' Local 340 of the Union of Needletrades, Industrial, and Textile Employees (UNITE) held spirited street rallies demanding a contract from Barney's, an upscale department store. One demonstration included a fashion show with members in drag. "Rallies were wildly colorful and dramatic, including a fashion-show spoof held on a make-shift runway right outside the main store," read the report in *UNITE!,* the national union's news magazine.[40] The decision not to mention the drag acts in the report probably reflects a reluctance to present sexual orientation issues in immigrant urban and rural textile manufacturing communities where UNITE has many of its strongholds.

Another example of struggle can be found in the UAW. The National Writers Union, UAW Local 1981, has a positive and welcoming relationship with its gay and lesbian members. In 1992, the union pushed the UAW international convention to adopt a constitutional sexual orientation discrimination clause. The January–February 1993 issue of *Solidarity,* the UAW national magazine, then ran a feature on Ron Woods, a gay auto electrician in Detroit who had come out and been harassed at his job.[41] The "Letterbox" column of the next three issues of *Solidarity* published correspondence reacting to the story. While many members wrote to support Woods's courage, others attacked: "when the UAW starts backing q——s you are very close to losing me," Iowa retiree Daryl L. Voshell complained in the May–June issue.[42]

Solidarity's publication of both sides of the controversy is an important example of the UAW's commitment to democratic debate. Many other American unions neither

broach the subject of sexual orientation issues to their members nor welcome the introduction of gay and lesbian issues into the union discourse. In the building trades, lesbian and gay construction workers routinely hide their identities, and even worksite
friendship cliques are suspect. In such unions, the open organization of gay, lesbian, or
other sexual minority union caucuses is not even a notion yet.

It remains to be seen whether the AFL-CIO's newly sanctioned Pride at Work will be
successful in opening a wider debate on sexual orientation issues throughout the U.S.
labor movement. Certainly the achievements of the many lesbian and gay union caucuses that helped bring the national organization to the attention of the AFL-CIO prove
that productive and progressive union work can grow out of a lesbian and gay dialogue
within the "House of Labor." Networks like SEIU's Lavender Caucuses and AFSCME's
issues committees have provided the international unions with reasonable organizing
models. Through PAW, a multitude of proud and open union activists can be empowered to reach out to brother and sister unionists within their locals and at national meetings. Labor and lesbian, gay, bisexual, and transgendered communities have everything
to gain from the integration of sexual orientation issues into the structures, programs,
and culture of the U.S. labor movement.

Notes

Acknowledgments: This chapter has benefited from the thoughtful comments of Debra Bern-
hardt and Desma Holcomb. Throughout the research and writing, I have been inspired and
informed by the work of the seventy-five gay and lesbian union activists whose life stories
I recorded for the *Out in the Union Oral History Collection* in the Robert F. Wagner Labor
Archives at New York University's Tamiment Library. I conducted the interviews in this collection with the support of the 1995 NYU Stephen Charney Vladeck Junior Faculty Fellowship.

1. Interview with Tom Ammiano, 10 April 1995, and Hank Wilson, 12 April 1995, *Out in
the Union Oral History Collection (1995–1997),* Robert F. Wagner Labor Archives, Tamiment
Library, New York University.

2. Gay Teachers Association leaflet, 1978, from GTA papers, International Gay Information
Center, New York Public Library.

3. Part of Proposition 6 proposed that "the State finds a compelling interest in refusing to
employ and in terminating the employment of a schoolteacher, a teachers' aide, a school admin-
istrator, or a counselor . . . who engages in public homosexual activity and/or public homosexual
conduct directed at, or likely to come to the attention of school children or other school employees." For a discussion of the campaign against the Briggs initiative, see D. Ehrensaft and R. Milkman, "Sexuality and the State: The Defeat of the Briggs Initiative and Beyond: Interview with
Amber Hollibaugh," *Socialist Review* 45 (May–June 1979): 55–72.

4. The 125,000 members represented by the UFT include approximately 65,000 classroom
teachers and approximately 60,000 school-related personnel, including social workers, school
nurses, secretaries, and dietitians. Current AFT president Sandra Feldman was the UFT representative who served as the regular point-person for GTA concerns (*Gay Teachers Association
Newsletter,* October 1979, February 1980). GTA regularly estimated that 10 to 15 percent of the
New York City teaching workforce was gay/lesbian (about 12,500 UFT members). Nowhere near
that number have participated actively, but over a twenty-year period, the organization's work

has touched the lives of thousands of gay, lesbian, bisexual, and transgendered teachers and their allies.

5. *Gay Teachers Association Newsletter,* January 1981, p. 7.

6. Interview with Peter Tenney, 10 April 1995, *Out in the Union Oral History Collection.*

7. Interview with Tenney, 10 April 1995.

8. *New York Teacher,* 22 October 1978, p. 19. Bay Area Teamster unions were involved because their organizing drive with Coors Beer workers had benefited powerfully from the gay community consumer boycott of Coors products. See D. Osborne, "Lavender Labor: A Brief History," in *Homo Economics: Capitalism, Community, and Lesbian and Gay Life,* ed. A. Gluckman and B. Reed (New York: Routledge, 1997), pp. 232–234.

9. Interview with Tenney, 10 April, 1995.

10. Interview with Tenney, 10 April 1995.

11. *Dishrag* 1, no. 1 (1980): 1.

12. Interview with Tenney, 10 April 1995.

13. *Dishrag* 1, no. 1 (1980): 3.

14. In New York City contract negotiations in 1986–1988, bereavement leave provisions were not necessarily the direct result of gay and lesbian caucus work. Bereavement language was sometimes championed by liberal negotiating committees aware of membership demographics. Sometimes the provision was high on the agenda of negotiators who were themselves gay/lesbian. See M. Frank and D. Holcomb, *Pride at Work: Organizing for Lesbian and Gay Rights in Unions* (New York: Lesbian and Gay Labor Network, 1990), pp. 40–45.

15. Interview with Jeff Weinstein, 3 March 1989, Lesbian and Gay Labor Network papers, Robert F. Wagner Labor Archives, Tamiment Library, New York University. For more analysis of the *Village Voice* breakthrough, see Frank and Holcomb, *Pride at Work,* pp. 46–48.

16. See Desma Holcomb's chapter in this volume, which analyzes the achievement of domestic partner benefits in public and private sector unions.

17. John Mehring, personal communication, 18 August 1997.

18. Interview with Bob Lewis, 28 June 1996, *Out in the Union Oral History Collection.*

19. Mehring, personal communication, 18 August 1997.

20. Mehring, personal communication, 18 August 1997.

21. Pat Hendricks, personal communication, 20 August 1997.

22. Interview with Becky Capoferri, 17 July 1995, *Out in the Union Oral History Collection.*

23. Interview with Ann Montague, 16 July 1995, *Out in the Union Oral History Collection.*

24. A. Montague, "We Are Union Builders Too: Oregon Union Tackles Discrimination Based on Sexual Orientation," *Labor Research Review* 20 (1994): 81–83.

25. S. Moir and E. Hunt, "Gaining a Voice in Gay Labor," *Forward Motion* 12 (1993): 5–8. Ten years of wide-ranging community coalition work by GALLAN are reviewed in an interview with founder Susan Moir in *Homo Economics,* ed. Gluckman and Reed.

26. Interview with Ginny Cutting, 24 March 1995, *Out in the Union Oral History Collection.*

27. Interview with Michael Dias, 29 April 1995, *Out in the Union Oral History Collection.*

28. M. Snider, "Gay, Proud & Union," *SEIU Union* (Winter 1993): 12–15.

29. Tom Barbera, personal communication, 21 September 1997.

30. Barbera personal communication, 21 September 1997.

31. Julie Schwartzberg, personal communication, 23 September 1997.

32. *Public Employee Press,* March 1988, p. 16.

33. *Lesbian and Gay Labor Network Newsletter* (November 1989), p. 1, Lesbian and Gay Labor Network papers, Robert F. Wagner Labor Archives, Tamiment Library, New York University.

34. Schwartzberg personal communication, 23 September 1997.

35. All New York City workers obtained domestic benefits by Mayor David Dinkins's Executive Order of 1993. See Desma Holcomb's contribution to this volume.

36. Schwartzberg personal communication, 23 September 1997.

37. Z. Allen, "Coming Out at Work: How the Union Helps," *Public Employee Press,* June 1997, p. 9.

38. Osborne, "Lavender Labor," pp. 223–224.

39. For a practical discussion on how to organize gay and lesbian union committees, see M. Frank, "How (and Why) to Organize Lesbian and Gay Union Committees," *Labor Notes* (March 1993): 12–13.

40. *UNITE!* (July–August 1996): 10.

41. M. Funke, "Pride and Prejudice," *UAW Solidarity* (January–February 1993): 18–19.

42. In spite of years of intense harassment, Ron Woods successfully brought sexual orientation language into the 1996 national bargaining demands. For an exploration of his ordeals, see T. Gold and K. Anderson, *Out at Work* (New York: AndersonGold Films, 1997), videotape; and J. B. Stewart, "Coming Out at Chrysler," *New Yorker,* 21 July 1997, pp. 38–49.

Desma Holcomb

---

6   Domestic Partner Health Benefits: The Corporate Model vs. the Union Model

Why Domestic Partner Health Benefits Became a Focus in the United States

Domestic partner health insurance benefits became big news in the United States in 1991 when *Business Week* reported on domestic partner benefits at the Lotus Development Corporation: "Lotus Opens a Door for Gay Partners; It's the First Big Company to Give Benefits to Gay Workers' 'Spouses.'"[1] The vice president for human resources at the computer software firm asserts in the article that "This is fair and equal." As the article reveals, however, these benefits would not apply to unmarried, cohabiting straight couples. Lotus's reasoning is that "straight couples have the option of marriage, while homosexual colleagues don't." When asked about limiting the scope of changes to lesbians and gays, a benefits consultant explained that, in trying to stem rising health care expenses, "The last thing an employer wants now is to add another group of dependents."[2]

The Lotus story highlights a number of important issues having to do with health care coverage in general, and with lesbian and gay partner benefit coverage in particular. In the United States, the lack of a national health care system has produced predominantly private sector, employer-sponsored health insurance schemes. This means that obtaining adequate coverage for individuals and their families is largely a workplace issue. The Lotus story also points to the struggles that occur to make health care coverage inclusive of all types of families.

This chapter explores the role of organized labor in fighting for domestic partner benefits in the United States. It examines why the health care insurance issue has become so important for lesbian and gay labor activists, how and where domestic partner benefits have been achieved, how these benefits later emerged in a much more restricted form in nonunionized settings, and how domestic partner coverage has sometimes been defeated by insurance industry resistance or right-wing backlash. The chapter concludes with a discussion of the broader political issues that this historic experience poses for lesbian and gay activism and the labor movement.

The campaign for domestic partner health insurance benefits has been one of the major focuses of lesbian and gay labor activism in the United States. Although the legal recognition of lesbian and gay families is a political and social issue of contention in many nations, the focus on health benefits is largely specific to the United States. This is a direct result of a predominantly private sector and employer-based health care system. The high-profile public debate over health care reform in the United States in the early 1990s made it widely known that the United States is one of the few countries in the industrialized world without a comprehensive national health care system. There is a "safety net" of basic government insurance for the very poor (Medicaid) and the elderly (Medicare), but together, these public plans cover only 20 percent of Americans. Most American families (60 percent) get health care through for-profit insurance provided by employers in the form of insurance for the employee and his or her immediate family.[3]

This system creates a number of social problems. There is no health insurance for unemployed people unless they are very poor and have the particular family structure—single mother with children—that is covered by Medicaid. Furthermore, many people with jobs are not covered. Many companies do not provide insurance to their workers; they are not required by law to do so. That many small retail stores and restaurants have trouble affording insurance for their workers is not surprising, but some huge corporations in the service sector, like McDonald's and WalMart, also neglect to cover all their numerous part-time employees. It is actually very common for part-time, temporary, and freelance workers to be uninsured, and these categories are a growing proportion of the U.S. workforce. Moreover, a wide disparity exists between the comprehensive plans (medical, hospital, dental, and optical) provided by large businesses, such as the Xerox Corporation, and the minimal plans (covering only major illnesses and injuries) provided by medium and smaller companies.

Finally, the proportion of health insurance costs that are borne by workers has increased steadily but varies widely among firms. Twenty years ago, employers who offered family benefits paid the total cost themselves. In 1996, the average cost of insurance per employee was $3,915 per year, and companies were increasingly demanding that workers pay a large part of that cost. In most unionized firms, workers have paid a very small fraction of that cost.[4] On the other hand, in many nonunionized firms, the cost of family coverage may be so great in comparison to take-home pay that workers cannot afford the percentage of insurance fees required of them to cover their spouses or children. A recent government study found that "more and more workers, especially those who earn low wages, are declining to take [family health insurance] benefits" because the average cost to the worker for that coverage is $1,596 a year. That comes to 11 percent of the total gross wages of an employee who earns $7 an hour.[5] As a result of these trends, almost 10 million children in the United States (14 percent of the nation's children) were uninsured in 1995. Most of these uninsured were not children of the unemployed, but children of people with jobs.[6] Overall in 1995, more than 40 million Americans were uninsured, over 17 percent of the population under age sixty-five.[7]

Barriers to Domestic Partner Health Coverage

Given the limits on the availability of health benefits, the disparities in coverage, and the increasing costs to workers, it is not surprising that one of the core demands of unionized workers has been that employers provide *comprehensive* and *affordable* health insurance for them and their families. The U.S. labor movement has been relatively successful in this endeavor, but until 1982, employers and insurers did not include lesbian and gay domestic partners in the definition of "immediate family." Securing health insurance for domestic partners required overcoming a long-held legal and historical definition of what constituted a family. Generally speaking, state law regulates marriage and defines families. Federal, state, city, and private sector benefits are then pegged to that state definition. For example, federal law gives tax deductions for spouses and children as defined by state law. State inheritance laws give automatic inheritance to spouses and children when there is no will, and state family law governs parental rights, divorce, and visitation, frequently discriminating against gay and lesbian parents and their partner coparents. Cities give spouses special visitation rights in hospitals and prisons, and employers give a host of family benefits to spouses and children.

The U.S. Census from 1970 to 1990, however, shows a fivefold increase in the reported number of unmarried couples—lesbian, gay, and straight. This reflects the growing phenomenon of lesbian and gay couples living openly together and the rising social acceptance of never-married and divorced or widowed adults cohabiting without marrying or remarrying. The gap has widened between the legal definition of family and the social reality of families. A union proposing domestic partner coverage has had to define what a partner is and then convince the employer to use that definition in the absence of any legal definition. This is why partner benefits became a lightning rod for the religious right. The benefits and the definition of partnerhood challenge the traditional and legal definition of family in American society.

The Service Employees International Union (SEIU) Local 790 in Berkeley created a definition in 1985 that has been widely adopted by other unions and employers. Couples register with an affidavit in which each partner affirms that he or she is over age eighteen, unmarried, unrelated to the other by blood, and that they have been cohabiting and sharing the necessities of life for six months. The document is legally binding, and both people are liable for the value of the benefits received if their affirmations are later found to be false. This affidavit means that the employer recognizes the children of the partner as children of the employee for purposes of insurance coverage and tuition benefits and acknowledges the partner's parents as parents-in-law for benefits such as bereavement leave.

Securing partner benefits began with the positive recognition of lesbian and gay families; a struggle to overcome homophobia was necessary to gain that recognition. But there was an additional barrier to securing partner benefits. Throughout the 1980s, the insurance industry actively tried to avoid covering workers with HIV/AIDS (and assumed that most domestic partners would be people with AIDS). Long before a physiological test existed, insurance firms had tried to exclude gays from their policies in an effort to avoid AIDS coverage. They refused to write policies for single men between the ages of 25 and 45 and employer group plans in stereotypically "gay" industries such as theater companies and hairdresser shops. Once an HIV test was discovered in 1985, gay rights activism led California, Florida, the District of Columbia, New York, and Wisconsin to pass laws prohibiting insurance industry HIV testing. By 1989, however, insurance industry lobbying had succeeded in reversing all but California's law. Insurance companies made testing mandatory and then refused to cover those who tested positive.[8] Because of these practices, an entire class of people was denied insurance to cover medical costs associated with a serious illness. This is a corruption of the purported function of health insurance, which is to share the risks of medical bills among the healthy and the ill.

Given these trends and the lack of a national health care safety net, whether or not lesbian and gay partners had family coverage could make the difference between getting medical treatment or not, and between affordable treatment or personal bankruptcy. In the documentary film *Out at Work*, Nat Keitt, a New York City public librarian, describes how his partner's uninsured medical costs quickly mounted to a substantial debt. "I woke up one day and realized I was $50,000 in debt just from David's medical [bills]."[9] Keitt is an African American member of District Council 37 of the American Federation of State, County, and Municipal Employees (AFSCME), the New York City municipal workers' union. His partner David, a Latino construction worker, was out of work on long-term disability, and David's workplace insurance coverage had lapsed. Keitt got involved in his union's campaign to establish domestic partner benefits for New York City workers.

The Role of Lesbian and Gay Labor Activism

Gay workers like Nat Keitt were able to create domestic partner health benefits through their unions because health insurance programs for unionized workers are constantly revised through collective bargaining. In fact, domestic partner benefits in the United States were first secured by lesbian and gay labor activists through collective bargaining. In the mid-1970s, Jeff Weinstein dreamed of a day when gay domestic partners would get family health insurance at work, but he never thought that dream would come true. Then he started to work for the *Village Voice*, a progressive and cultural weekly newspaper in New York City. Weinstein, a longtime activist in gay and union causes, discovered in 1981 that the *Voice* had an unofficial policy of covering unmarried, cohabiting straight couples for health insurance. District 65 of the UAW represented the editors, writers, and clericals at the paper, and Weinstein organized a caucus of lesbian and gay union members. The caucus proposed that the policy of providing health insurance for cohabiting couples be formalized in the contract for straights and gays. Weinstein got elected to the Negotiating Committee and helped overcome the management's reservations to create the first "spouse equivalent" health plan in the United States. Since 1982, about 10 to 15 percent of the *Voice*'s workforce of 170 have registered their spouse equivalents—about half straight and half gay or lesbian. Some of these families include children of *Voice* workers' partners, such as the son adopted by one gay couple.[10]

Three thousand miles away in Berkeley, California, city employee Tom Brougham had tried as early as 1979 to sign up his domestic partner for family health benefits.

The issue was later taken up by the East Bay Lesbian/Gay Democratic Club and then by the public employees union, SEIU Local 790. In 1984, the Berkeley City Council agreed to offer domestic partner benefits to city employees, but insurance companies refused to cover the benefits or quoted astronomical premiums. According to Claire Zvanski, a staff representative for SEIU Local 790 who was involved in negotiations with the insurers, the firms told the city and the union that they were afraid of adverse selection, that workers would sign up only sick partners or sick friends posing as partners.[11] There was a strong undercurrent of homophobia and AIDS phobia in these objections, even though the union proposal covered both gay and straight couples. A year of SEIU's relentless pushing at the bargaining table finally convinced the insurance companies to agree to try the benefits.

With the victory in Berkeley, thousands of public workers became eligible, and hundreds of couples won benefits. At first, the insurers demanded a surcharge as a hedge against a surge of partners with AIDS. The city and the union agreed, but only on condition that the surcharge be refunded if insurance company fears were not borne out in practice. A few years later, the surcharge was refunded because it had never been needed. On average, the health bills of domestic partners, even those with AIDS, were equivalent to the health bills of married couples. Although insurance companies continued to raise concerns about partners with AIDS, a movement for partner benefits had been generated, and armed with Berkeley's real-life cost data, the unions persisted and prevailed.[12]

By 1990, local movements for domestic partner benefits were active in most of the major cities on both coasts, based in the gay and lesbian rights movement and in city workers' labor unions. Each victory provided inspiration and actuarial data for the next round. Success followed in West Hollywood, Santa Cruz, San Francisco, Seattle, Los Angeles, New York City, and New York State. In each case, lesbian and gay labor activists and public sector unions such as SEIU and AFSCME were at the center of the struggle for policies that covered gay and straight families. In some instances, partner benefit movements failed to overcome insurance industry obstacles and homophobia. (I will address these setbacks later in this chapter.)

Preconditions for the Domestic Partner Benefits Movement

The movement for domestic partner benefits arose in major metropolitan areas in which several necessary preconditions existed: first, the lesbian and gay rights movement had achieved basic nondiscrimination municipal laws or ordinances; second, city workers were already organized in unions; and third, these unions were already bargaining creatively on "work and family" issues such as new parent, family, and medical leave, child care, and elder care. The gay civil rights victories emboldened workers not only to come out on the job and resist negative harassment, but also to demand positive recognition of their families in the form of domestic partner benefits. These public sector unions had gained experience in the 1980s in negotiating work policies that reflected the needs of *real* families—for example, with two working parents or a single working parent—as opposed to *mythic* families with a male breadwinner and a wife-and-mother at home. Most of the examples of innovative contract language in the Coalition of Labor Union Women's *Bargaining for Family Benefits: A Union Member's Guide* came from SEIU, AFSCME, and UAW District 65. Consequently, these unions were better able to accept the demand by lesbian and gay families for partner benefits as an extension of their own union's work-and-family campaigns.

Also in the 1980s, these same unions initiated landmark lawsuits and negotiated precedent-setting contract language around the issue of equal pay for comparable worth. Public sector unions criticized employers' salary systems, challenging the underlying assumptions that resulted in secretaries earning less than truck drivers, and child care workers earning less than zookeepers.[13] Thus, these unions were open to the argument that giving different benefit levels to similarly situated families constituted wage discrimination against workers with domestic partners. One SEIU Local 616 leaflet used in a domestic partner benefit campaign in Alameda County, California, made this explicit, using a mock want ad:

WANTED: ACCOUNT CLERK

Starting wage of homosexual or unmarried worker $9.02 per hour. For married worker $10.33 per hour. Apply at the County Personnel Office. Alameda County is an Equal Opportunity Employer.[14]

Gay and Straight Coalitions and Collective Bargaining

Union culture and core collective bargaining strategies critically shaped the demand for partner benefits. The following description of how the demand took shape is drawn from my experience as a union staff negotiator for UAW District 65 at the Museum of Modern Art and from conversations with the dozens of union activists nationwide who, beginning in 1988, called me through the New York City–based Lesbian and Gay Labor Network for advice on bargaining for partner benefits.

Early in the campaign to secure domestic partner benefits, gay and lesbian trade unionists formulated domestic partnership as including gay and straight unmarried, cohabiting couples and their children. Public sector unions had already been through a process of contrasting traditional family definitions and modern family realities, arguing that child care was an employer issue because of the decreasing numbers of home-based family members; more and more family members were out working. The unions further argued that workers need sick days to take care of sick children. Thus, when a lesbian or gay union member pointed out to her or his local the need for domestic partner benefits, the union would inevitably consider the question of how many heterosexual members were also unmarried domestic partners. Moreover, straight union members felt comfortable speaking up at meetings about themselves or coworkers who were in long-term unmarried relationships and suffering from lack of insurance. Unlike nonunion-based gay rights activists who challenged corporations through lesbian or gay employee interest groups, the trade unionists understood that the core issue was not that straight couples could marry. Many chose not to marry for a variety of important reasons, and the union respected that. The union perspective, and the lesbian and gay union perspective, was that if people cohabit and live as a family, they should get family benefits just as legitimately as lesbian and gay partners who cannot legally marry.

Furthermore, as soon as union leaders and gay union activists recognized that there was a broader constituency for domestic partnership than the gay and lesbian membership, they knew that a more broadly defined demand would have stronger support and therefore a better chance of winning. Thus, domestic partnership became incorporated into the long tradition of collective bargaining as workplace coalition politics. In this tradition, contract demands consist of two types. One type is special demands that meet the special needs of key constituencies, such as demographic groups like young families, long-term staff who are near retirement, or subgroups based on race, sex, or sexual orientation. Departmental or job classification groups might also have special needs. This collection of special demands and the coalition of interest groups is then bound together with the larger membership by a group of broader workplace demands for raises and basic benefits.

A savvy advocate of a constituency demand like partner benefits will define that concept as broadly as possible and then advocate equally hard for other subgroup demands as well as the overall wage and benefit program. Thus, the most effective gay labor proponents of domestic partner benefits tend to be shop stewards and bargaining committee members who have mastered these coalition skills and know how to earn the support of union members who do not have domestic partners but who want the reciprocal solidarity for their own bargaining demands. In practice, the number of domestic partners who register for benefits ranges from 1 percent (same sex only) up to 5 percent (same and opposite sex) of the workforce. The typical demographics of unionized domestic partnerships are 50 to 70 percent straight couples, with the rest evenly split between gay and lesbian couples, so the straight constituency for this issue is sizeable.[15]

The coalition bargaining that created unionized domestic partner benefits is a totally different process from the lesbian or gay committee in a nonunion corporation that petitions directly to the office of personnel. Such committees have neither the structure and traditions of collective bargaining nor the backing of a broad workplace coalition. The key difference is collective power.

Union Power Makes Partner Benefits Winnable

The original partner benefits victories were possible because the labor movement had the power to force insurance funds or companies to experiment with coverage they were actively trying to avoid. Whether the benefits were first tried in a joint labor-management health fund (as at the *Village Voice*), through a commercial insurance company that couldn't afford to lose a major client (City of Berkeley), or through self-insurance (as with City of West Hollywood), unionized workers had the leverage to move an extremely conservative industry.[16] Once the actuarial data started mounting up and showing that partner benefits cost the same as married family coverage, it became much easier for other cities, liberal corporations, and universities to agree to the benefits and to get more insurance companies to offer the coverage at appropriate prices.

To this day, domestic partner coverage usually takes one of these three original forms—joint funds, self-insurance, and insurance concessions to a major client. The *Village Voice,* like many unionized workplaces in the United States, was insured through a joint labor-company fund with trustees from both the union and management. Partner benefits got political support from the trustees, so the fund could simply decide to cover these new dependents without having to wrangle with for-profit insurance firms.

However, many unionized employers have commercial insurance and have had terrible fights with their insurance companies over proposed partner coverage. The City of West Hollywood, for example, could not find an affordable commercial policy that included partners; the solution was self-insurance. The city paid its employees' medical bills, using an outside firm to administer these payments and to provide inexpensive back-up insurance to cover any bills that were unusually high (over $100,000 for one employee). Because self-insurance eliminated insurance industry profit margins, the City of West Hollywood *saved* $65,000 in the first six months while covering partners, compared to its old premiums without partner coverage.

The third way that workers get partner coverage is through an employer that is too big a client for the insurance companies to ignore. This was true for pioneering larger cities such as Berkeley, San Francisco, and Seattle. Once the union had won management's agreement to partner coverage, the insurance carriers were forced to negotiate a price or risk losing a major client. Nevertheless, in these cities, the insurers insisted on a surcharge or reserve fund to cover their anxious estimates of excessive medical bills from domestic partners (i.e., partners with AIDS). However, in each case, the surcharge was refunded and the reserve fund was dismantled after a few years of actual experience with partner coverage. Indeed, married straight workers' childbirths, cancers, and heart attacks balanced out domestic partners' health bills, partly because 50 percent of insured domestic partners are straight; nor did the cases of AIDS and some lesbian child-bearing upset this equation.

Although insurance companies used high estimates of usage based on the guideline that 10 percent of Americans are gay, typically only 1 to 5 percent of all workers register their partners for benefits. There are several reasons for this. First, registering a lesbian or gay partner requires coming out at work, if only to the personnel office, which some people are reluctant to do because of fear of discrimination. Second, not all lesbian or gay employees have live-in partners. Third, many domestic partners carry insurance through their own jobs. The typical domestic partners insured through the new benefit plans are either unemployed, self-employed, or employed in an uninsured industry or job, or they have a benefit plan significantly inferior to their partner's.[17] This is how domestic partner benefits fill in the huge gaps in comprehensive, affordable insurance in the U.S. health care system.[18]

Multiple Tactics Yield Results

Even in a city like New York, with a municipal gay rights ordinance, powerful municipal unions, and bargaining power as a giant client of the health insurance industry, it took many years and a combination of tactics to win domestic partner health benefits. In 1987, Ron Madson, Ruth Berman, and another lesbian who withheld her name from publicity, all of whom were members of United Federation of Teachers (UFT) Local 2 of the American Federation of Teachers (AFT) and of the Gay Teachers Association (GTA), filed a lawsuit seeking domestic partner benefits for their long-term partners and the partners of all teachers and other public school employees. Municipal unions, led by AFSCME District Council 37, first put partner benefits on the bargaining table that same year. However, both groups faced a reluctant city hall and a hostile state insurance commissioner.

There were two breakthroughs in 1989. The highest state court, the New York Court of Appeals, ruled that the longtime partner of a man who had died of AIDS was a member of his partner's immediate family for the purpose of retaining the right to his partner's rent-controlled apartment.[19] The majority opinion of Judge Vito J. Titone stated that the term family "should not be rigidly restricted to those people who have formalized their relationship by obtaining, for instance, a marriage certificate or an adoption order." Judge Titone stipulated that protection against eviction "should find its foundation in the reality of family life," which he stated would include "two adult lifetime partners whose relationship is long-term and characterized by an emotional and financial commitment."[20] This was the first judicial ruling that equated domestic partners and blood/married/adopted kin. That same year, Mayor Ed Koch was in danger of losing the Democratic primary to David Dinkins, who was gaining lesbian and gay swing votes with his support of domestic partner benefits. On the eve of the primary, the mayor granted domestic partner bereavement leave for city workers through an executive order. AFSCME District Council 37 immediately locked this benefit into the contract to protect it from a mayoral change of heart.

In the end, David Dinkins won the primary, but he did not keep his election promise to settle the teachers' lawsuit and grant domestic partner health benefits to all city employees. His administration told AFSCME at the bargaining table that he couldn't agree to benefits as long as the teachers' lawsuit was in court. But the city's attorneys told the GTA that they couldn't unilaterally grant the benefits to settle the suit because the benefits had to be bargained with the unions.[21] The root cause of the delay was concern about how much the benefits would cost. Dinkins was being attacked by Republican mayoral candidate Rudolph Giuliani for excessive public spending, and once again, the insurance companies were making dire predictions about premiums for partner coverage.[22]

Knowing that partner benefits were affordable, based on other cities' experiences, the Lesbian and Gay Issues Committee within AFSCME organized a coalition of the city unions, the GTA, and the lesbian and gay rights movement to put coordinated pressure on Dinkins. AFSCME DC 37's Disability Rights Committee and Retiree Committee joined forces with the Lesbian and Gay Issues Committee in this campaign for partner benefits. The coalition was based on a related set of circumstances. Workers receiving government medical disability income and widows and widowers receiving surviving spouse government Social Security income risked losing those benefits (and their financial independence within the relationship) if they married their domestic partners. This provided a strong incentive not to marry. As unmarried partners, however, they could not share health insurance benefits, unless domestic partner health benefits were available.[23]

In the spring of 1992, Mayor Dinkins tried to respond to this election-year coalition by issuing an executive order creating a domestic partner registry for all city residents as of January 1993. Further, the order granted family-related leave for city workers with domestic partners, as well as hospital and prison visitation rights for all city residents with partners. But the Dinkins administration did not move on partner health benefits.

The coalition intensified the pressure over the summer leading up to Mayor Dinkins's increasingly tight race against Giuliani in November 1993. Dinkins needed the lesbian and gay vote and the voter-mobilization support of the teacher and municipal unions that were advocating partner benefits. Finally, in September, Dinkins joined forces with Democratic Governor Mario Cuomo to force the hostile state insurance commissioner to issue a ruling that partner benefits were permissible under state insurance law, even though New York state law still had a traditional definition of family.[24]

With that bureaucratic roadblock out of the way, Dinkins simultaneously settled the teachers' lawsuit and collective bargaining over partner benefits with AFSCME and the other municipal unions between October 29 and 30. Although the administration had predicted costs of $60 million, the negotiated estimate was only $15 million, to be financed by other health plan savings. Dinkins lost the election, but the benefits were safely secured in union contracts and not subject to elimination by a new mayoral executive order.

It took the combined power of lesbian and gay union activists fighting in many arenas at once—the courts, the bargaining table, the streets, and electoral politics—to make these benefits available to New York City's 350,000 municipal employees. As with all the other union-secured partner benefit plans, this one covered both gay and straight couples.

Emergence of the Corporate Model

This chapter began with the 1991 *Business Week* article that hailed Lotus, the computer software firm, as the first major corporation to grant domestic partner benefits. There is a single fleeting reference in that article to one of the dozen U.S. municipalities that had agreed through collective bargaining to domestic partner benefits beginning in 1985. Large city governments' years of actuarial experience with domestic partner benefits and costs made it possible for the three lesbian employees at Lotus to convince their company and its insurers to cover domestic partners.

Lotus was followed by liberal jeans manufacturer Levi Strauss & Co. and other nonunion computer firms, such as Apple Computer (maker of Macintosh personal computers), Microsoft Inc., Oracle Systems Corp., and Silicon Graphics. Another wave of domestic partner benefit gains in the entertainment industry began at MCA (1992) and was followed by HBO cable TV and Warner of Time Warner (1993), and by Viacom, Universal, Paramount Pictures, Sony, and Walt Disney (1996). During the same period, partner benefits were achieved at colleges and universities beginning with the University of Iowa and Stanford University in 1992. By 1994, domestic partner benefits had spread to schools like Harvard, the University of Chicago, the University of Pennsylvania, and New York University.[25]

With the exception of Levi Strauss (which will be covered in more detail below), these companies and schools have always followed the lead of the first corporation in covering *only* lesbian and gay couples. Even though almost every one of these companies (and many of the schools) had their corporate headquarters in a city with domestic partner benefits for both gay and straight couples, they chose to cover only lesbians and gays because it was much cheaper and because the employee advocates did not have the perspective or the power to gain broader coverage.

An early and significant example of this was the case of a lesbian doctor's lawsuit against the Bronx Montefiore Medical Center to get health insurance for her partner. In 1991, the medical center agreed to gay partner benefits in an out-of-court settlement—but only for doctors. They restricted the benefit not just to gays but to only a tiny portion of their employees. Because the media have given high-profile coverage to these corporate plans, it is still a common misconception that only lesbian and gay couples benefit from domestic partner health insurance. A further misconception is that the benefit was bestowed without a fight by a few enlightened corporations and colleges.

The Corporate Model vs. the Union Model

By the time the issue of domestic partner benefits for New York State public employees came to a head in early 1994, more corporations and universities offered the benefits than did municipalities, although municipal workers covered far outnumbered private sector employees. Both the state and the several unions that represented state workers were aware that including straight couples tripled or quadrupled enrollment and costs. In this instance, the cheaper, gay-only corporate model began to put pressure on the more inclusive union model of partner benefits.

Some background information is required to understand the political context for New York State employee negotiations. In 1982, Governor Cuomo issued an executive order prohibiting discrimination by the New York state government based on sexual orientation. This order was particularly important because the state legislature had never passed a statewide gay civil rights law. Especially after the partner benefit victory in New York City in 1993, the lesbian and gay political movement and the gay activists within the state unions increased their pressure on Cuomo to grant partner benefits as the logical extension of his executive order. There was some concern that George Pataki, a Republican candidate for governor, might rescind the executive order if he won in November 1994, and this made negotiations for the benefits that much more urgent.

The Public Employee Federation (PEF), representing many state professionals and jointly affiliated with the AFT and SEIU, supported domestic partner health coverage for gays and straights.[26] However, the Civil Service Employees Association (CSEA), which is part of AFSCME and represents the bulk of white- and blue-collar state workers, took the position in a letter to Cuomo from CSEA president Joseph E. McDermott on May 11, 1994, that it would be acceptable to CSEA if only lesbian and gay couples were covered.[27] This generated tension within the state coalition of unions because the unions all knew that covering only gays would be cheaper and very tempting for the governor in his race against the fiscally conservative Pataki.

On June 28, 1994, only days after the massive international gay rights demonstration in New York City commemorating the twenty-fifth anniversary of the Stonewall Rebellion, Governor Cuomo announced that he would extend benefits to domestic partners of gay and lesbian state employees as of January 1995. The governor added that he was uncertain whether or not to cover straight partners. Because the unions had already proposed partner benefits in the past, the governor's agreement to grant them virtually assured their inclusion in upcoming union contracts. The *New York Times* article covering this announcement included quotes from a CSEA leader, Ross D. Hanna, affirming the union's support for gay-only partner benefits.[28]

Ironically, it was the socially conservative prison guards' union, Council 82 of AFSCME, that tipped the scale toward covering both gays and straights. According to Vivienne Freund, a founder of PEF's lesbian and gay committee, there was concern that Council 82 would simply reject the governor's offer of partner benefits out of homophobia, but Council 82 leaders took a different tack. The prison guard bargaining representatives first argued that they had *no* lesbian or gay members; they then went on to insist that domestic partnership had to cover straight partners, because that was the only way that domestic partner insurance would benefit their membership. They refused to support the CSEA's gays-only position, and in tactical combination with PEF, they swayed the state union coalition to an inclusive partner benefit demand.[29] Based on discussions with the unions before the gubernatorial election, the governor agreed to institute inclusive partner benefits by executive order commencing in January 1995, with the understanding that the benefits would be formally incorporated in union contracts by March 31.

Only a few weeks later, however, Cuomo lost the election to Republican George Pataki, who had attacked Cuomo's support for partner benefits as a bald attempt to win gay votes. Pataki also criticized the benefits as bad policy because they were costly and because they endorsed the gay lifestyle. Shortly after taking office in January, Dennis Vacco, the new attorney general, rescinded the prior attorney general's sexual orientation nondiscrimination policy covering the office's staff. This move infuriated PEF members under Vacco's supervision, according to Tom Privitere, a PEF staff representative and staff liaison to the union's lesbian and gay committee.[30]

Right after Vacco's policy shift, the Republican state senate majority leader, Joseph Bruno, unilaterally rescinded domestic partner benefits for employees of the state senate. As Bruno explained in a press release a week later, "The former governor's unilateral action was opposed by state legislators and others concerned about its potential cost and the possibility of fraud. . . . In light of these facts and Governor Pataki's state[d] opposition to extend these benefits, the Senate decided to forego providing domestic partner health benefits to its employees."[31] The "possibility of fraud" refers to the old insurance industry fear that workers will sign up fake partners to get insurance for sick friends. In this environment, negotiations began between the Pataki administration and the state employee unions in February for a contract that was to expire on March 31.

Most of the unions were firm in their support of domestic partner benefits. PEF told the state's chief negotiator that they wouldn't sign a contract if it didn't include partner benefits, and the PEF negotiators' resolve was strengthened by organized agitation from lesbian and gay members (whether or not they had partners) as well as members who were already using the benefit. CSEA once again floated a trial balloon to management about covering only gay and lesbian partners, but this was the last thing the Pataki administration wanted to do, especially as they began to hear from hundreds of straight employees who were using the benefits.

After only three months of implementation, 800 domestic partners (including retirees) were registered for benefits; 75 percent of them were straight. Half of all the employees who wanted to cover partners were already receiving family health insurance because they had children, so adding the partner cost the state literally nothing. According to an oral history interview by Miriam Frank with Tom Privitere, "The Pataki administration finally backed off when they realized it would hurt straights and the elderly and that the fight wasn't worth the labor unrest."[32] The fact that partner benefits had been implemented for straight couples had saved partner benefits for lesbians and gays from a vigorous Republican fiscal and homophobic attack. According to Privitere, figures for New York State showed that by April 1996, 1,253 domestic partners were registered for health benefits; 75 percent were straight, with the remainder split evenly between gays and lesbians.

The Future Frontiers: Private Industry and Conservative States

The future frontiers for achieving partner benefits are in private industry and in more conservative cities and states. The first steps will be winning nondiscrimination policies in collective bargaining with industrial corporations. This is currently an area of contention between the UAW and the Big Three car companies, Ford, General Motors, and Chrysler.[33] However, this is almost an unmentionable issue in most locals within the building trades craft unions, which still have difficulty integrating women and racial minorities, much less sexual orientation minorities. If workers and union members are afraid to come out, there is no visible constituency to advocate bargaining for partner benefits.

Similarly, in more socially conservative parts of the country, it is difficult to pass nondiscrimination ordinances and secure partner benefits. Often, lesbians and gays leave their birth state and migrate to more liberal cities in order to avoid severe discrimination. Thus, even though lesbians and gays are "everywhere," they are present in smaller numbers in some communities, and these communities often disapprove of straight domestic partners as well. In this context, it is interesting to examine the theory and practice of domestic partner benefits in Levi Strauss & Co., which has its headquarters in liberal San Francisco but its factories in conservative states like Texas and Arkansas.

Levi Strauss & Co. is the largest apparel firm in the world, making jeans, other casual pants, sport shirts, and T-shirts in the United States and other countries.[34] It has a liberal reputation based on its business philosophy of combining employee personal fulfillment and profitable jeans production and its early adoption of nondiscrimination policies, including one on sexual orientation. Levi Strauss implemented partner benefits for gay and straight employees in 1992 and got extensive coverage in a *Newsweek* article on domestic partnership.[35] The human resources manager who was interviewed neglected to mention that a lesbian and gay employee committee at the corporation's San Francisco headquarters had been lobbying for these benefits for two years.

She also made no reference to bargaining demands for nondiscrimination and partner benefits that had been raised by garment workers in Levi's factories in Texas and Arkansas. These workers were members of the Amalgamated Clothing and Textile Workers Union (ACTWU), who are now merged into UNITE (the Union of Needletrades, Industrial, and Textile Employees), which has a nondiscrimination clause on sexual orientation in its constitution. It had been hard for lesbians in those factory locals to get their demands on the table because many of their coworkers disapproved of their "lifestyle." Nevertheless, they persevered, with support from union staff, and the benefits were incorporated into the next contract.

Three years later, at a national conference held in Oakland, California, by Pride at Work, the U.S. organization for lesbian, gay, bisexual, and transgender labor, a local UNITE activist from a Levi Strauss jeans sewing plant in Arkansas spoke at a workshop on domestic partner benefits. "I work for Levi Strauss in the town of Harrison, in the Ozarks of northern Arkansas," the activist stated, adding that "this very scenic and very tragic part of Arkansas" had become "the life support for a very evil organization—the Knights of the Ku Klux Klan." With the Klan headquartered a short distance from Harrison, the activist pointed out, "Your next door neighbor who greets you from his front porch may enter into his own home and devise a plan to run you out of town."[36]

Arkansas is also a "right-to-work" state in which membership in a union local is optional even if that union has a collective bargaining agreement at the plant. This means that the local is in a constant state of organizing workers to join and stay in the union. The UNITE activist recalled a survey that the union sent out to the Levi Strauss workers. "One question in particular asked those that were no longer in the union why they got out. Some of the comments were very disturbing. Our president is a lesbian, and anything that goes wrong they blame on her sexual orientation."

In this atmosphere of homophobia, only two out of 323 employees at the Harrison plant had signed up for domestic partner benefits, and both were straight women. At the corporate level, two-thirds of partners with benefits were straight, but in Harrison, Arkansas, the lesbian and gay one-third was still in hiding. One challenge for the lesbian and gay labor activists is to find concrete ways to encourage, support, and defend their union sisters and brothers in such places.

Another tough state for lesbians and gays is Texas, even in Austin, its fairly liberal state capital with the customary preconditions of a city gay rights ordinance and an active AFSCME municipal union. Lesbian and gay city and county workers were active in placing domestic partner benefits on their union's bargaining agenda. They also organized AFSCME to work with the Lesbian and Gay Rights Lobby of Texas to convince the city council to pass a domestic partner ordinance to take effect January 1994, despite opposition from the Christian religious right. According to the Lesbian and Gay Rights lobby, the day the ordinance was passed, the conservative Christians published a full-page ad in a local newspaper that said, "Shame on the Sodomites!"[37]

Having educated themselves about partner benefits and which companies provided them, this religious group was outraged to learn that Apple Computer was negotiating a tax break for a new Apple plant with neighboring Williamson County. The Austin right-wingers descended on Williamson's county commissioners, demanding that Apple rescind its domestic partner benefits or risk losing county subsidies for the new plant. When Apple held firm, however, and threatened to put the new plant elsewhere, the county voted in favor of badly needed jobs and subsidized the new plant, "sodomites" and all.

A few months later, the same right-wing religious coalition launched a referendum campaign to repeal Austin's gay rights ordinance. The consultant they hired persuaded them to keep the Bible-thumping, anti-gay preachers in the background. He also recommended that they name the coalition "Concerned Texans." The consultant recognized the power of Austin's lesbian and gay movement and its liberal sympathizers, so he shifted the focus of the attack to straight domestic partners—labeling domestic partnership a "Shack-up, live-in plan." He exaggerated the cost of the benefits and the impact on the city's tight budget. The referendum against partner benefits succeeded, and the anti-gay fanatics reemerged to celebrate their victory.[38]

In this case, domestic partnership suffered a setback from a combination of homophobia, fiscal conservatism, and moral opposition to straights who were "living in sin." Because they weren't organized as an interest group with their own lobbyist, straight domestic partners were the weak link in the Austin movement for partner benefits. Of course, a referendum against gay-only partner benefits might have succeeded as well.

Conclusion

Securing domestic partner health benefits has been a long-term focus of the U.S. lesbian and gay labor movement because of the gaps in coverage in the current for-profit, employment-based health insurance system in the United States. A straight, married individual can secure benefits through a spouse's employer; however, lesbian and gay domestic partners cannot get the same coverage because employers do not recognize them as "family." Because employers are not required to provide health insurance and because there is no guaranteed insurance for the self-employed and unemployed, many partners of unionized lesbians and gays have been uninsured.

In the last fifteen years, lesbian and gay union activists, particularly in municipal unions in cities that adopted local gay rights ordinances, were in a unique position to use the collective bargaining process to design and secure domestic partner health benefits. These unions, as well as District 65 of the UAW, had already negotiated protection against discrimination based on sexual orientation, litigated and bargained over pay equity, and developed an agenda of reforms to help workers deal with the conflicts between the demands of work and family. Therefore, these unions were receptive to the core issues of domestic partner benefits: concerns about discrimination, problems of benefit equity, and the need to broaden the definition of family.

Based on their experience with coalitions and collective bargaining, these union activists incorporated straight domestic partners into the new definition of family and marshaled their unions' strengths to win these benefits in the face of both homophobic and fiscal resistance by employers and the insurance industry. They organized alliances with other public sector unions and with the lesbian and gay rights movement because public sector bargaining raises issues of public policy and requires political action as well as workplace mobilization.

Lesbian and gay employee groups within liberal, nonunion corporations used the actuarial cost and benefit experience of city workers to campaign for partner benefits in their companies. However, lacking both the tradition of coalition organizing and the power of collective bargaining, these groups secured domestic partner health insurance for gay and lesbian families only. As the number of companies with gay-only partner benefits increased, public sector employers, such as the State of New York, tried to limit unionized partner benefits to homosexual families. These efforts were largely unsuccessful. In general, domestic partner benefits that cover both gay and straight families have been easier to protect from a conservative backlash precisely because they have a broader base of support.

As word of the financial viability of domestic partner health benefits spreads through the national media as well as through lesbian and gay labor publications and networks, an increasing number of unions in wider geographic and industrial settings have begun to show serious interest in these benefits. Usually, the first step is negotiating a nondiscrimination clause that covers sexual orientation. The process of proving that lesbian and gay workers are present and need protection from discrimination lays the groundwork for activists to come out and advocate for lesbian and gay family benefits. Some unions, such as the UAW, are currently wrestling with this first issue. In some cities and states where the religious right is a force in politics, it is extremely difficult to achieve nondiscrimination laws and contract language, much less domestic partner benefits. However, in an ever-increasing number of unions in a wider variety of locations and industries, lesbian and gay activists are demanding and winning domestic partner benefits. An important task for Pride at Work (which affiliated with the AFL-CIO in 1997) will be to give inspiration and technical assistance to the many lesbian and gay union activists who want to make domestic partner benefits a collectively bargained reality.

Notes

Acknowledgments: This chapter is based on a paper on domestic partner benefits, "On the Frontier of Work and Family Issues: Public Sector Unions and Domestic Partner Benefits," that I delivered at the Institute for Women's Policy Research Conference in Washington, D.C., 3 June 1994. I would like to gratefully acknowledge the encouragement and editing I have received in the preparation of this chapter from my life partner, Miriam Frank.

1. K. H. Hammonds,"Lotus Opens a Door for Gay Partners," *Business Week,* 4 November 1991.

2. Marie R. Dufresne, consultant with Hay/Huggins Company, quoted in *ibid.*

3. D. A. Stone, "AIDS and the Moral Economy of Insurance," in *Homo Economics: Capitalism, Community and Lesbian and Gay Life,* ed. A. Gluckman and B. Reed (New York: Routledge, 1997).

4. M. Freudenheim, "Health Care Costs Edging Up and a Bigger Surge Is Feared," *New York Times,* 21 January 1997.

5. A report by Schone and Cooper, cited in P. T. Kilborn, "Poor Workers Turning Down Employers' Health Benefits," *New York Times,* 10 November 1997.

6. R. Pear, "New Approach to Overhauling Health Insurance: Step by Step," *New York Times,* 11 November 1996.

7. E. Rosenthal, "New York Study Finds Uninsured Are on the Rise," *New York Times,* 25 February 1997.

8. D. A. Stone, "AIDS and the Moral Economy of Insurance."

9. T. Gold and K. Anderson, *Out at Work* (New York: AndersonGold Films, 1997), videotape.

10. M. Frank and D. Holcomb, *Pride at Work: Organizing for Lesbian and Gay Rights in Unions* (New York: Lesbian and Gay Labor Network, 1990), pp. 46–48; M. Frank, "How (and Why) to Organize Lesbian and Gay Union Committees," *Labor Notes* (March 1993): 12–13. See also Miriam Frank's chapter in this volume.

11. C. Zvanski, personal communication, May 1994.

12. J. Steinhauer, "Increasingly, Employers Offer Benefit to All Partners," *New York Times,* 20 August 1994.

13. D. E. Bell, "Unionized Women in State and Local Government," in *Women, Work and Protest: A Century of Women's Labor History,* ed. R. Milkman (Boston: Routledge and Kegan Paul, 1985), pp. 292–299.

14. Quoted by P. R. Roberts, "Comment on New Directions in Organizing and Representing Women," in *Women and Unions: Forging a Partnership,* ed. S. Cobble (Ithaca, NY: Cornell University Press, 1993).

15. G. Power, "Domestic Partner Benefits for Levi Strauss Employees," *San Francisco Chronicle,* 22 February 1992; T. Privitere, personal communication, 1997.

16. Frank and Holcomb, *Pride at Work.*

17. M. Winerip, "A Lesson from Teacher for City Hall," *New York Times,* 31 May 1992; M. Navarro, "New Choices in Health Care: New York Extends Health Benefits to Domestic Partners of City Employees," *New York Times,* 27 December 1993; Steinhauer, "Increasingly, Employees Offer Benefits to All Partners."

18. Some lesbian and gay labor activists such as Susan Moir have argued that the gay movement should have put more emphasis on winning universal health care instead of focusing on domestic partner benefits to fill in these gaps (A. Gluckman, "Laboring for Gay Rights: An Interview with Susan Moir," in *Homo Economics,* pp. 236–237).

19. In New York State, the rent and lease succession rights for certain older buildings' apartments are regulated by state law. These are known as "rent-controlled" apartments.

20. Cited in Frank and Holcomb, *Pride at Work.*

21. R. Madson, personal communication, 1997; E. Wolfson, personal communication, 1997.

22. E. Sachar, "Battle for Benefits: Gay Couples Seek Health Insurance," *New York Newsday,* 25 May 1992; C. W. Dugger, "Workers' Partners Added to Health Plan by Dinkins," *New York Times,* 31 October 1993.

23. J. Schwartzberg, personal communication, 1997.

24. S. Harrigan and M. Powell, "Ruling Boosts Benefit Plan for Partners," *New York Newsday,* 30 September 1993.

25. R. M. Anderson, "Domestic Partner Benefits: A Primer for Gay and Lesbian Activists," in *Homo Economics.*

26. V. Freund, personal communication, 1997.

27. J. Schwartz, personal communication, 1994.

28. J. Fisher, "Cuomo Decides to Extend Domestic-Partner Benefits," *New York Times,* 29 June 1994.

29. V. Freund, personal communication, 1997.

30. T. Privitere, personal communication, 1997.

31. C. L. Taylor, "Gay Rights Blast: Dems Demand Bruno Restore Health Benefits," *New York Newsday,* 7 February 1995.

32. M. Frank, interview with Thomas I. Privitere, 13 March 1996, in *Out in the Union Oral History Collection (1995–1997),* Robert F. Wagner Labor Archives, Tamiment Library, New York University.

33. J. B. Stewart, "Coming Out at Chrysler," *New Yorker,* 21 July 1997, pp. 38–44, 46–49.

34. Ironically, Levi Strauss did not have to extend its domestic partner insurance to its employees overseas because "most of those workers are in countries with some kind of national health care" ("Levi Strauss Oks Benefits for Unmarried Partners," *Los Angeles Times,* 24 February 1992).

35. K. Ames, et al., "Domesticated Bliss: New Laws Are Making It Official for Gay or Live-in Straight Couples," *Newsweek,* 23 March 1992.

36. Confidential interview, 1995.

37. D. Hardy-Garcia, quoted in D. Holcomb, "On the Frontier of Work and Family Issues: Public Sector Unions and Domestic Partner Benefits" (paper presented at the Institute for Women's Policy Research Conference, Washington, D.C., 3 June 1994), p. 6.

38. D. Hardy-Garcia, quoted in Holcomb, "On the Frontier of Work and Family Issues," p. 6.

Jonathan Goldberg-Hiller

7 The Limits to Union: Labor, Gays and Lesbians, and Marriage in Hawai'i

> *The People of Hawai'i realize that it is a great leap from passing laws that stop discrimination against homosexuals to passing a law allowing homosexuals to enter into society's most favored relationship. That is why in a state with an unparalleled history of tolerance and diversity, over two-thirds are against same-sex marriage.*
>
> (John Hoag, Co-chair of Hawai'i's Future Today, 1996)

> *We in the labor movement don't believe that civil rights is a special interest. It's all our interest. It's the interest of all of us to ensure that equality and freedom is extended to all the citizens of our country.*
>
> (John Sweeney, AFL-CIO Convention, 1983)

> *Affiliated unions and state and local bodies should take an active role in opposing measures which reduce the rights of people based on their sexual orientation and should participate in appropriate coalitions in order to defeat such measures.*
>
> (AFL-CIO convention resolution, 1993)

The strategies that have brought the labor movement in the United States to the same table as lesbian and gay organizations to dine on the fruits of common interest have had mixed success. Right-wing initiatives to deprive gays and lesbians of their civil rights in Maine, Oregon, and Idaho in recent years have been met by coalitions between labor and other progressive forces that helped defeat each, although by very slim majorities. In some public and private contract negotiations, labor has supported the extension of benefits to gay and lesbian partners, encouraging a "silent revolution" of progressive social policy even where public policy has officially remained mute. At the national level, in 1997—fourteen years after first going on record in support of gay and lesbian civil rights—the AFL-CIO made Pride at Work an official "constituency group" within the organization to foster mutual understanding of lesbian and gay and labor issues.

Despite these political successes and organizational achievements, the limits to cooperation and understanding have become increasingly evident. Spontaneous coalitions such as the one that defeated Oregon's discriminatory Measure 9 have been short-lived, and gay political action groups that emerged from the fight, such as Oregon Right to Privacy, have not always reciprocated later in support of labor's declared issues.[1] In Hawai'i, where gays and lesbians are poised to gain unprecedented rights to marriage through the courts, and where a well-funded right-wing backlash threatens to submerge far more than just the legal progression of the marriage case, labor has been disturbingly silent. In Hawai'i, the table of common interest is not yet set.

This chapter asks: What accounts for the present limits to cooperation between labor and lesbian and gay groups, and how might these frontiers be expanded? My focus will be on Hawai'i, an admittedly limiting case of cooperation but an appropriate point of inquiry. Hawai'i is a strong union state; it is presently ranked fourth in percentage of unionized workers, but for many years the state's labor density trailed only New York in national rankings. Its electorate has been committed to progressive politics, which made it the first state with universal health care and the first to vote to ratify the Equal Rights Amendment. Hawai'i's citizens are prideful of their reputation for social tolerance, first forged in the great wave of union organizing in the sugar fields that built the foundations for nearly four decades of uninterrupted Democratic Party rule. With this history, it seems almost natural that the state would be the first to add equal rights to marriage to what is already some of the nation's strongest anti-discrimination protection for gays and lesbians in employment and state services.

As reaffirmation of past practices—a valorization of the state's progressive legacy—much more could be done to meet our expectations of continued support for an expansion of civil rights by the labor community. The many years of ethnic-based divide-and-conquer strategies to control labor in the sugar and pineapple fields made union organizers keenly aware of the centrality of anti-discrimination principles in the construction of solidarity. The post-war political economy that emerged from labor's victories in agriculture and the tourist industry was based on relatively high wages and generous workers' rights, social rights to a bountiful welfare state, and strong support for immigrants. In addition, the special character of the tourist industry, predicated on the allure of a preserved Polynesian culture for a global clientele, made an appreciation for the civil rights of all an integral part of what makes Hawai'i work. Why, then, was this progressive legacy squandered when it comes to gay and lesbian demands for marriage?

Writing about the negative case—why union action to support the rights of gays and lesbians has *not* materialized—is an onerous task. The absence of evidence is paradoxically the best evidence, yet it necessarily speaks little. What it presents is an opportunity to see how political language constructs the issue as a nonproblem, that is, a problem not fit for labor's intervention. This chapter begins with an examination of the case of same-sex marriage in Hawai'i, pinpointing the political—as opposed to strictly legal—opportunities for strategic cooperation and opposition to dominant discourse. A subsequent section evaluates the nature of political argument to make sense of interviews

I conducted with several of Hawai'i's union leaders to learn why they have failed to support the marriage case. Comparing these unions with one committed to support, I speculate that unions with a strong democratic culture—one that encourages coalition building and tolerance for open gay and lesbian identities—may have more success in envisioning gay rights, identities, and citizenship in harmony with workers' interests. The concluding sections of the chapter consider a strategic framework for cooperation between labor and gay and lesbian activists, and the consequences if the present struggle is lost. Long-term union interests, especially in Hawai'i, depend on a broad commitment to civil rights.

Blue Hawai'i: Progressive Law and Reactionary Politics

In late 1990, when two lesbian couples and one gay couple requested marriage licenses in the state of Hawai'i, they were relatively certain that their requests would be denied. They had been in contact with a sympathetic lawyer who was prepared to take their case to the courts under the theory that the rights to privacy, equal protection of the laws, and due process as guaranteed by the Hawai'i state constitution forbade the discriminatory denial of a license to marry. The legal struggle was an uphill run; similar challenges in Minnesota, Kentucky, and Washington in the early 1970s had failed to produce such a ruling.[2] Marriage, in these earlier cases, was ruled by definition to exclude same-sex formations. Thus, there was little private surprise and little public notice when the Hawai'i circuit court in 1991 dismissed the complaint, ruling that the government's refusal to issue licenses to same-sex couples did not give rise to any constitutional question.

The expected appeal to the Supreme Court produced a ruling several years later that shook the legal world as much as it upset the foundations of the plaintiffs' arguments and their diminishing hopes. In 1993, the court held in *Baehr v. Lewin* that the circuit court had erred in not providing the plaintiffs a trial. The high court agreed that the gay and lesbian couples' right to privacy had been violated by the state, yet because the right to privacy had never been interpreted to encompass same-sex marriage, there was no remedy at law. There was, from this angle, no *right* to same-sex marriage. However, the denial of a marriage license also violated the state constitution's prohibition on state-sanctioned discrimination on the basis of sex. This form of discrimination, according to the court, was a parallel to the issues raised in *Loving v. Virginia* in 1967. That case had overturned anti-miscegenation laws by rejecting Virginia's metaphysical claim that interracial marriages could not exist because they were intrinsically unnatural, if not repugnant to custom. Just as the *Loving* court had argued that interracial marriage proscriptions were mainstays of white supremacy, designed as they were to keep the races separate, the Supreme Court argued that bans on same-sex marriage went to the heart of sex discrimination.[3] Here the ban could be legitimate only under a compelling state interest that would override the constitutional guarantee of equal protection of the laws. On this basis, the Supreme Court reinstated the lower court trial. The state was burdened with proving that same-sex marriage posed the highest threat to community or state policy—a threat so great it should be allowed to override the rights of each plaintiff to be free of sex discrimination. The law, which had always responded to gay and lesbian demands for marriage from the perspective of their novelty, now recognized that traditional civil rights law (itself secure in a strong web of precedent) anchored same-sex marriage firmly within its legal tradition.

The political and economic repercussions of the reinstatement of the trial were immediate. The plaintiffs, already heavily in debt to their lawyer, needed money. A fund raiser was held in 1993, and finally, the Marriage Project was organized to provide financial support for the plaintiffs and disseminate information to the community about the case. The Marriage Project raised about $100,000 annually, mostly from gay- and lesbian-friendly networks. Labor did not contribute, nor was it asked to support the plaintiffs, in part because the fund raisers were unprepared and, according to one organizer, too "timid" to engage the controversy that such a request might produce. Grass roots support grew without labor's involvement, sprouting organizations such as the Hawai'i Equal Rights to Marriage Project, the Alliance for Equal Rights, the Coalition for Equality and Diversity (which was coordinated by the state ACLU), and the Clergy Coalition. The Lambda Legal Defense Fund of New York, a powerhouse gay and lesbian public interest firm, furnished a lawyer to support local counsel and promoted regional Freedom to Marry Coalitions around the nation in order to keep public involvement high. Right-wing concern about the implications of the case began more slowly. Because the right was poorly organized in Hawai'i, there were few local exhortations of opposition, except within the Mormon and Catholic churches. This would change as the political maneuvering surrounding the case began to provide a more obvious set of opportunities to channel grass roots organizing.

In response to conservative and moderate voices, including the powerful labor unions, the legislature interceded before the court case could run its full course. An act was passed in 1994 asserting that any change in the regulation of marriage licensing is "properly left to the legislature or the people of the state through a constitutional convention"; the decision to allow same-sex marriage was "essentially one of policy, rendering it inappropriate for judicial response."[4] In support of this logic, the statutes were amended to define marriage as being between one man and one woman. Additionally, a Commission on Sexual Orientation and the Law was convened to examine the issue of extending domestic partnership benefits to registered same-sex couples. A 5–2 majority on the commission—reappointed after the efforts by conservatives to preserve several seats for clergy was ruled unconstitutional—upset many moderate legislators when it found "substantial public policy reasons . . . to extend all the legal and economic benefits . . . to same-gender couples who are willing to enter into the marriage contract."[5] The commission substantially agreed with the reasoning of the Supreme Court. To stop the trial from proceeding, however, the legislature busied itself with hearings to produce a constitutional amendment restricting the jurisdiction of the courts. During the 1996 legislative session, following highly emotional public hearings in which testimony of hundreds of supporters and opponents of same-sex marriage was taken, Hawai'i's house of representatives agreed on an amendment banning same-sex marriage, but the senate, lobbied hard by progressive forces, remained deadlocked.

When the trial was finally conducted in the fall of 1996, marriage law remained substantially unchanged. The state's case—unpopular with progressives and with many conservative groups who wanted to "defend traditional marriage" by trying homosexuality itself—rested on the argument that the best interests of children required two parents of opposite sexes, justifying the state's rejection of same-sex marriage. To no one's surprise, the court ruled that the state had not demonstrated a compelling reason for its discrimination. Public sentiment was again inflamed by the decision, and hearings and debate rigorously restarted in a legislature chastened by the November electoral defeat of several incumbents for their perceived sympathy to the plaintiffs' cause. This time a conference committee succeeded in bridging house and senate concerns. An amendment banning same-sex marriage was readied for the 1998 ballot, and a domestic partnership bill, giving some of the economic advantages of marriage to any two people legally precluded from matrimony, was passed in an eleventh-hour conference committee. This was a token effort to meet the demands of the Supreme Court for equal protection for gays and lesbians, but since it was appropriately seen as a choice between marriage or an inferior legal status, it had few supporters.[6] In the meantime, the Supreme Court has yet to rule on the state's final appeal or to lift the stay imposed by the lower court.

Fearing a repeat of the legislature's deadlock the year before, some conservative activists campaigned for a constitutional convention to end the chances of same-sex marriage. In the November 1997 elections, the proposal for a convention was passed. Unions, which to this point had remained publicly distant from the politics of marriage, challenged the vote in court out of a fear that a convention called mainly for the marriage issue would spill over to weaken collective bargaining rules and permit greater privatization of public contracts (a growing possibility in light of years of budget tightening). The state supreme court ruled on the vote challenge in early 1997, deciding that the large number of spoiled ballots denied the clear majority mandated by the constitution to call a convention. In reaction, several business people filed suit in federal court to uphold the original vote. Although their probable target was union power and the rights of Native Hawaiians to gather traditional resources on private land—rights which had been asserted to delay and obstruct new hotel developments—the same-sex marriage issue was used to gain popular support for this latest intervention. The federal court ordered a new vote on the basis that, without advance publicity about the status of the spoiled ballots, the original vote was fundamentally unfair, a decision later overturned in the Ninth Circuit Court of Appeals. At this writing, a new proposal for a convention has been passed by the legislature. Native Hawaiian groups, unions (especially the large and powerful public unions), and gays and lesbians interested in marriage rights—each group brooding separately in its own corner—all have deep concerns about the outcome.

Of course, the political ferment in Hawai'i begun by the marriage case was not contained by the Pacific. Panicked at the possibility of having to recognize same-sex marriages solemnized in Hawai'i, forty-eight states considered legislation that would prevent this obligation. Sixteen passed anti-recognition laws by 1996 (twenty-seven at this writing). The issue quickly spread to the U.S. Congress, where presidential candidate Robert Dole was one of the chief sponsors of the revealingly named Defense of Marriage Act designed to accomplish the same task at the federal level. The act sailed through both houses without significant opposition. Recognizing its popularity, President Clinton signed the legislation before the 1996 elections.

For our interests, two aspects of this history of the marriage issue bear emphasis. First, as studies of law and policy have repeatedly shown, court decisions are rarely taken in a political vacuum.[7] Throughout the four-year-long political crisis that the *Baehr* case initiated, citizen involvement was ample. From the writing of *amicus* briefs to grass roots campaigning, testimony before legislatures and Congress, and public declarations of support, numerous avenues of expression outside the courtroom have given this case a highly charged political character. Indeed, public debate has constructed this issue as popular spectacle. However, in Hawai'i, where the issue has dominated local politics for the past four years, only one labor union out of 118 made an affirmative declaration of support for marriage rights.[8] Even in the face of a constitutional convention directly threatening the interests of unions and gays and lesbians, there has been no movement towards common political opposition.

The second notable aspect of this history renders the sparse support of labor even more surprising. Despite the novelty of same-sex marriage, the principle by which *Baehr* was decided has become part and parcel of labor notions of fair play and due process: the right to be free of gender discrimination. Additionally, the idea that was solidified in public testimony and the findings of the Commission on Sexual Orientation and the Law, that the right to marriage has to be seen as a direct economic benefit denied gay and lesbian couples, is also a traditional issue of justice for unions: family benefits and their fair distribution.

Finally, this history demonstrates the critical importance of theorizing the public character of union support for gay and lesbian civil rights. As many of the chapters in this book demonstrate, labor has made accommodation with and directly supported gay and lesbian families, thereby actively participating in forging a new social revolution. In Hawai'i, the irrepressible politics of same-sex marriage have made domestic partnership and civil rights into issues of the public sphere where democratic demands and public policy rather than private accommodation matter most. This is especially the case for the powerful public unions in Hawai'i, whose bargaining is tightly constrained by the politics of marriage and domestic partnership. Additionally, incremental moves toward establishing domestic partnership agreements in the private sector are increasingly dominated by the marriage issue, appearing to some progressives as insufficient and to most opponents of gay and lesbian rights as an illegitimate recognition of status—an ersatz marriage.[9] Same-sex marriage is a unique and, to many, vexing political issue, but in Hawai'i, it has become *the* litmus test of civil rights commitments, especially for labor unions.

Labor's twentieth-century embrace of legal protection and civil rights as both "Magna Carta" and a language of citizenship (reflected in John Sweeney's quotation opening this chapter) has striking parallels to the commitments of same-sex marriage proponents.[10] In activist Barbara Cox's words, "Preventing same-sex couples from marrying treats us as second-class citizens. As long as this society refuses to legally recognize our relationships, gay men and lesbians cannot be equal members of the polity."[11] Acknowledging these common claims to equal citizenship voiced by workers, gays, and lesbians, we must again ask: Where have the unions gone on the marriage question?

Hawai'i Calls: Explaining Why the Unions Do Not Hear

Three structures of political language and argumentation—three discursive frames—surround the *Baehr* decision. Discursive frames are dominant structures of argumentation, oriented around a binary tension of competing ideas, through which political and social action is constructed. Discursive frames matter because of the underlying nature of collective action. As plummeting union density and the rise of new forms of collective action since the 1960s attest, the decline of the industrial economy has produced what Klaus Eder calls a decoupling of class and action, or an extinction of "once-natural" affinities between similarly situated class actors.[12] What has taken the place of traditional class politics is a complex field of interaction increasingly mediated by communication. For this reason, common interest and social attitudes are often insufficient to motivate action or alliance. Agency today is organized by discursive frames that provide meaning for signifiers used by collective actors to visualize social boundaries and reproduce identity. Relevant frames may be articulated by one party, or fixed through mutual conflict, but are just as often borrowed from previous struggles where they have been "secreted" within the hegemonic or commonsense "conception of the world."[13] Discursive frames resonate deeply with common cultural ideas, delimiting boundaries of action and identity or, because they expand that action in tactical ways, drawing in allies or electoral majorities larger than the size of the pool of primary identifiers might indicate.[14]

For example, unions have historically constituted themselves in opposition to capitalists and their market-based arguments as to why their interests in profit should be taken as the universal social interest. Union success has met with allegations of corruption, Communism, and lack of efficacy, while capitalists have been portrayed as rapacious, oppressive, and insufficiently nationalist. The articulated discursive frame—nationalist/anti-nationalist (or universalist/nonuniversalist)—makes a difference for the effectiveness of collective action by unions and business firms. In the case of gays and lesbians, their political actions to "come out" have led to conservative movements opposed to a liberalization of social mores that their presence is used to represent.[15] As Cindy Patton argues, these movements have relied on various claims about the value and meaning of civil rights to posture as an embattled minority deserving of public sympathy and support.[16] At issue are civil rights and the right to a public morality. The tactical reliance on discursive frames about "civil rights" in the struggle between conservative groups and their gay and lesbian opponents has made common cause between unions and gay and lesbian groups hard to produce.

To substantiate this argument, I would like to turn to a discussion of three discursive frames and how their activation within the debate over same-sex marriage has inhibited union support for same-sex marriage. Each frame marks a contest over the role of "civil rights" in democratic practice. The first relates to the social production of norms for social change; the second is an argument about the economic cost of rights and intervention into market relationships; the third is a political concern for the relationship between courts and electoral majorities. I call these frames activist/traditional civil rights, unlimited/scarce civil rights, and court/public democratic ideals.

Activist/Traditional Civil Rights

The Supreme Court opinion in *Baehr* acknowledged that there is no tradition of same-sex marriage in Hawai'i, or elsewhere, and thus, that there is no right to same-sex marriage which can be extracted from common practice. Nonetheless, the court reasoned that deep legal traditions of anti-discrimination, bolstered by the state constitution, prevent the state from limiting the recipients of marriage licenses. This ambivalence about the legal meaning of tradition has been further played out within the political debates and subsequent legal arguments surrounding the case. This discursive frame has had a direct impact on union commitments.

Perhaps the strongest tactical lines between opponents and proponents of same-sex marriage have been drawn with the rhetoric of "traditional marriage." For many conservatives in this debate, the tradition of heterosexual marriage is set against claims for civil rights by gays and lesbians that are said to be antagonistic to and even mock community values. As the leader of the largest coalition against same-sex marriage testified before one legislative committee, "It is clear that Hawai'i residents do not want to legalize same-sex marriage. It's time for the legislature to acknowledge this and put aside diversionary tactics, like specious civil rights arguments or twisting the equal rights amendment to achieve a purpose for which it was never intended."[17] Such a line drawn between "tradition" and "civil rights" is, for many conservatives, a barrier between valued ways of life on the one side, and complicity in extremism on the other. "I am opposed to compromising traditional marriage in an attempt to validate the alternative lifestyle of homosexuality.... We would be sacrificing what we know is right and what we know isn't," testified one conservative.[18] Arguments for changing tradition can only be seen in this frame as alien; as another opponent testified, "The well-financed push to weaken traditional marriage is a result of queer theory and the radical agenda.... Please don't kill the American family."[19] Even the state's attorney argued that "same-sex couples can be denied marriage on the strength of our cultural and moral traditions."[20]

In an attempt to resuscitate the traditional values embedded in the concept of "civil rights," supporters of the *Baehr* decision testified to the "state's long-held traditions of diversity, tolerance, acceptance of different cultures and family relationships, and a commitment to equality," to "traditional values and the principles of fairness and equity," and "Hawai'i's traditions of nondiscrimination and fairness to all."[21] This attempt to broaden the meaning of traditional practice reproduces the discursive frame distinguishing activist civil rights, and questions of what is right and civil, from what is commonly practiced, even while it embraces a progressive view of marriage rights. Those seeking access to marriage are asking for a traditional sanction of their relationship. That they must ask, and that such sanction must be given by courts, seems to support the conservative theme that same-sex marriage is something imposed according to the logic rooted in abstract ideals rather than custom.

One might expect that unions would feel an affinity with the more activist tradition and seek to support the side arguing for "civil rights." After all, there is much in the tradition of American labor, and the Hawaiian experience with labor in particular, that values activism. With John Sweeney's accession to the helm of the AFL-CIO came a stated commitment to recreate the traditions of activism that energized the labor movement of the 1940s, and to renew traditions to increase labor's organizing options.[22] Yet this discursive frame works against the call to progressivism by juxtaposing tradition against activism, a tension naturalized by the material context of labor's declining strength and its consuming efforts to hold on to what it once had, which displace struggles to expand its entitlements. In this way, the frame resonates with workers who see the commitment to civil rights protections for gays and lesbians, especially outside of the workplace, not as a matter of simple justice, as when something unfairly taken away is later returned, but something to be measured by the yardstick of appropriate activism or even personal energy and commitment. In this metric, the issue of marriage rights might be—and even should be—deferred to the future, even though it is present in legal time. This frame works against union assistance for marriage politics by making the costs of support seem "exceptional," defeating the idea of common interests.

The power of this frame was evident in my discussions with the leadership of major unions in Hawai'i. The head of the Hawai'i Carpenters Union made the political distinction between marriage and extended benefits for gay and lesbian partners, suggesting that his union could support the latter but not the former. Marriage "went too far and asked too much." Since gay and lesbian groups had not asked his support on the issue, he thought his union should remain publicly uncommitted.[23] The executive director of the Hawai'i Governmental Employees Association, the largest public union in the state, echoed the Carpenters' chief. He talked about his commitment to fairness, choice, and equal treatment in regard to benefits for nontraditional partners, but he drew the line at marriage. This was "not a good or timely idea," and he had privately told the legislature this during their deliberations, he averred.[24] The leader of the state teachers' union has long been committed to a public stance for her union in support of the *Baehr* decision and against the political machinations designed to weaken or kill it. However, with her board increasingly influenced by conservatives (who have been supported by conservative groups organized initially in opposition to the marriage issue), "the members are not ready for this."[25] Only the University of Hawai'i Professional Assembly (UHPA) overcame this frame, perhaps importantly because the leader of the Marriage Project sat on the board, as did three other gays and lesbians. This "personalized" the issue according to the union president and brought the legal time frame of the *Baehr* case into realistic alignment with the frame of traditional civil rights commitments. Rather than claiming that same-sex marriage was an open issue awaiting further decision making, UHPA's tactic was to argue that marriage, like other traditional equal protection issues, had been already decided. The union testified before the legislature that "Gays and lesbians comprise less than 3 percent of the population of Hawai'i, but they took on the State of Hawai'i in court, and they won fair and square.... To now change the rules on gays and lesbians is simply unfair."[26]

Unlimited/Scarce Civil Rights

If the activist/traditional civil rights frame erases the immediate pressure of the evolving court case from contemporary union commitments, a second frame reinforces the narrowing of union concern. This frame captures the essence of what I have called else-where "the political economy of civil rights," in which civil rights are depicted in a zero-sum relationship to one another. Some rights, particularly "special rights" for gays and lesbians, are seen as excessive or "inflationary" in the rights economy, threatening to crowd out other, more cherished rights and values.[27] The idea of a limit to governmental protection for individuals resonates with other contemporary discourses of scarcity and exclusivity endemic to American liberalism, but in the process it confuses civil rights based in the values of a free and democratic society with entitlements qualified by the level of economic development. Such rhetoric is especially appealing in the economic recession that has plagued Hawai'i since the early 1990s. This frame between scarce and unlimited rights establishes a tension between more recently articulated rights and older ones, valorizing older struggles such as the labor and civil rights movements over others such as that for equal marriage rights. It also encourages opposition to newer rights, as they may tend to devalue these other, more precious civil values.

Consider, for example, one central theme in the state's counter-intuitive argument to the court: that extending the proven benefits of marriage to gays and lesbians *harms* the rights and interests of heterosexuals. Using a market analogy, the state's attorney argued that policy preferences are directly threatened by the fiscal impact of extended rights: "Every dollar spent on a same-sex couple, or a cohabiting couple, of necessity strips a dollar from the [s]tate's ability to assist married couples."[28] This language was echoed by the Bank of Hawai'i, which published a letter in the Sunday newspaper explaining their lawsuit to halt the recently enacted domestic partnership law. "It is important for everyone in our community—individuals, unions and businesses—to aggressively address issues which impact the people of this state," the letter asserts, adding that, as a consequence of the domestic partnership law, "companies will no longer be able to control or even predict the cost of health care benefits. It will raise the costs of providing important benefits to those that are truly deserving and make it more difficult to provide quality dependent benefits. Indeed this legislation may have the effect of reducing dependent coverage—not increasing it." As the bank sees it, "We must maintain a cost structure which allows us to provide cost-effective products and services to our customers and to compete in today's global economy."[29]

The politics of scarcity sweeps along within its conservative economic logic a fond-ness for entrepreneurialism. Groups demanding rights should demonstrate not only that their demands cost little, but that they provide concrete benefits to the common-weal. As a leader of the largest anti-gay-marriage group testified before the legislature, in assessing the proposed bill to constitutionally block same-sex marriages, "we should be discussing the economic and sociological impact same-sex marriage would have on our community. However, debate is continually sidetracked with the issue of civil rights. . . . An equal status for same-sex couples is not supported by evidence of equal contributions to society."[30]

When this same entrepreneurial language is used by proponents to argue that same-sex marriage could have direct economic advantage to the state—by reaping the pent-up national demand for gay and lesbian nuptials—opponents argue that it cheapens and denigrates rights through the sale of the state's police powers over health and safety, thus delegitimating gays and lesbians who would stoop to talk about marriage in such materialist terms. As the State of Hawai'i sarcastically argued to the court, "If Hawai'i is willing to legalize same-sex marriage, why not legalize prostitution, gambling, marijuana, or even better, child prostitution? That would probably be even more lucrative—in the short term."[31]

The argument between those who see rights as expandable and ultimately beneficial to an economy and those who argue for their scarcity due to the limits of fiscal responsibility has direct consequences for union support. In the expanding, post-war, Fordist economy in which union wages regularly increased, fueling high levels of consumption and production, workers' rights could be neatly equated with the general interest. In this framework, those rights grew as economic health increased. The civil rights movement and the women's movement would follow in labor's wake through the 1960s and 1970s. However, once the economy ceased its expansion in the mid-1970s, labor experienced the tension between its demands and the profit expectations of the private sector, as well as the homologous concerns for fiscal solvency of the public sector. In the new political economy, workers' rights represent only a particular interest, and other rights claims make competing demands on a limited economic base. As Offe and Wiesenthal point out, mature unions can resort to "opportunistic" strategies of survival, minimizing the need for the democratic collective action that was present early in their formation, and reaffirming the logic of the market.[32] In the years since Offe and Wiesenthal wrote, the market and the state have demonstrated their commanding power to weakened American unions, which quickly learned to go along, often at the cost of principled support for democratic rights.

In Hawai'i, this trend has become most noticeable in the marriage case. Unions have borrowed heavily from conservative and state discourses about the scarcity of civil rights, contributing their voices to the chorus arguing for fiscal restraint. Private and state sector unions are frequently divided on macroeconomic strategy, especially the role of state budgets on economic health. However, in times of recession, both types of unions find themselves victims of cost cutting. This has pushed them to develop similar positions on the economic value of rights. Union leaders in Hawai'i argued in interviews that the cost of new benefits for gay and lesbian workers which would follow either legalized same-sex marriage or the recognition of domestic partnership status was too high to bear and would weaken labor's already precarious position by slowing the economy. Private sector unions involved in the building trades have shown that they believe in awaiting the economic tide that will float all boats; the added cost of new beneficiaries was, in their minds, too much added ballast. Public union leadership voiced similar concerns about the state's ability to afford the cost of new benefits in the midst of chronic budget shortfalls.

Even after the domestic partnership legislation was signed into law, many unions continued to thwart the law in its first few months, convinced by the growing clamor of business that it would cost too much. The force of this argument was evident in discussions about health benefit policies across the state. In their first meeting after the requirement to extend benefits took effect, union trustees for the Health Fund insurance pool accepted the legal requirement for inclusion of domestic partnerships but debated (without resolution) who should pay. Many argued that the added cost of beneficiary coverage should be absorbed by the workers requesting coverage and should not become a burden to the state. A settlement of the issue is still not apparent. The teachers' union, which offers an attractive private insurance plan, voted through its health trustees to exclude domestic partnerships because of the added cost. Those demanding such coverage are being urged to rejoin state insurance coverage instead.

Court/Public Democratic Ideals

Why have such obvious double standards that go against the grain of valued democratic traditions of solidarity been allowed to continue within Hawai'i's unions? The always complicated relationship between union leadership and rank and file has been exacerbated by a third discursive frame surrounding the marriage case, which has worked rhetorically to separate electorates from courts upholding civil rights, creating a tension that has important ramifications for union action.

The tension between courts and publics is raised in the marriage case through the common argument that the courts have usurped traditional legislative prerogative, thereby necessitating the patriotic restoration of democratic sovereignty. According to some revealing citizen testimony, gays and courts are "forcing" an interpretation of marriage onto a reluctant majority—a clear case of "judicial tyranny."[33] A co-chair of Hawai'i's Future Today, a conservative group opposed to same-sex marriage, testified before the legislature that, "given the results of several public opinion polls, it is clear that Hawai'i residents do not want to legalize same sex marriage." She held that it was "the responsibility of the legislature to act on behalf of the people" and pre-empt a contrary decision by the court. "It's times like these that make me grateful I live in a democracy," she stated.[34]

The state bolstered this conservative rhetoric with its arguments to the court that marriage was a special case and could not be subsumed under normal legal categories. According to the attorney general, the state cannot be neutral when it comes to domestic politics, and so must choose between wishes of the majority and the antagonistic rights of minorities. "Marriage is too deeply enmeshed in conventional morality to fit neatly into an equal rights analysis."[35] Legalizing same-sex marriages is an endorsement that will promote more same-sex couplings, encourage more same-sex families to have children, and lead to more social ills.[36] "To legalize same-sex marriage will send a message that will devalue and weaken the very relationship that is critical to draw men to their children," the state argued to the court, adding that it would encourage AIDS, harm women, and confuse children.[37]

These arguments have been used to support the claim that equal rights for gays and lesbians are "special rights" that impede the function and efficiency of democratic majorities. This idea has special relevance for labor unions, which have themselves been labeled as "special interest groups" seeking public rents without an equal exchange of public gains. Such rhetoric, however, has not made unions the natural allies of other "special groups"; instead, unions have tried to escape the contagion effect by backing away, unwilling to challenge the conservative implications of this discursive frame. As with the case of the constitutional convention, it is not that the unions actually endorse this notion of democracy. Rather, the matter is one of expediency. As long as law is open to challenge on grounds of majority rights, many unions are unwilling to act on any other principle. For this reason, the teachers' union, which had separated health benefits of domestic partnership families from families constituted through marriage, welcomes a legal challenge to their decision. "We have nothing to fear from litigation except clarity in this matter," the president reported in an interview with the author. Litigation would not only clarify the duties of leadership to members of the union who have domestic partners. It would also serve as a strong signal to the rank and file—who are not immune to the conservative backlash against the marriage case—that democracy cannot be opposed to equal protection arguments.

Indeed, legal uncertainty appears to be the very concern that killed an opportunity for the teachers' union board of directors to consider a policy statement advocating same-sex marriage. The union's Youth and Human Civil Rights Committee had endorsed support for the *Baehr* case but, according to the committee's chair, balked at submitting the resolution to the board for consideration. The committee feared that a refusal to endorse the issue would fuel conservatives within the union, and the public without, thereby doing more harm to the issue than silence ever could.[38] Democratic commitments could not be heard clearly amid the uncertain status of legal authority.

A Hawaiian Wedding Song

Impediments to successful alliances between unions and gay and lesbian groups concerned with the marriage issue are many and broad. The discursive frames that constitute democratic debates make most unions wary of defending rights, even when those rights directly impact some of their members. Equal rights for gays and lesbians are seen by unions to reach too far, cost too much, and further isolate unions already vulnerable to low public opinion. What, then, can be learned from the single case where an alliance was made?

The University of Hawai'i Professional Assembly, a union of university and community college professors, bucked the trend for several reasons. First, it had an understanding of the marriage case almost from its inception because one of its active board members and chair of the political action committee was also a leader of one of the first community groups organized to raise support for the plaintiffs. According to Tom Ramsey, this three-fold position allowed him to educate the union president, who came to slowly appreciate the justice in the position, and the union's responsibility for its gay and lesbian members. The cause became her personal passion. This, however, was prior to the construction of the issue through predominantly public discursive frames.

The support of the UHPA stands in contrast to the teachers' union, which also had gay and lesbian activists who were involved early in the case, and a president committed to the issue. However, unlike the UHPA, the teachers union had no formal and few informal channels of communication between the board of directors and the special committee that was empowered to consider civil rights issues. By the time the committee decided to bring its recommendation of support to the board—months after the professors had publicly announced their position—the stakes seemed too high, opposition on the board had already been voiced, and the issue languished.

Another reason for UHPA support of the marriage case was the presence of several self-identifying lesbians and gays on the board at the time this issue came up for discussion. According to many on the board, this personalized the issue to an important degree. Where discussions in the abstract can easily draw on dominant discursive frames for reference, personal accounts of discrimination, reminders of common goals, and the recognition of diverse interests can break through the bonds of convention and formulate commitments to the new opportunities at hand.

The membership of UHPA was a third factor. University and community college professors take occupational pride in free thinking. This often leads to explosive debates between union leadership and some rank and file, especially on controversial political issues. Polls taken shortly before the union's decision to endorse same-sex marriage (and reward political candidates with compatible positions) revealed that 25 percent of the faculty were strongly opposed to same-sex marriage, and another 24 percent were slightly opposed. That left only the barest of majorities who were in favor of or unconcerned about the issue, a poor base of support for a politically risky endeavor. However, in this particular case, outrage by those opposed was successfully deflected by another issue. The union leadership simultaneously voted to support a call for legalized casino gambling to bolster the economy, which they knew had even less support among the faculty. This other issue evoked a vehement set of responses from the membership, eclipsing same-sex marriage as a strong political litmus test.

In sum, the factors favoring UHPA's endorsement of same-sex marriage were fortuitous and enabled by organizational design. Although it is risky to pluck practical ideas from the winds of luck, this case does offer some insights into labor and gay and lesbian cooperation. The value of common projects engaging union and community interests, and the visibility of gays and lesbians within the union, stand in direct challenge to the discursive frames that tend to separate notions of gay and lesbian rights, identities, and even citizenship from those of other interested citizens and organizations. The "queering" of such boundaries through common endeavors may be an important strategy to consider in future struggles. Political theorist Shane Phelan captures this point with her notion of affinity politics. "The problem for coalition politics is not, what do we share?" she argues, "but rather, what *might* we share as we develop our identities through the process of coalition? Coalition cannot be simply the strategic alignment of diverse groups over a single issue, nor can coalition mean finding the real unity behind our apparently diverse struggles. Our politics must be informed by affinity rather than identity, not simply because we are not all alike but because we each embody multiple, often conflicting, identities and locations."[39]

Little suggests that professional or public unions have any organizational advantage over other unions in the practice of this type of coalition building. An exciting body of new literature is challenging the idea that blue-collar attitudes evince increased hostility toward or intolerance of gays and lesbians, suggesting little difference in structural homophobia between unions.[40] Additionally, public and private employers have voiced similar economic concerns about the increase in rights, militating against sectoral advantage when it comes to this issue. Nonetheless, the middle-class bias of many gay and lesbian organizations may increase the membership overlap with white-collar unions. Where strong democratic traditions (which can run in any union) permit dynamic coalitional politics between these organizations, then Phelan's vision can be realized.

Of course, legal cases often provide poor conditions for the development of these coalitions. Cases rarely progress as slowly as *Baehr*, or offer as many political opportunities for intervention. Even where there is opportunity for political organizing, coalitions that spring up in response to the sudden surprise of controversial legal decisions may not have the breadth or timeliness to combat the dominant discursive frames articulated in media and by political opponents. For this very reason, many union leaders privately wonder if there remains any effective role for labor in progressive politics, supposing they are willing to give voice to progressive issues. The window of opportunity is perhaps shut, or nearly so. The November 1998 vote on the constitutional amendment (which reads "The legislature shall have the power to reserve marriage to opposite-sex couples") soon showed 74 percent approval in opinion polls, and the influx of right-wing money from the Mainland to ensure its passage makes opposition a discouraging prospect for many.

Breaking the Limits to Union

That unions have missed the boat on same-sex marriage is tragic on a number of fronts. Trapped in dominant discursive frames that have reified tradition, issued a logic of scarcity, and overvalued electoral politics, unions have squandered their democratic legacy. In so doing, they have failed more than their gay and lesbian members demanding the benefits of full citizenship. They have also limited the transformational possibilities that their political weight could bring to a high-profile issue. Further, in failing to post a challenge to discursive frames, they have placed themselves in a vulnerable position when these same frames are used against generous public worker benefits and for the economic imperatives of privatization. As much as gays and lesbians have needed them in the past few years, unions themselves now need committed allies.

In attempting to build more effective coalitions and alliances, what can we learn from the Hawaiian situation? Hope for renewal of effective coalition politics in Hawai'i is perhaps best focused now on the constitutional convention where the overlap of concerned groups—from labor, to gay and lesbian, to Native Hawaiian—may permit affinity politics to emerge. Because the convention will culminate in an electoral referendum, conscious attention to the production of discursive frames and their hegemonic character to construct debates is an unavoidable political task. The hefty investments already made in rhetorical strategies surrounding the marriage issue make the tired tactics of reweighting the discursive frames unlikely to be successful, either in changing the tenor of the public debate or in building the common identities between various groups that could provide a new foundation for politics. Coalition politics focused on the convention may, however, produce a new frame capturing new lines of alliance.

Nascent groups now exploring broad alliances, especially Protect our Constitution, have begun to use a rhetoric of "citizenship," which could dominate the politics surrounding a constitutional convention and which holds a potential to play a significant role in the anti-marriage amendment vote. "No chinks in the armor of the

Constitution," and "a Constitution for all" are slogans under consideration by progressive alliances. They are designed to substitute a common political symbol for what has become a divisive set of frames isolating gays and lesbians. Asserting a common commitment to which diverse groups can adhere, a new frame of citizen/noncitizen generalizes the heart of the marriage debate and so raises the political stakes of exclusion. This frame can easily subsume the discourse that has made "civil rights" equivalent to "special rights" in the minds of many and, instead, assert a common sovereign status extending beyond the jurisdictional interests of courts and legislatures. At the same time, the opportunity for diverse progressive groups to work together in such a coalition may build mutual understanding and commitments, and transform identities to the degree needed for such a coalition to weather the future politics of division.

What is at stake for gays, lesbians, and labor? Here the lessons are easily stretched beyond the mid-Pacific. At a time when economic opportunities have stagnated, state budgets are tight, and social scapegoats are hunted, rights are not only essential to marginalized groups but are politically vulnerable to attack. Unions and gays and lesbians have much to gain from discourses that champion common citizenship and respect the value of collective action in its defense. There is an economic prize for labor here as well. The economy of scarcity—of opportunity and of rights—can be reorganized for the benefit of workers (and most citizens) when civil rights are successfully defended. The increase in economic security provided by increased access to marriage rights is similar to the concerns of public workers whose rights to bargain for benefit-rich contracts are threatened by calls for privatization. The same can be said for Native Hawaiians defending access rights for traditional gathering and the preservation of their culture. Defense of the commons—in this case, citizens' access to benefits: the closest approximation to a defense of social rights that America has to offer—is imperative when the options and their consequences are considered. The continuation of a rhetoric of scarcity, of blame, and of demagogic politics prevents the types of alliance that can make a difference.

Postscriptum

In November 1998, the constitutional amendment designed to derail the *Baehr* case passed with 69.2 percent voting in favor—far beyond what even the proponents predicted. In the waning weeks of the campaign, several unions lent their names to the fight against the amendment, but only the UHPA and the local International Longshore and Warehouse Union actively campaigned against it. To many insiders and observers of the campaign, it was little support too late. Opposition to the constitutional convention was led by a phalanx of public and private sector unions fearing alteration of the collective bargaining laws, and was vocally supported by both candidates for governor. The convention went down to defeat. The day after the election, the reelected governor, who supported the anti-same-sex marriage amendment, called for a new and extensive domestic partnership law for gays and lesbians in the interests of fairness. This was immediately denounced by the still-celebrating anti-marriage activists, who promised to fight on. As one activist stated, "It's a sad day for Hawai'i. Just one day after the people made it absolutely clear that we don't want same-sex marriage, the Governor declares that he will push for legalization of same-sex marriage in the legislature, but in the disguise of a different name.... This is an outrageous attempt to undermine the will of the people."[41] Whether labor unions will now use their legislative clout on behalf of domestic partnership in the face of such vocal opposition is the pressing concern for a chastened civil rights community in Hawai'i.

Notes

1. D. Osborne, "Lavender Labor: A Brief History," in *Homo Economics: Capitalism, Community, and Lesbian and Gay Life,* ed. A. Gluckman and B. Reed (New York: Routledge, 1997), p. 226.

2. See *Baker v. Nelson,* 191 N.W.2d 185 (Minn. 1971), appeal dismissed, 409 U.S. 810 (1972); *Jones v. Hallahan,* 501 S.W.2d 588 (Ky. Ct. App. 1973); *Singer v. Hara,* 522 P.2d 1187 (Wash. Ct. App. 1974).

3. C. R. Sunstein, "Homosexuality and the Constitution," *Indiana Law Journal* 70 (1994): 1–28.

4. Act of 22 June 1994, No. 217, Section 1 (p. 526), 1994 Haw. Sess. Laws. Act 217.

5. State of Hawai'i Report of the Commission on Sexual Orientation and the Law, 1995, p. 23.

6. Although it is the most extensive domestic partnership legislation ever passed in the United States, the Reciprocal Beneficiaries Act, as this legislation is known, was opposed by most gay and lesbian rights activists as insufficient. It was also opposed by the governor (who let it become law without his signature), the attorney general (who wrote an opinion gutting its most important provisions for medical insurance of domestic partners), and by the right wing (which assailed it as just another unmerited step on the path towards marriage). Unions wisely stood their distance.

7. D. Horowitz, *The Courts and Social Policy* (Washington, D.C.: Brookings Institution, 1977); H. Jacob, *Silent Revolution: The Transformation of Divorce Law in the United States* (Chicago: University of Chicago, 1988); M. McCann, *Rights at Work: Pay Equity Reform and the Politics of Legal Mobilization* (Chicago: University of Chicago Press, 1994).

8. The University of Hawai'i Professional Assembly testified before the legislature and gave vocal support to the Marriage Project. I will talk more about this union and the source of its political commitments later in this chapter.

9. J. Goldberg-Hiller, "The Status of Status: Domestic Partnership and the Politics of Same-Sex Marriage," *Studies in Law, Politics, and Society* (forthcoming).

10. The words are from AFL president Samuel Gompers about the Clayton Antitrust Act of 1914, which exempted labor unions from anti-trust actions under the Sherman Act. For a discussion of labor's early-twentieth-century attitude toward the law, see M. Dubofsky, *The State and Labor in Modern America* (Chapel Hill: University of North Carolina Press, 1994); and K. Orren, *Belated Feudalism: Labor, the Law, and Liberal Development in the United States* (Cambridge, UK: Cambridge University Press, 1991).

11. B. Cox, "The Lesbian Wife: Same-Sex Marriage as an Expression of Radical and Pluralist Democracy," *California Western Law Review* 33 (1997), p. 158.

12. K. Eder, *The New Politics of Class: Social Movements and Cultural Dynamics in Advanced Societies* (London: Sage, 1992).

13. A. Gramsci, *Selections from the Prison Notebooks of Antonio Gramsci* (New York: International Publishers, 1971), pp. 197, 199.

14. See A. Melucci, *Nomads of the Present* (Philadelphia: Temple University Press, 1989).

15. D. Herman, *The Antigay Agenda: Orthodox Vision and the Christian Right* (Chicago: University of Chicago Press, 1997).

16. C. Patton, "Tremble, Hetero Swine!" in *Fear of a Queer Planet: Queer Politics and Social Theory*, ed. Michael Warner (Minneapolis: University of Minnesota Press, 1993); and C. Patton, "Queer Space/God's Space: Counting Down to the Apocalypse," *Rethinking Marxism* 9 (1997): 1–23.

17. Testimony of Debi Hartmann, Co-chair of Hawai'i's Future Today, House Hearing on Constitutional Amendment Relating to Marriage, 21 January 1997.

18. Transmitted testimony of Scott VanInwagen, dated 19 January 1997, for House Hearing on Constitutional Amendment Relating to Marriage, 21 January 1997.

19. Transmitted testimony of Janis Judd, dated 20 January 1997, for House Hearing on Constitutional Amendment Relating to Marriage, 21 January 1997.

20. State's post-trial brief, *Baehr v. Miike*, 25 October 1996, p. 4.

21. Transmitted testimony of Vanessa Chong, Coalitions Coordinator, Coalition for Equality and Diversity and Clergy Coalition; of the Japanese American Citizens League; of Patrick Taomoae, American Civil Liberties Union of Hawai'i; dated 19, 20, and 18 January 1997, respectively, for House Hearing on Constitutional Amendment Relating to Marriage, 21 January 1997.

22. F. Gapasin and M. Yates, "Organizing the Unorganized: Will Promises Become Practices?" *Monthly Review* 49 (1997): 46–62; and K. Moody, "American Labor: A Movement Again," *Monthly Review* 49 (1997): 63–79.

23. Interview with Walter Kupau, Financial Secretary-Treasurer, Carpenters and Joiners of America, United Brotherhood of Local 745, 6 August 1997.

24. Interview with Russell Okata, Executive Director of Hawai'i Governmental Employees Association, 13 August 1997.

25. Interview with June Motokawa, President, Hawai'i State Teachers Association, 20 August 1997.

26. Testimony of University of Hawai'i Professional Assembly, for House Hearing on Constitutional Amendment Relating to Marriage, 21 January 1997.

27. J. Goldberg-Hiller, "'Entitled to Be Hostile': Narrating the Political Economy of Civil Rights," *Social and Legal Studies* 7, no. 4 (1998): 517–538.

28. State's post-trial brief, *Baehr v. Miike*, 1996, p. 34.

29. *Honolulu Advertiser*, 13 July 1997, p. A33.

30. Testimony of J. S. Keali'iwahamana Hoag, for House Hearing on Constitutional Amendment Relating to Marriage, 21 January 1997.

31. State's post-trial brief, *Baehr v. Miike*, 1996, p. 55.

32. K. Offe and H. Wiesenthal, "Two Logics of Collective Action: Theoretical Notes on Social Class and Organizational Form," *Political Power and Social Theory* 1 (1980): 67–115. See also K. Moody, *An Injury to All: The Decline of American Unionism* (London: Verso, 1988).

33. Peter Brandt, Testimony for House Hearing on Constitutional Amendment Relating to Marriage, 21 January 1997.

34. Testimony of Debi Hartmann, for House Hearing on Constitutional Amendment Relating to Marriage, 21 January 1997.

35. State's post-trial brief, *Baehr v. Miike*, 1996, p. 10.

36. *Ibid.*, p. 24.

37. Transmitted testimony of Professor Lynn D. Wardle, dated 17 January 1997, p. 12, for House Hearing on Constitutional Amendment Relating to Marriage, 21 January 1997.

38. Interview with Tom Aitken, former chair of the Youth and Human Civil Rights Committee of the Hawai'i State Teachers Association, 26 September 1997.

39. S. Phelan, "The Space of Justice: Lesbians and Democratic Politics," in *Social Postmodernism: Beyond Identity Politics,* ed. L. Nicholson and S. Seidman (Cambridge, UK: Cambridge University Press, 1995), p. 345.

40. Gluckman and Reed, *Homo Economics*; and S. Raffo, ed., *Queerly Classed: Gay Men and Lesbians Write About Class* (Boston: South End Press, 1996).

41. Press release of Mike Gabbard, Chairman of Alliance for Traditional Marriage.

Jacqueline Leckie

---

8   **Silence at Work: Trade Unions,
Gender, and Sexual Diversity
in the South Pacific**

Peni lives on one of the islands in the South Pacific. He has a reputation as an excellent nurse and aggressive unionist. His coworkers and patients respect his decisiveness and strong personality, but they know little of the contradictions he has battled throughout his working life. His conversation ranges from in-depth analysis to sharp, campy humor, and he reflects warmly on a childhood spent in the company of strong professional women. His mother and many of his aunties were nurses, a respectable career for Pacific Islands women, typifying the feminine virtues of caring, devoted service, and long working hours with little financial reward. Peni, although male, chose to follow in their footsteps and became one of the few men in this particular women's domain. Although his career choice was liberating, allowing him to develop traits considered effeminate, he fell into another gender trap; he was forced to accept the inadequate pay and skills recognition, limited promotion, and demanding stressful work considered natural to a woman's lot. In reaction, Peni has become an outspoken union and health advocate. At the end of the day, however, he cannot legally declare his homosexuality. To break this silence could cost him not only his career but his personal liberty. He can publicly agitate for workers' rights, but even this liberty is tenuous in a political, economic, and ideological context where employers and the state resist independent unionism.

Peni's story is not unusual. Throughout the South Pacific islands, the rule has been silence on sexual diversity issues, and trade unions have not broken it. This silence can be partly explained in terms of the contradictory ideologies in Pacific Islands societies—conflicts about sexuality and gender and about workers' rights and representation. This chapter explores some of the sources and consequences of the silence, first by outlining the cultural context within which sexual diversity and gender is understood within the Pacific region, then discussing the legal frameworks that impede progressive change. From there, the chapter shifts to an examination of the emergence and character of trade unions in the Pacific region and their lack of response to sexuality and gender issues. Ultimately, trade union timidity on issues of gender and sexual diversity must be understood as a reflection of the legacy of colonialism, current economic and legal realities, impediments in law, and contradictions in cultures. Despite the forces arrayed on the side of silence, however, the human rights environment of the Pacific region is on the threshold of change, and this may have a liberating effect on labor unions.

The South Pacific refers to a vast area, covering the world's largest ocean, in which there are thousands of islands and diverse cultures. The region includes American Samoa, Cook Islands, Fiji, French Polynesia, Kiribati, Nauru, New Caledonia, Niue, Papua New Guinea, Samoa (formerly Western Samoa), Solomon Islands, Tokelau Islands, Tonga, Tuvalu, and Vanuatu. Although Aotearoa (New Zealand), Hawai'i, and some states within Micronesia are often identified as part of this oceanic grouping, they do not feature in this chapter. Many of the populations in the South Pacific are tiny, such as Niue's 2,300, but bigger concentrations include Fiji (800,500) and Papua New Guinea (4,141,800).[1] Differences in natural resources have contributed to varying levels of economic development. Most Pacific societies retain a strong subsistence base but also have increasingly become dependent on a cash economy.

The legacy from the colonial past figures strongly today. From the nineteenth century, Pacific societies became incorporated through differing political arrangements under British, German, French, New Zealand, Australian, Japanese, and American domination. Tonga escaped this colonial path, declaring its sovereignty in the nineteenth century as an autocratic Christian monarchy. In 1962, the New Zealand trust territory of Western Samoa was the first nation to achieve independence. Decolonization proceeded in most South Pacific colonies during the 1970s, although this step is yet to be taken in the French territories of New Caledonia and French Polynesia.

The cultural context is paramount in understanding patterns of sexual diversity in the Pacific and why unions have been silent on this issue. Historically, the region has been segmented into Polynesia, Melanesia, and Micronesia. Cultural generalizations based on these categories can easily become superficial, but the terms are still popular denominators of subregional identity. Polynesia lies in the central and eastern Pacific, covering a huge triangle with Hawai'i, Rapanui (Easter Island), and Aotearoa forming the axes, and Samoa and Tonga at the center. Fiji, also at the center of the South Pacific, contains Polynesian cultural patterns but is more generally considered part of Melanesia. Thousands of differing cultures in the western Pacific form Melanesia, including the states of Vanuatu, New Caledonia, Solomon Islands, and Papua New Guinea. Melanesian cultures have been essentialized as more egalitarian and less hierarchical than the chiefly societies of Polynesia, although such dichotomies have proved problematic. Fiji particularly defies rigid categorization, not only because of the wide range of chiefly traditions there, but also because almost half the population are of Indian descent. Thousands of tiny islands in the central and northwest Pacific constitute Micronesia. A wide diversity of indigenous cultures were subjected here to Asian and European influences, especially American colonialism.

Contemporary Sexual Diversity in the Pacific

Pacific cultures are still characterized by many outsiders as exotic and sexually permissive, based on simplified representations such as Gauguin's paintings, the movie *South Pacific,* and advertisements to entice the tourist dollar. European missionaries and explorers condemned and admired what they perceived as "Oceanic sexuality," including that of Polynesian men who identified as females. Such a man is known today in Samoa as a *fa'afafine,* a "man who behaves in the fashion of a woman"; in Tonga as *fakaleiti* (or the preferred self-identity *leiti*), "biologically male but widely recognized as woman-like"; in Tahiti and Hawai'i as *mahu*; and in Fiji as *wadua*.[2] Western obsession with the exotic is one explanation for the disparity between academic fascination with flamboyant transgender practices (and Melanesian "ritualized homosexuality") on the one hand, and disinterest in "ordinary" homosexuality on the other hand. Hidden and illegal activities are admittedly hard to study, but even homosexual court cases have attracted little academic analysis.

Transgendered people have long been part of Polynesian societies, although they were not accepted by all Pacific communities.[3] Transgender identities were less common in Melanesia, for example. In other cultures, young men were socialized to engage in ritualized homosexual activities, including anal and oral sex with older men.[4] Judy Bennett reports historical evidence of considerable homosexual activity among male migrants working on plantations in Solomon Islands. This contravened the mores of most Solomon Islands societies, which opposed any form of male homosexuality: "In the light of the prevailing sexual ideology, it was an admission of male weakness as much as a source of shame."[5] Similarly, Kerry James stresses divergence between practice and attitudes: "Tongan men generally show strong homophobia whether or not they sexually use *fakaleiti*."[6]

Contradictions between overt values and covert practice, different behavior standards for "home" and "away" communities, and differences within Pacific Islands cultures help us to understand the absence of gender and sexual issues in the political agendas of seemingly progressive organizations such as unions. Oversimplified assumptions about Polynesian tolerance of transgender identity are also confused when all *fa'afafine, fakaleiti,* or *mahu* are labeled homosexual, transvestites, or prostitutes, or when any Polynesian homosexual is called *fa'afafine*. Niko Besnier emphasizes the "complex, fluid and ambiguous" identity of gender-liminal people, noting that terms like homosexual, gay, transsexual, and transvestite "capture only one aspect of the category and at worst are completely miscontextualized."[7] As Besnier states, "Neither complete men or full women, fa'afafine waver back and forth between male privilege and the covert authority of women, between status degradation and social visibility. While some position themselves as pillars of fa'a-Samoa [Samoan culture] and can ascend the ladder of power and prestige in one or the other sphere of the Samoan social world, others emerge as rebels, whose playful defiance of the received order, particularly in matters of gender and sex, provokes the amusement, consternation, contempt, or a complex blend thereof among mainstream Samoans."[8] Transgender sexuality is part of Samoan and other Polynesian cultures, but this acceptance remains ambiguous, particularly when it merges with overt homosexual identity.

One of the biggest areas of silence is around female sexuality, whether heterosexual, homosexual, or transgender.[9] Besnier notes, "in contemporary Polynesian contexts, one does find women who dress like men, perform certain tasks for men, are traditionally responsible, are sexually aggressive with women and are given labels that mirror terms referring to liminal men."[10] These terms include *fakatangata* in Tonga and *fa'atama* in Samoa, meaning "in the fashion of a man," or *akin-on,* or *bayot,* the term for male cross-dressers, referring to Polynesian females who cross-dressed and engaged in male occupations.[11] The implication in the literature is that many fewer women than men identify as gender liminal or lesbian. The silence that allowed this misconception to develop, however, has been challenged by the more assertive feminist movements in the Pacific. Feminist academics have written and spoken about the complexity of same-sex relationships between women and courageously described the issues facing lesbians of Pacific Islands descent. However, no academic investigation of the double (or triple for ethnic minorities) barriers faced by lesbians has been undertaken in the Pacific Islands.

Tradition and Silences

Sexual and gender identities in the Pacific need to be considered within the context of local cultures. While there may be a general consensus among Pacific Islanders over what they identify as core to their separate and common cultures, there is still much contestation over the meaning of tradition. Today's "traditions" may stem from precolonial cultures but also reflect colonialism and Christianity, and they are being renegotiated within contemporary global change. Pacific Island traditions stress respect for hierarchy and authority, which in practice has resulted in unquestioning obedience to authority and severe limitations on collective and individual rights. There is little space for the concept of gender-based rights. Tradition, heavily influenced by Christian morality, has impeded public discussion of sexuality issues. The subject remains taboo within many Pacific Islands cultures.

Tradition in the contemporary Pacific also has implications for workers' representation. Neoliberal ideology reinforces anti-union sentiments that sprang from elements of original cultures in the Pacific Islands and colonial traditions. Appeals to an invented nationalism have been used by the state and customary authorities to inhibit the establishment and operation of trade unions. Unions have been dismissed as a foreign import, antithetical to the "Pacific Way." Where the weight of tradition and hierarchical authority is strongest, for example in the Kingdom of Tonga, workers' organizations are weakest. In the Pacific, ethnic solidarity and nationalism have been utilized to promote compliant unions—for example, the Fijian unions encouraged by some employers and chiefs in the aftermath of industrial unrest during 1959–1960. Some indigenous-based unions returned after Fiji's 1987 coups but did not attract sustained support.[12]

Tradition is integrally linked with kinship in Pacific cultures. Such ties can be fiercely protective of differing sexualities, especially of *fa'afafine,* but equally can restrain homosexual identity. Kinship loyalties have also tested workers' cohesion in the Pacific. During a prolonged public service strike in 1981 in Western Samoa, industrial action was portrayed as not just against fa'a-Samoa but a threat to kinship ties. Many families were divided over support or opposition to the strike. Personal ties, patronage, and authoritarian management still complicate labor relations in the Pacific. Consider the statements of Samoa's prime minister, Tofilau Eti Alesana, during a strike at Samoa's Yazaki industrial plant. "If you're Samoans who love your country, return to work," he advised, adding that the workers' appearance before the members of parliament was disrespectful. "I am a Samoan, I know the respect of a Samoan." Tofilau warned workers who were his kin or from his village that "you're wrong . . . being misled."[13]

Deference by young people for elders, and by women towards men, is a continuing cultural value in conflict with legislation and attitudes that endorse equality. Union organizers have frequently had to negotiate kinship bonds in the public sector, in larger industrial plants (such as Yazaki Samoa), and in smaller family enterprises. The intersection of kin-linked labor relations with moral or religious issues is a further cultural constraint on organized labor advocating sexual diversity concerns.

Colonialism has left Pacific Islands societies with ample reasons to be suspicious of outside influences. This caution can spill over into bigotry and repression. Rather than positively nurturing dynamic cultures, such caution can articulate conservative moralities and political and economic power. Challenges to these ideologies and structures have come from labor and women's movements, although within these movements there is a wide diversity of attitudes to traditional values. Colonial and indigenous authorities dismissed workers' unrest and collective organizations as infiltration by foreign dissidents that were not part of Pacific cultures.[14] Feminism has frequently been brushed aside as a foreign, middle-class preoccupation. This dismissal extends to silence over issues of violence and sexual abuse against women and children. Although gender-liminal people (such as *fa'afafine*) as individuals are accepted as part of Pacific cultures, contemporary gay or queer culture is often feared as another foreign scourge. Hostility to this style of overt homosexuality is evident, for example in Fiji, in negative reactions to the region's first openly gay tourist resort, "Man Friday." Such attitudes have been heightened by popular perceptions that AIDS is a Western contamination, spread by homosexuals. These attitudes may mean that discrimination against gay foreigners will increase. In 1996, Samoan authorities refused a reentry immigration permit to the male partner of a New Zealand male lecturer simply because it was "a very delicate matter."[15]

Tradition and culture in the Pacific have been thoroughly penetrated by the ideologies of the Christian churches. Until recently, the issues of homosexuality and gender diversity have been excluded from the public agenda, partly because of the churches' silence over all aspects of sexuality. This morality stems from missionary influence, a fundamentalist interpretation of the Bible, and a widespread, mistaken myth that Pacific Islands cultures do not discuss sex. However, as Sitiveni Vete (the South Pacific Commission's AIDS specialist) wryly observed, church officials do not hesitate to give public space to homophobic views. Archbishop Mataca, head of the Roman Catholic Church in Fiji, articulated a widely held view when he declared: "Homosexuality has no place in the church. The only legitimate sexual union can take place between a husband and a wife. . . . All cultural and religious groups in Fiji treasure family values."[16] A spokesperson for the Methodist Church condemned "Westernized homosexuality" creeping into Fiji. "Fiji must also be cautious of Western influences. Not all good things come from Western civilization. We must base our future with sound Christian doctrine," he stated, noting, "we should treasure family values and teach our people to live a healthy moral standard." He warned that "Fiji is on the verge of a wrong and drastic turn."[17] The Catholic Church of Fiji continues to condemn homosexual activity as "intrinsically disordered" and "contrary to the natural law"; homosexual behaviors are "acts of grave depravity," and "under no circumstances can they be approved."[18]

Religious fundamentalism and indigenous nationalism returned in Fiji after military coups there in 1987. This was also a period of intensified opposition to organized labor. The hardening of such attitudes in some workplaces does not augur well for toleration of sexual diversity. For example, at the fish processing factory of PAFCO in Fiji, the company stepped up regular prayer meetings following an industrial dispute in 1993. The meetings attempted to quiet militancy by preaching the virtues of nonconfrontation, love, unity, and the ideology of "family togetherness" in the factory.[19]

The influence of conservative traditions and religious fundamentalism in labor relations and gender relations is strongly contested in the Pacific. To counter repressive rhetoric, some trade unionists, such as Kolonio Matala, general secretary of the Fijian Affairs Board and Provincial Council Employees' Association, have tried to turn the tables by appealing to Christian values: "when we workers want to enforce our God given rights to withdraw our labor in support of our opposition to the unfair wage freeze, fingers are quickly pointed at us that we are sabotaging the economy. This reminds us of the Bible story about the Lord's sermon to those people casting stones at a prostitute [let he who is without sin cast the first stone]."[20]

Progressive sections of the churches have networked with unions and activists to condemn abuses of human rights, nuclear and environmental destruction, the impact of structural adjustment programs, and the rise of poverty in the Pacific.[21] Recent public debate over the rights of homosexuals and people with HIV/AIDS has also swept through Pacific churches. Father Winston Halapua, dean of the Anglican Church in the diocese of Polynesia, has offered an alternative view to conservative attitudes. "There is no religious constraint to talking about sex when it is in relation to better physical and spiritual health," he asserts. "Where we see injustices, it is our duty to speak out and work towards changing things."[22]

The Law

The legal framework governing employment practices in the Pacific imposes further barriers to the discussion of gender and sexual diversity issues in the workplace and by unions. Most countries lack any legislation to promote equal opportunity or provide affirmative action in the workplace. The Samoan and Fijian governments have not ratified Convention No. 100 of the United Nations on equal pay for work of equal value, or Convention No. 111, which prohibits discrimination in employment. Although these countries ratified the United Nations Convention on the Elimination of All Forms of Discrimination Against Women (CEDAW), they have not translated it into practice in many employment areas. Indeed, legislation enacted during the colonial years still discriminates against women, for example, by restricting evening work and employment underground.[23] Progressive labor legislation, where it exists, is often not enforced for economic reasons or because of apathetic attitudes or corrupt public services.

Pacific women's groups are working to expose these discriminatory employment laws and win protection for the majority of women who are in casual, unregulated, and nonunionized work.[24] Any success they have in eliminating discrimination and promoting equity for women workers will eventually have positive implications for gender-liminal and homosexual workers. For them, however, the immediate problem is more basic. Pacific Islands countries, with the exception of Vanuatu, still have criminal laws against consensual homosexual behavior between adults.[25] Section 177 of Fiji's penal code states: "Any male person, who whether in public or private, commits any act of grotesque indecency with another male person or procures another male person to commit any act of grotesque indecency with him or attempts to do so is guilty of a felony and is liable for imprisonment for five years with or without corporal punishment."

No law in the Pacific Islands safeguards a person's HIV status or prohibits discrimination against HIV-positive persons. At least one employer is alleged to have dismissed an employee because of HIV-positive status. The legality of HIV screening in the workplace has not been determined in the South Pacific, but this would contradict professional confidentiality: "Where a special relationship exists, such as between doctor and patient, solicitor and client, or employer and employee, a common law duty binds the professional person not to disclose information about their client."[26]

Laws that discriminate on the basis of sexual orientation are likely to be challenged in Fiji because of the new 1998 constitution, which establishes a bill of rights. Under Section 38(1)(a), "A person must not be unfairly discriminated against, directly or indirectly on the ground of his or her actual or supposed personal characteristics or circumstances, including race, ethnic origin, color, place of origin, gender, sexual orientation, birth, primary language, economic status, age or disability."[27] A Human Rights Commission will enforce this, and a test case may be the recent employment dismissal of two women because of their declared lesbian identity.[28] Meanwhile, the existing penal code for male homosexuals will remain in force until parliament passes specific legislation changing or revoking it. Attempts to remove or amend Section 177 (quoted above) are evoking fanatical opposition. Archbishop Mataca warns: "To revoke anti-homosexual laws would mean a break-up of the family unit and a degradation of moral standards." Muslim leader Maulana Bashir Ahmad Diwan predicts that "if gay laws were legalized there would be social chaos."[29]

Fiji's new constitution offers a breakthrough for human rights and equity in the Pacific. Among the many progressive provisions, it allows affirmative action programs to be instigated for any community—a radical change from Fiji's 1990 constitution, which provided such policies only for indigenous Fijians. The new constitution also reconstitutes the appeals system against discrimination in promotions and appointments, which was suspended after the coups in 1987. Although the old system did not specify gender bias as grounds for appeal, the proposed new mechanism will do so.

The guidelines for Fiji's 1998 constitution were reached after intensive debate about the undemocratic nature of the 1990 constitution, which discriminated against Indo-Fijians, about 43 percent of the population. The Constitutional Review Commission, however, tackled more than the politically burning issue of race and ethnicity.[30] The findings of the many submissions to this review encouraged a general shift to greater recognition of individual rights and differences, while continuing to protect Fijian culture. International pressure pushed in the same direction, largely from within the ideology of unfettered global capitalism. Thus, although individual liberties may be extended, anti-union sentiments seem likely to persist in Fiji and the rest of the Pacific.

The Emergence and Character of Pacific Unions

Workers' collective organization in the Pacific Islands has long faced legal and ideological constraints of major proportions. Colonial heritage, cultural context, and economic and structural realities have shaped contradictory forms of assertiveness and accommodation within organized labor. Basic struggles for union recognition and wages above local poverty levels continue to preoccupy many workers. Human rights and equity issues have been threaded into demands for material betterment, but only recently has the gender dimension had overt recognition from unions. The following sketch of the checkered history of union development in the Pacific shows the context within which workers' divergent sexual identities have been silenced.

The relatively recent emergence of trade unions in the Pacific Islands reflects uneven industrial and capitalist development and the continued centrality of the subsistence base in these economies.[31] Workers' organizations came much earlier to Hawai'i and Fiji than to the rest of the Pacific Islands, particularly in the early days of the sugar industry.[32] The first trade union on record in Oceania was formed in 1884 in Hawai'i, the site of future militant and bloody struggles for workers' collective rights. In Fiji, an early attempt to unionize by the Fiji Wharf Laborers' Union was crushed, but this did not deter other workers and farmers from forming organizations.[33] The Fijian colonial state and employers used force, legislation, and the manipulation of ethnic loyalties to thwart assertive unionism. Other colonial states in the Pacific resisted militant unionization, but some encouraged compliant professional organizations among their civil servants. In 1943, the Fiji Public Service Association was formed and became one of the leading unions in the South Pacific.[34]

World War II had a profound impact on the growth of organized labor in the Pacific. Islanders fought alongside and worked for overseas armed forces, gaining an awareness of international workers' rights, trade unions, and the value of their labor. Workers in Fiji demonstrated their refusal to accept low wages and poor working conditions in several strikes during the 1940s. During the same period, laws for the recognition and functioning of trade unions were introduced in British and New Zealand colonies.

With the exception of Hawai'i and Aotearoa, trade union development within Polynesia and Micronesia was slow compared to most Melanesian countries. In some states, such as Tonga, even now there is no legal provision for workers' organizations (although the Tonga Nurses' Association and the Friendly Island Teachers' Association are active). In contrast, Cook Islands trade unions date back to World War II but became confined mainly to the public sector.[35] Unionization in Samoa has centered on the Western Samoa Public Service Association, which emerged in 1969. Private sector workers became organized during the 1990s, although there is still no legal provision for the registration of trade unions under Samoan law. As in many Pacific Island states, workers' freedom of association is guaranteed under the country's constitution. Waterside workers in Tahiti established a union there in 1946. Later, twelve other unions, organizing seamen, machinists, printers, nurses, police, and teachers, formed the Trades Council, affiliated to the Confédération générale du travail (General Confederation of Labor) in France.

Trade union legislation in Papua New Guinea stemmed from the 1963 Industrial Relations and Industrial Organizations Ordinances.[36] Following Australian models, this legislation legalized trade unions and established industry councils, boards of inquiry, industrial negotiation, and compulsory conciliation and arbitration. Even so, colonial labor legislation remained in place long after independence in 1975.

Since 1990, most national union centers in the Pacific have been part of the South Pacific and Oceanic Council of Trade Unions (SPOCTU), which is strongly committed to trade union education, human rights, and empowerment.[37] It has taken up the labor issues associated with political and economic restructuring in the Pacific and the increasingly globalized labor markets and concentrations of capital during the late twentieth century. At the same time, regional union issues—such as a nuclear-free, decolonized Pacific—continue to earn the attention of the SPOCTU.

Heated controversy throughout the Pacific over the proper political role for trade unions has led many members to take a negative view of activism on the wider social stage. From their inception in the region, however, workers' organizations have always provided important avenues for political expression, especially given the absence of political parties and universal suffrage through much of the colonial Pacific. Unions have played a part in social and democratic movements in the postcolonial Pacific. In the French Pacific colonies, for example, anti-colonial and anti-nuclear activism is a priority for the labor movement. In New Caledonia, the Union des syndicats des travailleurs kanak et exploiters, or USTKE, split from other unions to advocate independence from France and improvement in the welfare of indigenous workers. As late as 1995, a general union in French Polynesia, A Tia i Mua, was proactive in community protests about nuclear testing, which put its leader, Hirohiti Tefaarere, in jail for four months.

Fijian unions have been preoccupied by political issues after the 1987 coups. Indigenous and ethnic issues fomented divisions within and between unions. This has distracted attention away from common economic grievances.[38] Questions of gender diversity and parity in the workforce were sidelined by ethnic nationalism, such as a postcoup decree that 50 percent of the civil service be composed of indigenous Fijians and Rotumans. The sidelining of women's working issues on many union agendas in the South Pacific requires closer scrutiny. Rectification of this anomaly is fundamental to addressing the silence over sexual diversity by organized labor.

Women, Sexual Diversity, and Trade Unions

Early trade union development in the Pacific faced not only constraints from employers but also opposition from the colonial state. The transition from prohibiting to guiding collective workers' organizations was grounded in paternal, racial, and patriarchal

TABLE 8.1. Estimated Percentage of Female Members in
South Pacific Trade Unions

	Total membership	% female
Fiji	47,000	22
Papua New Guinea	130–140,000	*
Samoa	10,000	55
Solomons	30,000	25
Vanuatu	4,800	35
Cooks	2,000	45
Kiribati	4,800	40
Tonga	350	*
French Polynesia	*	10–20
Tuvalu	700	*

Source: South Pacific and Oceanic Council of Trade Unions, Survey of Trade Union
Development in the Pacific, 1993.
* Data not available.

relations and aspects of indigenous cultures. Local elites often felt threatened by workers' organizations. Although the trade union arena did become locally controlled, it was
overwhelmingly male and heterosexual. Women workers took covert action to improve
their pay and working conditions, but until the late 1970s, there was virtually no record
of women's issues making the agenda of Pacific Islands unions.

With the exception of Samoa, women are under-represented within unions in the
Pacific, in terms of numbers, leadership, and having specific concerns addressed (see
Table 8.1). Women's limited participation in the paid, unionized workforce is one reason given by unionists for ignoring gender issues. In Fiji, for example, one of Oceania's
more industrialized states, women were only 14 percent of the formal workforce in
1970. During the past two or three decades, there has been a noticeable rise in female
formal workforce participation throughout the Pacific; in Fiji, it jumped to 30.5 percent by 1993.[39]

Another factor in organized labor's silence over gender diversity was the concentration and marginalization of women at lower employment levels, often with inferior conditions. Two-thirds of women in paid labor in Fiji, for example, are employed in government and manufacturing. The public service in Fiji and Samoa is almost equally
composed of males and females but segmented by gender, with females concentrated in
health and education.[40] Here, as throughout the public and private sectors, more women
are employed at lower levels than men.[41] Following global trends, much of the growth
in new employment is among women workers in the service and manufacturing sectors. This work is generally poorly paid, casual, not unionized, and offers little security of employment. A 1994 report found the minimum wage in the Fijian garment
industry to be 85 cents an hour, which was much lower than in other manufacturing
areas.

Employers' preference to hire women for particular kinds of jobs draws on the traditional gender division of labor and creates a concept of "natural" women's work.
Global stereotypes about female work attributes are reproduced in the Pacific; nimble

fingers, dexterity, patience, speed, and efficiency are perfect qualifications for low-level jobs in the manufacturing and service industries. Poverty and desperation push women to accept their assigned place in the segmented labor market, as well as the unequal opportunities and exploitation they face in the workplace.

Gender stereotypes that structure employment patterns are formed long before women reach working age. Despite some changes, conscious and unconscious gender stereotyping persists within schools and homes in the South Pacific.[42] Many young women are pressured into pursuing occupations in "feminine" caring or service industries and are given little encouragement when they show interest in training in traditionally male-dominated courses. "It remains a standard practice that a wife subordinates career development to that of her husband, and the education of daughters to that of the sons. Consequently, equality of opportunity and treatment in training and education and employment is also dependent on a household's expectations of men's and women's roles in society."[43]

Many families in the Pacific show a reluctance for their daughters to take up tertiary trade or agricultural training. At the Universities of the South Pacific and Papua New Guinea, where over half of the undergraduates are women, there is a marked decline in female participation in postgraduate and advanced professional studies. Vocational-orientated tertiary education requires special targeting to enhance gender equity.[44]

The liminal role of transgendered people has particular relevance to this discussion of gender and work stereotypes. Extreme stereotypes about gender and work have mixed implications for the protection of working rights for transgendered people and homosexuals in the Pacific. Besnier stresses that labor participation is what fundamentally distinguishes gender-liminal men. They tend to follow what is locally considered women's work, such as crafts including mat and tapa making, paid and unpaid domestic activities, and employment in the manufacturing, hospitality, clerical, health, and education sectors. According to Besnier, "the gender-liminal person in Polynesia is commonly thought to excel in women's tasks: his mats are said to be particularly symmetrical and regular in shape, his domestic chores singularly thorough, and he is more resilient to tedium than the average woman. In urban settings, liminal men are superb secretaries and coveted domestic help. In this sense, liminal persons are more womanly than women, a theme that recurs elsewhere."[45]

Chris Peteru reiterates the "strong work ethic among queens" that leads to "plenty of employment offers in a country now demanding better standards from its work force."[46] But this is just one side of the story. Although the gender-liminal person may shine at "women's work," this can mean entrapment in the "women's room." Peni, whose story began this chapter, points out that not only are nurses exploited because they are mostly women, but many female nurses are resigned to their undervalued role. When it comes to the status of women in his country, Peni notes, "it's not much, their voice and their rights are not much." Peni finds the discrimination frustrating and "not fair to the women. I keep telling these women every time it happens, like they take away night allowance, I say you know they do it to you because you are women. If men were working here, if nurses were all men, it wouldn't happen. If they did it to the teachers, the teachers wouldn't stand up for it; they would strike immediately. But none of the women have responded; they all sit down and accept it, and that's why they continue to do it."[47]

Women's participation, as members and as leaders, is the biggest issue facing Pacific unions if they are to be representative of gender diversity in the workplace. Few women occupy executive positions in employment sectors or in unions with high female participation. For example, in 1990, 49 percent of Western Samoa Public Service Association (WSPSA) members were women, but only a few were union officers.[48] The number of female leaders in the banking and teaching unions in Fiji does not correlate with the high levels of female membership.

Male leaders have often attributed the discrepancy in participation rates to women being "passive and submissive" about union matters.[49] More recently, some men have recognized that this explanation "blames the victim" and that men have to take responsibility for their lack of gender sensitivity.[50] Another barrier to women's participation in unions is the male orientation of trade union culture. Fa'amanatu Osasa Nielsen, president of the Western Samoa Registered Nurses' Association, recalls "rude, undisciplined behavior" at WSPSA meetings.[51] Further, women face difficulties in attending meetings held outside office hours because of family responsibilities and opposition from their partners or elders about participation in male-dominated activities. Separate organizational forms for men and women may be appropriate in those Pacific cultures where public gender segregation is the norm. However, the multitude of labor, time, and emotional commitments to paid and unpaid work, family, community, and church would remain a continuing block to women's participation in union activities and leadership: "our traditional and cultural obligations ... [are] the hardest barrier to overcome."[52] Informal networking that integrates cultural and other identities offers the best hope of improving women's union commitment.

Until recently, women workers lobbied for separate sections within those unions with relatively high female membership. In 1979, the Fiji Public Service Association (FPSA) was one of the first unions to establish women's committees.[53] Their fate was similar to that of women's subgroups in bureaucratic, male-dominated institutions elsewhere: marginalization. Although the women's committees began with a promising agenda to tackle gender discrimination in the public service, few concrete measures were taken. Instead, women's committees took a prominent role in organizing sporting and social events.

It was not until the 1990s, partly under pressure from international union agencies, that Pacific Islands unions began to adopt structural and constitutional changes so that women's committees could be an integral part of the executive organization. More progress on this front is likely to come with increasing union amalgamation and the strengthening of national centers. Fijian unions have been the trailblazers, giving space to a national institution based on gender: the Fiji Trades Union Congress (FTUC) Women's Wing, established in 1983.[54] There was considerable debate over the extent to which the Women's Wing was marginalized from central union issues, with the result that some activist women chose to focus their energies as representatives of FTUC affiliates rather than of the Women's Wing. The FTUC constitution was amended in 1994 to specify that at least three members of the National Executive must be women.

Women have taken a proactive role in unions in Samoa, Tonga, and Cook Islands. WSPSA has a Women's Advisory Committee, and a woman, Vaosa Elisaia, is the director of WSPSA. Since 1994, the Solomon Islands Council of Trade Unions has included a Women's Committee and attempted to organize women's committees in each affiliate. Moreover, SPOCTU, the Pacific's leading regional union organization, has prioritized women's representation since 1990. A deputy chair position is reserved for a woman, and female unionists Elisaia, Ollie Pokana, and Susana Tuisawau have in turn been chairpersons of SPOCTU.

Significant investments of money and energy have been poured into educational programs to address gender discrepancies in Pacific Islands unions and workplaces. Initially, these were often couched within the framework of "women and development"; for example, the FTUC along with the International Confederation of Free Trade Unions (ICFTU) and Asian Pacific Regional Office (APRO) organized a seminar on women workers' problems and status in overall development.[55] A similar symposium in 1981 discussed ways to achieve greater involvement of women in trade unions, family health and working women, and employment prospects for "career women." Again, this came under the rubric of the contribution women could make to national development.[56]

By the 1990s, postcolonial states had come under widespread criticism about the beneficiaries of national development. Union and workers' gains were also under attack, while women were identified as the major group most vulnerable to poverty and exploitation in the workplace.[57] SPOCTU and the ICFTU-APRO inaugurated a major project in 1990 to integrate new and established women workers into trade unions in Fiji, Kiribati, Papua New Guinea, Vanuatu, and Samoa. The objectives of the project were to try to change attitudes, create women's awareness of their rights as union members, discuss issues specifically of concern to women, strengthen networking, and develop guidelines on all these issues. Positive outcomes included decisions by some unions to reserve official positions for women, to require equal participation by women in all union education programs, and to ensure that women's education would be facilitated by women.[58]

Six years later, addressing a FTUC/ICFTU-APRO seminar on gender perspective, Padma Dorai (ICFTU-APRO Director of the Women's Department), stated that globally and in the Pacific Islands, despite costly union educational projects, there had not been a commensurate impact on gender awareness at the grass roots levels of unions. This echoed an earlier concern raised by Ollie Pokana over poor communication and consultation by national union centers with women workers regarding SPOCTU's gender policies.[59] Other female unionists have denounced the entrenched resistance by union leaders to the need to seriously address gender perspectives in all facets of trade union activity. Consequently, a major education project from ICFTU's Equality Department for 1996–1998 has tighter guidelines and less ambitious goals than in the past. All teaching must involve male and female trainers, and 50 percent of participants should be male. This contrasts with earlier programs in which most facilitators were male and participants were female. Dorai urged that "change is not to be forced down people's throats" but brought about gradually through promoting gender awareness. One concrete goal of this project is the recruitment of new members, among which many are likely to be women. Each participating union must also set up a gender perspective team to monitor progress.

Diverse Issues, Diverse Silences

Toward the close of the twentieth century, the meaning and practice of human rights are under extensive debate in the South Pacific. It might be expected that this debate would embrace workers' rights and gender/sexuality issues. Yet, as we have seen in this chapter, these largely remain areas of silence. The silence surrounding workers' rights comes partly as a legacy from the colonial past, but it is reinforced by the continuing power of traditional hierarchies and stereotypes of ethnicity. Similarly, in the post-colonial Pacific, "culture" intersects with the demands of restructured labor markets to resist workers' organization.

Paradoxically, however, culture, gender, and ethnicity are increasingly being used as means to promote workers' organizations, that is, to develop proactive unions with a Pacific style. The report from a recent workshop held by the Western Samoa National Union of Workers shows how apparently contradictory elements are combined in one union's agenda: "Unemployment, family obligations to cultural activities, health and education are among some of the most important issues that concern union members. The union has a duty to address these issues."[60]

Unions in the South Pacific have tended to be silent on women's issues, let alone gay and lesbian issues. This is partly because women's work is located mainly in subsistence and informal sectors which unions have seen as outside their jurisdiction. The recent growth in export manufacturing has brought a marked feminization of the formal workforce in the Pacific, but women are still poorly paid and have little employment security. Although many of the new industrial workers are women, existing unions have been slow to act on their specific problems. Much of the impetus to recognize the gendered composition of the workforce came from other women-centered, non-governmental organizations. Recognition of women's potential to strengthen (even salvage) the labor movement has been slow in coming. The treatment of women's working rights and gender sensitivity most likely will provide a benchmark for future issues of sexual diversity in the workplace.

Increased awareness of gender inequality is a major objective for Pacific Islands unions, but recognition of the wider issues of sexual diversity has not been of concern to the leaders of trade unions or openly raised by workers. This silence seems to reflect the taboos of strongly Christian societies. As noted, transgender or liminal gender identity is accepted in many Pacific societies, but homosexuality that does not fall within such cultural limitations arouses more negative responses. In the contemporary Pacific, there is a growing polarization of public opinion between tolerance for diverse sexual identities and rejection amounting to homophobia. Union leaders claim that their primary role is to protect and reflect members' views—conveniently ignoring the fact that members are sharply divided over morality, sexuality, and the roles and status of women.

As long as Pacific Islands states continue to classify homosexual behavior as criminal, it is unlikely that labor discrimination due to sexual orientation will be a cause pursued by unions. However, *fa'afafine,* gays, and lesbians are certainly among the Pacific Islands workforce, and like Peni, they are active in their unions. Will sexual diversity make it onto the social agenda for the future? This author believes they should. Pacific unions have an important role as nongovernment community organizations, and especially as advocates of human rights and democratic development. The complex and shifting strands of identities involving sexuality, gender, and ethnicity need to be more seriously considered by unions so that all Pacific Islands workers are supported and protected as their region becomes integrated into the globalized labor and investment market.

Notes

1. United Nations Development Program, *Sustaining Livelihoods. Promoting Informal Sector Growth in Pacific Island Countries* (Suva, Fiji: United Nations Development Program, 1997), p. 10.

2. N. Besnier, "Crossing the Boundaries," *Illusions* (Winter 1996): 43; N. Besnier, "Sluts and Superwomen: The Politics of Gender Liminality in Urban Tonga," *Ethnos* 62, no. 1–2 (1997): 9; J. Mageo, "Male Transvestism and Cultural Change in Samoa," *American Ethnologist* 19 (1992): 443–459; and R. Watts, "The Polynesian Mahu," in *Oceanic Homosexualities,* ed. S. O. Murray (New York: Garland, 1992).

3. Besnier, "Sluts and Superwomen," pp.13–14.

4. G. Herdt, ed., *Ritualized Homosexuality in Melanesia* (Berkeley: University of California Press, 1984); and B. M. Knauft, "Homosexuality in Melanesia," *Journal of Psychoanalytic Anthropology* 10, no. 2 (1987): 155–191.

5. J. Bennett, "'We Do Not Come Here to Be Beaten': Resistance and the Plantation System in the Solomon Islands to World War II," in *Plantation Workers: Resistance and Accommodation,* ed. B. Lal, D. Munro, and E. Beechert (Honolulu: University of Hawaii Press, 1993), p. 148.

6. K. James, "Effeminate Males and Changes in the Construction of Gender in Tonga," *Pacific Studies* 17, no. 2 (1994): 65.

7. Besnier, "Sluts and Superwomen," p. 10; and N. Besnier, "Polynesian Gender Liminality Through Time and Space," in *Third Sex, Third Gender: Beyond Sexual Dimorphism in Culture and History,* ed. G. Herdt (New York: Zone Books, 1994), p. 287.

8. Besnier, "Crossing the Boundaries," p. 43.

9. S. O. Murray, "Female Homosexuality in Pacific Societies: Introduction," in *Oceanic Homosexualities,* ed. S. O. Murray (New York: Garland, 1992).

10. Besnier, "Polynesian Gender Liminality," p. 288.

11. Herdt, *Ritualized Homosexuality in Melanesia,* p. 75, n. 10; Hart cited in Murray, "Female Homosexuality in Pacific Societies," p. 399.

12. J. Leckie, *To Labour with the State: The Fiji Public Service Association* (Dunedin, New Zealand: University of Otago Press, 1997), pp. 133–139.

13. *Samoa Times,* 15 January 1993.

14. J. Leckie, "Nurturers or Watchdogs of Labour? New Zealand and Trade Union Internationalism in the South Pacific Islands," in *Pioneering New Zealand Labour History,* ed. P. Walsh (Palmerston North, New Zealand: Dunmore Press, 1994), pp. 80–101.

15. C. Peteru, "The Gay Life," *Pacific Islands Monthly* (October 1996), p. 43.

16. S. Vete, "Sex and AIDS: Myths That Kill," *Pacific Health Dialog* 2, no. 2 (1995): 134–137; and *Fiji Times,* 11 July 1994.

17. *Fiji Times,* 13 July 1994.

18. *The Sunday Times (Suva, Fiji),* 12 April 1998.

19. A. Emberson-Bain, "Backbone of Growth: Export Manufacturing and Fiji's Fish Tuna Wives," in *Sustainable Development or Malignant Growth? Perspectives of Pacific Island Women,* ed. A. Emerson Bain (Suva, Fiji: Marama Publications, 1994).

20. *Fiji Times,* 28 April 1989.

21. K. Barr, *Poverty in Fiji* (Suva: Fiji Forum for Peace and Justice, 1990).

22. Vete, "Sex and AIDS," p. 135.

23. M. Pulea, "The Legal Status of Women in the South Pacific," in *Women in Development in the South Pacific* (Canberra: Development Studies Centre, Australian National University, 1984), pp. 52–54.

24. A. Emberson-Bain and C. Slatter, *Labouring Under the Law* (Suva, Fiji: Fiji Women's Rights Movement, 1995).

25. United Nations Development Program, *Time to Act,* pp. 79–80.

26. *Ibid.,* pp. 89, 79.

27. *The Sunday Times* (Suva, Fiji), 26 July 1998.

28. *The Sunday Times* (Suva, Fiji), 12 April 1998.

29. *Fiji Times,* 11 July 1994.

30. P. Reeves, T. Vakatora, and B. Lal, *The Fiji Islands: Towards a United Future (Report of the Fiji Constitutional Review Commission 1996),* Parliamentary Paper 34/1996 (Suva: Government of Fiji, 1996).

31. C. Moore, J. Leckie, and D. Munro, eds., *Labour in the South Pacific* (Townsville, Australia: James Cook University of North Queensland, 1990).

32. E. Beechert, *Working in Hawaii: A Labor History* (Honolulu: University of Hawaii Press, 1985); N. Kent, "The Development of Trade Unionism in Hawai'i," in *Labour in the South Pacific,* ed. Moore, Leckie and Munro; and J. Leckie, "Workers in Colonial Fiji," in *Labour in the South Pacific,* ed., Moore, Leckie, and Munro.

33. K. Hince, "The Earliest Origins and Suppression of Trade Unionism in the Fiji Islands," *New Zealand Journal of Industrial Relations* 10 (1985): 93–101.

34. Leckie, *To Labour with the State.*

35. Leckie, "Nurturers or Watchdogs of Labour?"

36. M. Hess, *Unions Under Economic Development: Private Sector Unions in Papua New Guinea* (Melbourne, Australia: Oxford University Press, 1992.

37. J. Leckie, "Labour Regionalism and Internationalism: A Case Study of Fiji," in *Pacific History: Papers from the 8th Pacific History Conference,* ed. D. Rubenstein (Guam: University of Guam Press, 1992).

38. Leckie, *To Labour with the State,* chapter 6.

39. Fiji Bureau of Statistics, "Annual Employment Survey, Provisional Report, 1993" (Suva: Government of Fiji, 1996).

40. H. Booth, *Women of Fiji: A Statistical Gender Profile* (Suva, Fiji: Department for Women and Culture, 1994); Ministry of Women's Affairs, "A Statistical Profile of Women and Men in Western Samoa: Western Samoa Country Report," for United Nations Fourth World Conference on Women, Beijing, People's Republic of China, 1–15 September 1995.

41. International Labour Organization, United Nations Development Program, *Towards Equality and Protection for Women Workers in the Formal Sector,* South East Asia and Pacific Multidisciplinary Advisory Team (Suva, Fiji: International Labour Organization, 1997); and Ministry of Women's Affairs, "A Statistical Profile," pp. 4–5.

42. J. Leckie, "Gender and Work in Fiji: Constraints to Re-negotiation," *Women's Studies Journal* 13, no. 2 (1997): 127–153; and K. Thaman, "Women, Education, and Work," in *Women and Work: Proceedings of the Fourth Conference of the Fiji Association of Women*

Graduates, 29–30 January 1994, ed. Jean A. Maybin (Suva: Fiji Association of Women Graduates, 1994).

43. South Pacific Commission, *National Review of the Nairobi Forward-Looking Strategies for the Advancement of Women* (Noumea, New Caledonia: South Pacific Commission, 1995).

44. Fiji Trades Union Congress, "ICFTU/APRO Women's Symposium on Equality: Continuing Challenges and Future Strategies," 1989.

45. Besnier, "Polynesian Gender Liminality," pp. 296–297.

46. Peteru, "The Gay Life," p. 42.

47. Interview with Peni, October 1996.

48. K. Hince and M. McFarland, *The Western Samoa Public Service Association: A Brief History* (Wellington, New Zealand: Industrial Relations Centre, Victoria University, 1997), p. 50.

49. *News from F.P.S.A.* 4, no. 1 (April 1977), p. 3.

50. International Labour Organization, *Towards Equality and Protection.*

51. Hince and McFarland, *The Western Samoa Public Service Association,* pp. 50–51.

52. Fiji Trades Union Congress, *Report of Activities: June 1994–May 1996* (Suva: Fiji Trades Union Congress, 1996), p. 71. See also A. Chhachhi and R. Pittin, "Multiple Identities, Multiple Strategies," in *Confronting State, Capital and Patriarchy: Women Organizing in the Process of Industrialization,* ed. A. Chhachhi and R. Pittin (Houndsmills, UK: Macmillan, Institute of Social Studies, 1996).

53. Leckie, *To Labour with the State,* pp. 62–64.

54. *Fiji Labour Sentinel* 6 (July 1983).

55. *Fiji Labour Sentinel* 2 (October 1979).

56. *Fiji Teachers' Journal* 3 (1981).

57. J. Bryant, *Urban Poverty and the Environment in the South Pacific* (Armidale, Australia: University of New England, 1993); Emberson-Bain, "Backbone of Growth; C. Harrington, "Impact of Global Restructuring on Women in the Garment Industry," paper presented to Women in Politics Conference, UNIFEM, Fiji, 18 November 1996; Leckie, "Gender and Work in Fiji."

58. South Pacific and Oceanic Council of Trade Unions, "Survey of Trade Union Development in the Pacifics" (Brisbane, Australia, 1993), unpublished report.

59. *Pacific Unionist* (newsletter of SPOCTU/ICFTU/APRO) no. 12 (April 1993).

60. *Pacific Unionist,* no. 22 (September 1997).

Shane Ostenfeld

9   Sexual Identity and the Australian Labor Movement in Historical Perspective

Employment discrimination against sexual minorities, ranging from nonhiring to harassment and violence on the job, has been just as prevalent in Australia as in comparable countries.[1] The masculinist Australian labor movement might be presumed complicit in this discrimination. From the time that lesbians and gays began to organize into a social movement in the 1970s, however, the industrial and political wings of labor have proved to be the most receptive and actively supportive institutional forces within Australian society.[2] This receptivity can be attributed in part to the growing strength of white-collar workers in the organized labor movement and in part to the alliance that united the women's and students' movements with the gay liberation movement and labor in an attempt to ward off the forces of the right within labor and in wider Australian society.

With employment discrimination high on the agenda of the nascent gay and lesbian liberation movement, Australia's centralized industrial relations regime meant that gay and lesbian activism was directed at legislative action by the state. To this end, gay and lesbian liberation groups worked within trade unions toward union policy formulation aimed at influencing state and federal Labor party governments. The leadership role played by the Labor party, and by the unions directly, while not unfaltering, was decisive in achieving positive change. This chapter describes the Australian labor movement and recounts some of the history of the accomplishment of progressive legislation in support of gay and lesbian issues in Australia, on a government by government basis. The focus is on legislative attempts to address employment discrimination and the reform of criminal law.

Some background on the Australian political system is required to clarify the intricacies of the political history to be described. Originally inhabited more than 40,000 years ago, Australia met with a white invasion dating from 1788, when the first fleet of soldiers, convicts, and free settlers arrived from Britain. A series of six colonies were established through the course of the nineteenth century: New South Wales, Tasmania,

Victoria, Queensland, Western Australia, and South Australia. These became the states of the Commonwealth of Australia upon federation in 1901. At the same time, the Australian Capital Territory was established as the site of the nation's capital, Canberra. Remaining territories and protectorates include the Northern Territory, a large land mass with relatively sparse population.

In the post–World War II era, the major political parties in Australia have been the Labor party and the more conservative Liberal/National Party coalition. The parties engage in electoral combat for lower house majorities in Australia's national (commonwealth) and state parliaments. A lower house majority enables a party to form a government. An upper house is also found in all Australian parliaments except that of Queensland. In the commonwealth parliament, the lower house is called the House of Representatives and the upper house is called the Senate. The senate is designed to protect the interests of the states, each of which is represented by twelve senators. In operation, party lines are dominant. In the state parliaments, the lower houses are known as legislative assemblies and the upper houses as legislative councils. The role of the upper houses is mainly to review government legislative proposals, although the upper houses may also initiate legislation.

Labor in Australia

Noteworthy features of the Australian labor movement include its level of institutionalization within Australian society, its "masculinism," and its ideological cleavages. An understanding of these features is crucial to an understanding of the importance of labor to the gay and lesbian movement and the nature of their interaction. The early history of Australian trade unionism sheds some light on the institutional importance of labor in Australia. The masculinism of the labor movement, compounded by a strong Catholic right wing, means that the only hope for positive interaction between labor and the gay and lesbian movement in the 1970s and later would come through unions of the left.

The early trade unions of Australia date from the 1820s, beginning as small, craft-based organizations. Unionism later spread to include miners, transport workers, shearers, and factory workers. Workers formed confederations in the form of peak union councils in major cities, with links between the unions in the various colonies beginning in 1879.[3] The great strikes and economic depression of the 1890s followed. The role of the state in developing the Australian economy in the nineteenth century provided a base for state intervention, which brought about commissions to conciliate industrial disputes and arbitrate where agreement between unions and employers could not be reached. This was seen by liberals as an elixir against a repetition of the social disruption caused by the strikes. With this state machinery in place in the first decade of the twentieth century, encompassing the recognition and registration of trade unions, union membership rose to around 50 percent of the workforce, where it remained until decline commenced in the 1980s.[4]

Given their defeat in the strikes, and the coalition of employer and state against labor, Australian unionists perceived that the influence of employers on the state would diminish if labor won direct representation in parliament. In New South Wales, the

Labor party won 35 out of 141 legislative assembly seats in the 1891 elections, but the party soon split over protection and other issues. Nevertheless, Labor won enough seats to be an influential player, and by 1910, the party won majority government both in New South Wales and federally. The Labor party has been particularly successful at state level. There, unions have won major concessions through legislation rather than industrial action.[5] This would be the pattern of achievement in relation to the rights of gay and lesbian workers during the latter part of the twentieth century.

Tolerance for unionism and a Labor party in Australia are partly explained by the notion of "mateship," the myth of the practical, egalitarian, and hospitable Australian male.[6] Mateship might not necessarily translate to a positive disposition toward gays and lesbians, however. Turn-of-the-century foundations led to the veneration within the Australian labor movement of frontier masculinity. As industrialization took place, the rough masculinism of the Australian bush was supplanted by craft masculinism, whereby the collective image of the skilled worker was transmitted by a "guarded system of apprenticeship." The trade workshop underscored the link between skill and patriarchy in Australian working life. The trade apprenticeship initiated boys into skilled manhood with the rites and rituals of nineteenth-century apprenticeship, including ritual sexual humiliation, playing a central role in the reproduction of a masculinist craft identity. In some key industrial areas, craft culture and practices persisted in Australia until well beyond World War II.[7] This masculinist legacy fueled the perception that gay and lesbian movements of the 1970s and later would not get a hearing from the blue-collar-dominated Australian trade union movement.

Compounding the problematic relationship between sexual minorities and masculinist labor, the trade union movement and the Labor party have been subject to the moral conservatism of widespread Catholic Church influence. The Catholic Church challenged the growing strength of Communist Party of Australia influence in the trade unions from the 1930s. In 1937, the Australian National Secretariat of Catholic Action was formed, and groups began to form in trade unions in opposition to communist leadership. By 1941, with the establishment of the Catholic Social Studies Movement, right-wing mobilization began to be highly structured. By 1946, the Labor party had established formal "Industrial Groups" to fight Communism. These Industrial Groups, formed with Catholic Social Studies Movement support, competed within the unions against Communists and were later endorsed by several Labor party state branches.[8] The Catholic "Groupers" had the support of federal opposition leader H. V. "Doc" Evatt, who continued the anti-communist policies of the Ben Chifley Labor government until the influence of the Groupers began to threaten him. In 1954, Evatt attacked the Catholic Social Studies Movement, and the federal party moved against the Grouper-controlled Victoria executive of the Labor party. Thus occurred "the split" whereby a breakaway Democratic Labor party was formed, an event particularly damaging to the party in Victoria, where Labor would not regain government until the 1980s. In New South Wales, the deftness of the Labor party leadership averted federal intervention and a split in that state.[9]

After the split, the industrial and political wings of the New South Wales labor movement became separated, although the Australian Workers Union was able to create a majority for the right at the Labor party conference.[10] With the right in control in

New South Wales, and the labor movement split in Victoria, Catholic influence was strong. The resulting moral conservatism of this influence amplified the patriarchy of the craft masculinism in Australian labor. But some unions retained left-wing strongholds in the ideological battles of the 1950s. These included the unions that responded positively to the later struggles of lesbians and gays for union recognition. These unions provided the means for the adoption of the supportive peak union confederation policies that facilitated Labor party legislative action.

The existence of the Labor party adds an extra dimension to all political mobilization in Australia. Engagement with the labor movement means engagement at two levels. The political and industrial wings of labor have differing spheres of influence. Trade unions have traditionally acted to redress the grievances of individual members and to negotiate collective award conditions and rates of pay in the centralized state and federal industrial tribunals. The Labor party, on the other hand, is either a party of government or opposition in Australia's two-party Westminster system. Government legislation and policy regulate matters as diverse as the various state Crimes Acts, service in the armed forces, and anti-discrimination. The trade union movement has close links with the Labor party and is influential in the formulation of Labor government policy to variable degrees in the state and federal jurisdictions. Trade union policies for the protection of gays and lesbians would provide the basis not only for the redress of individual worker grievances, but also for Labor-government legislation to remedy employment discrimination.

The Australian Council of Trade Unions, the key national confederation of peak union councils, had by 1981 been bolstered by the affiliations of its counterpart white-collar bodies. Although the Australian Council of Trade Unions is not affiliated with the Labor party, its leading figures have usually been prominent members of the party. These links between the industrial and political arms of the Australian labor movement have supported "the modification rather than the enforcement of extreme union claims."[11]

In the states, the various trade and labor councils have provided links between the industrial and political wings of the labor movement. The Labor Council of New South Wales, for example, has always enjoyed significant representation on the Labor party state executive.[12] The labor councils are branches of the Australian Council of Trade Unions. For the advancement of anti-discrimination measures and reform of the various Crimes Acts, state activity has been of paramount importance to the lesbian and gay movements. Because the labor councils have influence with state branches of the Labor party, the lesbian and gay movements have focused on gaining labor council support for reforms in the state arena.

Policy Development in Unions in Australia

Government action on employment discrimination in the late 1960s was tentative. What galvanized trade union resolve to eliminate discrimination in employment was the rising volume of discrimination cases associated with the gay and lesbian movements' coming-out agenda of the 1970s, followed by the HIV/AIDS crisis in the 1980s.

The establishment by the national Gough Whitlam Labor government of the state-based Employment Discrimination Committees created a snowball effect. These committees did their job of investigating the incidence of discrimination but were frustrated in turning the tide. By the early 1980s, teachers', social workers', and public servants' unions called for specific national anti-discrimination legislation. Their calls for legislation were boosted by the support of the peak union confederations.[13] At the same time, employer associations and the New South Wales Labor Council supported a statutory base for the Employment Discrimination Committees, to keep employment matters under the aegis of the industrial tribunals. The Australian Council of Trade Unions and others promoted an alternative to legislation: inserting anti-discrimination clauses in federal awards. Until the mid-1980s, the tussle between these competing remedies for the deficiencies of the Employment Discrimination Committees constituted the debate over union policies in relation to lesbian and gay employment discrimination.

National policy evolved from branch discussion in the case of the social workers' and teachers' unions. These affiliated unions proposed policy motions to the Australian Council of Salaried and Professional Associations and the Australian Council of Trade Unions. Women provided the impetus for the adoption of policy at the Council of Australian Government Employee Organizations and, in tandem with national union policy development, the Australian Council of Trade Unions.

In 1975, a government grant of $40,000 was made to the Australian Council of Salaried and Professional Associations to set up a resource center for working women. This center was established in Melbourne as the Working Women's Center, with parallel groups operating in other states. In August 1976, the Working Women's Center, along with the Queensland Women's Trade Union Committee and the Women's Trade Union Commission, Sydney, convened an Australian Women's Trade Union Conference. This conference, held in Sydney, expressed support for a Working Women's Charter campaign throughout Australia. The charter was among the first calls within the union movement for employment rights for gays and lesbians; it called for "The right to paid work for everyone who wishes to do so; an end to discrimination on the basis of sex, race, country of origin, age, religious or political belief, appearance, marital status or sexual preference."[14]

Recommendations from the Women's Trade Union Conference formed the basis for the discussion on employment discrimination at another peak union confederation, the Council of Australian Government Employee Organizations. This council had established a Standing Committee on the Status and Employment of Women at its 1971 conference. In May 1977, the Council of Australian Government Employee Organizations adopted a general policy calling for anti-discrimination legislation specifically identifying sexual preference as a grounds of complaint. This policy emanated from the third report of the Committee on the Status and Employment of Women. The Council of Australian Government Employee Organizations also endorsed the Working Women's Charter at this 1977 conference. Statements affirming the Council of Australian Government Employee Organizations' support for homosexual workers appeared in the council's anti-discrimination legislation policy and its Working Women's Charter policy from this time.[15]

The Working Women's Charter was also adopted by the Australian Council of Trade Unions, during its 1977 congress. Two amendments relating to the grounds of discrimination came from the right-wing Federated Clerks' Union, but these were not related to the inclusion of sexuality, and in any case, they failed at the vote. The equally right-wing Shop Distributive and Allied Employees' Association put forward an amendment to reword the preamble in support of full-time homemakers. This also lost at the vote. No discussion was recorded concerning the inclusion of "sexuality" in the policy. With the affirmation of the resolution, the position was adopted that "The Australian Council of Trade Unions supports, consistent with its policy, the right to paid work for all who want to work, irrespective of . . . sexuality."[16] Through the Working Women's Charter, two national union confederations, the Council of Australian Government Employee Organizations and the Australian Council of Trade Unions, had adopted supportive statements in relation to gay and lesbian workers. These policy statements provided points of departure from which to evolve more developed policy initiatives in support of these workers.

In the Australian Council of Salaried and Professional Associations, initial policy development took place in affiliates such as the Australian Social Welfare Union and in teacher union forums such as the Victorian Secondary Teacher Association's Open Committee on Homosexuality. Then, following the 1978 Sydney National Homosexual Conference, the Salaried and Professional Associations determined to convene meetings of homosexual unionists; to work with groups, including gays and lesbians; to fight unjust discrimination against workers; and to seek that the Australian Council of Trade Unions, as the major peak union confederation, consider adoption of the same detailed action policy.[17]

The newspaper media was skeptical of a positive reaction from the Australian Council of Trade Unions to these proposals. Sylvie Shaw, representing the Australian Social Welfare Union at the conference, explained to the press that homosexuals "would be discriminated against in their jobs if they declared their homosexuality," especially in the teaching and welfare fields. The press commented that "union observers believe it may be an uphill battle for reformers to get the blue collar unions actively on side." This was put down to the "hearty male comradeship that nearly all union officials appear to enjoy in the country's pubs and clubs [which] leaves little room for any 'deviant' behavior."[18]

Union receptivity to the demands of gays and lesbians had been addressed by Australian Council of Salaried and Professional Associations federal secretary Bill Richardson. In his speech to the National Homosexual Conference, Richardson noted the propensity for unions to be masculinist and patriarchal but tempered these comments with the assertion that "they also attract people who are receptive to progressive social change and the protection of human rights." Later, Richardson commented to the press that "the union movement must regard discrimination against any section of working people as an issue of top priority demanding attention. To do otherwise will be to lay the ground for attacks in the foreseeable future on such people as a means of dividing the class to which we belong."[19]

At its January 1979 conference, the Australian Teacher's Federation supported the Australian Council of Salaried and Professional Associations' decision to convene national meetings of homosexual unionists. Furthermore, the Teacher's Federation decided to put to the next Australian Council of Trade Unions congress detailed motions in the same terms as those adopted at the Australian Council of Salaried and Professional Associations conference.[20] In August 1979, the Australian Council of Trade Unions executive considered these agenda items and referred the matters "back to the Affiliates to raise at congress."[21] Although the Teacher's Federation and the Social Welfare Union listed motions in similar terms to their recently adopted policies as agenda items for the 1979 Australian Council of Trade Unions congress, the congress did not reach these items on the agenda.[22]

The Australian Council of Salaried and Professional Associations' decision to convene meetings of homosexual unionists was put into effect through a National Union Meeting on Homosexual Workers, held at the Victorian Teacher's Union in August 1979. The Teacher's Federation gave "full support" to the national meetings and asked its affiliates to provide the same.[23] "Full support" meant at least some financial input. At the August 1979 meeting, Secretary Richardson of the Australian Council of Salaried and Professional Associations affirmed that the push for homosexual rights within the union movement had started with small groups of individual unionists taking up the issue within their own mainly white-collar unions.[24]

The failure of the Australian Council of Trade Unions Congress to reach the Teacher's Federation and Social Welfare Union motions on its agenda is indicative of the strength retained by the right, particularly the National Civic Council, within the Australian labor movement at this time. During his speech to the Australian Council of Salaried and Professional Associations' national meeting, Richardson focused on the "extreme right-wing elements in Australian society," identifying these with fundamentalist Christian groups. Mindful that the Briggs amendment's defeat in California was contingent on support from the AFL-CIO and individual unions, Richardson made a call for resistance against any National Civic Council moves "to deny homosexuals the protection of the Australian Council of Trade Unions."[25] These words were spoken with the foreknowledge that the Australian Council of Salaried and Professional Associations would not for long be in the vanguard of progressive union policy development. The council held a final national conference in December 1979 to formalize an amalgamation with the Australian Council of Trade Unions. The wind-up motion paid tribute to the leading role of the council in taking up the fight over discrimination against homosexuals. In light of the amalgamation, the meeting called on the Australian Council of Trade Unions to formulate a policy to protect all unionists, regardless of sex, sexuality, and marital status, and to adopt policies in support of the rights of all oppressed groups.[26]

The Australian Council of Salaried and Professional Associations was joined by the Council of Australian Government Employee Organizations in calls for the Australian Council of Trade Unions to adopt a comprehensive anti-discrimination policy. A discussion at the National Labour Consultative Council, a forum of the federal government and the national union confederations, clarified the Australian Council of Trade Unions' position.[27] The Australian Council of Trade Unions executive had debated a resolution on discrimination at its February 1980 meeting. The resolution mentioned only sex or marital status as grounds for which discrimination should be prohibited but joined a growing chorus of discontent with the performance of the Employment Discrimination Committees.[28] Concerns with the Australian Council of Trade Unions' proposal to provide a statutory base for the Employment Discrimination Committees, however, led to further policy development, which resulted in support by the Council of Australian Government Employee Organizations for specific anti-discrimination legislation.[29]

As in 1979, the 1981 Australian Council of Trade Unions congress did not reach the discrimination policy proposals on the agenda. Policy recommendations for this congress reaffirmed support for the inclusion of sexual orientation in anti-discrimination measures and reaffirmed the call for "effective national anti-discrimination legislation." While noting the support given by the union movement to the Employment Discrimination Committees, this policy recommendation decried the lack of financial resources available to the committees and called for "much more effective machinery at national level to fight discrimination." As part of this, the resolution called for state legislation and the insertion of anti-discrimination clauses in awards. The agenda papers for this 1981 congress also contained a proposal from the Teacher's Federation to amend the Working Women's Charter to include a further section covering partner benefits in allowances and entitlements. Included was a call for an end to discrimination in superannuation on the basis of sex, marital/de facto spouse status, or sexual preference. This agenda item also asked that no distinction be made between male/female, married/single, or homosexual/heterosexual workers in the provision of remote, removal, meal, travel, or other allowances.[30]

Although the 1981 congress did not reach these proposals, they were handed on to the executive for consideration. As a result, the Council of Trade Unions did adopt a policy. This opened with the statement: "There is no place in Australian society for discrimination on the basis of . . . sexual orientation."[31] The Council of Trade Unions then disseminated an amended draft anti-discrimination clause suitable for insertion into federal awards. This covered both sexuality and sexual orientation and named the Employment Discrimination Committees as Boards of Reference under the award, with unresolved matters to be referred to the Conciliation and Arbitration Commission.[32] The New South Wales Anti-Discrimination Board met with the Australian Council of Trade Unions to discuss some amendments to the proposed clause. Also discussed at this meeting was a draft bill from one of the employers' peak representative bodies, the Confederation of Australian Industry, seeking to entrench the Employment Discrimination Committees in statute. The confederation wanted to add to collective agreements a clause that respondents "shall not discriminate against an employee . . . unless such discrimination is based on the inherent requirements of a particular job." The Australian Council of Trade Unions said that it most certainly did not agree to the employers' draft.[33]

In an illustration of the institutional significance of union and employer representative bodies in Australia, draft anti-discrimination legislation was presented by the Confederation of Australian Industry in 1982. Homosexuality was not specified as an area of protection from discrimination in the bill, and there was no provision for the inclusion of other grounds by any mechanism other than legislation. Another area of trade union concern, reflecting long-standing qualms over the operation of the Employment Discrimination Committees, was that there was no provision for the inclusion of members of disadvantaged groups on the proposed state committees.[34]

The coverage of gays and lesbians in any anti-discrimination legislation was a demand affirmed by the Council of Australian Government Employee Organizations. Government employee organizations also sought action from the federal government as an employer. The Council of Australian Government Employee Organizations federal executive at its February 1981 meeting carried a resolution seeking legislation to outlaw discrimination on grounds including sexual preference in all agencies of the federal government. The Confederation of Australian Industry's qualifier was included, though affirmative action was supported.[35]

Affiliated unions and labor councils, the state peak union confederations, prepared to follow the line of dual attack favored by the Australian Council of Trade Unions. This meant working toward legislative action and the insertion of anti-discrimination clauses in industrial collective agreements. In New South Wales, however, concerned unions meeting in February 1983 resolved to seek amendments to the New South Wales Industrial Arbitration Act to save the "long and costly process" of pursuing anti-discrimination clauses in state agreements.[36] In May 1985, the New South Wales Labor Council undertook an active campaign directed at removing references to employment in the Anti-Discrimination Act. These would be replaced by the insertion of a new part in the New South Wales Industrial Arbitration Act covering discrimination at work. The rationale for this was that "events at the workplace are primarily industrial matters and should be handled as such.... Accordingly, the appropriate bodies to deal with such problems are unions and the appropriate forum to solve such problems is the Industrial Commission."

This campaign provoked conflict within organized labor, and between organized labor and the new movements. The Campaign Against Discrimination mobilized in order to fight the New South Wales Labor Council proposals, preferring the retention of employment matters in the Anti-Discrimination Act. The Campaign Against Discrimination boasted a long list of endorsements, including trade unions and women's, aboriginal, religious, human rights, and migrant organizations. This groundswell had an effect. By October 1986, the labor council campaign was defeated. It was not enough for the new movements to place their trust in organized labor; a new, separate machinery was demanded.

The defeat of the New South Wales Labor Council proposals provided some rationalization of the alternate remedies being pursued within the trade union movement to address the issue of employment discrimination. The trade union movement was united in a call for more effective anti-discrimination machinery, but a statutory base for the Employment Discrimination Committees and the inclusion of anti-discrimination clauses in awards now seemed ruled out. Along with this clarification of its agenda, by the mid-1980s, the trade union movement evinced a heightened consciousness with regard to lesbian and gay issues. A submission from the Australian Council of Trade Unions to the Human rights Commission sought that the exemption given in the Sex Discrimination Act to superannuation be removed. Going further, the Australian Council of Trade Unions noted "that there are factors other than sex or marital status discrimination that have denied equality of treatment in superannuation to members of the Australian workforce and that concerted efforts on the part of the union movement will be necessary to ensure that all workers have reasonable access to superannuation."[37]

With the advent of the HIV/AIDS crisis by the mid-1980s, the union movement, through the Australian Council of Trade Unions, was able to respond rapidly. AIDS policy was on the Australian Council of Trade Unions executive agenda in May 1985. The ratified policy endorsed education campaigns, the negotiation of Occupational Health and Safety agreements, and that "unionists in high risk groups form support networks in the workplace."[38] Cliff Dolan, president of the Australian Council of Trade Unions, contributed to the work of the Victorian Aids Council Unions Working Group through a special Australian Council of Trade Unions Health and Safety Bulletin on AIDS. The Victorian AIDS Council described Dolan's Health and Safety Bulletin as "the best summary of the occupational aspects of AIDS yet produced in the world."[39] In addition, several unions were publishing informed articles on AIDS in their journals. The Liquor and Allied Trades Union journal carried a full-page article, explaining to members that AIDS could not be caught from cups and plates. The Municipal Officers' Association journal published a full-page article, based partly on a leaflet produced by the Plumbers and Gasfitters Union. When the Hospital Employees' Federation published an article on AIDS in its journal, it included translations in several community languages.[40]

Through the mid-1980s, the trade unions and peak union confederations developed anti-discrimination policies supporting gay and lesbian workers. The defeat of the New South Wales Labor Council campaign for redress of employment discrimination only via industrial awards meant that the legislative route was the only way for the labor movement to make further reform happen. The rest of this chapter examines the legislative record of the Labor party in relation to the demands of gays and lesbians.

Labor Politics and Employment Protection

Although none of the anti-discrimination legislation enacted in Australia by the end of the decade of the 1970s included sexuality or homosexuality as grounds of discrimination, the Employment Discrimination Committees had discretion over whether they could hear such complaints. The committees, however, were widely seen as "nothing less than diversionary and a means of containment." Of the twenty-six cases of sexuality discrimination reported to the committees by 1981, only one was successfully resolved.[41] During the first decade of the emergence of the gay and lesbian movement in Australia, a void of protective legislation was only tentatively being redressed through the Employment Discrimination Committees. The gay and lesbian communities sought the assistance of trade unions in approaching Labor governments to provide enhanced legislation. In doing so, the representatives of a new social movement reached out to governments formed by the political representatives of the labor movement. The characteristics of the various Labor parties of the states colored the subsequent history of the Labor party.[42] The sections that follow examine the characteristics of the various state branches of the Labor party and the state response to the demands of the lesbian and gay movements.

The various branches of the Labor party were restructured after the election of Gough Whitlam as federal parliamentary leader in 1967. This restructuring encouraged the emergence of formalized factions within the Labor party. Incorporated within the dominant right is the remnant of the Catholic right of the 1950s: "essentially laborist, not socialist . . . and conservative on social issues."[43] Whether progressive policies could jump the hurdle of this conservative rump in transferring from the industrial to the political wing of labor was a major concern for gays and lesbians. First examined is activity in the central, federal arena. (The Commonwealth of Australia and the Australian Capital Territory are discussed separately.) Next addressed is state activity, commencing with those states and territories that figured early in this history. The approach taken is to unravel the historical development of Labor government support for lesbian and gay employment equity.

Central Activity

The Commonwealth

The federal arena constitutes an important site in overcoming discrimination against lesbians and gays.[44] Although the federal government has limited powers, it is a large employer. Further, the federal government sets the rules with regard to eligibility for service with the Australian armed forces. In addition, the federal government has responsibilities in relation to the promulgation of international treaties to which Australia is a signatory.

Just as gay and lesbian consciousness was awakening in Australia, the reformist Whitlam Labor government was elected to government in 1972. This broke twenty-three years of continuous conservative Liberal/National Party coalition rule. The Whitlam government held power for three years, to be followed by eight years of further coalition control. The Hawke and Keating Labor governments first came to office in 1983, remaining in power until 1996.

The strength of the New South Wales Catholic right during the Hawke and Keating Labor governments tempered reformism. Although gays and lesbians in particular may have felt excluded by the Labor program, Labor opened opportunities that were taken up by the progressive parties of the Senate. There was progress in the public service and defense force. The use by Labor of instruments such as the Australian Industrial Relations Commission and the parliamentary committee system enabled advances in family leave. This, and the Toonen case, best illustrate the minimalist approach to progressive social policies adopted by Labor under Hawke and Keating, building on the earlier moves of Whitlam.

Soon after its election, the Whitlam government established the advisory Employment Discrimination Committees at federal and state levels and ratified International Labour Organization Convention No. 111 "Concerning Discrimination in Respect of Employment and Occupation."[45] It also turned its attention to the employment policies of the Defence Department.

Australian government labor practices, especially in the armed forces, had been an early area of concern for the first gay and lesbian activist groups, particularly the Campaign Against Moral Persecution (CAMP). In January 1971, CAMP raised questions to the Minister of Defence about the sacking of gays by the Navy. The sacking of lesbians by the Army was made into a public issue in 1973, as was the dismissal of two alleged lesbians from the Air Force. The next controversy was over Naval Orders 2/72 and 3/72, which styled homosexuality as a "weakness of character" and a "regression to adolescence." CAMP feared these definitions were to be extended to cover the entire armed forces. Seeking assurances that this would not happen, CAMP was satisfied when its concerns were referred to the newly established Employment Discrimination Committee in New South Wales.[46] By 1974, the Minister of Defence could no longer avoid a full review of the policy on homosexuals in the armed forces. During this review, the Department of Defence advocated that there was no room for homosexuals in the armed services. A new policy provided for an investigation to be "carried out as discreetly and with as little publicity as possible." With the substantiation of an allegation of homosexuality, where charges were not laid, and if it was "apparent that the serviceman or servicewoman is a confirmed homosexual who cannot or will not refrain from further involvement," administrative action would be taken. This was defined as "release from the Service." With a ban on homosexuality still in place, there had been no advance for gays and lesbians serving in the armed forces.[47]

Just before its defeat, the Whitlam government established a Royal Commission on Australian Government Administration. The report of this commission acknowledged that homosexuals suffered from disadvantage in seeking public service employment or promotion.[48] Further progressive action by the Whitlam government was not possible before its defeat at the polls in 1975, but the Whitlam reforms had generated some momentum. The Commonwealth Public Service Board made a mixed statement in relation to the employment of homosexuals, recommending that the federal government should follow "a policy of non-discrimination in employing homosexuals as an example to all employers," but warning that "caution should be exercised in employing homosexuals where access to secret material is involved."[49]

This two-faced approach to equality of treatment for gays and lesbians continued under the Malcolm Fraser Liberal government. In 1979, for example, the Department of Immigration and Ethnic Affairs adopted the view that "the non-discriminatory character of Australian immigration policy extends to questions of sexual orientation," but only marriages between males and females were to be recognized for family reunion.[50] The government considered introducing legislation covering discrimination in its own employment but did not follow through.[51] The government's Public Service Acts Amendment Bill was debated in the Senate in October 1982. Amendments seeking to prohibit discrimination on the grounds of homosexuality were defeated.[52]

The Bob Hawke Labor government was elected in 1983 and almost immediately introduced a Sex Discrimination Bill to provide protection in employment and other areas for women. During the Senate debate, the Democrats pressed for protection against discrimination for lesbians and gays.[53] They were not successful. In December 1983, the Hawke government made a commitment to a Public Service that "precludes discrimination" on a number of grounds, including sexual preference. But it was clear that the government would concentrate its implementation effort on only four designated groups: women, Aborigines, migrants, and the disabled.[54]

By 1986, the AIDS crisis brought into focus the wider issues raised by earlier gay and lesbian employment rights activists. The partners of dying gays were struggling for the same rights to time off and survivor benefits that the partners of heterosexual workers received. A document, *Guidelines on the Management of Occurrences of AIDS in the Australian Public Service Workplace,* had been issued in December 1985 and was followed by government working-party discussion on a draft of guidelines for the employment of homosexuals. These discussions concluded in August 1986. With the expiration of the Pubic Service Board in 1987, however, the matter went no further.[55] While individual departments could regulate partner benefits, there would be no servicewide policy for equal rights.

At long last, limited anti-discrimination reform took place federally in 1989. Labor's attorney general announced in December of that year that the Human Rights and Equal Opportunity Commission would be able to investigate discrimination in employment over several new grounds, including "sexual preference." It was a limited gain. The new provision did not make any such discrimination unlawful.[56]

Reform was also forced on the military. A 1992 report called for an end to the ban on homosexuals in the armed forces, but new draft instructions on "Homosexual Behavior in the Australian Defence Force" were introduced by a clause stating, "Homosexual behavior is not accepted or condoned in the Defence Force." The federal Human Rights Commissioner expressed "extreme disappointment" with the government's announcement. Under pressure from the Democrats, who held the balance of power in the Senate, the government established a special caucus committee to make further investigations into the armed services ban. In September 1992, this committee recommended major changes.[57] Again the Human Rights and Equal Opportunity Commission leaned on the government to "do the right thing." Unable to withstand the pressure, the Labor government lifted the ban on gays and lesbians serving in the Australian armed services in November 1992.

The process of reform under Labor continued when the Keating government amended the Industrial Relations Reform Act 1993 to give the Industrial Relations Commission responsibility for preventing and removing discriminatory provisions from collective agreements. The grounds of discrimination referred to in the act now included sexual preference. This was a result of a successful Australian Democrats amendment in the Senate. The act also instructed the Australian Industrial Relations Commission to hear a special family leave test case for the determination of whether family leave provisions would be included in collective agreements.

The family leave test case was heard during July and August 1994 in Melbourne and Sydney. Of most interest to lesbian and gay workers was the extent of access to this leave. The Australian Council of Trade Unions took the view that the act excluded gays and lesbians from the provisions for family leave by its definition of "immediate family."[58] This prompted the Australian Federation of AIDS Organizations, along with the Australian Council for Lesbian and Gay Rights, to formally intervene in the case. The Federation of AIDS Organizations protested that "workers have been dismissed or denied leave to care for terminally ill partners or to attend their partner's funerals." The Australian Education Union, which had evolved from the Teacher's Federation, urged the Australian Council of Trade Unions to widen its definition of care givers to include same-sex partners and broaden its definition of family to include gay and lesbian relationships.[59]

Responding to an Australian Council for Lesbian and Gay Rights mail-out, white- and blue-collar unions showed their support for liberal definitions. The Finance Sector Union, one of the three unions involved in the case, wrote that they would push the Australian Council of Trade Unions to take the view that any outcomes "should have a non-discriminatory application." The Construction, Forestry, Mining, and Energy Workers Union (West Australia Branch) wrote directly to the president of the Industrial Relations Commission in support. Support also came from the New South Wales Nurses' Association, the Australian Nursing Federation, the National Union of Workers, the state Public Services Federation, the Independent Education Union of Australia, the Public Sector Union nationally, the National Tertiary Education Union, and the Australian Services Union Queensland Executive Council.[60] The commonwealth's submission on the case proposed the use of the definition of "immediate family" contained in the Sex Discrimination Act 1984, where "partner" and "de facto spouse" are defined as referring to persons "of the opposite sex." It was plain that the Keating Labor government did not support the inclusion of same-sex partners within the ambit of family leave.

In response, the Australian Council for Lesbian and Gay Rights collected examples of progressive employment practices in the private sector. A *Sydney Morning Herald* survey of company policies indicated that firms such as American Express, Qantas, Ansett, Microsoft, Lotus Development Corporation, Lend Lease Holding Company, Carlton United Breweries, and the retail giant Myer/Grace Brothers had progressive leave policies. The Australian Tax Office, Queensland Professional Officers' Association, Brisbane Workers' Health Cooperative Limited, Sydney City Council Enterprise Agreements, and the Victorian AIDS Council Inc./Gay Men's Health Centre Inc. all included same-sex partners within the parameters of care-givers leave.[61]

The family leave test case decision was handed down in November 1994 and finalized in February 1995. Rejecting the Australian Council of Trade Unions position, the Australian Industrial Relations Commission decided to extend access to sick leave to allow for the care or support of a family member, which they defined as "a member of the employee's household or a member of the employee's immediate family (as defined in the Sex Discrimination Act)."[62] While same-sex partners were not to be considered "immediate family" members, family leave would be available should they be members of the same household. This was greeted as a victory by gay and lesbian groups, and it raised hopes for further recognition of the partnerships of lesbians and gays in other areas.[63]

During these deliberations, a collective agreement covering the 18,000 federal employees of the Australian Tax Office was ratified. The agreement provided for special care-givers leave to gay, lesbian, bisexual, and transgendered workers. The Community and Public Sector Union Queensland Branch lesbian and gay caucus claimed "a significant victory."[64]

Overlapping these events was the development of the Human Rights (Sexual Conduct) Bill. In 1991, Australia had ratified the First Optional Protocol to the International

Covenant on Civil and Political Rights. This allowed Australians to complain directly to the United Nations Human Rights Committee if all domestic remedies had been exhausted. As soon as the protocol came into effect, a complaint was lodged by Nick Toonen, who claimed that sections 122 and 123 of the Tasmanian Criminal Code, which criminalized homosexual acts, breached his right to privacy under article 17 of the International Covenant and his right to equality before the law under article 26. The United Nations Human Rights Committee upheld Toonen's complaint in April 1994, finding that he was entitled to an effective remedy. The conservative Tasmanian government, however, refused to repeal the anti-homosexual provisions of its criminal code. The commonwealth stepped in, proposing a general guarantee of privacy for the sexual conduct of consenting adults.[65] With the opposition split during debate, the Human Rights (Sexual Conduct) Bill passed through both houses of parliament in late 1994.

The Australian Capital Territory

The Australian Capital Territory, the site of the nation's capital, Canberra, was granted self-rule in 1989, but between 1974 and 1989 a legislative assembly exercised limited self-government. Although the first elections to form the new Territory Legislative Assembly in 1974 gave the Labor party only four seats out of eighteen, in 1975, one of its members (Kep Enderby, the Labor party member for the federal parliament) proposed an ordinance to decriminalize male homosexual activity. To a charge of "the abominable crime of buggery," the ordinance would allow as a defense that the couple "were consenting adults doing their thing in private."[66] No dissent was recorded to the ordinance. However, amendments to eliminate the new offense of homosexual incest and to lower the age of consent for male homosexual activity to that for heterosexual activity were defeated. The Australian Capital Territory ordinance to legalize same-sex private sexual activity was proclaimed in November 1976.[67]

A powerful "sisterhood" in the Australian Capital Territory Branch of the Labor party led the way toward anti-discrimination legislation in the legislative assembly.[68] The Trades and Labor Council, the Council of Australian Government Employee Organizations, and the Women's Union Committee all supported legislative intervention to prohibit sex discrimination in employment. But the unions and employers were unable to agree on the terms to be included in the ordinance.[69] The election of the Hawke federal Labor government in 1983 provided the Capital Territory with some anti-discrimination protection, covering sex, marital status, and pregnancy. Not until 1991, however, did the territory's legislative assembly pass its own Anti-Discrimination Act. Under this legislation, "homosexuality" and "sexuality," broadly defined, gained coverage.[70] Facilitating this legislative victory was a Labor party with power devolved to the local branches, and an active women's movement. Another factor was the early support of key workers' representative agencies dominated by white-collar unions; these agencies included the Council of Australian Government Employee Organizations and the Australian Capital Territory Trades and Labor Council.

State Activity

New South Wales

New South Wales has led the way in terms of state response to lesbian and gay employment discrimination. A long period of Conservative rule from 1965 was broken in 1976 with the election of the Wran Labor government. Neville Wran, an urbane lawyer, had been maneuvered into the party leadership by John Ducker, leader of the right-wing faction.[71] Although structural changes in the state branch during the 1960s assured the party's left wing of some institutionalized representation within decision-making bodies, the "New Right," under Ducker, was firmly in control. This control, signified by the elevation of Wran to party leadership, marked the return of the state peak union confederation, the Labor Council of New South Wales, to dominance in the Labor party.[72]

Lesbian and gay political activists had worked hard to establish their credentials within the labor movement up to this point, although the battle over union policies was only just beginning. The earliest gay and lesbian group was the Campaign Against Moral Persecution (CAMP). With the 1976 election of the Wran government, CAMP's hopes were raised. After all, the New South Wales Branch of the Labor party had adopted policy supportive of lesbians and gays at its 1973 Women's Conference.

CAMP began discussions with the parliamentary leadership about the government's planned Anti-Discrimination Bill. After only one CAMP deputation to Premier Wran, agreement was reached for the inclusion of "homosexuality" in the bill.[73] But Wran could not ensure that the bill would be adopted. Although a new "technocratic" right was in control of the Labor party machine, including the labor council, the old Catholic right was still strong in the state parliamentary caucus.[74] The New South Wales Legislative Council, the state's upper house, at first blocked its passage.[75] The bill was later passed, but only with watered-down clauses in relation to homosexuality; the New South Wales Anti-Discrimination Board, for example, was now able to "investigate, research and inquire into a number of matters, including homosexuality, which are not at present grounds upon which it is unlawful to discriminate."[76] This nevertheless opened the door to gay and lesbian demands.

At this time, CAMP was also lobbying for reform of the anti-homosexual provisions of the New South Wales Crimes Act. The perceived inadequacies of earlier South Australian and Australian Capital Territory legislation led CAMP activists to develop a model for criminal law reform that could be advanced to all Australian legislatures.[77] The government, however, was still wrestling with its anti-discrimination measures. A review of government practices had heard submissions drawing attention to discrimination "against both male and female homosexuals in government employment."[78] At the same time, the Anti-Discrimination Board commenced its research on discrimination on the grounds of homosexuality.[79] Published in 1982, the Anti-Discrimination Board's report, *Discrimination and Homosexuality,* was the result of surveys, submissions, and a "phone-in." Employers, employment agencies, government departments and statutory authorities, and trade unions were surveyed. The report indicated widespread discrimination against lesbians and gays, who had achieved some measure of equal treatment only in the trade unions. To put an end to the homophobia that was found in their investigations, the Anti-Discrimination Board recommended "that the Anti-Discrimination Act be amended to render unlawful discrimination in employment on the ground of homosexuality."[80]

The trade union response was immediate. The Australian Theatrical and Amusement Employees Association wrote to Premier Wran urging implementation of the report's recommendations. The association also wrote to the Labor Council of New South Wales, reminding them of the council's October 1980 motion opposing discrimination against homosexuals. The labor council, too, wrote to Wran seeking talks. Wran replied that he preferred to defer a meeting until some future time, for by this time he was grappling with parliamentary opposition to a series of attempts to make changes in the criminal law in response to gay and lesbian demands.[81]

By November 1982, there were four failed attempts to decriminalize homosexual acts in New South Wales. The Labor backbencher, George Petersen, a member of the Socialist left faction, made the first attempt in April 1981. This was an amendment to the Sexual Assault Act that would have removed all homosexual offenses from the Crimes Act. The Gay Rights Lobby supported the move and mobilized around it. The proposed amendment was publicly supported by Young Labor and by Frank Walker, the attorney general. The New South Wales Independent Teachers Association took the view that "the amendments and reforms were long overdue, would be welcomed by the community and that the government ought not be intimidated by certain reactionary opposition."[82] But retaining power was the main priority of the Wran government. With an election coming up, Labor shied away from "such a contentious issue." In the parliament, the speaker of the legislative assembly ruled Petersen's amendment out of order. Given a threat of expulsion from the Labor party, Petersen did not challenge the speaker's ruling.[83]

With the return of the Wran government after the September 1981 state elections, another attempt was made by Petersen. This bill was overwhelmingly defeated in the legislative assembly in December, with half the Labor party joining the coalition block in opposition, having been provoked into this rebellion by the government's inclusion of an equal age of consent clause in the bill.[84] A December 1981 attempt at reform by Michael Egan, a Labor-party member of the legislative council, also failed. On this occasion, the bill was opposed by not only the right, but also the gay and lesbian communities, who objected to the retention of homosexual offenses in the bill.[85]

In February 1982, Barrie Unsworth, a Labor-party member of the legislative council and secretary of the New South Wales Labor Council, introduced the Crimes (Homosexual Behaviour) Amendment Bill into the legislative council. His attempt at law reform was, in part, aimed at deflecting criticism from the Labor government for its ineffectuality in this area, highlighted by the anomaly whereby the Crimes Act imposed a heavier penalty for consensual homosexual activity than the 1981 Sexual Assault Act did for heterosexual rape. The Unsworth approach also was an attempt at keeping the Catholic Church satisfied by retaining the offense of buggery and proposing a higher age of consent of eighteen for homosexual sex, compared to sixteen for heterosexual sex. In addition, his bill proposed a new offense of "gross indecency" between males in public, with a penalty of two years jail. The gay and lesbian community was generally in disagreement with these items. Lex Watson, co-convener of the Gay Rights Lobby, argued that the police crackdown that had been evident since the defeat of the Petersen and Egan bills in December 1981 ought not be allowed to continue, and that the wider community would infer government support for such crackdowns should the New South Wales parliament refrain from law reform again at the fourth request.[86] A conscience vote was allowed in the upper house, the legislative council, and the bill passed by a narrow margin. (A "conscience vote" meant that members could vote as they pleased, rather than having to toe the party line.) However, the bill was defeated in the lower house, the legislative assembly, by 47 votes to 42, when Unsworth was unable to deliver the right.[87]

Later in 1982, the Anti-Discrimination Act was successfully amended to make it unlawful to discriminate against a person on the ground of their homosexuality in employment and other areas. This brought about the anomalous situation in which it was illegal to discriminate against homosexuals in New South Wales, but homosexual acts remained illegal.

The police crackdown continued, and police raids on homosexual meeting places served as a focus for lobbying efforts. The Theatrical Employees Union, for example, registered a strong protest against the January 1983 raid on Club 80.[88] Two further raids on Club 80 were executed by the New South Wales police during 1983, and a total of twenty-seven gays were arrested and charged with offenses such as indecent assault on a male and the common-law offense of engaging in "scandalous conduct." A Gay Rights Embassy was established on the lawns of Premier Wran's suburban residence for two weeks in September 1983. Statutory declarations admitting to engagement in consensual sexual acts with other adult males contrary to the Crimes Act were delivered personally to the head of the police vice squad. Pressure was on Premier Wran, still seen as a civil libertarian, to "show personal leadership on this issue." The pressure increased when, in April 1984, three openly gay candidates were elected to the Sydney City Council.[89]

Following his return to power in the 1984 state election, Wran indicated that homosexual law reform was back on the agenda. In April, Wran announced that he would introduce a bill to parliament, and that on this occasion, no conscience vote would be allowed. Although the bill removed all references to offenses relating to consensual sex between two males over eighteen, it contained two new offenses applying to situations in which one of the males was under eighteen, and it failed to include an equal age of consent clause. With the imprimatur of the premier, the bill passed in May 1984 and was proclaimed in June 1984.[90]

In 1986 Barry Unsworth, leader of the New South Wales Labor party New Right faction, succeeded Wran as premier but proved an electoral liability. He was succeeded in 1988 by a Liberal/National Party coalition government, followed by the Fahey Liberal government. These Liberal governments led to further reform in anti-discrimination measures. In 1994, the exemption for collective agreements was removed from anti-discrimination measures, and the vilification of homosexuals was outlawed.

After the election of a Labor government led by Bob Carr in 1995, the New South Wales labor movement's political and industrial wings were again called on for support by the lesbian and gay communities. A family leave test case was to be heard by the

New South Wales Industrial Relations Commission. The Gay and Lesbian Rights Lobby liaised closely with the New South Wales Labor Council during preparations for this case. Negotiations proceeded between various employer groups and the labor council to define the classes of persons eligible for the leave. After three attempts at agreement, a draft was put to the commission by the Retail Traders' Association. Their suggested language was designed to include same-sex partners provided the partner "lives with the employee as the de-facto partner of that employee on a bona fide domestic basis." It was accepted by the labor council, the new Carr Labor government, the Motor Traders' Association, and the Chamber of Manufactures, but rejected by the New South Wales Employers' Federation and others. Given this lack of unanimity, and the limited inclusiveness of the wording of the draft, the Gay and Lesbian Rights Lobby sought to intervene in the case. The commission declined to give leave for such an intervention and adopted the wording of the draft, notwithstanding the opposition.[91]

In New South Wales, the positive response of the political wing of the labor movement to lesbian and gay demands was tempered by the negative influence of Catholicism. A "technocratic gloss," however, under the urbane Wran as party leader, allowed some progressive measures, including the Anti-Discrimination Act, eventual coverage of gays and lesbians under that legislation, and criminal law reform. The resistance to these progressive measures emanated from right-wing Labor-party members of the New South Wales legislative council. At the time of the Unsworth bill, only four of the twenty-four Labor members of the legislative council were aligned with the left.[92] Measured reform was epitomized by the Carr Labor government's accession to only limited recognition of gay and lesbian partnerships in employment leave entitlements in the state family leave test case.

South Australia

While New South Wales led the way in Australia toward protection of gays and lesbians through anti-discrimination legislation, South Australia was the leader in the decriminalization of homosexual acts. Success in this area is partly attributable to the nature of the South Australia Branch of the Labor party, which at this stage was characterized by the consensus-driven politics of the leadership clique. Contributing to the absence of an ideological dimension to the party was the lack of an Irish-Catholic convict base in South Australia, unlike the other ex-colonies. This lessened the Catholic influence in the party, so that the branch was more open than other Labor-party state branches to social reform. The South Australian Branch of the Labor party was also less subject to the influence of trade unions than other branches. A number of university-educated ministers in the Dunstan Labor government came from nonunion backgrounds. The nature of union affiliation to the Labor party also contributed. The four largest of the sixty-five Labor-party affiliated unions in 1973, for example, could muster only 40,883 votes, which was short of the 51,522 needed for a simple majority. The inclusion of the Australian Government Workers' Association in this group of four also provided some left-wing balance, something lacking in the other branches. Likewise, public sector unions have affiliated to the Labor party in South Australia, unlike in other branches.[93]

The murder of Adelaide academic George Duncan in May 1972 spurred the first moves for decriminalization of homosexual acts in Australia. Duncan had been thrown into the Torrens River and drowned at a place where police practiced harassment of homosexuals, including entrapment procedures.[94] His death sparked outrage in the general community in Adelaide, with the Moral Freedom Committee emerging to lobby parliament for homosexual law reform. Their argument was that if sex between men had been legal, then more witnesses might have been willing to come forward and give evidence. In July 1972, Murray Hill, a Liberal, introduced a private member's bill to amend the Criminal Law Consolidation Act along these lines. Hill's amendment was limited in scope, merely allowing as a defense to prosecution for buggery or gross indecency evidence "that the act had been between consenting adult males in private." After a free vote, the amendment passed in both houses.[95]

The timidity of that reform prompted the Labor-party left into action. The first step toward substantive reform in South Australia came during the second term of the Don Dunstan Labor government. Dunstan's left-wing attorney general, Peter Duncan, introduced a bill in September 1973 designed to remove specific references to sexual acts between males in the criminal law, and to provide a single code of sexual behavior regardless of sex or sexual orientation. After lobbying from CAMP (South Australia) and the Gay Liberation Front, the bill passed in the lower house but was defeated on the casting vote of the speaker in the legislative council.[96] After another attempt, again defeated in the upper house, Duncan offered a new bill in August 1975.[97] This bill passed in both houses.[98]

Legislation to outlaw discrimination in employment because of a person's sex or marital status was also introduced in 1975 in the South Australian parliament.[99] The Sex Discrimination bill was proclaimed in August 1976, and the Commissioner for Equal Opportunity took up office in that same month.[100] In its first years of operation, the office of the commissioner received several complaints of discrimination on the grounds of homosexuality and transexuality. As a result, she recommended that the act be extended to give such coverage. A working party to review anti-discrimination legislation reported during 1983–1984, recommending that sexuality be included as grounds of discrimination in the South Australia legislation.[101] Amendments to encompass sexuality and HIV/AIDS status proceeded on the commissioner's recommendation in 1993, just prior to the demise of the Arnold Labor government.

One impetus for these anti-discrimination amendments was the landmark Jobling case, which arose in 1992 when South Australia's director general of education canceled a drama program David Jobling was to conduct at Jamestown Primary School on account of Jobling's homosexuality and HIV-positive status. The South Australian Commissioner for Equal Opportunity assisted Jobling to argue his case at the Equal Opportunity Tribunal. When the decision was handed down, Jobling received $30,000 compensation for loss of earnings, $5,100 for ongoing psychiatric treatment, and $25,000 damages. In addition, he received a public apology and an acknowledgment of his excellent qualifications, reputation, and fitness to work with children.[102]

Western Australia

Domination by the urban blue-collar unions isolated the Western Australia Labor party from the electorate and kept it mostly out of office in the postwar era. Before 1983, Labor governments held office in that state only during 1953–1959 and 1971–1974. In the 1970s, a younger generation of parliamentarians came to the fore. This new generation was inspired by the successes of the reform-minded Dunstan in South Australia and Wran in New South Wales.[103] A bill similar to the 1972 initiative taken in South Australia to decriminalize homosexual acts was introduced by the Tonkin Labor government in Western Australia in November 1973. The bill was defeated, but a Royal Commission was appointed to look into the issue. Although limited in its terms of reference, this commission recommended decriminalization. No steps were taken to implement the commission's findings, however.[104]

A second attempt at law reform was made by Labor party upper-house member Grace Vaughan in 1977. Her bill, which advocated an equal age of consent, was passed in the upper house in October 1977 but defeated in the legislative assembly on a conscience vote. Although a majority of Labor opposition members were in favor, only nine members of the Conservative government were of like mind.[105]

Following the election of the Burke Labor government in 1983, a third attempt at law reform was launched. Controversy erupted within the Labor party over the equal age of consent provision in the bill. Young Labor gave strong support, as did various unions from the center and left, but the bill was defeated in the Conservative-dominated upper house. A fourth attempt at reform of the criminal law in Western Australia was finally successful in 1991. John Haldon, Labor-party left convener and upper-house member, used his roots in the Miscellaneous Workers' Union to ensure en bloc support from the left of the Labor party.[106]

Despite these achievements in criminal law reform, no anti-discrimination measures are in place in Western Australia to protect gays and lesbians against employment discrimination. Western Australia remains a backwater of condoned employment discrimination within the nation. With Labor out of office, this situation has little hope of change.

Tasmania

Tasmania's unique system of electoral politics has generally worked to keep Labor out of control of the upper house, but in control of the lower house.[107] Labor governments ruled continuously in Tasmania from 1934 to 1969. A three-year interregnum was then followed by Labor government over the period 1972–1982. In 1989, a minority Labor government in alliance with five independents (Greens) regained office, governing until 1992. The Catholic influence has been a powerful force in the Tasmanian Labor party. The split of the 1950s continues to affect the state; the Catholic conservative Brian Harradine, expelled as Tasmanian Labor Council secretary, has been returned to the Australian Senate as an independent in every election since 1975.

Gay and Lesbian activists have been prominent in Tasmanian politics since the mid-1970s. They presented a petition, calling for homosexual law reform, to the Royal

Commission into Human Relationships when it visited Launceston in 1975. In 1976, following an attempt by the executive of the Tasmanian Labor party to stifle discussion on homosexual law reform at its annual conference, the Tasmanian Homosexual Law Reform Group was formed. The group gained credibility when the prominent Green, Dr. Bob Brown, came out as gay. Group leaders met with Labor Premier Neilson later in 1976 to put forward an agenda for reform.[108]

The Labor government responded well to the demands of the lesbian and gay movements. In 1977, it set up a committee of the legislative assembly to conduct an inquiry into victimless crimes. The committee heard evidence for and against decriminalization of homosexual acts and eventually recommended that homosexual acts between consenting adults in private be legalized.[109] At the same time, the state council of the Labor party made the same call, with only a minority of union delegates voting against.[110] Two years later, the Tasmanian Labor government allowed the introduction of a private member's bill to implement the new policy. It created a storm of protest, with a public opinion poll showing 51 percent of Tasmanians opposed. The party's resolve was not tested, as the bill lapsed in February 1980 when its sponsor lost his seat in a by-election.[111]

A further setback occurred in 1981 when a legislative committee recommended that the government not proceed with any anti-discrimination legislation. The committee found "that the evidence does not disclose even a moderate degree of discriminatory practice in Tasmania."[112] Before it could react, Labor lost office in Tasmania. Progress was stalled on law reform and anti-discrimination measures, so the gay and lesbian movements increased their activities. Arrests of gay law-reform supporters at Salamanca market in Hobart in 1988 sparked a picket of the Tasmanian Travel Centre in Melbourne.[113]

Labor was returned to power in 1989, forming a minority government with the Tasmanian Greens. The new government put forward legislative proposals on HIV/AIDS issues in 1990. The decriminalization of homosexual acts was included in this legislation, but the provisions on HIV/AIDS provoked such concern that the Australian Federation of AIDS Organizations was moved to strongly reject the package. The preamble to the bill was seen as "offensive and unnecessary." A clause allowing medical professionals to require a person to undergo an HIV test before routine surgical or dental procedures was also unpopular.[114] There was some relief when the bill was rejected in parliament.

During 1991, a first in Australia occurred in Tasmania when the lower house passed an anti-vilification bill to protect gays and lesbians. Predictably, the upper house blocked the bill.[115] Not until 1994, under international pressure over the Toonen case, was criminal law reform successfully carried out. The federal government was forced to legislate in relation to sexual conduct in private in Tasmania. International humiliation over the Toonen case stirred the voters to shake up the upper house in elections, removing the most virulent anti-gay campaigner. With a chastened upper house, the Tasmanian parliament amended its criminal code in May 1997 to fully decriminalize homosexual acts.

Tasmania's humiliation was in a period of Liberal Party government, and it was the conservatives who undertook full decriminalization. Labor had attempted to have anti-discrimination passed in parliament but passage was blocked in the legislative council in November 1996. The conservative government then proposed its own anti-discrimination legislation in this period of armistice; however, the Tasmanian Gay and Lesbian Rights Group led opposition to the use of the term "lawful sexual activity." The election of the Bacon Labor government in August 1998 then saw anti-discrimination legislation using the term "sexual orientation" introduced. As well as outlawing discrimination, the bill prohibited the incitement of hatred or severe ridicule on sexual orientation and other grounds. The bill was passed in December 1998 and was lauded as "a huge turnaround."[116]

Although the negative influence of the Catholic right in the Tasmanian Labor party has been substantial, the response of successive Tasmanian Labor governments to the demands of gays and lesbians has been mostly positive. The wresting of control from the right in 1976 facilitated this response, and the influence of the Greens in Tasmania has helped keep Labor honest in their support for the disadvantaged. On the other side of the ledger, the conservative, anti-Labor upper chamber was able to frustrate all attempts at reform until 1997.

Victoria

The liberalism of the Victorian anti-Labor forces, incorporating an acceptance of equality of opportunity, helps to explain the progressive approach of the Liberal party in Victoria, as well as the lack of success for Labor in that state until the 1980s.[177] The ability of the Victorian Liberal party to govern as a majority, without the encumbrance of coalition arrangements, provided them with further freedom to pursue progressive policies.[118] The Liberal party in Victoria has legislated for criminal law reform and anti-discrimination measures for gays and lesbians.

Conservative power in Victoria came to an end in April 1982 with the election of the Cain Labor government. The previous Labor government had collapsed in the split of 1955. Until then, the Victorian Labor party had been "dominated by Catholics." With the split, however, the left came to dominate the Labor party state branch.[119] The relationship between the Victorian peak union confederation, the Trades Hall Council, and the Labor party in Victoria has been more distant than in other branches. Many influential unions, including the white-collar clerks and shop assistants, chose to affiliate with the Democratic Labor party to escape the polarization between the Communist and Grouper camps in the Labor party. As in New South Wales, a renewed will to regain government in the 1970s led to the rise of a leadership that emphasized "professional competence." The wisdom of this strategy was evident in the successful 1982 state election campaign when the Labor party was able to attract 40 percent of its funding and organizational support from the three (unaffiliated) Victorian teacher unions.[120]

Homosexual law reform had been on the public agenda in Victoria since the Humanist and Rationalist Societies prompted debate on the issue in 1969. Bypassing a comparatively isolated labor council, gay and lesbian groups lobbied parliament directly in Victoria. Society Five, the earliest Victorian lesbian and gay organization, established a subcommittee to look at the issue of law reform shortly after its formation in 1971. Bipartisan lobbying led to motions of support at the Liberal party state council in 1974 and the Labor party state conference in 1975. The first attempt at law reform came in October 1975. Barry Jones, a member of the Labor opposition, introduced a private member's bill to bring about partial reform. Jones's bill was an attempt to preempt the government's foreshadowed sex-discrimination legislation, which would not cover homosexuality.[121] Although Jones's bill was introduced into the lower house, it was not debated and did not proceed beyond the first reading stage.[122] The Black Rock Beach arrests of homosexuals in 1976–1977 were followed by a second attempt at reform by Barry Jones. This second bill was more comprehensive, but it did not go any farther than the second reading stage.[123]

Haddon Storey, the Liberal attorney general, introduced the Hamer government's Crimes (Sexual Offenses) Act in 1980. The legislation found strong support within the gay and lesbian communities in Victoria because, following the South Australian example of 1975, it proposed to treat homosexual and heterosexual conduct equally.[124] A backbench revolt within the Liberal party resulted in the inclusion of the new offense of "soliciting for immoral sexual purposes." But even this did not prevent nine Liberal members crossing the floor to vote against the bill. The Labor party voted as a block in support of the legislation, however, and the legislation passed in December 1980.[125]

In 1982, Labor regained office in Victoria. A proposal by the government for a provision prohibiting discrimination on the ground of sexuality was defeated by the opposition in the Victorian upper house in 1984. On that occasion, the leader of the opposition stated clearly a determination to "continue to stand firmly" against such a provision. Given such resistance, the Labor party decided against introducing a new bill. At the end of the decade, the attorney general concluded that "there is no reason to believe that the opposition's attitude has changed."[126]

The Gay Electoral Lobby met with all parties prior to the 1988 Victorian state election, and with the returned Labor government's attorney general afterwards.[127] Fulfilling a commitment to the Gay Electoral Lobby, the attorney general referred the idea of legislative protection for gays and lesbians to the Law Reform Commission. The commission recommended that the Equal Opportunity Act be amended to include "sexual orientation" as prohibited grounds of discrimination. The act was amended to include actual or presumed HIV/AIDS status, but the recommendation to include sexual preference was not taken up.

During 1992, a new activist group, Buggers and Dykes, highlighted the lack of progress made in over a decade of Labor government. Just before the 1992 election, in a move that reeked of empty political opportunism, the Joan Kirner government gave notice in parliament of pending anti-discrimination legislation. Labor lost this election to the Liberal party. It was the Liberals who finally expanded the grounds of the Victorian Equal Opportunity Act to include sexual preference, using the term "lawful sexual activity" to overcome the resistance from the forces of Victorian conservatism.[128]

Queensland

Until the election of 1989, Queensland had been known as Labor's "resting place of dead electoral hopes and lost political souls."[129] The new Wayne Goss Labor government, following decades in opposition, adopted a cautious, pragmatic, and controlled approach. The largest faction in the party at that time was the Australian Workers' Union. With 50,000 members and an influential leader in the right wing of the party, the Australian Workers' Union remained dominant throughout the 1980s.[130] Respect for the strength of fundamentalist groups, which were still influential in matters of sexual morality, also tempered the Goss government's nerve. Its goal was to contain public opposition, thus minimizing potential political damage. Criminal law reform took place under the Goss government, which also legislated to protect gays and lesbians from employment discrimination.

The cautious approach of the Goss government resulted in inquiry-led reform. Parliament established a Criminal Justice Committee, which investigated the laws relating to homosexuality in 1990. The Public Sector Union and the Miscellaneous Workers' Union called for reform in similar terms, and it did take place in 1990. Community groups were persuaded that an offensive preamble to the legislation was designed to satisfy the "troglodytes" in the Labor party and that it would not hold up if tested in court.[131]

Law reform was followed by a debate on anti-discrimination legislation during 1992. Much of this debate concerned the use of the term "lawful sexual activity" to give coverage under the Equal Opportunity Act to lesbians and gays, as had worked in Victoria. "Lawful sexual activity" was not defined, leaving room for competing interpretations. The attorney general explained that "lawful sexual activity" was a precise term in Queensland, which was not a state with a common-law jurisdiction,[132] unlike New South Wales and Victoria. However, teachers' unions, along with the Public Sector Union and the Liquor, Hospitality, and Miscellaneous Workers' Unions, pressured the government over the perceived ambiguity of the term, especially in light of the state's "offensive behavior" statutes, under which homosexual behavior could be seen as offensive, and thus unlawful. The legislation passed in late 1991.[133]

Conclusion

Gay and lesbian movements all over Australia recognized that winning over the trade union movement was one of the keys to winning the struggle for equality. Because of the institutional importance of trade unions in the lives of working people and in the politics of the nation, activists reached out to the unions as part of a strategy to stop state oppression and to further the identity/life politics of the movement.

The response of the trade unions to the demands of the gay and lesbian liberation movement was considered, incremental, and hotly debated among members. By 1980, progressive trade unions representing white-collar workers, including teachers, social workers, and public servants, adopted anti-discrimination policies inclusive of their lesbian and gay membership. National white-collar union confederations promoted such policies to the Australian Council of Trade Unions. The masculinity of the predominantly blue-collar peak body was able to stymie policy development through only a couple of attempts at its congress.

The adoption of progressive policies by the unions created pressure for wider change, but the Australian labor movement has been a site of activism for conservative as well as progressive forces since its inception. Because a moderate laborist tradition has held sway, the movement has been spectacularly successful. The unions and the Labor party, that is, the industrial and political wings of the movement, have become institutionalized as the partners of government. The industrial wing was institutionalized through the industrial relations apparatus of the state; the political wing won legislative power at the federal and state levels. This accumulation of political leverage made the institutions of the labor movement an attractive arena for those seeking power.

Both the left and right use industrial relations as a site of contestation. Within the union movement, it is not always easy to draw a neat line between the two. In general, the social-democratic left has dominated unions of white-collar public servants, teachers, and social workers. The moral-conservative forces of the right have in general had more appeal for unions of shop assistants and clerks.

The religious right, which promotes the negative stereotypical images of homosexuality underlying employment discrimination, has long been the main opponent of the gay and lesbian movement, in the labor movement in particular and in society in general. The Catholic Church extended the influence of the religious right into the organized labor movement, and into the Labor party. Although its past actions created many enemies within the party, the influence of the church remains strong.[134]

Left-leaning Labor governments have provided most of the breakthroughs in redressing discrimination against gays and lesbians. The "incrementalism" associated with laborism in Australia has typified their approach. The first breakthroughs came at the national level with Whitlam's establishment of committees of inquiry such as the Royal Commissions and Employment Discrimination Committees. In the late 1970s, discrimination on the basis of sex or marital status was gradually outlawed by each state in turn. While Labor government played an important role in this, the conservatives in their ranks posed endless challenges and objections to the extension of anti-discrimination moves to provide for the protection of gays and lesbians.

In all cases of legislative reform in support of lesbians and gays, trade unions played an important role in lobbying government. Of particular importance in the "outlying states" were blue-collar unions on the left. The Miscellaneous Workers' Union, because of its members' front-line role as workers in hospitals in the midst of the HIV/AIDS crisis, was especially attuned to the problems of gay and lesbian discrimination. Teachers' unions were also sensitive, playing an important role in the Queensland reforms and in the development of peak union confederation policy. Public sector unions were instrumental in achieving breakthroughs in their own arena. The support of trade unions and peak bodies in lobbying for legislative protection for lesbians and gays was also important, especially in New South Wales and the Capital Territory.

The Labor party was the only major party to fight for progressive change for gay and lesbian workers, which demonstrates the possibility of links between old and new social movements. Coalition building between labor and the gay and lesbian liberation movement has been underway in Australia for two decades. Posing a new challenge, however, is the move to decentralize industrial relations and de-institutionalize the federal and state systems.[135] Although anti-discrimination measures are in place in all but one Australian jurisdiction, equity has not yet been achieved in recognition of partnership rights in employment leave and superannuation benefits, and in the need for affirmative action. A centralized system of industrial relations has been a leveling influence in Australia, resulting in low wage differentials and generalized social change. (At the same time, local negotiations can result in positive outcomes, as the enterprise agreement evidence presented at the federal family leave test case indicates.) With decentralization of industrial relations, lesbians and gays will have to become active in local firms and trade union organizations to achieve new forms of social justice.

Labor's receptivity to the demands of sexual identity movements will be further tested as Australian industrial relations undergoes even more change. The removal of trade restrictions that protected workers' wages and conditions is part of continuing government competition policy.[136] The "arbitral" model is coming to an end, meaning a transfer of negotiations from the industry or national level to the level of the enterprise. As a result of a reliance on the arbitration system, however, unionism in Australia is relatively weak at the workplace level. This, along with a continuing decline in total union density, to 31 percent in 1996, means that the achievements of Australian labor with respect to sexual identity may have reached a plateau.[137] Whatever the future holds, as the 1990s draw to a close, it is timely to look back and recognize, and indeed celebrate, what has been achieved by the Australian gay and lesbian movement's alliance with organized labor.

Notes

1. Gay Men and Lesbians Against Discrimination found that around 32 percent of respondents to its survey reported being harassed at work; 14 percent of women and 11 percent of men reported being pressured out of a job or sacked. In all, 45 percent of women and men responding reported experiencing the kinds of discrimination listed. See Gay Men and Lesbians Against Discrimination, *Not a Day Goes By: Report on the GLAD Survey into Discrimination and Violence Against Lesbians and Gay Men in Victoria* (Melbourne: Gay Men and Lesbians Against Discrimination, 1994) pp. 10, 28. These results indicate a higher incidence of discrimination at work in Australia than in the United Kingdom or in North America. See P. Greasley, *Gay Men at Work: A Report on Discrimination Against Gay Men in Employment in London* (London: Lesbian and Gay Employment Rights, 1986); J. Woods, *The Corporate Closet* (New York: Free Press, 1993), pp. 268–269, 271.

2. In Australia, the labor movement comprises two wings. The political wing is the Australian Labor party, to which many trade unions are affiliated. The industrial wing is the trade union movement, encompassing blue- and white-collar trade unions.

3. G. Patmore, *Australian Labour History* (Melbourne: Longman Cheshire, 1991), pp. 36–39, 56–63.

4. Ibid.

5. Ibid., pp. 74–82.

6. Ibid., pp. 36–39, 56–63.

7. B. Shields, "Craftsmen in the Making," in *All Our Labours: Oral Histories of Working Life in Twentieth Century Sydney,* ed. B. Shields (Sydney: New South Wales University Press, 1992), pp. 86–122, 89–90.

8. A. Parkin, "Party Organizations and Machine Politics," in *Machine Politics in the Australian Labor Party,* ed. A. Parkin and J. Warhurst (Sydney: George Allen and Unwin, 1983), p. 24.

9. G. Maddox, "The Australian Labor Party," in *Political Parties in Australia,* ed. G. Starr, K. Richmond, and G. Maddox Heinemann (Richmond, Victoria: Heinemann Educational Australia, 1978), pp. 219–220; T. Wheelwright, "New South Wales: The Dominant Right," in *Machine Politics in the Australian Labor Party,* ed. Parkin and Warhurst, pp. 33–34.

10. Ibid., pp. 31–34.

11. D. W. Rawson, *Unions and Unionists in Australia* (Sydney: George Allen and Unwin, 1978), pp. 14–16.

12. R. Markey, *In Case of Oppression: The Life and Times of the Labor Council of New South Wales* (Sydney: Pluto Press, 1994), p. 6.

13. S. Ostenfeld, "Interactive Movements: Gay Lib, the Women's and Student Movements, and the Trade Unions," in *Gay and Lesbian Perspectives III: Essays in Australian Culture,* ed. G. Wotherspoon (Sydney: Department of Economic History with the Australian Centre for Lesbian and Gay Research, University of Sydney, 1996).

14. Australian National University and Archives of Business and Labour (ANU/ABL): ACOA National Office Z237/258 File 138/1, "Working Women's Centre"; "Working Women's Charter Campaign Conference: Resolutions Carried at Conference Held August 12, 13 and 14," ANU/ABL Council of Australian Government Employee Organizations N87/95.

15. Australian Council of Salaried and Professional Associations (ACSPA) 1974 National Conference, Record of Major Decisions, ANU/ABL: ACSPA Z140/1, "Papers from ACSPA National Conference."

16. Australian Council of Trade Unions Decisions 1977, 10, ANU/ABL: Australian Council of Trade Unions S784/4; Minutes, Australian Council of Trade Unions Congress, 13 September 1977, second session, 7-10, ANU/ABL Australian Council of Trade Unions S784/4. In a display of inconsistency, however, the Australian Council of Trade Unions' executive recommendation to the 1977 congress with regard to Australian Government Employment did not include "sexuality" in the schedule of areas to be covered by the requested anti-discrimination legislation (see "F" Australian Council of Trade Unions Executive Recommendation to the 1977 Congress: "Australian Government Employment," ANU/ABL Australian Council of Trade Unions S784/4; "1977 Australian Council of Trade Unions Congress, Ref: R.4 [131]," 19 September 1977, ANU/ABL Council of Australian Government Employee Organizations N87/94).

17. Document A3: "Homosexuals at Work Conference"; "1978 National Conference (Melbourne, 16–20 October) Record of Major Decisions," ANU/ABL ACSPA Z140/1, and "ACSPA 1978 National Conference," ANU/ABL ACSPA N10/460.

18. "Gays in Jobs: Unions to Act." *The Age,* 18 October 1978, ANU/ABL Australian Council of Trade Unions N58/595; "Unions Will Give Homosexuals a Say," *The Australian,* 18 October 1978, ANU/ABL Australian Council of Trade Unions N58/595; "Gay Clerks Seek Rights," *The Sun,* 18 October 1978, ANU/ABL Australian Council of Trade Unions N58/595; "The Battle for Gay Rights," *The Sun,* 24 October 1978, ANU/ABL Australian Council of Trade Unions N58/595.

19. "Leader Talks on ACSPA Conference," *Direct Action,* no. 232, 9 November 1978, p. 4, ANU/ABL ACSPA N10/460.

20. "Correspondence to Federal Secretary ACSPA from General Secretary Teacher's Federation, 5 June 1979," ANU/ABL ACSPA Z140/1.

21. Executive Meeting Fourth Day, 23 August 1979, Australian Council of Trade Unions Executive Minutes, ANU/ABL Australian Council of Trade Unions N68/835.

22. "1979 Australian Council of Trade Unions Congress Agenda Papers," ANU/ABL Australian Council of Trade Unions S784/4.

23. Correspondence Teacher's Federation, ACSPA 5 June 1979, ANU/ABL ACSPA Z140/1.

24. "ACSPA National Union Meeting on Homosexual Workers," ANU/ABL ACSPA N10/139, Reports for 1978 National Conference; Handwritten Notes from Meeting (no author noted), Australian Lesbian and Gay Archives (ALGA)/ACSPA; "Special Circular: Homosexuals in the Workplace Meeting," 2 August 1979, ANU/ABL ACSPA N10/141; "ACSPA Fed Exec Circulars 1979"; "Record of Decisions of Federal Executive Meeting, 14 June 1979," ANU/ABL ACSPA Z140/1.

25. Three other large unions not affiliated with the labor umbrella organization (the teamsters, auto and aero industry workers, and the machinists). "ACSPA National Union Meeting on Homosexual Workers," ANU/ABL ACSPA N10/139, Reports for 1978 National Conference.

26. "Background Paper on Homosexual Unionists," prepared for ACOA Queensland Branch Conference, March 1984.

27. File Council of Australian Government Employee Organizations, Council Minutes 1978–1980, ANU/ABL ACOA Z237/302 CAGEO Council Minutes.

28. Ibid.; File 227 "Discrimination," ANU/ABL ACOA Z237/258.

29. Ibid.; Minutes, 102nd Meeting of the ACOA Federal Executive, March 1981, p. 9, item 53.

30. Policy Recommendations and Agenda Papers, 1981 Australian Council of Trade Unions Congress, pp. 20, 28, 45 (Section M, part 3), 1981 Australian Council of Trade Unions Congress Papers, ANU/ABL Australian Council of Trade Unions s784.

31. Ibid.; Australian Council of Trade Unions circular 133/1983, file 227/1, part 1: "Discrimination Legislation," ANU/ABL ACOA Z237/195.

32. Outline of proposed clause dealing with Discrimination in Employment—attached to Australian Council of Trade Unions circular 373/1981, 24 August 1981, File 227, Discrimination, ANU/ABL ACOA Z237/258.

33. Notes, Paul Stein, relating to a meeting between the New South Wales Anti-Discrimination Board and the Australian Council of Trade Unions on 3 June 1981, pp. 2–3, file 227/1, part 1, "Discrimination Legislation," ANU/ABL ACOA Z237/195.

34. File 227/1, part 1, "Discrimination Legislation," ANU/ABL ACOA Z237/195.

35. Minutes, Council of Australian Government Employee Organizations Federal Executive, February 1981, File Council of Australian Government Employee Organizations Council Minutes 1980-81, ANU/ABL ACOA Z237/302.

36. Correspondence, from Sams, Labor Council Industrial Officer to Pat Hills, Minister for Industrial Relations and Technology, 25 February 1983, ANU/ABL FEDFA N129/67. See also Circular C6/83 from Labor Council Industrial Officer to Affiliates, 11 January 1983, ANU/ABL FEDFA N129/67.

37. Submission from Australian Council of Trade Unions to Human rights Commission re Superannuation and the Sex Discrimination Act, file Discrimination—Sexual Preference, ANU/ABL PSU Z237/265.

38. Executive Report, p. 62, 1985 Australian Council of Trade Unions Congress Papers, ANU/ABL Australian Council of Trade Unions s784.

39. Australian Council of Trade Unions Bulletin on AIDS, 1 May 1986, file Discrimination—Sexual Preference, ANU/ABL PSU Z237/265.

40. AIDS Action: A Newsletter From the Victorian AIDS Council, no. 5, July 1985, p. 5.

41. National Employment Discrimination Committee, Annual Report 1976–1977, pp. 25–26, ANU/ABL ACOA Z97/139.

42. Patmore, Australian Labour History, pp. 74–82.

43. Parkin, "Party Organizations and Machine Politics," pp. 26–28; Wheelwright, "New South Wales," p. 34; J. Jupp, "Victoria: Left, Right and Centre," in Machine Politics in the Australian Labor Party, ed. Parkin and Warhurst, p. 70; D. Jaensch, The Politics of Australia

(Sydney: Macmillan, 1992), pp. 231, 239; Maddox, "The Australian Labor Party," pp. 205–208, 215–217.

44. This material with regard to the federal arena was presented as a conference paper; see S. Ostenfeld, "Identity Politics and Trade Unions: The Case of Sexual Minorities in Australia," in *Current Research in Industrial Relations: Proceedings of the 12th AIRAANZ Conference,* Wellington, 1998, pp. 289–298.

45. "Equal Chance for Jobs," *The Australian,* 26 June 1973, ANU/ABL: Australian Council of Trade Unions N58/165.

46. Press Release, 8 December 1973, ALGA: CAMP New South Wales.

47. Correspondence, Department of Defence/Clohesy, 20 June 1975, ALGA: Department of Defence; "Policy Regarding Homosexuals in the Armed Services," ALGA: Department of Defence.

48. "Report to the Nation '76," p. 20, ALGA: CAMP New South Wales.

49. "Equal Work Rights for Gays Urged," *The Age,* 13 September 1978, ANU/ABL Australian Council of Trade Unions N58/595.

50. "Homosexuality as a consideration in applications for resident or temporary entry and change of status," Department of Immigration and Ethnic Affairs, Executive PC 7, 28 August 1979, ALGA: Dept Immigration, Hxl relationships.

51. News Release, Minister for Home Affairs, 21 December 1979, ALGA: Australian Commonwealth Government (also in file "Cageo Australian Capital Territory Div. Discrimination," ANU/ABL Council of Australian Government Employee Organizations N88/85).

52. Senate Hansard, 26 October 1982, pp. 1821–1826, ALGA: Australian Commonwealth Government.

53. Press Release, "Democrats to Press Again for Affirmative Action and Anti-Discrimination Legislation," 25 August 1983, ALGA: Australian Democrats.

54. "Reforming the Australian Public Service: A Statement of the Government's Intention," December 1983, pp. 32–33, file 190/4/1 PS Inquiry—White Paper re 1984 PS Reform Legislation, ANU/ABL ACOA Z237/130.

55. Minutes of Working Party on Guidelines on Employment of Homosexuals in the APS— first meeting 1 August 1986, file Discrimination—Sexual Preference, ANU/ABL PSU Z237/265.

56. Press Release, Lionel Bowen, "New Grounds of Discrimination in Employment," 8 December 1989, ALGA: Jamie Gardiner.

57. Press Release, "Army Coup Entrenches Sex Discrimination: Powell," 18 June 1992; Defence Instructions, "Homosexual Behaviour in the Australian Defence Force"; Hansard Pink, Senator Robert Ray, 18 June 1992; Press Release, "Human Rights or Factional Deals: Powell to Force Government's Hand on the Floor of the Senate," 26 August 1992; Press Release, "Statement on ADF Policy on Homosexuals," Human Rights Australia, 18 June 1992, ALGA: Brother/Sister Newspaper.

58. Correspondence, Shayne Wilde / Sir Ronald Wilson, President, HREOC, 3.6.94, GLRL Files; N. Johnston, "Gay Family Leave Claim Gets a Boost," *The Age,* 4 July 1994, p. 7.

59. *Workforce,* no. 975, p. 1; no. 979, p. 2, GLRL Files.

60. Correspondence, Kevin Davern, FSU / Shayne Wilde, 14 July 1994; Bill Ethel, CFMEWU (WA) / President AIRC, 1.5.94; Kerry Lewis, NTEU / Jenny George, 7 July 1994; Patricia J. Staunton / Ms. S. Wilde, 13 July 1994; M. Beaumont, ANF / Ms. Jennie George, Australian Council of Trade Unions, 14 July 1994; Greg Sword, NUW / Mr. B. Kelty, Australian Council of Trade Unions, 28 June 1994; Jennie George, Australian Council of Trade Unions / Shayne Wilde, 4 July 1994; plus file note "Trade Unions Who Have Shown Support Thus Far" (not dated), GLRL Files.

61. "How Gays are Treated," *Sydney Morning Herald,* 15 June 1994, p.15; Correspondence, Brian Grieg, ACLGR / American Express, Qantas, Ansett, Microsoft, Lotus Development

Corporation, Lend Lease Holding Company, Carlton United Breweries, Myer / Grace Brothers, GLRL Files.

62. Australian Industrial Relations Commission, "Decision, Family Leave Test Case," pp. 39–40, GLRL Files.

63. Australian Industrial Relations Commission, "Decision, Various Industries," Dec 207/95 S Print L9048, Sydney, 3 February 1995, pp. 5–7.

64. D. Southorn, "Gays Win Work," *Courier-Mail,* 19 August 1984, p. 1.

65. Parliamentary Research Service, "Bills Digest No. 149 1994," pp. 1–2; News Release, Attorney-General The Hon. Michael Lavarch MP, "Burdekin Report on Tasmanian Criminal Code," 23 August 1994.

66. L. Bebbington, "Australian Capital Territory Law Reform," 13 June 1975, ALGA: AUS; "Is the Law Behind the Times?" *The Age,* 15 July 1976.

67. Australian Capital Territory Ordinance Proclamation No. 55 of 1976, ALGA: Australian Commonwealth Government; Hansard, Australian Capital Territory Legislative Assembly Proceedings, 22 July 1975, ALGA: Australian Commonwealth Government.

68. B. Juddery, "Australian Capital Territory: Social Democrats," in *Machine Politics in the Australian Labor Party,* ed. Parkin and Warhurst, pp. 210–217.

69. Record of a meeting between Office of Women's Affairs and Unions and Employer Representatives 22 May 1980, ANU/ABL Council of Australian Government Employee Organizations N88/85, Cageo Australian Capital Territory Div. Discrimination.

70. R. Hunter, *Indirect Discrimination in the Workplace* (Sydney: Federation Press, 1992), pp. 24, 32.

71. Markey, *In Case of Oppression,* p. 487.

72. Wheelwright, "New South Wales, pp. 33–34, 41–42.

73. Correspondence, Clohesy / Neville Wran, Premier, 24 September 1976, ALGA: CAMP New South Wales.

74. C. Johnston, "Social Democracy Versus Social Reform: New South Wales Labor and Homosexual Law Reform," paper presented at the Australasian Political Studies Association, Perth, 18–20 August 1982, p 8.

75. "Report to the Nation '76," p. 19, ALGA: CAMP New South Wales.

76. Correspondence, Anti-Discrimination Board of New South Wales/Camp Inc, 21 September 1977, ALGA:ADB New South Wales.

77. Correspondence, Clohesy, 28 August 1976, ALGA: CAMP New South Wales.

78. "Discrimination 'Indictment,'" *Sydney Morning Herald,* 27 January 1978, file Discrimination, ANU/ABL Australian Council of Trade Unions N58/595.

79. Correspondence, D. Moore, President Anti-Discrimination Board / The Federal Secretary, ACOA, 5 January 1978, file Discrimination, ANU/ABL Z237/258.

80. New South Wales Anti-Discrimination Board, *Discrimination and Homosexuality,* 1982, p. 399.

81. Circular C450/82 from Secretary, Labor Council to Affiliated Unions, 16 November 1982, ANU/ABL FEDFA N129/67; Correspondence, from Australian Theatrical and Amusement Employees' Association (New South Wales Branch) to Wran (23 Sept 1982) and Unsworth (25 August 1982), ANU/ABL FEDFA N129/67; Correspondence, Wran to Unsworth, 3 November 1982; Correspondence Unsworth to Wran, 18 November 1982, Correspondence, Premier Wran to Jenkins, Theatrical and Amusement Employees' Association, 3 November 1981, ANU/ABL FEDFA N129/67.

82. Correspondence, M. Raper to B. Ralph, 26 May 1981, ALGA: New South Wales ITA.

83. Johnston, "Social Democracy Versus Social Reform," p. 12.

84. Australian Lesbian and Gay Archives, "New South Wales," in *Homosexual Law Reform in Australia* (Melbourne, 1993), pp. 1–2; Johnston, "Social Democracy Versus Social Reform," p. 15.

85. Australian Lesbian and Gay Archives, "New South Wales," pp. 15–16.

86. L. Watson, "Why Lex Watson Does Not Demand Unsworth's Defeat," *Oxford Weekender News,* no. 26 (March 1982), p. 6, ALGA: Bright, Mervyn John.

87. Australian Lesbian and Gay Archives, "New South Wales," pp. 2–3; Johnston, "Social Democracy Versus Social Reform," p. 22.

88. Watson, "Why Lex Watson Does Not Demand Unsworth's Defeat," p. 6; Correspondence, from Jenkins, Theatrical Employees, to Unsworth, Secretary, New South Wales Labor Council, 14 February 1983, ANU/ABL FEDFA N129/67.

89. P. Blazey, "The Sad State of Gay Politics," *The Australian,* 20 September 1983 (G. Weir 1984 archive document 25); Australian Lesbian and Gay Archives, "New South Wales," pp. 4–5.

90. Australian Lesbian and Gay Archives, "New South Wales," pp. 6–7.

91. State Family Leave Case: Judgment of the Industrial Relations Commission of New South Wales, 12 May 1995.

92. Johnston, "Social Democracy Versus Social Reform," p. 17.

93. G. Stokes, "South Australia: Consensus Politics," in *Machine Politics in the Australian Labor Party,* ed. Parkin and Warhurst, pp. 134–147.

94. T. Reeves, "The 1972 Debate on Male Homosexuality in South Australia," in *Gay Perspectives II: More Essays in Australian Gay Culture,* ed. R. Aldrich (Sydney: Department of Economic History, University of Sydney, 1994).

95. Australian Lesbian and Gay Archives, "South Australia," in *Homosexual Law Reform in Australia,* p. 1.

96. Ibid., p. 2.

97. P. Holloway, "Anti-Homosexual Laws Repealed in SA," 2 October 1975, ALGA: Duncan, Peter (MP).

98. Australian Lesbian and Gay Archives, "South Australia," p. 2.

99. "Equality Bill Recognised De Facto Marriage," *The Australian,* 16 October 1975, ANU/ABL: N58/105.

100. Office of the Commissioner for Equal Opportunity, South Australia, *Annual Report,* 1976–77.

101. Ibid., p. 15; 1978–79, p. 16; 1983–84, pp. 62–63; 1984–85, p. 33.

102. Ibid., 1992–93, pp. 63–64; 1993–94, pp. 42, 71–72. The respondents appealed this decision to the Supreme Court, with a confidential settlement negotiated between the parties finalizing the case during these proceedings.

103. D. Mitchell, "Western Australia: The Struggle to Adapt," in *Machine Politics in the Australian Labor Party,* ed. Parkin and Warhurst, p. 165.

104. Australian Lesbian and Gay Archives, "Western Australia," in *Homosexual Law Reform in Australia,* p. 2.

105. *Ibid.*

106. Interview, S. Ostenfeld / Mark Cuomo, Perth, 6 October 1993; Interview, S. Ostenfeld / Darren Ray, Perth, 8 October 1993. See M. Beasley, *The Missos: A History of the Federated Miscellaneous Workers Union* (Sydney: Allen and Unwin, 1996), for an appraisal of the importance of the union in relation to the Labor party, particularly the Labor party left (pp. 75–81, 137–157).

107. R. Davis, "Tasmania: Premiers and Parochial Politics," in *Machine Politics in the Australian Labor Party,* ed. Parkin and Warhurst, p. 186–87; R. Wettenhall, *A Guide to Tasmanian Government Administration* (Hobart: Platypus, 1968), p. 33.

108. Australian Lesbian and Gay Archives, "Tasmania," in *Homosexual Law Reform in Australia*, pp. 1–4.

109. Ibid.

110. C. Johnston, "Victimless Crimes Inquiry," *Homosexual News Service*, no. 1, 27 July 1977, p. 4, ALGA: AUS.

111. Australian Lesbian and Gay Archives, "Tasmania," pp. 1–4.

112. File 227/1, part 1, Discrimination Legislation, ANU/ABL ACOA z237/195.

113. "Support Gay Law Reform in Tasmania," broadsheet, ALGA: Sheril Berkovitch; R. Croome, "Setting Our World on Fire," keynote address at Mardi Gras forum "Activism in the 1990s," 22 February 1992, ALGA: Rodney Croome.

114. Press Release, "National Body Rejects Tasmanian AIDS Legislation," 10 September 1990, ALGA: AFAO.

115. Press Release, "Attention All Gay Media Editors and Journalists," R. Croome, 28 August 1992, ALGA: Brother/Sister Newspaper.

116. J. Counsel, "Lobbyists Push for Anti-discrimination Law on Sexuality," *The Australian*, 11 December 1998, http://www.theaustralian.com.au/state/4357082.htm; Tasmanian Gay and Lesbian Rights Group, "Campaign Updates," 1998, http://www.tased.edu.au/tasonline/history/country/st/tasqueer/may1998/updates/updt9_html; Australian Broadcasting Corporation, "Gay Groups Praise New Anti-discrimination Laws," 10 December 1998, Anti-discrimination Campaign; http://ausqrd.queer.org.au/qrd/news/aus/1998/Q4/newsnat-10dec1998-32htm.

117. Jaensch, *The Politics of Australia*, p. 275.

118. Interview, Ostenfeld/Starr, 21 November 1996.

119. Jupp, "Victoria," p. 90.

120. Ibid., pp. 72–77; J. Warhurst, "Group Pressure," and L. Sonder, "Labor and the Unions," in *Labor to office: The Victorian State Election 1982*, ed. B. Costar and C. Hughes (Melbourne: Drummond,1983), pp. 90, 242–243.

121. "Hamer Plans to Outlaw Sex Barriers," *The Age*, 27 September 1975, ANU/ABL: Australian Council of Trade Unions N58/105.

122. Australian Lesbian and Gay Archives, "Victoria," in *Homosexual Law Reform in Australia*, pp. 1–2.

123. Ibid., p. 2.

124. Minutes of Meeting to Discuss Action on Homosexual Law Reform, Plumbers Union, 8 October 1980, ALGA: Campaign 4 Gay Equality.

125. Correspondence, Laurie Bebbington to Haddon Storey, 14 September 1980, ALGA: Laurie Bebbington.

126. Correspondence, Kevin Pittman, Attorney General's Department of Victoria, to S. Berkovitch, "Discrimination on the Ground of Sexuality" (n.d.), ALGA: Sheril Berkovitch.

127. Meeting with the Attorney General, 8 November 1988, ALGA: Gay Electoral Lobby; Dissection of Polling Results, St. Kilda; ALGA: Gay Electoral Lobby.

128. Office of the Commissioner for Equal Opportunity, Victoria, *Twelfth Annual Report*, 1988–89, pp. 2, 44; Equal Opportunity Commission of Victoria, *Annual Report, 1994–95*, pp. 11–12.

129. W. Swan, "Queensland: Labor's Graveyard?" in *Machine Politics in the Australian Labor Party*, ed. Parkin and Warhurst, pp. 100–104.

130. M. Hearn and H. Knowles, *One Big Union: A History of the Australian Workers Union 1886–1994* (Melbourne: Cambridge University Press, 1996), pp. 179–180, 310, 334–336; R. Wear, "Wayne Goss—A Leader in the Queensland Tradition," and J. Wanna, "Managing the Politics: The Party, Factions, Parliament and Parliamentary Committees," in *The Goss Govern-*

ment: Promise and Performance of Labor in Queensland, ed. B. Stevens and J. Wanna (Melbourne: Macmillan, 1993), pp. 25, 54–60.

131. Federated Miscellaneous Workers' Union, July Meeting 1990, Correspondence G. Smith / G. Weir, 17 July 1990; PSU Queensland Branch, "Reform of Laws Relating to Homosexuality," July 1990, G. Wier Archives; Interview, S. Ostenfeld / Gerry Smith, 17 September 1993, Brisbane.

132. The criminal laws of New South Wales, Victoria, and South Australia include specific statutes as well as the common law (judge-made law), and the Australian Capital Territory applies the NSW Crimes Act and supplements it with local statutes. The common law is displaced by criminal codes in Queensland, Western Australia, Tasmania, and the Northern Territory. They also have statutes that concern specific types of crimes such as narcotics offenses. See Queensland Right to Life, "Overview of Law in Australian States and Territories," 1997, http://www.qrtl.org.au/euthanasia/legal.htm.

133. Queensland University of Technology media release, 28 November 1991, G. Weir Archives; Correspondence, G. Weir / Sue Yarrow, Federated Miscellaneous Workers' Union (n.d.), G. Weir Archives; P. Tahmindjis, "The New Queensland Anti-Discrimination Act: An Outline," *Queensland Law Society Journal* 22 (February 1992): 9.

134. Although one commentator suggests that "The virtual ending of religious sectarianism in Australia, and the wash-up of the Labor Split of the 1950s, has led to a situation where Catholics in Australia's conservative parties are at historically high levels. What's more, there is now a group of Catholic fundamentalists who have more in common with other Christian fundamentalists than with liberal Catholics." See G. Henderson, "Don't Mention the War to Members of the Lyons Forum," *Sydney Morning Herald,* 1 April 1997, p. 15.

135. R. Naughton, "The De-Institutionalization of Australian Industrial Relations—Temporarily Stalled?" *Current Research in Industrial Relations: Proceedings of the 11th AIRAANZ Conference,* Brisbane, 1997, pp. 518–524.

136. E. Davis and R. Lansbury, "Industrial Relations in Australia," in *International and Comparative Industrial Relations: A Study of Industrialised Market Economies,* 2nd ed., ed. G. Bamber and R. Lansbury (Sydney: Allen & Unwin, 1993), p. 103.

137. M. Gardner and G. Palmer, *Employment Relations: Industrial Relations and Human Resource Management in Australia,* 2nd ed. (Melbourne: Macmillan, 1997), p. 97.

Mazibuko K. Jara, Naomi Webster,
and Gerald Hunt

10   At a Turning Point: Organized Labor, Sexual Diversity, and the New South Africa

Collin Ndaba, the general secretary of a trade union, calls Charity into his office with a very somber expression on his face. He says, "Charity, I have something serious to tell you. Mazibuko has been hiding something from you and Cornelia. Do you know he is gay? He has spoken to me about protecting the rights of gay and lesbian workers, but I am going to ignore him." Charity is thinking: Mazibuko is working for a lesbian and gay rights organization. He does not have to be gay to work for lesbian and gay equality. Why does it matter one way or the other? Anyway, why should a trade union official be thinking this way? Shouldn't unions be supporting equal rights? However, Charity feels she cannot express what she is thinking because the union's policies do not yet include provisions for lesbian and gay equality.

The above story is one example of a continuing but slowly changing attitude toward sexual minorities within post-apartheid South Africa. Although there have been significant legal and constitutional changes in relation to gays and lesbians, many South African individuals, organizations, and institutions have been slow to rethink long-standing prejudicial attitudes and to alter practices toward sexual minorities. So far, organized labor appears not to be a notable exception to this trend. On the one hand, many labor leaders supported the new government when it was enacting change in the legal and constitutional apparatus of the post-apartheid Republic of South Africa, including the incorporation of sexual orientation as a category for nondiscrimination. On the other hand, very few labor federations or trade unions have changed their internal policies, procedures, and collective agreements to reduce or eliminate discrimination on the basis of sexual orientation in areas such as hiring, firing, and benefit coverage. Nevertheless, South Africa continues to be in the midst of enormous change in relation to human rights and equity issues. There are encouraging signs, especially within the judiciary, that discriminatory attitudes and practices toward sexual minorities are changing. Moreover, organized labor seems increasingly committed to gender and other equity issues and now might be more amenable to initiatives directed at equality for sexual minorities than at any other point in its history. This chapter undertakes to review, assess, and analyze these developments.[1]

The New South Africa

Collective applause was heard throughout the world in April 1994 when Nelson Mandela's African National Congress Party (ANC) was swept into power through a massive victory in the first-ever democratic, nonracial elections held in South Africa. After years of civil riots, bloodshed, and protest, South Africa finally entered a post-apartheid period. Once the celebrations were over, work began in earnest to restructure the political and social landscape of the country. Expectations were high, especially from the large black majority, many of whom had been living in abject poverty but now had hopes for a much improved life politically, socially, and economically. Equally hopeful about the prospects for change were other groups, not the least of which were gays and lesbians, who had lived under a cloud of oppression, inequality, and intolerance.

Since 1994, human rights issues have been at the forefront of debate and legislative change in South Africa. Soon after coming into power, the ANC government passed the Human Rights Commission Act (1996), which created a central commission and regional offices to hear complaints and undertake educational initiatives. In 1996, a new constitution was enacted, guaranteeing protection and outlawing unfair discrimination by the state or individuals on thirteen grounds, including race, gender, sex, and marital status. Also included, after considerable lobbying and pressure, were gays and lesbians, making it the only constitution in the world specifically guaranteeing protection, nondiscrimination, and equality for this minority group.

In tandem with the new constitution and the creation of a Human Rights Commission, the ANC brought forward several important pieces of legislation designed to protect and enhance workers' rights and generally reinforce broader equity initiatives. A new Labor Relations Act (LRA) was enacted in September 1995, and a Basic Conditions of Employment Act (BCEA) and an Employment Equity Act (EEA) were enacted in 1998. The new LRA has been widely seen as a victory for organized labor and reinforces the anti-discrimination clauses of South Africa's constitution. It specifically includes sexual orientation as grounds for nondiscrimination in the workplace. The BCEA includes provisions for such things as "humane" working hours and conditions, maternity leave, and the elimination of child labor. It also includes a clause acknowledging the "life partner" of any employee for the purposes of family responsibility, thus recognizing and potentially accommodating all types of families inside and outside of traditional marriages, including same-sex couples. The LRA provisions were transitional until the passing of the EEA. The EEA outlaws unfair discrimination on seventeen grounds including race, gender, sex, sexual orientation, marital status, and HIV/AIDS status. The EEA also requires employers to develop and implement employment equity initiatives to help address and correct apartheid inequities in the workplace. Designated groups under the EEA are black people, women, and people living with disabilities. The EEA defines family to include partners in the same way as the BCEA.

The terms of the EEA were quite controversial and strongly opposed by many white people in positions of power. The provisions in the EEA were only achieved through an employment and equity alliance made up of twenty-two organizations, including the National Coalition for Gay and Lesbian Equality, the South African Council of Churches, the Southern Africa Catholic Bishops' Conference, and a number of trade unions. Notably, the South African Council of Churches did support the expanded definition of family to include same-sex partners, even though some coalition members were opposed to the idea.

Also contributing to a much more progressive environment has been the creation of a number of investigatory commissions. A Human Rights Commission was established by the Human Rights Commission Act to promote respect for human rights and a culture of human rights, as well as to investigate and to report on the observance of human rights and take steps to secure appropriate redress where human rights have been violated. It also has a research and education role. The Commission of Gender Equality Act, passed in 1996, created a Commission on Gender with the power to monitor, investigate, research, educate, lobby, advise, and report on issues concerning gender inequity. The Truth and Reconciliation Commission, headed by Bishop Desmond Tutu, was created to explore and expose apartheid-era injustices in business, policing, the law, and the church, and to recommend corrective action and compensation plans for victims.

Thus, the ANC set itself a massive agenda with an overarching goal: to unify South Africa as a model of democracy after years of having being ruled by a powerful white-minority regime—all to be achieved within a country in the throws of an economic downturn, very high unemployment and underemployment, enormous income disparities, an extremely serious violent crime problem, and significant emigration of professionals. In spite of the enormity of the task, though, this emerging political order has created the framework for the transformation of South Africa toward a people-centered, democratic state based on equality, respect for human rights, dignity, and justice for all. In so doing, it has offered the lesbian and gay rights movement a unique moment in history to demand full membership and equality in the new South Africa.

The Rise of a Gay and Lesbian Rights Movement

At a press conference held in Washington, D.C., in December 1996, the well-known activist Zackie Achmat indicated that the fight for gay and lesbian rights in South Africa would continue to be "part and parcel" of the larger liberation movement.[2] Early organizing for gay and lesbian rights, however, reflected the racially divided nature of the country; the movement was primarily white and conservative. The rise of gay and lesbian activism in South Africa, as a result, is closely linked to its transition from a uniracial to a multiracial movement, and one much more aligned with broader civil rights goals.[3]

The first wave of political activism emerged in 1968 in response to a law reform movement aimed at making virtually any homosexual activity a serious criminal offence. Up until this period, gay life had focused on underground bars, house parties, and cruising, all within an environment where public, but not private, male homosexual acts were unlawful. However, when a draconian anti-gay bill was introduced by the government in 1968 to amend the Sexual Offences Act, designed to make homosexuality itself statutorily illegal and to bring lesbians within the scope of the law, gays and lesbians started to mobilize. The first "public" meetings aimed at gay rights within South Africa were organized mainly by an urban and professional group of white men and women, with the singular goal of preventing the passage of the proposed bill. These meetings had the effect of bringing together for the first time a group committed to political activism, helping to forge a sense of a community with a common purpose. Their initiatives drew attention to the worse excesses of the bill but did not prevent its passage in a somewhat modified but still outrageous form in March 1969. Among other things, the amendments raised the age of consent for male homosexual activity from sixteen to nineteen, outlawed dildos, and criminalized almost all male sexual activity within the public and private domain. So stern was the new law that it became illegal for a male person to commit any act designed to stimulate sexual passion at a "party"; where a party was defined as any occasion involving more than two people, sexual passion could be something as innocent as dancing. Sodomy became a schedule 1 offense, lumping it together with serious crimes such as murder, rape, and treason. Nevertheless, there was some very slight cause for celebration because the original bill had proposed making it illegal for two women to live together and contained provisions for a mandatory three-year prison term for all homosexual acts.

Ironically, these new and harsh measures ushered in an era in which gay and lesbian life, including a degree of activism, began to flourish. While all public spaces such as parks and washrooms were even more closely monitored for homosexual activity, and house raids on private parties remained common, the police appeared prepared to look the other way when it came to bars and private clubs, as long as minors or liquor were not in evidence. In other words, homosexuality continued to be tolerated in spite of the repressive laws, as long as it took place indoors, especially in ghettoized commercial spaces, and out of sight. This in turn lead to the creation of "meeting spaces" and the beginnings of a community based on a shared sense of isolation and oppression. At the same time, though, the already stratified feature of gay and lesbian life was reinforced. Those without the money to go to bars, and those too frightened to be seen in a gay place, had few other options. Oddly as well, even under apartheid, blacks were allowed to enter bars that did not serve alcohol, and although some of the few that had sufficient funds did try, they were often refused admission by the management.

Within these constraints and contradictions, a gay and lesbian subculture took root during the 1970s. On the one hand, nearly any kind of homosexual activity was illegal; on the other hand, a vibrant urban commercial scene began to emerge, tentative as it was, since it existed at the whim of the authorities. The government, police, and military were increasingly preoccupied with growing tensions and rebellion in the black townships rather than the private diversions of homosexuals. For most of the gays and lesbians enjoying the outlets provided by bars and private clubs, the primary goal was social rather than political, a fact that may also have helped to foster a certain level of tolerance by the police.

Toward the end of the 1970s, however, there was a resurgence of more enthusiastic policing of places where gays and lesbians gathered, fueled in part by a political and media-driven campaign equating gay life with pedophilia. In response to this renewed sense of vulnerability and oppression, a new wave of activism began to take shape in the early 1980s. The Gay Association of South Africa (GASA) formed in 1982, an amalgamation of several other smaller groups, and although largely a socially oriented, white middle-class and conservative mix of people, it provided a forum for political discussions. Although its main publication was banned by the authorities, the group was able to organize social events and meetings and hold an annual convention. In October 1982, GASA organized the largest gay event ever to take place up until that time, a Gay Jamboree held in the Transvaal Country Club attended by over 3,000 people. By May 1985, GASA was holding conventions at a downtown Johannesburg hotel, complete with speeches on gay liberation. Brazenly, given the legal situation, it opened an office in 1983 and subsequently a community center, and by 1984 it had spawned one of the first women's interest groups. For all its advances, however, GASA espoused and tried to foster an apolitical stance. Its manifesto specifically required the organization to be a "moderate, non-political answer to gay needs."

By the mid-1980s, the emerging AIDS crisis, more vigorous policing, the rise of a gay and lesbian presence in the black townships, and a growing mass of anti-apartheid and pro-democracy individuals provided the impetus for more activist-driven and less racially divided gay and lesbian organizations. The Gay and Lesbian Organization of Witwatersrand (GLOW) started in 1983; the Organization of Lesbian and Gay Activists in Cape Town (OLGA) followed in 1987. Partly the result of softening of apartheid rules in 1989 and 1990, these groups were able to organize the first gay and lesbian rights march held in Johannesburg in 1990, drawing a crowd of around 800. These marches became annual events and were expanded to include theater events, film festivals, and sporting activities. During the late 1980s, these groups developed manifestos that were expressly nonracist, nonsexist, nondiscriminatory, and pro-democracy. As a result, blacks became more active participants in the groups, leaders began to forge alliances with the growing anti-apartheid movement, and alliances with the African National Congress were forged. These alliances, however, were not without conflict and difficulties. Winnie Mandela's assertion in 1991 that "Homosex is not in black culture" spoke to a deeply rooted feeling among many black freedom fighters that homosexuality was "un-African," a byproduct of colonial capitalism, something "circumstantial" rather than "organic." Still, in 1991, an ANC Constitutional Committee drafting a bill of rights included a provision to outlaw sexual orientation discrimination, largely the result of lobbying by GLOW and other national and international groups. Subsequently, in 1993, the ANC incorporated protection on the basis of sexual orientation into its draft constitution, albeit in the face of considerable internal dissent and once again under pressure from national and international gay and lesbian rights groups.[4]

A regrouping and amalgamation of organizations in the early 1990s resulted in the birth of the National Coalition for Gay and Lesbian Equality (NCGLE) in December 1994. This umbrella organization, representing over eighty urban and rural gay and lesbian organizations in South Africa, along with one from Zimbabwe and one from Swaziland, was created with a mandate to insure sexual orientation remained a listed ground of nondiscrimination in the final constitution. Once that goal was achieved in 1996, the coalition set to work on a much broader agenda aimed at the elimination of sexual orientation discrimination in South Africa through education and lobbying efforts, as well as initiating court challenges based on the new constitution. In 1997, the coalition and the statutory Human Rights Commission applied to the High Court to have the sodomy laws declared unconstitutional. In spite of opposition from a variety of groups, in a 1998 decision, they were successful. The eleven-judge panel also declared that men who had been convicted of sodomy since 1994 could demand monetary damages and have their criminal records cleared.

From the beginning, one of NCGLE's major objectives was to confront discrimination in the workplace. By 1996, it was ready to focus more attention and resources toward achieving this goal. One of NCGLE's actions was to set up an Equal Rights Project (ERP) with the express purpose of examining all aspects of the lives of gays and lesbians in South Africa, but with a particular focus on the workplace. The ERP led to the formation of a Johannesburg-based gay and lesbian legal advice center in August 1997. The center has since dealt with more than eighty cases of workplace discrimination and harassment. Most of these cases were resolved within the new statutes and rules set out by the constitution, LRA, EEA, and the BCEA.

Sexual Orientation Issues in the Workplace

As the new millennium approaches, South Africa is similar to many other countries in the issues that remain contested terrain for sexual minorities. Although the 1990s witnessed enormous change in the laws affecting the lives of sexual minorities, prejudicial attitudes, policies, and practices in many facets of life, especially in the workplace, have been much more resistant to change. Here as elsewhere in the world, sexual minorities face discrimination in hiring, firing, and promotion decisions, violence and harassment, and the failure to have same-sex relationships recognized for legal and benefit coverage.

The most obvious form of discrimination takes place when a person applying for a job or promotion does not get it, or is fired or demoted because of his or her sexual orientation. Obviously, an employer can attempt to cover up and disguise the real motives for these decisions, making it difficult to establish a case. Another related area of concern is the threat of harassment and violence, since gays and lesbians are often subject to jokes, taunts, and beatings based purely on their sexuality. Outlawing these forms of discrimination is an important first step, one the government has initiated by provisions in the new constitution, Labor Relations Act, and proposed Code of Employment Practices on Sexual Harassment. However, legal change, important as it is, does not mean the problems disappear, only that legal recourse is available. Many people are reluctant to take legal action. Instead, they look to employers to institute measures aimed at preventing and confronting discrimination within specific work sites. Sexual minorities also look to trade unions for assistance. Unions can engage in collective bargaining with employers for agreements that articulate these issues and provide mechanisms for their resolution. Moreover, unions can provide financial and moral support in mounting legal challenges against employers.

Perhaps the most blatant form of discrimination related to sexual orientation is the failure to recognize same-sex relationships for the purpose of legal and benefit coverage. Most workplaces offer at least some benefits to employees and their families but routinely exclude people who do not fit the heterosexual norm. In South Africa, this is particularly problematic because many people obtain their medical coverage through workplace-based schemes, and because medical aid is enjoyed by a very small minority of South Africans, it is one of the most appealing and crucial benefits offered by employers. Most medical plans allow for the registration of legally married spouses and children but specifically exclude unmarried couples, even though the new constitution and LRA provisions prohibit discrimination on the basis of marital status. As a result, access to medical benefits for same-sex couples and their families is often denied. In addition, especially in unionized settings, a wider range of benefits may be available. These benefits include superior medical aid, pension schemes, housing supplements, and retirement provisions. A few employers also provide benefits related to education and training, as well as various forms of leaves for such things as child care and bereavement. As with medical coverage, these benefits tend to be restricted to employees and their legal spouses and do not provide for same-sex or common-law couples.

Although it is widely believed by gays and lesbians that the above forms of workplace discrimination are everyday occurrences, and there is no evidence to suggest otherwise, little research has documented the extent of the problem. What is perhaps most telling is that employers continue to deny medical, pension, and housing benefits to gay and lesbian employees when requested, forcing workers to appeal to the courts for assistance. Even then, employers contest the legitimacy of the claims and seem prepared to expend considerable sums of money on litigation. One of the few ways to examine the extent of the problem is by considering the issues brought to the Equal Rights Project of NCGLE. Of the fifteen cases brought forward between September 1996 and 1997, seven had to do with refusal to include a same-sex partner for medical aid; three had to do with dismissal on the basis of sex orientation; five involved harassment. It must be kept in mind, though, that these figures probably represent the tip of an iceberg, since most people would be extremely reluctant to lodge a formal discrimination charge on the basis of sexual orientation. It should also be noted that the majority of cases were brought forward by white gays and lesbians, who are more likely to have access to support and legal advice favoring such actions.

A similar sense of the problem comes from data collected by the Center of Applied Legal Studies at the University of Witwatersrand. The center began in 1980 in an attempt to address human rights violations, and it has been involved in legal issues related to labor, gender, land rights, and AIDS. The center's Gender Research Project (GRP) incorporated issues related to sexual orientation and undertook research in this area. In June 1996, the GRP convened a workshop to look at issues that could best be addressed by unions. The results showed that hiring and firing issues ranked as most important, followed closely by refusal of medical aid for partners, and harassment. If we combine the information from NCGLE and the GRP, the issues that emerge as most critical are medical aid coverage, fear of not being hired or of being dismissed if found out to be gay or lesbian, and harassment. Even though the data arise from very limited sampling, these findings provide a picture of what people believe to problematic, and they help to prioritize concerns that could be addressed by unions.

As we will highlight in the next sections, the labor movement played a direct role in the creation of new human rights legislation and institutions. It is therefore reasonable to expect that labor might lead the way in developing policies and practices designed to insure that equity initiatives actually are implemented, especially within the workplace. As we will see, however, labor has so far been reluctant to push forward further reforms.

Organized Labor in the South African Context

Trade unions have existed in South Africa since the 1890s but have paralleled the racially divided history of the country. The first black trade union was the Industrial and Commercial Workers Union (known as the ICU—"I see you white man"). Formed by dock workers in 1919 in Cape Town, the ICU became one of the first major mobilizing tools for black workers against exploitation and national oppression. However, the ICU was short-lived; by 1930, it was dead in all but name. Between 1930 and the banning of the ANC and the Pan African Congress in 1961, there were attempts to build trade unions and federations among black workers, especially in light of the fact that black workers represented the majority of workers in the country. This period also saw the rise of a number of socialist organizations committed to building a stronger labor movement. Unions that emerged during this period included the African Mine Workers Union, the African Federation of Trade Unions, the Council of Non-European Trade Unions, and the South African Congress of Trade Unions. These organizations remained largely powerless, since white workers continued to organize separately in so-called "sweetheart" unions. Nevertheless, these unions and federations became sites where workplace struggles were articulated and links were made to broader struggles for national liberation.

The upsurge in racial repression during 1960–1992 effectively crushed these unions and moved their political operations underground. White workers' unions, however, continued to grow during this period but tended to offer little resistance to the apartheid state. In spite of these enormous roadblocks, the beginnings of a strong and progressive, nonracial trade union movement was taking place in the 1970s, with organizing activity in the major industrial cities of Durban, Cape Town, and Witwatersrand. These developments led to the birth of several trade unions and federations, some of which continue today.

Since 1992, organized labor in South Africa has been in a much more stable period. It now has the distinction of having the fastest growing trade union membership in the world. The 1997 Annual Report of the International Labor Organization (ILO) reported that, between 1985 and 1995, trade union membership had fallen in seventy-two of the ninety-two countries it surveyed, but that membership in South Africa had increased by nearly 127 percent. According to the ILO report, union density in South Africa in 1995 was 41 percent of the economically active population, compared to 37 percent in 1992, giving it the highest unionization rate of any developing country. The largest growth in membership has occurred in the public sector. South Africa now has several trade union confederations, including the Coalition of South African Trade Unions (Cosatu), the Federated Unions of South Africa (Fedusa), and the National Congress of Trade Unions (Nactu).

Cosatu is overwhelming the largest, most progressive, and important union confederation.[5] It was founded in 1985, the result of an amalgamation of several other federations at the height of anti-apartheid conflict. Cosatu is now the fastest growing federation of its type in the world, with nearly 2 million members drawn from nineteen affiliates covering a wide range of unions in manufacturing, public services, mining, transportation, construction, and the service sector. Although an explicitly nonracial and nonsexist union, historically most of Cosatu's membership has been black males in blue-collar occupations. These demographics, however, have been in a state of accelerated change in the post-apartheid period, mainly the result of large increases in public sector membership (which now accounts for 19 percent of Cosatu's members) and recent affiliations with white-collar bank employee and teachers' unions. One of the most dramatic changes at Cosatu, given its history as a "black" federation committed to the overthrow of the apartheid state, has been the recent addition of prison warders and police to its membership ranks. Female membership has been on the rise, and Cosatu now has a woman vice-president.

In addition to its strategic position within the labor movement, Cosatu is a key player in political and government circles. It is a member of the influential tripartite alliance with the governing ANC and the South African Communist Party, and many former Cosatu leaders now serve as ANC cabinet ministers, members of parliament, provincial premiers, and government officials. The organization has played a significant role in the development of new human rights legislation and helped to draft the new Labor Relations Act.

Thus, after a long history of oppression and struggle, South Africa now has a growing and vibrant trade union movement with very strong links to the ANC government and other centers of political influence. As a result, alliances and links with organized labor in South Africa are an important and necessary component of any social change momentum, no less so for the gay and lesbian rights movement.

Labor's Response to Gender and Sexual Orientation

Organized labor in South Africa has a mixed history in relation to equity issues. Although long-standing divides and tensions along racial and class lines have been hugely narrowed in the post-apartheid period, they still exist. Cosatu, for example, is grappling with recent influxes of white, professional members, such as teachers, who arrive with somewhat different issues and concerns from the predominately black, working-class membership base. However, Cosatu is formally committed to accommodating these developments in its organizing campaigns, education programs, and collective bargaining strategies.[6] Less open to change has been the heterosexual, male-dominated power base of the labor movement. Struggles to incorporate issues related to gender and sexual orientation have been fraught with tension and conflict.

Although some notable achievements have been made, gender discrimination and issues related to the empowerment of women within labor organizations remain highly contested. As early as 1984, female labor leaders were calling for more priority to be placed on women's issues; women's forums were established to push their unions toward improved harassment and violence policies, maternity leave provisions, pay equity, occupational equity, and union representation.[7] But even in Cosatu, arguably the most progressive federation, the development of policies and practices related to gender issues has been haphazard and slow. Cosatu sponsored a women's conference in April 1988 and has organized several since then. However, as recently as the 1991 Cosatu General Congress, women had to fight to maintain these gender forums as places where women's confidence and skills could be fostered, a struggle that ended with the explicit provision that men could be part of these gatherings. Debate and conflict over these forums continues, and a 1995 report indicated that "women were still taking responsibility for organizing them but that men tended to dominate the discussions in these forums when they attended." More dramatically, in a few instances, women were literally dragged away from meetings by a husband or brother.[8]

Over the years, though, a number of the issues raised by women have been addressed. In areas such as sexual conduct, sexual harassment, organizing campaigns, collective bargaining provisions, and policy interventions, progress has been made. For example, when allegations of serious sexual harassment arose at the 1994 Cosatu conference, a new code of conduct on sexual behavior and harassment for its member unions was quickly drafted and made policy by May 1995. As well, a growing number of unions have successfully negotiated collective agreements with good provisions for maternity leave and child care facilities and allowances. Unions such as Numsa (National Union of Metalworkers of South Africa) and CWIU (Chemical Workers' Industrial Union) have made commitments to fight for such things as pay equity and free pap smears. FAWA (Food and Allied Workers Union) has gone so far as to take the employers of one of its members to court in a sexual discrimination case, and CWIU was able to get a manager fired for sexually harassing a woman worker at a tire factory.

While gains have been made in issues most affecting women, women remain underrepresented in positions of power. A 1994 survey found that only one regional union secretary was a woman, and that no general secretary or union president had ever been a woman. At the same time, the survey found that by 1994, 8 percent of national officers of Cosatu and its affiliate unions were women, compared to only 5 percent in 1990. Also as a measure of at least some change, by 1997, Cosatu had a woman in a senior executive role.[9]

Women activists are cautiously optimistic, reporting that gender issues are on labor's agenda and that more and more unions have taken up issues related to child care, parental rights, and sexual conduct. They assert, however, that action has been sporadic and inconsistent, and every advance has been an uphill battle. At the current time, Cosatu is leading the parade on women's issues and has appointed a full-time national gender coordinator to oversee activities in this area.

In contrast, organized labor has not been nearly as open to change on issues related to sexual orientation. As we have already noted, alliances between gay and lesbian rights activists and the labor-infused ANC have been in place since the late 1980s, but they have a history of conflict. Most components of the labor movement supported, or at least did not oppose, the new constitution and several other important pieces of legislation that include sexual orientation as protected grounds. It has, however, been slow to move beyond these initiatives. Overall, organized labor appears at best unresponsive, and at worse antagonistic, in the fight to change prejudicial attitudes and practices related to sexual orientation.

Cosatu is the only federation that has a general policy committing it to equality for gays and lesbians. So far, it has only taken a few steps to act beyond its policy statement. Although Fedusa, with a primarily white constituency, does not have a formal policy statement in this area, the loosely organized Fedusa Equity Forum is aimed at discussing affirmative action and employment equity issues within the union, and this may be a site where sexual orientation issues will emerge in the future. To date, no other federation has shown any activity on issues of concern to sexual minorities. Several indicated when contacted by phone that they expect to develop policies in the near future, but so far there has been no concrete action.

The Transport and General Workers Union (TGWU), a Cosatu affiliate, is the only trade union known to refer specifically to gay and lesbian equality. In an August 1995 revision to its constitution, it states: "we are committed to build and maintain a democratic worker-controlled union based on the principles of non-racism, non-sexism, and non-homophobia." Until recently there had been little action, but in 1998 the union's education department, in conjunction with the NCGLE, decided to run courses for staff and members highlighting sexual diversity issues. TGWU is expected to pass a further resolution at its August 1999 congress affirming its commitment to gay and lesbian rights, placing it at the forefront of unions active in the area of sexual minority rights. As a result, the TGWU stands out, since no other union is known to have adopted a formal policy or program based on the interests or demands of gays and lesbians.

Another union that has recently shown some interest in confronting the discrimination sexual minorities face is the National Education, Health and Allied Workers Union (NEHAWU). This very large union of 250,000 members in the public sector has now adopted a positive position on gay and lesbian rights, and has been the site of courses and presentations run by the NCGLE.

In several cases, workers have been demonstrably "out" within their unions, but without much in the way of formal support or recognition from their union leadership. The mines are a good example. Several historical and contemporary texts document a lengthy tradition of same-sex relationships among mine workers in South Africa.[10] The mining industry has always represented a good job for black men, and the lack of opportunities in general has meant that more gay men found their way into this occupational category than might be expected by people unfamiliar with the indigenous history of the country. Over the years, informal and formal gay social and support groups developed in the major mining regions of South Africa, the best organized in Newcastle (KwaZulu Natal coal mining region) and Welkom (Free State gold fields). These gay miners' support groups were able to create an environment of tolerance and acceptance in what might otherwise have been a fairly hostile situation. There are reports of gay marriages taking place within these mining communities, but most of the activities have been sports-related or purely social. Gay and lesbian support groups in the gold fields, for example, organized soccer tournaments between its members and straight coworkers, an arrangement that appears to have produced considerable goodwill and little conflict. Recently, however, the mandate of these groups appears to be changing; some have started to raise questions and make demands within their union (NUM) related to discriminatory practices by employers. At the mining conglomerate Anglo-American, for instance, a gay group of employees indicated they would file a suit to win medical and other benefits for same-sex partners. This case appears to be proceeding, but so far with little support from the union.

Another interesting case is within union members of the police force. In May 1997, lesbian and gay members of the South African Police Services launched the Gay and Lesbian Police Network with the approval of their management and union. This network was aimed at securing employment equity in the ranks and improving relations between the police and the gay and lesbian community more generally. Supported by this network, Jolande Langemaat, a Johannesburg police officer, filed suit against the South African Police Service when they refused to extend medical coverage under the Police Medical Aid Scheme to her partner of eleven years. In February 1998, the Pretoria High Court ruled in her favor and declared the medical plan regulations unconstitutional. Even though asked to do so, the South African Police Union (SAPU) and the Police, Public, and Civil Rights Union (POPCRU) did not offer any support in the case. Recently, though, the SAPU has become more supportive of sexual minority issues and is now involved in the resolution of the Langmaat case.

In summary, South African unions have done little to take up issues important to gays and lesbians in the period following enactment of the new constitution. Some unions have opposed initiatives and court challenges. For example, between August 1997 and October 1997, several organizations, including labor- and union-affiliated groups, linked the court application for the decriminalization of same-sex activity to child molestation, some going so far as to suggest it might be justifiable to explore the limitation of constitutional rights of lesbians and gays. So far, unions have been an absent voice in supporting specific court challenges arguing for same-sex employment benefits, in some cases denying that discrimination had even occurred. While most unions will not publicly oppose equality for lesbian and gay workers because they do not wish to be seen to oppose the constitution or the LRA, they stop short of any other type of support. Some union leaders have gone on record as not wishing unions to get sidetracked from other priorities. Some have gone so far as to use the argument that "homosexuality is un-African" and that "workers will not understand lesbian and gay issues."

A Strategy for Change

Why have labor federations and unions been mostly unsupportive in fighting for an end to discrimination based on sexual orientation? Why have so few lesbian and gay workers organized themselves within their unions with the aim of forcing change? In those unions where support groups do exist, such as the police and miners, why have they not been able to bring their unions more directly onside? While there are no single or simple answers to these questions, it is useful to explore some of the factors that may be at play, as a starting point for mapping a strategy for change.

South Africa has traditionally been a society with an overlay of conservative religions and cultures, and until very recently, sexuality issues of any type were not generally a discussion topic. It is also a country only recently released from the horrors of a racially divided system, and one where human rights amendments are relatively new and untested. The racist and colonial past left many attitudes and practices that are hard to change. This is particularly the case in relation to sexual diversity. The labor movement is no different from most other institutions in embodying all of the conflicts and contradictions of the new Republic of South Africa. Although an activist-driven gay and lesbian rights movement has existed for some time, it has been preoccupied with broader reforms and only recently focused more of its attention on workplace issues. In other words, the legal and constitutional architecture for gay and lesbian rights has only recently been put into place, and the identification and analysis of issues affecting this group is a relatively new and controversial phenomenon for labor organizations. That said, the timing is ideal for accelerating the pace of change.

Unions and labor federations in South Africa are growing in size and importance, have well-established links with the political process, and are positioned to be key players in the social transformation of South Africa. Therefore, forging an alliance with organized labor must remain a critical goal for the gay and lesbian rights movement if workplace equity goals are to be achieved, in spite of the fact that labor has until now shown little enthusiasm for the project. Activists must identify the issues that trade unions share with sexual minorities, as well as the opportunities and new approaches that will promote alliances. Achieving these goals will necessitate a multifaceted strategy involving data collection, litigation, education, and coalition building.

The first step toward bringing about change is to better document the extent of the problem. Such information and statistics would help convince organized labor that inequities do exist, in particular that blatant income disparities are created when some workers are denied access to the benefits and perks available to others. The ERP project of the NCGLE has already started to compile this sort of information, and a database of this type is beginning to take shape.

The new legislative environment in South Africa is very amenable to litigation in the area of sexual minority rights. Nevertheless, initiatives are hampered by a judiciary largely from the old political order, some of whom appear to be opposed to progressive change in this area. Of note, though, is the recent appointment of Edwin Cameron, a noted gay activist, to the high courts. Overall, the new Constitutional Court, the highest court in the land, is made up of judges who are likely to support equality on all grounds. Careful selection of cases to go forward at this level will provide the most promising opportunities. However, litigation must be coupled to effective engagement with independent statutory institutions such as the Commission on Gender Equality and the Human Rights Commission, since these institutions have powers to investigate and litigate as well as advise the government.

Litigation requires careful planning and large financial commitments. This is where labor can play a significant role because it has the human and financial resources to undertake such activities. Convincing unions and federations that such commitments are necessary and appropriate must become a strategic goal of the movement for sexual minority rights. Recent policy statements by such key players as Cosatu open the door for further dialogue, and recent successes, such as Jolande Langemaat's suit against the Police Medical Aid Scheme, should help define the necessity and parameters for such discussions. Closely related to litigation is the potential offered by collective bargaining and arbitration. Significant change could occur very quickly if trade unions were persuaded to take sexual orientation issues related to hiring, firing, harassment, and benefits to the bargaining table.

Education is another important area for action. Activists must be instrumental in the development of educational programs designed to insure their concerns are not avoided or overlooked, within and outside the labor movement. Again, the new human rights and employment legislation opens doors for activists to position their concerns within the broader educational efforts that are taking place.

Finally, coalition building should be part of any overall strategy. Building relationships with women's groups, anti-poverty groups, the disabled, and other minorities would strengthen the potential access to organized labor and draw attention to the common demand for equal and fair treatment in the workplace. Alliances with women's forums in unions could prove to be the single best way to penetrate labor's agenda, since relationships of this type have been so successful in other countries profiled in this book. Lesbian and gay caucuses in some trade unions, such as the miners and police, are also important sites for coalition building. These caucuses have a good chance of being seen as legitimate and not outsiders by trade union members and represent important entry points for action.

Conclusion

The political articulation of issues related to sexual diversity is relatively new in South Africa, and only recently emerging as a workplace concern. Progress has been swift at the level of constitutional and legal change, but so far few individuals, organizations, or institutions seem to have altered their long-standing prejudicial attitudes and practices. Organized labor appears not to be an exception to this trend. Although Cosatu, the largest and most influential labor federation in the country, includes sexual orientation in its nondiscrimination statement, trade unions as a group have been reluctant to take up these issues in any tangible way. As a result, litigation based on the provisions of the new legislation have been the primary mode for activists.

Nevertheless, there is room for optimism. South Africa is in a process of accelerated transformation, and perhaps nowhere else on earth are the opportunities for social change more abundant. Although there are forces who long for a return to the oppressive, racist past, and other forces with a very conservative agenda, the overwhelming momentum is toward change that will establish equality and human rights as the sustaining architecture of the new social order. Given this new era, minorities of all kinds, including sexual minorities, have an unparalleled opportunity to acquire equal rights, and the responsibilities that go with them. It will be increasingly difficult for political, business, judicial, and labor leaders who espouse unequivocally a philosophy of equal rights to turn around and say, "But we didn't mean gays and lesbians." To gain ground, though, activists must act quickly and assertively to forge better alliances with key players such as organized labor, and by using every other resource at their disposal, including but not limited to the judiciary.

Within the new South Africa, equality for gays and lesbians must be positioned as a national reconstruction issue and a trade union issue. As Carl Stychin notes, gay and lesbian rights issues in South Africa cannot be divorced from the problems in housing, jobs, and safety nor from the gender, racial, and sexual oppression that has for so long plagued the country.[11] The trade union movement is sufficiently powerful and mature to discuss sexual minority issues openly, and with sufficient pressure could be transformed from sideline observer to ally.

Notes

1. We have prepared this chapter by drawing on our personal experience within the Equal Rights Project (ERP) of the National Coalition for Gay and Lesbian Equality (NCGLE) based in Johannesburg, as well as our telephone and personal contacts with labor federations, trade unions, and activists.

2. Quoted in the *Washington Blade*, 13 December 1996, p. 24.

3. A comprehensive account of early and recent gay and lesbian life and activism in South Africa can be found in M. Gevisser and E. Cameron, eds., *Defiant Desire: Gay and Lesbian Lives in South Africa* (New York: Routledge, 1996). Much of the information for this section is drawn from this resource, with additional insight taken from B. Adam, *The Rise of a Gay and Lesbian Movement,* rev. ed. (New York: Twayne Publishers, 1995); C. Dunton and M. Palmberg, *Human Rights and Homosexuality in Southern Africa* (Uppsala, Sweden: Nordiska Afrikainstitutet, 1996); C. Stychin, *A Nation by Rights* (Philadelphia: Temple University Press, 1998), chap. 3.

4. See Gevisser and Cameron, *Defiant Desire,* pp. 63–74.

5. See Cosatu website for details at www.cosatu.org.za.

6. See Cosatu website section, "Changing with the Times."

7. See "Women Workers," report prepared by Fosatu (now defunct Federation of South African Trade Unions), 1984; and "No Turning Back," report prepared by the Witwatersrand University Women's Forum, 1992.

8. See Cosatu website section, "No Woman, No Cry, Zabalaza," where there is a report on the Cosatu Gender Winter School held in 1995.

9. "No Woman, No Cry."

10. See N. Miller "Going Underground," in *Defiant Desire,* ed. Gevisser and Cameron; V. Ndatshe "Two Miners," in M. Krouse, ed., *The Invisible Ghetto: Lesbian and Gay Writing from South Africa* (Johannesburg: COSAW Publishing, 1993); M. wa Sibuyi "Tinkoncana Etimayinini: The Wives of the Mines," in M. Krouse, ed., *The Invisible Ghetto.*

11. See Stychin, *A Nation by Rights,* p. 76.

David Rayside

11   On the Fringes of the New Europe: Sexual Diversity Activism and the Labor Movement

From the early 1980s, transnational European institutions have given lesbian and gay activists opportunities to challenge the most oppressive laws and regulations of their native countries. In recent years, these openings appear to have widened and are being used more frequently to provide leverage against reluctant governments and legislatures. Hesitantly and unevenly, labor unions have also been developing a presence at the European level. They were long wary of the European Economic Community and its successors, treating it for good reason as a one-sided accommodation to corporate interests. The recognition that transnational corporate growth would threaten union leverage at the national level, and that some social policy gains might be possible through their own transnational cooperation, increased attention to Europe.

Serious questions remain, however, as to how wide the openings are for European-level social policy innovation, and how substantial the opportunities are for labor unions and human rights groups to intervene. There are also serious questions about how much common ground union leaders and lesbian and gay activists are building. The energies of union representatives in Brussels are not focused much beyond the core economic issues with which national labor movements in Europe have been long pre-occupied. The very newness and small size of the openings provided for them at the European level may have reinforced the narrowing of focus on traditional union issues. There are signs that the unions are prepared to include in their agenda some equity issues, though generally in areas in which the EU has already exercised authority—for example, gender. The very unevenness of labor's engagement with equity issues in general, and sexual orientation issues in particular—unevenness across and within member countries—slows the uptake of new issues by union organizations in Brussels.

In the European Union generally, policy rarely leaps ahead of the pack of constituent member states, especially on social policy issues. Even the shift toward majority voting in selected policy areas of the European Union has not fundamentally altered the pattern of European policy trailing national policy. For that reason, understanding developments at the European level requires tapping into the range of national policies toward sexual diversity. In this chapter, France, Germany, the Netherlands, and Britain provide illustrations of the range of national industrial-relations systems, sexual-minority movements, and social policy mixes that shape increasingly significant pan-European institutions.

France

The development of French political groups articulating sexual-minority concerns has always been fragile. The country's politics have traditionally been riven by deep divisions, with the left particularly centered on the profound class inequalities that still characterize French social and economic life. Social movements outside labor cannot escape the power of the class divide, and union engagement with new social issues is framed by a class ideology that has tended to place other issues on the margins.[1]

French gays have not confronted quite the sweeping legal prohibitions that their British counterparts have experienced, but they have faced a repressive social climate more deeply entrenched than statutory discrimination, and a judicial system still reluctant to recognize gay and lesbian rights. The notion of a distinctive identity based on sexual orientation never had the resonance that it did in the Anglo-American countries and some parts of northern Europe, to some extent hampering the development in France of a distinctively gay and lesbian politics. This reflected the depth of social and political differences among gays and lesbians themselves, and the "Jacobin" resistance in French political life to forms of identity autonomous of integrated French nationality. Late 1960s and early 1970s activist waves acquired some profile, though like other movements they had weak and divided foundations. In the 1980s and early 1990s, a form of community-identity politics developed on a relatively modest scale, influenced by U.S. examples.

The Mitterrand candidacy on behalf of the much strengthened Socialists attracted a great deal of extraparliamentary activist attention, and his victory in 1981 fueled great optimism. The Communist Party seemed relatively closed to or uninterested in gay-related initiatives.[2] However, the Parti Socialist (PS) seemed open to new social movements while in opposition during the 1970s, and structured itself as a broad coalition allowing considerable diversity within. In 1976, the party formally committed itself to a pro-gay position, and five years later the very high-profile Jack Lang joined activist leaders at the head of thousands of others in a pro-gay march.[3] This did not in itself cement closer ties between such movements and organized labor, however, for the Socialists never had the close and organizationally structured relationship to unions of its socialist or social-democratic counterparts in most other countries.

The Mitterrand-appointed government that took office in 1981 followed through on some promises given to feminists, anti-racism activists, and gays and lesbians. In 1982, it equalized the age of consent for homosexual and heterosexual activity, a move opposed almost unanimously by the parties of the right. In 1985, anti-discrimination legislation was passed that has come to be interpreted to cover sexual orientation even though it did not explicitly include it. In a general way, however, the Socialists adhered to established French state traditions in keeping social activists at some distance, doing little to strengthen movements that had vested so much hope in the Parti Socialist electoral victory. Political activism declined significantly in the aftermath of the early 1980s statutory gains, reviving only briefly in response to a 1986 attempt by the interior minister in Prime Minister Jacques Chirac's government to threaten the widely read gay magazine *Gai Pied*.

The Socialists returned to power with the 1988 legislative elections but provided as many disappointments as advances for gay and lesbian activists. The French government put into place wide-ranging AIDS plans, but they were very very late in coming and much compromised by blood-supply decisions. Prime Minister Edith Cresson made disparaging remarks about homosexuality in two separate media interviews in 1991. Socialists in the National Assembly equivocated in their support for same-sex relationship recognition in late 1992. Through this period, public opinion surveys indicated a significant shift toward acceptance or at least toleration of sexual diversity, though there are no indications of the French standing out among other Europeans in that regard. Even in highly educated circles, the fears, antipathies, and hesitations remained substantial enough to make it difficult even for leading intellectuals to come out as gay or lesbian.[4] In 1997, the justice minister declared the new PS-dominated government's intention to grant same-sex couples and cohabiting heterosexuals some of the rights of married couples, but pointedly excluded were adoption, access to state-funded artificial insemination, and automatic residency rights for foreign partners. The legislation was presented in the following year, encountering fierce opposition from the parliamentary and extraparliamentary right, but likely to complete passage by the end of 1999.

Lesbian and gay activists made no significant attempts to invoke the cooperation or support of labor unions, nor did any of the major unions provide more than token signs of support. Late 1960s activists had an interest in alliance with other left forces, including labor, but such interest was not much translated into close and productive linkages. The Comité d'urgence anti-repression homosexuelle, established in 1980, attached some importance to establishing dialogue with unions and political parties, but it is not obvious that much happened in respect to labor. By the 1990s, the highest profile mobilization on sexual orientation issues was by ACT-UP, focusing all of its energies on the appallingly high HIV infection rate among French gays. That activism, based on a newfound sense of gay and lesbian identity, was not as drawn to the traditional alliances of the left that had interested earlier activists. Political activism was relatively low-key through the 1990s, though the growth of a commercial subculture and the dramatic growth in popularity of Paris's Gay Pride marches contributed significantly to the visibility of sexual diversity.[5]

The utility of gaining union allies was compromised by the unions' relative weakness. By the 1990s, unions represented less than 10 percent of the workforce and exercised relatively little influence over state policy.[6] Labor openness to sexual diversity issues was also compromised. The Confédération Générale du Travail (CGT) retrenched somewhat in its relationship to feminist issues during the course of the 1980s, and its attitude toward sexual diversity would have reflected the most traditional of Marxist dismissals.[7] The Confédération Française Démocratique du Travail (CFDT) would have been more ideologically flexible but in the 1980s would have insisted on a class framework relegating sexual orientation issues to second tier status. In the 1990s, the labor movement was still shaped by class radicalism and unease about the resurgence of identity politics.

The labor and sexual diversity movements in France have devoted little attention to Europe. Both are sufficiently weak to have few resources for intervention at that level, and the largest among the labor confederations is among the few in Europe still opposed ideologically to the European project. The periods of Socialist government focused the attitudes of many activists on domestic openings to change. Moreover, because French activists have not faced as much of an explicitly discriminatory statutory apparatus as, for example, the British, they have had fewer incentives to use European-level courts to challenge domestic laws as oppressive.

Germany

As Ronald Holzhacker argues in his contribution to this volume, the Federal Republic and the united Germany have occupied something of a middle ground between the more progressive European countries like the Netherlands, Denmark, and Norway, and the more officially discriminatory like pre-Blair Britain. For example, a few of the German states have passed legislation prohibiting discrimination based on sexual orientation, some establishing administrative offices and centers to address sexual-minority issues, but only limited gains have been made in the realm of relationship recognition for same-sex couples.[8]

The established German political parties in the West did not offer much sustained encouragement to progressive social activists until the success of the Greens shocked them into at least partial accommodation to new causes such as environmentalism. The center-right Christian Democratic Party (CDU) has held to traditional views on gender, sexuality, and cultural diversity, substantially slowing progress at the federal level during the party's long period in government from 1983 to 1998, as well as in states where they have held power. The Free Democrats, coalition partners with the Christian Democrats, might have been expected to adopt an individualistically framed acceptance of diversity and equality, but they did not actively embrace causes that challenged traditional constructions of sexuality. The Social Democratic Party (SPD) was open to influence from new movements in the early 1970s, but its move to the right, particularly under Helmut Schmidt, curtailed that tendency.[9] The federal structure of the SPD prevented the complete marginalization of these movements, but from the 1980s on, many lesbians and gays, as well as activists in other social causes, abandoned the Social Democrats for the Greens.

Through the 1980s, the Greens included explicit support for sexual diversity among the rainbow of causes it espoused. The very breadth of the range of causes embraced by the Greens and the constant struggle between "realists" and "fundamentalists" have at times weakened their electoral standing, but not their influence over the body politic as a whole. The influence on the Social Democrats was particularly pronounced, the middle and late 1980s witness to important party resolutions on foreign policy, energy, the environment, and gender.[10] Sexual orientation issues were less obviously a part of this shift toward green, but portions of the SPD were pulled toward support of more progressive positions. In 1989 in Berlin, for example, before unification, an Alternative List/SDP coalition government established the Federal Republic's first public office to address the concerns of lesbians and gays.[11] Since then, SPD-dominated governments in a number of states and municipalities have adopted pro-gay measures.

As a result of the 1998 federal election, the SDP came to power in coalition with the Greens. Because of Green pressure, and in the face of SDP resistance, the coalition "contract" committed the government to strengthening minority rights and incorporated in its objectives explicit reference to sexual orientation. The contract referred specifically to the development of a regime of registered partnerships, and it talked of consulting recommendations of the European Parliament on the equal rights of lesbians and gays (see below), which interpreted the right to relationship recognition in very wide-ranging terms. The Social Democrats, however, quickly signaled their intention to exclude adoption rights in the German plan, and in early 1999 there were fears of further watering down of commitments in the wake of electoral losses in the state of Hesse.

The social activists who coalesced in the Greens did not particularly view labor as an ally. The environmental movement, for example, saw the industrial working class and its unions as tied to traditional models of economic growth and consumer spending.[12] The organizational strength and institutionalized access accorded German unions made them seem insinuated into the established order that social activists were challenging. Lesbian and gay activists had reason enough on their own to be wary of the likelihood of alliance with the union movement, and their association with the other elements in the green coalition reinforced that distance. Andrei Markovits and Philip Gorski point out that feelings were mutual, with unions more hostile than the SDP to the New Left of the 1960s, and to the social movement activism that emerged from it.[13]

The postwar Federal Republic had institutionalized a system of codetermination that was never quite as radical in practice as it seemed on paper, but it gave German workers more workplace leverage than their European counterparts. The labor-relations system helped produce large centralized unions with relatively little of the oppositionist relationship to management and the state that was characteristic in less corporatist systems. The unions therefore had few incentives to search for allies among other activists. (As Holzhacker points out, too, some of the issues that motivated sexual-minority mobilization in other union systems have been at least partially addressed in Germany.)

On the other hand, German unions, like most of the European labor movement, have always seen their mandate extending far beyond the negotiation of economic gains. Like a number of unions elsewhere, they had begun to approve policies on issues being raised by new social movements during the 1970s.[14] In 1990, the DGB—Germany's largest labor federation—acknowledged its slow progress in attaining gender-related objectives. Within a few years of that, IG Metall—the country's largest union—developed proactive policies on racial discrimination.[15]

On gay-specific issues, as Holzhacker points out, the German public service and transport workers union (ÖTV) was in the lead. It was the first to take proactively gay-positive measures, establishing staffed working groups in a number of regions during the 1980s. In 1996, the union's chair, Herbert Mai, publicly affirmed the organization's commitment to combating animosity and discrimination against lesbian and gay colleagues in the workplace.[16] In 1998, the ÖTV was one of the major sponsors of an international conference in Amsterdam on "Trade Unions, Homosexuality, and Work."[17] This sort of commitment stimulated the development of groups in a few other unions and in the DGB, supported with official recognition and funding. A number of these working groups have been successful in securing passage of anti-discrimination resolutions through their unions and securing union support in political lobbying campaigns. Where they have been most notably unsuccessful is in convincing unions to take gay-related issues, particularly those related to same-sex benefits, to the bargaining table.

The collapse of the Berlin Wall and of the East German regime in late 1989 began a lightning-fast unification of East and West Germany that posed great challenges to the union system. Between 1990 and 1994, employment in the new eastern states plummeted by 40 percent, and the absorption of lower-paid East German workers into the country's labor-relations system was creating downward pressure on wages and benefits. This, combined with the increased competitive pressures on German industry from outside the country and a shift toward more decentralized collective bargaining, focused union energy on employment security and wages. All of this reduced the likelihood that union interest in green issues would be much translated into demands at the bargaining table.

German unions have until now not focused much attention on Europe. Like their counterparts in most of northern Europe, they have retained employment benefits and social policy protections that are better than the European average, and they certainly have more bargaining strength than could be conceived of within the European framework. The extent of their interest in the EU has been in preventing the development of a supranational system so deregulated that it would further ease the flight of investment to low-wage and ununionized environments.

Lesbian and gay activists, inside and outside the union movement, were for a time looking toward Europe with some hope of progress there. This was in part a reaction to the anti-gay sentiments that persisted in the CDU-led federal government and a belief in the possibility of effective end runs around that government through the use of European institutions. On the other hand, sexual minorities in Germany do not suffer the same degree of blatant discrimination in law that has motivated their British counterparts to seek redress in Europe. In addition, Germany's progressive activists—for example in the Green movement—are distrustful of the centralization and bureaucratization they see as embodied in Brussels.[18]

The Netherlands

For sexual minorities, the Netherlands provides one of the most politically inclusive environments to be found anywhere. Discrimination on the basis of sexual orientation is prohibited in the constitution, though as a result of court interpretation rather than explicit inclusion. Same-sex couples have as much legal recognition as in any country.

State agencies support gay and lesbian access to the media and recognition of homosexuality in immigration, housing, and education. Several Dutch municipalities have had offices for homosexual emancipation since the early 1980s, and by the 1990s such offices numbered more than two dozen. Public opinion is unusually accepting, one survey indicating that only 10 percent of the Dutch public disapproves of homosexuality, a much smaller rate of disapproval than in just about any other country in the world.[19]

The Netherlands has the strongest and longest lasting national gay and lesbian organization of any country in Europe, and probably the world. Cultuur- en Ontspannings-Centrum (COC) was formed in 1947, and for most of the time since then it has benefited from well-established systems of subsidization and support from all levels of government.[20] State policy-making reflects a general pattern of interest-group inclusion in elaborate consultative exercises designed to arrive at consensus. As Hanspeter Kriesi argues, "Dutch authorities tend to integrate, coopt and subsidize challengers rather than repress and marginalize them."[21] This did not occur in the first years of COC's existence, but gradually authorities began treating the group as representative of a mini-"pillar," with its leadership given a certain access to policy makers.

Prior to 1983, statutory prohibitions on discrimination of all sorts were limited and frail.[22] A new constitution coming into effect in that year opened with a prohibition of discrimination on the grounds of religion, belief, political opinion, race, or sex "or on any grounds whatsoever." The open-ended phrase was widely seen as encompassing sexual orientation, not least because 90 percent of the Chamber of Representatives had asked the government to submit legislation prohibiting such discrimination as early as 1978.

The development of an explicit legislative or constitutional prohibition on anti-gay discrimination was much delayed because of the complex task of reconciling such a ban with the rights of religious groups. The issue was finally resolved in the 1990s with the passage of the General Equal Treatment Act, which allows exemption from the anti-discrimination prohibition for religious institutions, including schools (an exemption much opposed by lesbian and gay activists). Immigrant policy was changed in 1984 to allow gay and lesbian foreigners to join their Dutch partners in the Netherlands, and in 1992, refugee policy changed to admit asylum seekers claiming persecution on the grounds of their sexual orientation.[23] National legislation in 1997 placed same-sex relationships on the same legal footing as heterosexual common-law couples but rejected full equivalence to marriage.[24] In 1998, the government announced its intention to introduce legislation allowing same-sex couples adoption rights and reversed its earlier position by announcing a proposal to allow same-sex marriage.[25]

As in all political systems, the parties of the left in this country have been closer than those of the right and center to social causes such as sexual minority rights. In the 1970s, the electoral success of the Christian Democratic Appeal (CDA)—an amalgam of three major religious parties—had led the Socialists (PvdA) to a strategy of connecting to social movements of the New Left. The CDA's continued success and government dominance in the 1980s, though, contributed to the Socialists' abandonment of their polarization strategy and to an increased willingness to cooperate with the CDA. For social activists, this restored elements of the previous state of affairs, in which cross-party contacts were more fruitful of policy success than reliance on any single party.

The Dutch union system had been segmented along religious and political lines in much the same way as the party system, but less bitterly split along ideological lines than the French, and less fragmented between industrial and trade unions than the British. In 1981, social democratic and Catholic labor federations amalgamated to form the Dutch Federation of Trade Unions (FNV) representing close to 60 percent of the country's union membership. From the late 1970s on, the power of Dutch unions had been declining significantly, the fall in membership during the 1980s rivaled only by that of French and U.S. labor movements (among industrialized countries)—taking it down to 25 percent of the workforce in 1990. Shifts in state policy deprived unions of crucial corporatist channels for political influence, and they faced decentralizing trends in bargaining, for which they were ill prepared.[26] Confronting the need to drastically redeploy resources, the leading unions narrowed their agendas.

During the 1970s, when the Socialist Party was drawing closer to social movements, union linkages to such activism were more tenuous. Unions were seen by many social activists as heavily bureaucratized and resistant to change—a view persisting through the 1980s.[27] Ben Valkenburg argues that even in the 1990s, Dutch unions have not engaged in the fundamental reassessment of the notion of solidarity that would be called for to respond fully to the challenges of diversity facing them along racial, gender, and other lines.[28]

In more recent times, shifts in the balance of union membership away from the industrial working class have opened up unions to social causes.[29] This has been accompanied by some effective gay and lesbian activism in the union movement.[30] ABVAKABO, the very large public sector union, has an institutionally supported lesbian and gay committee, publishes the group's journal *Inzake,* and sponsored a comprehensive survey of the experience of lesbians and gays at work.[31] The Dutch police union (NPB) has adopted a high profile on sexual orientation issues, with a working group established in 1994 and a Homosexuals Secretariat created in 1996 to serve the interests of lesbian and gay members. The following year, the NPB negotiated a national collective agreement stipulating that police organizations had to draw up plans to improve their work climates and accessibility in relation to sexual minorities. In late 1997, the union actively supported and participated in a large conference on "pink in the blue."[32]

Both NPB and ABVAKABO are members of the FNV. As early as 1979, a gay and lesbian working group was formed within FNV by teachers as a reaction to the dismissal of some of their colleagues because of their homosexuality. Activism at the federation level has not been particularly high profile, and the current FNV publication on the federation's anti-discrimination policy is virtually silent on sexual diversity.[33] On the other hand, FNV was one of the major sponsors of the 1998 Conference on Trade Unions, Homosexuality, and Work, and publicized the conference in its newsletter.[34]

The National Federation of Christian Trade Unions (CNV) is not nearly as proactive as the FNV, though it is worth noting that the Christian Police Union (ACP Politiebond) has had a lesbian and gay working group since 1997. The union was a party to the 1997 collective agreement calling for an improvement in the working climate for gays and lesbians, and it was in the aftermath of this agreement that the union affirmed its support for an equal opportunities policy that extends to sexuality. The union's publication on homosexuality acknowledged, however, that the union's Christian origin "still complicates the full acceptance of people's different sexuality."[35]

The progress made within the political realm and the shift in Dutch attitudes more generally, even if easily exaggerated, have reduced the urgency for union intervention in lesbian and gay issues. Movements such as that for sexual minority rights have built their own connections to parties and policy makers in the Dutch state, making the role of unions less crucial than it otherwise might be. Even in the heyday of a more centralized corporatist system, the unions' own centralization meant relatively weak presence in the actual workplace. Their importance for sexual minority activists was thereby diminished, since they offered little prospect of being able to challenge workplace practices beyond the level of formal policy. Moreover, because governments were key players in corporatist bargaining, leverage at that level could be as easily obtained through party connections as through union engagement.

What about Dutch social activism at the level of European institutions? As with their German counterparts, Dutch unionists have only modest incentives to devote attention and resources to Europe, except to prevent the EU from being so deregulative as to accelerate downward pressure on wages and benefits. This lack of incentives is even truer of lesbian and gay activists because of the substantial gains they have made and the consultative access they have acquired at the national level. The contrast between those gains and what would be possible in Europe is as stark as for their union counterparts. Balancing these disincentives somewhat is that the Netherlands, like the other Benelux countries, tends to see itself as at the heart of Europe. Its relative smallness may well have deepened the commitment among citizens and policy makers to the view that the gains of integration are substantial, and the risks entailed in reductions of national sovereignty worth the price.

Britain

Britain has had a statutory regime more explicitly discriminatory than most of Europe, alongside vibrant cultural and political movements expressing sexual difference and mounting challenges to state regulation. Even if British attitudes to homosexuality were not unusually prejudicial, the obviousness of officially sanctioned discrimination presented a target against which a community could be mobilized to produce both cultural and political challenges.[36] Tony Blair's Labour government, elected in 1997, promised to eliminate or change a number of discriminatory laws but so far has proceeded slowly and cautiously. Officially supported discrimination led British activists in the 1980s to work at gaining union support. It also led activists to look to Europe for remedies unavailable at home. Paradoxically, then, the country in which suspicion of European institutions has been greatest (on the left as well as the right) has been that country in which sexual minority activists, in and out of unions, have been most prepared to avail themselves of the openings created for legal and political appeals in the EU.

Sexual orientation activism inside the British Labour Party and the union movement intensified in the early 1980s, a period when the party seemed open to leftist social activists and when the Thatcherite threat made gravitation toward an opposition party seem a worthy project. The organizational links between party and union movement meant that the successful raising of sexual diversity issues required activist intervention in unions as well as in the nonunion constituency base of the party. White-collar unions were the most obvious targets, but overt lesbian and gay participation in the campaign to support the coal miners in resisting Thatcher government moves to close pits in the mid-1980s created surprising support for pro-gay resolutions in a few of the traditional and heavily male industrial unions.

The absence of legal prohibition on anti-gay discrimination and the more general absence of a bill of rights gave unions a potential role in supporting grievances based on prejudicial treatment in the workplace and in developing collective agreement language prohibiting discrimination. The relative decentralization of the union movement in Britain also accorded major significance to individual unions, allowing gay and lesbian inroads at times when national institutions were slow or reluctant to move. The Labour Party moved toward political moderation during the 1980s, trying to marginalize the most clearly left elements that had been drawn to the party at the beginning of the decade, and trying to establish some distance from the unions. However, that did not prevent activists within particular unions from continuing to engage their unions in sexual diversity issues.

As Phil Greasley and Fiona Colgan point out in their contributions to this volume, some unions, most notably the National Association of Local Government Officers (NALGO), adopted pro-gay policies as early as the mid-1970s. In 1985, the Trades Union Congress passed a wide-ranging resolution acknowledging the role of the union movement in supporting equal opportunities for gays and lesbians. By the early 1990s, a significant number of unions, particularly in the public sector and in areas with substantial numbers of women members, had pro-gay policies. The new public sector amalgam UNISON treated diversity issues in general, and sexual orientation in particular, as part of its core mandate.

The progress in British unions has constituted an uphill struggle against a union culture long shaped by the very traditional family and social values of the English industrial working class. "Cloth-cap" unionism was not a friendly environment for feminist initiatives starting in the late 1970s, nor for gay and lesbian activism. Persistent elements of such a culture should not be underestimated, though the dramatically altered demographics of union membership have contributed to change. By the late 1980s, over 35 percent of union members were women, far more, for example, than in the Netherlands. At the same time, close to half of union members were in white-collar sectors.[37] The lack of ideological fragmentation characteristic of the French union system also meant that the British movement was not as dominated by the view that class conflict subsumed all other political divisions and issues.

Litigation was not heavily used by activist movements in Britain, largely because of the lack of statutory prohibition against anti-gay discrimination and because of the tendency of courts to defer to Parliament. The judicial openings created at the European level, however, stimulated some interest in using the courts to circumvent reluctant politicians and employers. In a few such ventures into the very expensive litigation route, union support has been critical. In 1995, a gay worker took a complaint of unfair dismissal to an industrial tribunal with the help of his union and the activist group

Lesbian and Gay Employment Rights (LAGER).[38] In the late 1990s UNISON supported Lisa Grant in her action against South West Trains (see below).

Britain long excluded itself from the European Union's Social Chapter, but that did not prevent British labor unions from looking to Europe for help on a range of workplace and union-related issues. The very ferocity of the government's anti-union policies during the Thatcher and Major periods, in fact, increased unionists' attention to the potential of using European institutions to raise local workplace standards to continental norms. It is in Britain, therefore, that sexual minority activists and union officials have been most hopeful of using European institutions to make gains that have been slowed or blocked at home. Though it would be easy to overestimate, it is also in Britain that sexual-minority activism and union activism have intersected most substantially.

European Institutions: The Council of Europe

Sexual diversity activism directed at European institutions has been motivated in part by the increased significance of European-level policy making, and in part by the prospect of creating leverage at home.[39] The very unevenness of progress toward equity at the national level, evident in the case studies above, creates especially strong incentives for activists in "laggard" countries to pursue objectives at the supranational level. In precisely those countries, however, activist movements often are weakest and therefore least able to muster the resources required for intervention within or beyond the national system. The unevenness of progress creates challenges for activists seeking advances at the European level, too, because progress has tended to depend on broad consensus among national leaders—especially in social policy fields.

Two distinct sets of European institutions are relevant for sexual minorities: the Council of Europe and the European Union. The oldest institutions are those that arose from the 1949 establishment of the Council of Europe. Foreign ministers representing more than two dozen member states constitute its Committee of Ministers. The Parliamentary Assembly essentially lacks legislative power and has only slight political visibility. The most important offspring of the council is the European Convention on Human Rights (ECHR), administered by the European Commission on Human Rights and adjudicated by the European Court of Human Rights.

The ECHR contained no explicit ban on discrimination based on sexual orientation, though Article 14 stipulated that "the rights and freedoms set forth in this Convention shall be secured without discrimination on any ground such as sex, race, color, language, religion, political or other opinion, national or social origin, association with a national minority, property, birth or other status." Other articles spoke to the right to privacy and the right to family life. These provisions provided an inducement for activists to use court challenges to embarrass national governments, the incentives perhaps increased by political support within other Council of Europe institutions. In 1981, the Parliamentary Assembly adopted a recommendation calling not only for the legalization of homosexuality, but also for a common age of consent for homosexual and heterosexual activity, for equal treatment in the workplace, for the abolition of police files on homosexuals, and for the right of gay and lesbian parents to have access to their children without discrimination.

In 1981, the European Court of Human Rights delivered its first gay-related judgment, ruling in favor of Jeffrey Dudgeon's claim that the criminalization of all homosexual activity in Northern Ireland was a violation of the ECHR. Even if the court had no powers of enforcement, the court victory effectively forced the British government to partially reform the law in 1982. In 1988, the court ruled in favor of David Norris, who argued that the Irish Republic's prohibition of all homosexual acts was also illegal, that decision adding considerably to the pressure for law reform even in a country with deeply entrenched religiously based resistance to change. Both cases were judged on the basis of the right to privacy (Article 8), the court not yet ready to adopt an expansive reading of Article 14. Other attempts, several from Britain, to challenge other statutes or policies discriminatory against gays and lesbians fared less well than the Dudgeon and Norris cases.[40]

By the second half of the 1990s, the European Commission on Human Rights and the European Court of Human Rights were opening the adjudicative door wider to plaintiffs seeking remedy against discriminatory laws in the home states. Once again, British activists were taking the lead, faced as they were with a broad range of explicitly discriminatory statutes and regulations and the absence of constitutional protection against discrimination at the national level. In 1997, the European Court ruled unfavorably on a British case begun years before, following a 1985 arrest in the "Spanner" case, involving consensual sado-masochistic sex. In the same year, however, the European Commission considered the admissibility of an age of consent case brought by Euan Sutherland (with the help of the highly effective lobby group Stonewall) as a preliminary to transferring the case to the European Court. (Groups like Stonewall were now soliciting and supporting cases with the ECHR in mind, knowing the likelihood of defeat in British courts.) The commission ruled that the case had sufficient merit to oblige response from the British government. The commission later released a report on the case, agreeing with the plaintiff that the unequal age of consent was an infringement of the European Convention on Human Rights. It argued that there was no reasonable justification for a higher age of consent for homosexuals than for heterosexuals.[41] Shortly thereafter, the British government assured the plaintiffs that legislative moves would be undertaken within two years to equalize the age of consent in Britain. In 1998, the House of Commons voted to do just that, though opposition in the House of Lords both in that year and again in 1999 delayed final legislative approval.

However significant the positive outcomes under the ECHR, they have been based primarily on the narrow ground of a right to privacy.[42] In addition, neither the court nor the commission has the same enforcement mechanisms as the European Court of Justice, though most European Union members have incorporated the European Convention into national law, including Britain as of 1998. Cases that center on workplace discrimination, in any event, are more likely to require the kind of enforceability given to decisions taken through EU channels which unlike Council of Europe institutions can override national legislation.

The European Community and the European Union

The European Union is far more significant than the Council of Europe as a trans-nationally integrative institution, but until now it has provided little room for decisions on most equity issues and has encouraged only a narrow construction of rights.[43] As Carl Stychin puts it, "Citizenship, to the extent that it has been a meaningful concept within European law and politics, has focused on the individual as economic actor, as opposed to a more social or political conception of the relationship of the citizen to the polity."[44] A rights "discourse" within the EU context, then, does attract activists who work in national settings without much constitutional leverage in favor of individual or group rights, but it has been almost entirely a market-driven conception more restricted even than that employed by the ECHR.

Established first in 1957 as the European Economic Community, with a membership of six (West Germany, France, Italy, Belgium, the Netherlands, Luxemburg), the European Union has expanded to a membership of fifteen, with additional memberships being considered. Since 1992, the EU has moved toward closer political coordination and the establishment of a common currency. The major EU institutions are the European Court of Justice (in Luxemburg), the European Parliament (in Strasbourg), and the two most powerful bodies—the Council of Ministers (comprising heads of government or cabinet ministers from member states), and the European Commission (the Brussels-based administrative apparatus).

The European Parliament has been gradually increasing its profile and leverage—having long had little of either. The 1987 Single European Act (SEA) gave it some power through what was called "cooperative" procedures, and in 1993, it acquired certain "co-decision" rights. In a number of issue domains, the EP was now able to force negotiations with the Council of Ministers on amendments to legislation, and in some circumstances it was able to defeat legislation backed by a majority of the council. Among European institutions, it was in this legislative body that sexual orientation issues first found political support. In 1984, the European Parliament approved recommendations of the Squarcialupi Report on sexual discrimination in the workplace. (These recommendations were similar to resolutions adopted by the Parliamentary Assembly of the Council of Europe three years earlier.) The parliament also called on the European Commission to report on discrimination against lesbians and gays and to submit proposals for outlawing such discrimination in the workplace. Over the next several years, parliamentary majorities reiterated the call for prohibiting discrimination against sexual minorities.

Parliamentarians had long been interested in developing good relationships with a variety of pressure groups, in part to avail themselves of whatever expertise might be lodged within such groups. Increases in the EP's leverage intensified that interest, especially in areas that would increase the legislature's profile and its connections to grass roots political activists—areas such as environmentalism, consumer rights, and human rights.[45] Among the groups drawn into relationships to legislative networks was the International Lesbian and Gay Association (ILGA).

The European Commission at first did not heed the calls for action from parliamentarians, claiming that the absence of explicit reference to sexual-minority rights in the treaties establishing the Union, and the EEC before it, precluded action. Several writers have argued that openings were available under existing treaty provisions, and others have pointed out that the absence of environmental references had not prevented the issuance of regulations on green issues.[46] A Social Charter signed at Turin in 1961 had little substantive impact on policies developed within the European Commission or the Council of Ministers. To the extent that initiatives were undertaken, they were spillovers from the drive to create a single market, intended to contribute to the free movement of factors of production—market "building" initiatives rather than market "correcting."[47] Jacques Delors's assuming of the commission presidency in 1985, however, increased attention to the social dimension of Europe. Delors was outspoken on social policy—a 1988 speech to the Trades Union Congress, for example, was thought pivotal in drawing British union attention toward the potential for policy gains through European institutions.

In 1989, eleven of twelve European Community members (Britain excluding itself) approved the Community Charter of the Fundamental Social Rights of Workers. This helped secure social rights as a principle underlying the European Community, although it contained little more than solemn declarations of principle and reinforced the narrow identification of "social policy" with workplace rights and labor-management relations. The Treaty on European Union (TEU) agreed to at Maastricht and taking effect at the beginning of 1993 included an Agreement on Social Policy. The "Social Chapter," this too applying to eleven of the twelve, reaffirmed the principles of the 1989 Social Charter but facilitated the passage of EU legislation by extending the realm in which qualified majority voting in the council would apply—the principle of QMV having been introduced in 1987. It would now apply to workers' health and safety, working conditions, the information and consultation rights of workers, gender equality, and the integration of persons excluded from the labor market.[48] (It also increased the role of "social partners" in formulating social policy; see below.) The Social Chapter did not have the force of law, requiring implementation at the level of member states, but it brought a range of social issues within the EU's mission by specifically enabling the EU to legislate in these areas. Even if the EU was still driven primarily toward market-centered goals, social rights had been given some life of their own under the Maastricht regime.

On the other hand, the Social Chapter increased member-state fears of EU intrusiveness, exacerbated by the increased scope given to majority voting in the Council of Ministers. The principles of "subsidiarity" and "proportionality" were built into the Maastricht Treaty, stipulating that community action was justified only if the objectives in question were not sufficiently achievable by member states, and limiting action to what was necessary to achieve the ends of EU treaties. Evidence derived from European Community jurisprudence prior to Maastricht suggests that the latitude for EU initiatives would continue to expand, but subsidiarity could be cited by member states determined to prevent the enactment of equity measures.

The explicit inclusion of gender discrimination in the list of issue areas to which qualified majority voting would apply reflects its legal standing in comparison to other equity issues. Article 119 of the Treaty of Rome, requiring that women and men be paid equally for equal work, lay dormant for two decades but, from the 1970s on, was taken up by some important European Commission directives on equal pay and equal treatment in state benefit policies.[49] It was also taken up by the European Court of Justice, which during the 1970s and 1980s adopted relatively expansive readings of Article 119 (while still limiting the scope of European Community law to workplace issues).[50] Beyond the issue of gender, the court also used arguments based on the mobility of labor and services to make forays into the social policies of member states. It did so armed with the power to declare actions of European institutions and member states in violation of European Community law, and with treaty provisions requiring the application of its decisions by member-state courts and tribunals.

That said, the European Commission and its president were still treating gender issues as marginal. Women's policy networks were sidelined during the 1980s discussions leading to the single market.[51] Even within the directorate general responsible for social policy (DG V), the concerns of women were marginal. Delors was interested in expanding the social policy envelop, but he was preoccupied with providing openings for discussions between the "social partners"—i.e., labor and management. Positive steps were taken in 1991 and 1992 when the commission acknowledged that harassment was to be included in the interpretation of the 1976 Equal Treatment Directive and approved the Protection of Pregnant Workers Directive. It also agreed to "recommendations" on child care, though the latter were entirely nonbinding and shaped by a view still prevailing that such issues lay beyond the European Community's competence. As recently as 1994, the newly arrived European Commissioner for Sweden was dismayed at the predominance of "gray-suited men" in the upper echelons of the organization.[52]

In 1994, the European Commission acknowledged that the existing treaty framework did not address discrimination on grounds of race, religion, age, and disability, and admitted that this was "an omission that is becoming increasingly difficult to justify in today's Europe."[53] In 1995, a three-year Action Program included reference to these and other social issues. Later that same year, the commission issued its first "communication" on the issue of racial discrimination (including anti-Semitism), stating that a nondiscrimination clause would be included in future legislative proposals, a clause inspired by Article 14 of the European Convention of Human Rights.[54] At this stage, there was no specific mention of sexual orientation.

Back in 1990, Jacques Delors asserted that the commission had no power to act on sexual orientation matters even while broadening its interest in discrimination generally and suggested that the ECHR was the appropriate vehicle for confronting the issue. By the end of that year, however, there were encouraging developments. First, a European Community directive called on member states to prohibit the automatic processing of data on such factors as citizens' opinions, ethnic and racial origin, religious affiliation, and "sexual life." Then, the Social Affairs Commissioner met a delegation of lesbian and gay organizations from across the member states and agreed to appoint a senior official with formal responsibility for sexual orientation issues. In the following year, the commission issued, as a recommendation to member states, a code of practice on sexual harassment that included reference to sexual orientation.

In 1996, the European Commission extended some recognition to same-sex relationships in staff regulations covering EU employees, but it still reacted with caution when faced with proposals from the European Parliament for fully equal treatment. In a response to an inquiry from ILGA, the president's office wrote that the European Commission was not ready to propose that cohabiting couples (including same-sex couples) be put in the same category as married couples, "because the law in the Member States is still too diverse in this area and the Staff Regulations of officials and other members of the European civil service must, up to a point, take this into account."[55] In 1997, the commission intervened in the Lisa Grant case before the European Court of Justice (see below) to argue that the imposition of same-sex benefits would interfere with the principle that family law was a matter for member states to decide for themselves.[56]

The Council of Ministers seems even more reluctant to take up the issue, illustrated by an EU directive on parental leave. In the course of 1995, representatives of the European Trade Union Confederation (ETUC), the Union of Industrial and Employers' Confederations of Europe (UNICE), and the European Center of Enterprises with Public Participation (CEEP) were taking advantage of a procedure introduced in 1993 to forge an agreement on parental leave. This was a provision by which these social partners, if agreeing among themselves, could propose measures that could then be enacted by EU institutions proper.[57] The draft parental leave directive was the first to include the nondiscrimination clause envisaged by the European Commission itself, indicating that when member states adopted provisions implementing it, they should prohibit discrimination based on race, sex, color, religion, nationality, and sexual orientation. This was distinctive in its inclusion of race, color, religion, and nationality for the first time in European Community legislation, and in its addition of sexual orientation. Faced with the draft directive in 1996, however, the Council of Ministers deleted the anti-discrimination section, inserting a more innocuous, nonbinding statement that cited the Social Charter's recognition of discrimination, specifying a variety of grounds but excluding sexual orientation.[58]

The negotiations culminating in the mid-1997 Treaty of Amsterdam, in which a variety of amendments to EU treaties were agreed to by all member states (this time including Britain), signaled cautious movement from such exclusion. Social rights in general were given more profile in this agreement. An affirmation of the social charters of 1961 and 1989 was included in the preamble, and thereby enshrined as one of the general principles underlying the union.[59] A new clause on nondiscrimination (originally Article 6a and then Article 13) was added to the treaty, covering a great deal of new ground: "Without prejudice to the other provisions of this Treaty and within the limits of the powers conferred by it upon the Community, the Council, acting unanimously on a proposal from the Commission and after consulting the European Parliament, may take appropriate action to combat discrimination based on sex, racial or ethnic origin, religion or belief, disability, age or sexual orientation." This was certainly an advance, but substantially watered down from earlier drafts.

In late 1996, the Irish council president had proposed stronger language: "Within the scope of application of the Treaties on which the Union is founded and without prejudice to any special provisions contained therein, any discrimination on grounds of race, sex, national or ethnic origin, disability, age, sexual orientation, religion, social origin . . . shall be prohibited." The earlier draft of Article 6a stipulated that the council "shall take the necessary measures to prohibit discrimination" rather than it "may take appropriate action." In early 1997, the Dutch president of the council proposed substantial watering down by deleting explicit reference to social origin, disability, age, and sexual orientation.[60] The final version of the nondiscrimination provision includes sexual orientation but has no direct impact, simply enabling the European Commission and Council of Ministers to proceed, and only on the basis of member-state unanimity. Whether these changes will create additional openings for gays and lesbians remains uncertain, not least because the provision awaits member-state ratification. On the other hand, inclusion of reference to sexual orientation might provide room for interpretive expansiveness by the European Court of Justice, as might the treaty's provision for litigating cases through the ECJ on the basis of provisions in the European Convention on Human Rights.

The record of the European Court of Justice until now has not been particularly encouraging. As indicated earlier, the court's judgments have teeth and played an important role in expanding the EU's intervention in social issues, largely on the basis of securing free movement for services and labor. The court has been cautious, however, in moving into equity areas beyond ground clearly and explicitly staked out by treaty articles. On gender, the equity issue with the strongest treaty foundation, the court has tended toward a view that European Community competence lies only in workplace-related issues. Even within that domain, the court has resisted arguments that the effect of family responsibilities must be considered in assessing equal treatment at work, and it has applied a narrow interpretation of equality that stipulates identical treatment.[61] As Stychin points out, the court looks for a common ground that is relatively elusive amid the quite different constitutional traditions of member states.[62]

Only weeks after the June 1997 signing of the Amsterdam Treaty, though before its ratification, the court heard the case of a British lesbian, Lisa Grant, claiming that her employer, South West Trains, was discriminating in its refusal to grant a travel benefit to her same-sex partner—a benefit that would have been extended had she been in a heterosexual relationship.[63] The case had been referred to the ECJ by a British tribunal, asking clarification of the applicability to this case of the EU Commission's Equal Treatment Directive (the 1976 directive focused on gender). In September, the court's advocate general agreed that Grant had been a victim of sexual discrimination (since her partner would have received the contested benefit if Grant had been a man), and argued further that "there was nothing in the EU's treaties to indicate that the right not to be discriminated on the basis of gender should not apply to homosexuals, to the handicapped, to persons of a particular ethnic origin, or to persons who hold particular religious views."[64] "Equality before the law," he argued, "was a fundamental principle." Optimism that the court would eventually rule positively was fueled by a 1996 judgment in favor of a British transsexual, using the same Equal Treatment Directive cited in the Grant case.

In February 1998, however, the court ruled against the plaintiff, arguing that this was not a case of sex discrimination. It ruled further, and also against the advice of the advocate general, that discrimination based on sexual orientation was not covered by EU law as it stood.[65] The judgment noted that the European Commission on Human Rights had not recognized homosexual relationships as covered by the European Convention's provisions on respect for family life. The president of the court indicated further that it was up to national legislatures to adopt measures favorable to homosexual couples, point-ing out that the wide divergence of national laws on relationship issues was an argu-ment against siding with the plaintiff. This was obviously a retreat to the narrowest pos-sible interpretations of European law, and clearly a setback. It did not take away fully the openings in the EU's political institutions that had been so noticeably created in recent years, but it acted as a sobering reminder of the slowness of EU movement, and the reluc-tance in most EU institutions to move ahead of member-state policy development.

The one arena in which significant progress was still most obvious was the European Parliament. In 1994, building on earlier pronouncements, parliamentarians approved a resolution calling for the elimination of statutes criminalizing homosexuality and other measures discriminating against gays and lesbians—specifically targeting unequal age-of-consent laws and Britain's Section 28 (legislation passed in 1988 prohibiting local authorities from "promoting" homosexuality). The resolution called for equal legisla-tive treatment in areas like social security, inheritance, housing, and adoption, effec-tively asking member countries to fully accept same-sex relationships. It also called on the European Commission to draft a directive banning discrimination on the grounds of sexual orientation and recommended the creation of an agency dedicated to fight-ing discrimination against gays, lesbians, and other minorities. The resolution passed 159–96, despite the vocal opposition of the Vatican.[66] In May 1995, parliamentarians approved a resolution calling for the addition of a clause prohibiting discrimination on the grounds of sexual orientation in the revisions to the Maastricht Treaty, culminat-ing in the Treaty of Amsterdam.

In February 1997, the EP adopted amendments to EU draft legislation aimed at guar-anteeing equal treatment to the EU's own gay and lesbian employees, including "mar-ital" benefits to staff who registered partnerships in their home countries or with their employer.[67] (As indicated above, the commission later rejected the proposals on rela-tionship recognition.) In the autumn of 1997, an EP "intergroup" on Equal Rights for Gays and Lesbians was founded, with support from green parties, socialists, and even Christian Democrats. In early 1998, an EP resolution repeated the call on member states to recognize equal rights for homosexuals and to create provisions for civil con-tracts between same-sex couples.[68] It then repeated support for the full recognition of such relationships for EU employees. Another resolution, passed in September of the same year, reaffirmed commitments to lesbian and gay rights and bluntly condemned Austria's failure to equalize its age of consent. It also condemned discriminatory statutes in Cyprus and Romania—both countries in the queue for EU membership—and declared the EP's intention to refuse consent to accession of any country that, "through its leg-islation or policies, violates the human rights of lesbians and gay men."[69]

In September 1998, the European Commission launched a discussion process over the EU's human rights agenda "for the year 2000," including the appointment of a "Comité des Sages" (Committee of the Wise) to report on the topic. This highly pres-tigious group, which included the UN High Commissioner for Human Rights and a former secretary general of the Council of Europe, concluded that "discrimination based on sexual orientation continues to be widespread and should be more systemat-ically addressed through a Commission action plan and the development of a draft direc-tive on equal treatment."[70]

Activism's Influence in European Institutions

The success of resolutions in support of sexual minorities has been due in part to the work of the International Lesbian and Gay Association, which improved its effectiveness in Europe through a semi-autonomous European regional group. ILGA-Europe has held meetings with a few of the Commission's directorates general, most notably DG V (responsible for the social affairs portfolio),[71] and coordinated a particularly effective lobbying effort, alongside its own member groups, to ensure the passage of the European Parliament's September 1998 resolution on lesbian and gay equality. It has also worked with Egalité, a group representing lesbian and gay EU employees that now has over 350 members. Groups such as ILGA and Egalité are still marginal, though, not least because the entire European enterprise is tilted in favor of interests representing industry and commerce. Even in the 1990s, two-thirds of all European groups actually based in Brussels, the home of the European Commission, are business groups.[72]

The challenges facing equity-seeking groups aspiring to influence in Europe are daunting indeed. Member states guard their social policy prerogative with some firmness and retain dominant roles in policy implementation. Interest groups and social activists, therefore, incur the costs of maintaining pressure on national institutions while at the same time building linkages to European bodies.[73] Intervention in Europe, in fact, can sometimes undermine whatever relationships a national group may have with its own national government, especially if such intervention is designed to challenge domestic policy.

European institutions are highly complex and slow moving, and policy networks are ever changing.[74] Policy-making can involve an unpredictable mix of national-level interveners, individual commissioners, and more than one of the directorates general, each of the latter being relatively isolated from the others and likely to have distinctive decisional processes and group networks. Even if access to officials is secured, most groups lack the resources required to simply keep track of policy development. The resource problem is exacerbated by the need to intervene over a long period, from the first stages of formulating recommendations to the very last stages of implementation.[75]

To secure status in European policy-making, a group must make itself indispensable as a supplier of expertise, an aid to policy implementation, and a vehicle for securing the allegiance of an important constituency. As Mazey and Richardson point out, officials also expect groups to be "responsible"—willing to work respectfully with other groups interested in the same issues, to compromise, and to do so without publicity.[76] This does not create much room for rocking boats!

The dilemma facing activist groups is that the expectations imposed on them by Brussels blunt some of their most valuable strategic tools—for example, the use of media publicity—and alienate many of the activists and supporters who constitute their lifeblood. Yet activist groups that represent interests thought to be peripheral to the EU have to use media publicity, as they do the European courts, to challenge inaction by national governments and push envelopes within the EU itself. As Mazey and Richardson point out, "The trade-off may be between maintaining a high public profile through an action-oriented approach to lobbying, and sacrificing a chance of long-term influence in the processing of issues."[77]

Some activist groups have worked within these constraints with considerable success. The environmental movement has devoted major resources to EU policy-making, with noticeable impact. It has benefited enormously, though, from the active support of the European Commission, and in particular, the directorate-general responsible for environmental affairs (DG XI).[78] Groups representing most human rights and diversity issues have far fewer resources than the environmental movement, and while they have some support in DG V, they have nothing like the support among senior commissioners that environmental issues have sometimes had. Feminist networks have made gains, their status bolstered by the inclusion of gender in the Treaty of Rome and subsequent legislative enactments, and by relatively expansive court judgments.[79] Catherine Hoskyns points out, however, how difficult it was to establish a feminist presence in Brussels.[80] Policy networks such as the Women's Committee of European parliamentarians and the European Commission's Women's Bureau (later reconstituted as the Equal Opportunities Unit) began to form in the mid-1980s. The European Women's Lobby was inaugurated in 1990, but its relative lack of resources, the narrowness of room for maneuver in the EU, and the cumbersomeness and secrecy of Brussels decision-making impeded its linkage to feminist activism in member states.

The physical remove and structure of the EU's institutions discourage radical challenge of any sort, and little in the policy development of the last forty years suggests that anything other than incremental change is possible, with the possible exception of policies in aid of capital mobility. Groups operating in any political arena, including Brussels, need some hope of success to sustain themselves, and they need concrete achievements to ensure member support. That creates great pressure to work within the existing legal and political frameworks. The argument against discriminatory treatment of sexual minorities is put in terms of inefficiency, and the case for same-sex relationship recognition is put in terms of impediments to labor mobility—in other words, free-market frameworks. Any claims made for a more inclusive notion of "European citizenship" tend, for example, to leave unexamined the racially exclusionary elements in that construct.[81]

Sexual diversity activists in the new Europe have a few advantages. They are relatively united behind their demands, without the sorts of competitiveness between national agendas that is so often characteristic of groups at the EU level. Sexual diversity finds contrasting expression and political activism in the various countries of Europe and the regions within them, but there is not much disagreement on the basic demands of the Brussels-centered activists. Radical challenge is difficult enough and the footholds for sexual diversity politics are fragile enough that those who favor transformative politics tend not to bother intervening in Europe at all. Such unity helps in putting a case in Europe. That the activist agenda is relatively low cost, in contrast to much other social policy, also helps. Sexual diversity issues run up against "moral" objections from many European quarters, and certainly very widespread indifference, but much less resistance than high-cost social policy demands from those whose preoccupation is the construction of a deregulative environment for business and a minimalist state.

Labor's Engagement with the European Union

An analysis of the role of labor unions in furthering sexual minority equality at the European level requires first a consideration of union interest in Europe and influence within EU institutions. In the first three decades of the EEC and EC, the dominance of market-related considerations was incontestable, tilting the policy process substantially in favor of corporate interests. Even in the new Europe created by Maastricht and laid out in the Treaty of Amsterdam, business remains more influential than any other set of interests, including those of organized labor.[82] The 1987 Agreement on Social Policy, for example, instituted mandatory consultation for the social partners but provided no right to collective action and no particularly significant impetus to collective bargaining.

Steps toward increasing union strength in Europe inevitably collide with business determination to increase workforce flexibility, reduce wage costs, and deregulate markets—these objectives largely shared within EU institutions. Steps to strengthen labor would be complicated as well by highly variegated labor-relations systems at the national level, some centralized, others decentralized, some unified, others divided along ideological or religious lines, some relatively independent of government intervention, others not, some based on high union memberships, others low.[83]

Since the late 1980s, though, attention to social policy has increased, in large measure motivated by a European drive to create genuinely free movement of the factors of production. Because the social policy envelop has always emphasized workplace rights, the expansion of that envelope has created some openings for labor. There might well be an emergent role for unions in shaping policy on such matters as health and safety, education and retraining, the environment, and policies related to gender and other forms of workforce diversity. On some such questions, there may well be room for agreement between labor and management, since an increasing number of private firms now recognize the profitability in appearing to be environmentally friendly in their production practice and inclusive in their employment practice. Some observers argue, too, that the prospects of serious social dialogue are increased by the changed composition of the Council of Ministers brought on by the new membership of countries like Austria, Sweden, and Finland, with relatively positive views of "social regulation."[84]

Increasingly, labor union participation in European institutions has been under the rubric of the European Trade Union Confederation (ETUC), though the formation of a genuinely representative and effective peak organization is still very much a work in progress.[85] The ETUC is made up, first, by national federations of labor, and second, by sector-specific European federations. The European Union has recognized the ETUC as the peak organization representing organized labor in its member states, although the ETUC membership extends beyond the fifteen countries of the EU.

Since its formation in 1972, the ETUC has faced the challenge of representing a highly diversified labor movement. At the very least, it has to mediate between more than fifty national union federations and sixteen industry-specific federations. Despite their differences, and the tilt of EU policy-making in favor of capital, European unions have increased their interest in the ETUC and seem to have overcome some of the divisiveness that long characterized the organization. National unions have been weakened within their own countries by a variety of forces, not least of them globalization, and have seen European institutions become increasingly important in social policy development. Even the modest institutionalization of union participation in EU decision-making processes has added to the incentives for European involvement. As a result, the ETUC has moved from being a relatively ineffective and politically marginal organization to one with significantly increased effectiveness and importance, though like many of the other interests represented at the European level, its resources are spread very thinly and are inadequate for the challenges facing any group seeking influence within the complex institutional apparatus of the EU.

The ETUC depends greatly on the expertise and staff of its constituent members. A number of national unions and union confederations have appointed officers and created departments to deal with European affairs, generally under the ETUC rubric. The British union movement is among these, having dramatically shifted its view of Europe in the late 1980s. On the other hand, most national union movements are restrained in their enthusiasm for shifting energy to Europe. Relatively strong union movements have few incentives to shift resources toward a political jurisdiction in which the chances of gain are small.[86] Some countries with weak union movements may have strong incentives to support transnational institutions but few resources to contribute. Low-wage countries with weak unions, in fact, have fewer incentives, since the establishment of higher standards of wages and benefits would carry the risk of shifting investment and jobs away. Across all of Europe, union movements face traumatic changes at home. As a result, then, few national confederations are willing or able to commit significant resources to the development of a genuinely supranational union organization.[87]

In the last few years, despite the impediments in its way, the ETUC has secured a degree of access to some portions of the European Commission (especially DG V) and the European Parliament (especially the Socialist group). Even with limited resources, it is thought to have contributed in important ways to the final shape of the 1993 Works Council Directive, requiring worker consultation in large firms, and the 1993 Working Time Directive. It cooperated in the Commission's development of the 1996 voluntary code of practice on equal pay. The inclusion in the Treaty of Amsterdam of a commitment to the promotion of employment as one of the EU's core objectives could well provide additional openings for labor. The very severity of the threats that national union movements face as a result of restructuring might in the long run impel greater interest in Europe to ensure their continued relevance.

European Labor's Commitment to Equity

Labor organizations operating at the European level have taken some steps to recognize diversity issues, though generally they have been late and slow to take them up and have done so in relative isolation from groups and networks focusing on those issues. The limits on their resources and the need to represent diverse national movements within a highly restrictive institutional environment have also limited their agenda.

In most of Europe and North America, union embrace of gender issues has preceded the recognition of other issues. On that front, though, change has only begun to appear at the European level. In the 1970s and 1980s, union groups operating at the European level opposed the creation of autonomous feminist groups did little to encourage the creation of women's groups within union structures.[88] This helped ensure that the women's lobby organizations had a largely middle-class and professional composition, and it led to a degree of isolation between feminist work in European Community institutions and labor-oriented work. In any event, the union organizations themselves, reflecting national patterns, were relatively rigid and hierarchical—difficult for feminists to work with. Even at the national level, women had barely begun to make union inroads—in most countries succeeding only in the 1990s in effecting substantial improvement in the representation of women on decision-making bodies.

In European-level union organizations, some progress is evident in recent years. One early-1990s survey showed that a majority of sectoral federations had departments for equity or women's issues and some sort of positive action program.[89] The ETUC had an active women's committee and officers responsible for women's affairs. The 1995 Parental Leave agreement contained anti-discrimination language that broke new ground, and it specifically included sexual orientation, even though the final version approved by the Council of Ministers watered down that language. To be sure, their agreement followed a European Commission initiative in respect to leave policy and anti-discrimination riders, but it went beyond the norm in extending anti-discrimination language to include gays and lesbians. Labor's readiness to pursue equity issues was also apparent at a social dialogue summit in Florence at the end of 1995, when three peak organizations (ETUC, UNICE, and CEEP, the latter representing public sector institutions) adopted a declaration on measures to combat racism and xenophobia, promising active participation in a joint effort to prevent racial discrimination in the workplace.[90]

Still, the depth of labor's commitment to such issues is unclear, and the demographics of union representation at the European level do not generate confidence.[91] Women are even more underrepresented in the decision-making bodies of the ETUC than they are in national-level confederations and unions, where they are usually underrepresented to a significant degree.[92] This is relevant to sexual minorities, since the record of policy development and practice in unions across a large number of countries indicates that women and women's caucuses are often central to the extension of equity policies beyond gender. If union structures at the European level are slow to translate formal policy commitments on gender into practice, they are even slower on matters related to race, and still slower on sexual orientation.

The snail's pace on equity issues reflects to some degree the great disparities in the relationships between national union movements and other equity-seeking groups. Hanspeter Kriesi and collaborators in a comparative analysis of European social movements suggest that there are systematic national differences in the alliances between labor and the newer social movements that focus on issues such as gender, race, peace, environmentalism, and sexual orientation.[93] They argue, for example, that where governments have tended toward "exclusive" strategies that keep labor out of decision-making arenas, the union movement and old-left parties are more likely to have an interest in the newer movements. In an exclusivist regime such as France, however, the strength of radicalism reinforces labor's tendency to support other movements only on its own terms. In inclusive regimes such as the Netherlands, characterized by values of compromise and negotiation, social movements usually seek direct relationships with state authorities rather than using unions as external levers. Their very engagement in state institutions may limit union scope to the traditional agendas of organized labor. In systems as different as the Dutch and French, then, only modest incentives exist for collaboration between unions and sexual diversity activists.

Data compiled by Kriesi and his colleagues for France, Germany, the Netherlands, and Switzerland suggest that in none of these countries is the level of engagement in "new" social activism by unions or social democratic parties all that great. For example, they tabulated the participation of unions and parties of the left in "protest events" sponsored by the newer social movements and found that unions were involved in about 9 percent of such events in France and Germany, and less than 3 percent in the other two countries. Social democratic parties participated in just over 8 percent of these events in France and Germany, and around 4 percent in the other two.[94]

Counteracting this trend somewhat, as we saw in the German case, would be the emergence of new left or green parties posing electoral challenges to traditional working-class parties on the basis of appeals to new social agendas. As Kriesi and his colleagues point out, social-democratic parties in opposition will benefit from challenges directed to governments by movements other than labor, especially as these parties take their distance from traditional forms of laborism. Labor unions are beginning to recognize the importance of speaking to diversity issues as their own demographics change. The increased willingness of lesbian and gay workers to come out inevitably adds sexual orientation issues to the diversity agenda. The prominence given to relationship-recognition issues during the 1990s highlights discrimination in workplace benefit programs that activists readily see as causes worthy of union attention.

Factors operating at the European level will increase the connection between these movements. The absence of supranational collective bargaining pulls the ETUC into those policy areas in which there is potential for influence, including equity issues. In addition, however diverse the views of union members on such matters, they can often be more easily overcome than differences over issues closer to the traditional core of union agendas. Greenwood points to the development of policy in areas such as the environment, women's issues, racial discrimination, and assistance to the disabled, for example, as "relatively uncontentious."[95] It may well be too early for such language to be applied to sexual diversity issues, but they are still less complex than a number of other issue areas. Furthermore, the European Commission's directorate general with which the ETUC has its closest and most influential relationship is DG V, with responsibility for a wide range of social issues that takes in anti-discrimination policy. To the extent that the International Lesbian and Gay Association has a firm relationship with any directorate general, it is also DG V. ETUC perspectives likely will be shaped in some measure by the work of other groups interested in social rights, and like unions, traditionally on the margins of EU institutions.

Conclusion

The relationships between sexual diversity activists, labor unions, and Europe are symptomatic of the troubled relationships between "red" left, "green" politics, and transnationalism. Difficulties and uncertainties are embedded in the turbulent transition from the fordist regimes of the postwar settlement to another stage in political economy more dominated by corporate interests, by individualism, and by the assertiveness of new forms of identity. The development of European institutions adds to the complex challenges already facing labor movements. It also poses significant challenges to activist movements, such as the gay and lesbian, traditionally strongest at the local level and having to intervene at both national and international levels.

As we have seen, lesbian and gay national movements have differing degrees of incentive to devote significant energy to European-level institutions. Those movements like the Dutch that have had relative success in achieving objectives at the national level have no obvious self-interest in focusing on Europe, since there would be little chance of making gains in European bodies exceeding their gains at the national level. Even the German and French movements, less advantaged than their Dutch colleagues, do not face the sort of legal discrimination that would be an obvious target at the European level. Sexual minorities in parts of southern Europe may be the most disadvantaged of all, but not necessarily in ways that allow for obvious redress within EU institutions. Activist movements in such areas also tend to be weak and underresourced. The British are the most obviously positioned to be advantaged by European channels. However, they as well as their counterparts elsewhere face the difficulties of allocating already scarce organizational resources to a highly complex institutional environment at the supranational level.

The impediments in the path of establishing links between sexual-minority activists and unions at the European level are formidable. Unions and activist networks focusing on diversity issues have worked in relative isolation from one another. Unions are unevenly committed to devoting significant resources to Europe, especially in light of the crises they face at home. In any event, until now, there has been uneven interest in equity issues beyond formal pronouncement. Those countries in which most progress has been made toward equality for gays and lesbians (in northern Europe) are also the countries with the most advanced labor-relations systems, with unions standing to gain little from Europe. Thus, there is often only modest interest in Europe in those countries where union movements might be most open to equity issues.

For all the important advances made since the late 1980s, the policy issues that most concern union representatives and sexual minority activists remain on the margins of the new Europe. That said, some equity issues have been taken up as "spillovers" of the drive toward economic integration—always the focus of EC and EU concerns. The attractions of intervening in Europe are increasing for those movements interested in the rights of workers as well as those of such marginalized groups as lesbians, gays, bisexuals, and the transgendered. The European Commission has been more encouraging of equity initiatives than before. The European Parliament's declaration in favor of equity for gays and lesbians had little impact until recently, but the persistence of legislators on the subject has played a role in convincing the social partners and the officials of the commission that at least some of the commitments on equity and diversity might as well include sexual orientation. The growing evidence that accommodation to sexual diversity demands entails very little market "regulation" and even less cost will reduce the risks of incorporating them into broader equity programs.

The European Court of Justice has not until now played a leadership role on sexual orientation issues, but it has in the past used moderately expansive readings of treaty provisions on equal pay for women. The court has intervened in social policy in the interests of securing greater labor mobility between member states, and it has specifically ruled that the treatment of dependents is an important component of such mobility. Legislative discrimination against sexual minorities in member states has for some time been characterized as a barrier to labor mobility. Now, with such vast differences in legislative recognition of same-sex relationships, activists can reasonably argue that gays and lesbians with partners employed in countries that recognize those relationships are inhibited from moving to jobs in countries denying such recognition. The court may well take advantage of specific mention of sexual orientation in the Treaty of Amsterdam when it comes into force, although the weak phrasing of the relevant provisions of that treaty and the court's recent record should limit optimism.

Policy advances in Europe will never lurch ahead of the pack of member states, but they could well provide a boost for sexual minorities in member countries that have taken the fewest steps toward equity and inclusiveness. Improvements in the visibility and effectiveness of lesbian and gay organizations operating within the EU environment are making sexual diversity issues more inescapable than they ever have been. National public sector unions such as UNISON in Britain, ABVAKABO in the Netherlands, and ÖTV in Germany have played invaluable roles in taking on and providing visibility for activist concerns, broadening awareness of sexual orientation initiatives within their own countries' union movements and in the international arena. Union organizations operating at the European level, who have gained small footholds inside EU institutions, may have not until now done very much on sexual orientation issues, but they will at some point recognize the inevitability of including such issues in their equity agendas.

There is much risk of EU policy resorting to lowest common denominators, and near certainty that the EU as a whole will continue to attach priority to free-market principles. Notions of European civilization and citizenship, increasingly current in the post-Maastricht environment, are also built on highly exclusionary foundations.[96] Historically, national communities in Europe were defined so as to treat non-Christians and non-Caucasians as "other." Gender and sexual "deviation" were also treated as threats to cultural health and political security. Carl Stychin sees no evidence that the contemporary construct of European citizenship challenges those restrictive historical roots, and he fears that sexual minority activists are mistakenly trying to work within the narrow confines of that construct. Union interventions in Europe might be seen in a similar light, as posing few radical challenges to the concept of citizen emerging within EU institutions.

Nevertheless, the long-term impact of the small steps being taken now, however confined by the ideological and institutional characteristics of the EU, cannot be easily predicted. The European Court of Human Rights's 1988 ruling against Ireland's sodomy law was based on narrow grounds and had no enforcement mechanism, but it helped provoke national-level activism and significant reform. As Stychin points out, too, the Irish Republic's membership in the EU has helped stimulate a reconstitution of the notion of citizenship, moving toward a degree of inclusiveness and openness that scarcely could have been predicted a decade earlier.[97] Small gains made by the labor movement and by sexual diversity activists could well provide leverage for large-scale change and could weaken the most restrictive of the historical roots of European citizenship. Alliances between them will significantly increase the chances for such gains.

Notes

Acknowledgments: This chapter was greatly improved by comments from Ronald Holzhacker, Barry Adam, Gerald Hunt, and especially Alan Butt Philip, and by assistance from Michael Johnson. It was largely written in Australia, where I benefited from the generosity of Jude Irwin, Robert Aldrich, and Maude Frances, of the Australian Centre for Lesbian and Gay Research at the University of Sydney, Michael Pankhurst of the University's Student Union Computer Lab, Garry Wotherspoon, and especially Peter Caldwell.

1. See J. W. Duyvendak, *The Power of Politics: New Social Movements in France* (Boulder, Colo.: Westview, 1995).

2. C. Robinson, *Scandal in the Ink* (London: Cassell, 1995), p. 30.

3. For developments through this period, see F. Martel, *Le Rose et le noir: les homosexuels en France depuis 1968* (Paris: Seuil, 1996), pp. 143–152.

4. Some of the French polling evidence is distilled by Robinson, *Scandal in the Ink*, pp. 31–32.

5. See Martel, *Le Rose et le noir*, chaps. 14–16. It is Duyvendak's view in *The Power of Politics* that French gay activism was small scale and low key by this time, a view echoed to some extent in F. Anal, "The Gay Press and Movement in France," in *The Third Pink Book: A Global View of Lesbian and Gay Liberation and Oppression*, ed. A. Hendriks et al. (Buffalo: Prometheus, 1993).

6. In 1990, union members constituted 9.8 percent of all employees, down 12.5 percent from 1970. See R. Mouriaux, "The Disarray of the Trade Unions in a State of Crisis," in *The Lost Perspective? Trade Unions Between Ideology and Social Action in the New Europe*, vol. 2, ed. P. Pasture et al. (Aldershot, UK: Avebury, 1996), p. 50. Union weakness persists despite Mitterrand government legislation strengthening union bargaining rights. There may be some reason to anticipate increased union involvement in plant-level and national bargaining, but this would be an improvement on a very weakened base. See J. Goetschy and P. Rozenblatt, "France: The Industrial Relations System at a Turning Point?" in *Industrial Relations in the New Europe*, ed. A. Ferner and R. Hyman (Oxford: Blackwell, 1992).

7. On feminist issues, see J. Jenson, "Representations of Difference: The Varieties of French Feminism," *New Left Review* 30 (1991): 127–160.

8. Article 3 of the Basic Law of the Federal Republic prohibits discrimination based on gender, race, language, national origin, religion, or political persuasion. Article 5 guarantees freedom of expression, association, and movement. There is some uncertainty as to how much protection such provisions would give lesbians and gays. See, for example, P. Tatchell, *Europe in the Pink: Lesbian and Gay Equality in the New Europe* (London: GMP, 1992), pp. 112–113.

9. See C. E. Zirakzadeh, *Social Movements in Politics: A Comparative Study* (London: Longman, 1997), chap. 3.

10. A. S. Markovits and P. S. Gorski, *The German Left: Red, Green, and Beyond* (New York: Oxford University Press, 1993), pp. 268–269.

11. I. Kokula, "The Lesbian-Gay Interface Between East and West Germany," in *The Third Pink Book,* ed. Hendriks et al., p. 140.

12. Zirakzadeh, *Social Movements in Politics,* p. 60.

13. Markovits and Gorski, *The German Left,* p. 270.

14. See M. Baethge and H. Wolf, "Continuity and Change in the 'German Model' of Employment Relations," in *A Changing World Economy,* ed. R. Locke et al. (Cambridge, Mass.: MIT Press, 1995), pp. 252–253; J. Verberckmoes, "Germany: Inner Trade Union Diversity," in *The Lost Perspective,* ed. Pasture et al., pp. 180–214; and J. Hoffmann, "Trade Union Reform in Germany: Some Analytical and Critical Remarks Concerning the Current Debate," *Transfer* 1 (January 1995): 98–113.

15. "Racial Discrimination and Trade Union Policy," *European Industrial Relations Review,* no. 277 (February 1997): 26–28.

16. See *Lesbian and Gay Working Group in the ÖTV Berlin,* brochure.

17. Other major sponsors were UNISON, the largest public sector union in Britain, the Dutch labor federations FNV and CNV as well as the FNV-affiliated public sector unions ABVAKABO, and the Canadian Labour Congress.

18. E. Bomberg, "The German Greens and the European Community: Dilemmas of a Movement-Party," in *A Green Dimension for the European Community: Political Issues and Processes,* ed. D. Judge (London: David Cass, 1993).

19. See M. Hoogma, "The Netherlands: A Fifteen Year Fight for Equal Rights," in *The Second ILGA Pink Book: A Global View of Lesbian and Gay Liberation and Oppression* (Utrecht: International Lesbian and Gay Association, 1988).

20. There are now about fifty COC branches across the country. For an historical overview of lesbian and gay political development, see R. Tielman, "Dutch Gay Emancipation History (1911–1986)," in *Interdisciplinary Research on Homosexuality in the Netherlands,* ed. A. X. van Naerssen (New York: Haworth, 1987), pp. 9–17. See also J. K. van Wijngaarden, "The Netherlands: AIDS in a Consensual Society," in *AIDS in the Industrialized Democracies: Passions, Politics, and Policies,* ed. D. L. Kirp and R. Bayer (New Brunswick, N.J.: Rutgers University Press, 1992), pp. 252–280.

21. H. Kriesi, *Political Mobilization and Social Change: The Dutch Case in Comparative Perspective* (Aldershot, UK: Avebury, 1993), p. 170.

22. K. Waaldijk, "Constitutional Protection Against Discrimination of Homosexuals," in *Interdisciplinary Research on Homosexuality in the Netherlands,* ed. van Naerssen.

23. A. Hendriks and W. Ruygrok, " 'Strangers' in the Netherlands: Dutch Policy Toward Gay and Lesbian Aliens," in *The Third Pink Book,* ed. Hendriks et al.

24. " 'In Between Law' Gives New Recognition to Dutch Gay Couples," *Gay Times* (September 1997): 58.

25. Only Dutch children would be adoptable under the plan approved by the cabinet. The earlier partnership legislation followed a model used in the Scandinavian countries requiring one of the parties to be a Dutch citizen resident in the country.

26. On changes in industrial relations, see Kriesi, *Political Mobilization and Social Change,* chap. 5; and J. Visser, "The Netherlands: The End of an Era and the End of a System," in *Industrial Relations in the New Europe,* ed. Ferner and Hyman.

27. A. Kaplan, *Contemporary Western European Feminism* (London: Allen and Unwin, 1992), p. 153.

28. "Individualization and Solidarity: The Challenge of Modernization," in *The Challenges to Trade Unions in Europe: Innovation or Adaptation,* ed. P. Leisink et al. (Cheltenham, UK: Edward Elgar, 1996).

29. Kriesi, *Political Mobilization and Social Change,* pp. 238–239. The FNV has recognized the importance of targeted strategies to attract additional membership, but despite their declared intentions, unions have not been particularly successful in attracting women members, visible minorities, or young members, and diversity issues have had relatively little play in collective bargaining.

30. M. Odijk, "Homosexuality and Work: Individuals, Rights, Atmosphere," unpublished manuscript, n.d.

31. T. Sandfort and H. Bos, *Sexual Preference and Work: A Comparison Between Homosexual and Heterosexual Persons* (Utrecht: Nisso and Gay and Lesbian Studies, commissioned by ABVAKABO FNV, 1998).

32. See W. Koeslag et al., eds., *Roze in het Blauw: Verslag van een Conferentie,* the report of a conference on homosexuality and policing in the Netherlands held on 25 September 1997; and Nederlandse Politiebond, "Being Gay in the Dutch Police Force," a report prepared at the time of the 1998 Conference on Trade Unions, Homosexuality, and Work, Amsterdam, 23 July 1998. Participants in the Roze in het Blauw conference reported the persistence of widespread anti-gay sentiments in police forces and that, in a nationwide force of 40,000 police employees, only 200 were "out."

33. *Non-Discrimination Code for the FNV and Its Unions: Guidelines for the Union and Work Organization* (June 1993).

34. According to an article on the upcoming conference in the August 1997 *FNV News,* organizers stated that, although support for gay rights was gaining ground, few unions were really doing anything about it (p. 8).

35. ACP Politiebond, *ACP Policy on Homosexuality* (April 1998). See also *Roze in het Blauw,* pp. 80, 98.

36. See D. Rayside, *On the Fringe: Gays and Lesbians in Politics* (Ithaca: Cornell University Press, 1998), chaps. 1–3.

37. On this and other features of union movement change, see P. Edwards et al., "Great Britain: Still Muddling Through," in *Industrial Relations in the New Europe,* ed. Ferner and Hyman. By the late 1990s, over half of union members were white collar. Overall, union membership constituted 39 percent of all employees in 1990, down just over 4 percent from 1970.

38. "Industrial Tribunals Support Gay Employment Rights," *Gay Times* (June 1995): 40.

39. This section draws substantially from Tatchell, *Europe in the Pink.*

40. The earliest gay attempts to invoke the convention were by Germans in the 1950s, challenging the criminalization of all homosexual activity. On this and other litigation, see E. van der Veen et al., "Lesbian and Gay Rights in Europe: Homosexuality and the Law," in *The Third Pink Book,* ed. Hendriks et al.

41. See "Government May Abandon European Court Case Over Unequal Age of Consent," *Gay Times* (August 1997): 43; and "Government 'Promises Equal Age of Consent Within Two Years,'" *Gay Times* (November 1997): 39.

42. On the limitations of the ECHR's nondiscrimination provisions, see S. Palmer, "Critical Perspectives on Women's Rights: The European Convention on Human Rights and Fundamental Freedoms," in *Feminist Perspectives on the Foundational Subjects of Law,* ed. A. Bottomley (London: Cavendish, 1996).

43. This section draws not only from Tatchell, *Europe in the Pink,* but also from K. Waaldijk and A. Clapham, eds., *Homosexuality: A European Community Issue: Essays on Lesbian and Gay Rights in European Law and Policy* (Dordrecht, Netherlands: Martinus Nijhoff, 1993).

44. C. Stychin, *A Nation by Rights* (Philadelphia: Temple University Press, 1998), p. 116.

45. This is a point made by B. Kohler-Koch, "Organized Interests in European Integration: The Evaluation of a New Type of Governance," in *Participation and Policy-Making in the European Union,* ed. H. Wallace and A. R. Young (Oxford: Clarendon, 1997), pp. 55–56.

46. On sexual orientation issues, see the various contributors to *Homosexuality: A European Community Issue,* ed. Waaldijk and Clapham.

47. On this, see S. Leibfried and P. Pierson, "Social Policy," in *Policy-Making in the European Union,* 3rd ed., ed. H. Wallace and W. Wallace (Oxford: Oxford University Press, 1996), pp. 186–189.

48. J. T. Addison and W. S. Siebert, "Recent Developments in Social Policy in the New European Union," *Industrial and Labor Relations Review* 48 (October 1994), especially pp. 19–22.

49. The most important was the Equal Treatment Directive of 1976. Article 119 had been drafted initially not because of a commitment to genuine equality but to impose limits on the possibility of unfair wage competition across national borders.

50. For a critical treatment of these and subsequent developments, see G. More, "Equality of Treatment in European Community Law: The Limits of Market Equality," in *Feminist Perspectives,* ed. Bottomley.

51. C. Hoskyns points out that there was not a single woman in the core group established in 1986 to prepare the way for the SEA, in *Integrating Gender: Women, Law, and Politics in the European Union* (London: Verso, 1996), p. 153.

52. Cited by Hoskyns, *Integrating Gender,* p. 1.

53. "Disability, Employment, and the Law in Europe—Part One," *European Industrial Relations Review,* no. 251 (December 1994): 14.

54. Hoskyns argues that the European Commission and European Council have been almost entirely ineffective on race issues, in *Integrating Gender,* chap. 9.

55. "Answer from the EU Commission on the Lindholm Report," *ILGA Euroletter,* no 52 (August 1997). The commission's decision was then upheld in the European Court, in a decision announced in early 1999. See "EU Employers Will Not Recognize Gay Relationships," *Gay Times* (March 1999): 56.

56. "Lisa Grant vs South West Trains," *ILGA Euroletter,* no. 52 (August 1997).

57. The application of such measures would not include Britain, which at this point had opted out of the provisions of the Social Charter. See "Intro the Unknown: Implementing the Parental Leave Agreement," *European Industrial Relations Review,* no. 267 (April 1996): 19–24.

58. "Problems with the Parental Leave EU-Directive," *ILGA Euroletter,* no. 46 (December 1996). For an excellent overview of developments on sexual orientation, see M. Bell, "An EU Human Rights Agenda for the Year 2000," *ILGA Euroletter,* no. 62 (August 1998).

59. "Social Policy Under the Treaty of Amsterdam," *European Industrial Relations Review,* no. 283 (August 1997): 14–16. See also "Backlash in EU Treaty Negotiations," *ILGA Euroletter,* no. 46 (December 1996).

60. "Dutch EU Presidency Has Abolished Non-Discrimination Based on Sexual Orientation," *ILGA Euroletter,* no. 48 (March 1997).

61. Court judgments have tended not to take into account, for example, the differential burdens of domestic responsibilities and have tended to take a highly restrictive view of what sorts of affirmative action policies are permissible. See More, "Equality of Treatment in European Community Law."

62. Stychin, *A Nation by Rights,* pp. 129–130.

63. Among the groups donating money to help defray litigation costs was UNISON, the largest of Britain's public sector unions.

64. "Landmark European Employment Rights Victory for Lesbian Couple," *Gay Times* (November 1997): 41. See also "We Are Asking for Equal Treatment," *Gay Times* (July 1997): 43; and "To Luxembourg with Cherie Booth," *Gay Times* (September 1997): 7–8, 54.

65. "EU Law Does Not Protect Same Sex Couples, Says EU Court," *Sources Say* (17 February 1998), p. 1.

66. A. van Hertum, "Pope Blasts Europeans' Call for Gay Civil Rights," *Washington Blade,* 25 February 1994.

67. "European Parliament for Gay and Lesbian Rights," *ILGA Euroletter,* no. 48 (March 1997). This approval followed a surprise rejection the month before by the Legal Affairs Committee, reported in "MEPs Withhold Equal Treatment for Gays and Lesbians," *ILGA Euroletter,* no. 47 (February 1997).

68. "European Parliament Adopts Resolution on Human Rights," *ILGA Euroletter,* no. 58 (March 1998).

69. Passage of this resolution required active lobbying by ILGA-Europe and its member groups, particularly directed at the social-democratic parliamentary group, which had failed to support the resolution earlier.

70. ILGA-Europe, "European Union Launches Its Human Rights Agenda for the Year 2000," *ILGA Euroletter,* no. 65 (November 1998).

71. For reports on lobbying, see "Let the Lobbying Begin," *ILGA Euroletter,* no. 45 (November 1996); and "Third Series of Meetings Between European Commission Officials and ILGA-Europe," *ILGA Euroletter,* no. 58 (March 1998).

72. J. Greenwood, *Representing Interests in the European Union* (Basingstoke, UK: Macmillan, 1997).

73. On this point, see Kohler-Koch, "Organized Interests in European Integration."

74. S. Mazey and J. Richardson, "Environmental Groups and the EC: Challenges and Opportunities," in *A Green Dimension for the European Community,* ed. Judge, p. 110. This is a first-rate analysis based on speaking with officials and activists, and it informs a number of the points made in this section.

75. The commission subsidizes a number of groups that would otherwise have difficulty maintaining any kind of a presence in Europe, but such subsidies are insufficient to meet the full burdens of effective intervention.

76. Mazey and Richardson, "Environmental Groups and the EC," p. 110.

77. Mazey and Richardson, "Environmental Groups and the EC," p. 127.

78. G. Majone, "Regulating Europe: Problems and Prospects," *Jahrbuch zur Staats- und Verwaltungswissenschaft* (Baden-Baden: 1989), reported in Mazey and Richardson, "Environmental Groups and the EC," p. 114.

79. See, for example, Hoskyns, *Integrating Gender*; and G. Kaplan, "Feminism and Nationalism: The European Case," in *Feminist Nationalism,* ed. L. A. West (New York: Routledge, 1997).

80. Hoskyns, *Integrating Gender,* especially chap. 10.

81. This is a point made by Stychin, *A Nation by Rights,* especially pp. 140–144. It is also a point frequently made by writers in the critical legal studies tradition.

82. Greenwood, *Representing Interests in the European Union,* p. 155.

83. W. E. Lecher and H.-W. Platzer, "Introduction: Global Trends and the European Context," in *European Union—European Industrial Relations? Global Challenges, National Developments, and Transnational Dynamics,* ed. W. E. Lecher and H.-W. Platzer (London: Routledge, 1998), pp. 12–13. A similar argument is made by D. Buda, "On Course for European Labour Relations? The Prospects for the Social Dialogue in the European Union," in the same volume, p. 34. Other

contributors to the volume are equally pessimistic about the possibility of a genuine collective bargaining system developing at the European level, as is Greenwood in *Representing Interests in the European Union.*

84. See, for example, H.-W. Platzer, "Industrial Relations and European Integration: Patterns, Dynamics and Limits of Transnationalism," in *European Union—European Industrial Relations,* ed. Lecher and Platzer, p. 85.

85. On the ETUC's development and functioning, see Greenwood, *Representing Interests in the European Union,* chap. 7.

86. The DGB opened its own office in Brussels, though it remains relatively small. Berndt Keller describes trade union "internationalism" as purely verbal and argues that unions have provided only meager financial support to the development of transnational institutions such as the ETUC. See B. Keller, "National Industrial Relations and the Prospects for European Collective Bargaining: The View from a German Standpoint," in *European Union—European Industrial Relations,* ed. Lecher and Platzer, p. 51.

87. See Mouriaux, "The Disarray of the Trade Unions," pp. 3–18; J. Vilrokx, "Trade Unions in a Postrepresentative Society," in *Challenges to Trade Unions in Europe,* ed. Leisink et al.; and Buda, "On Course for European Labour Relations," pp. 34–36. A. Ferner and R. Hyman caution against exaggerating the uniformity of these changes across countries, or the extent of decline in union strength, though they still acknowledge large-scale forces for change, in "Introduction: Industrial Relations in the New Europe: Seventeen Types of Ambiguity," in *Industrial Relations in the New Europe,* ed. Ferner and Hyman.

88. This is a point made by Hoskyns, *Integrating Gender,* pp. 203–204.

89. Survey undertaken by M. Braithwaite and C. Byrne, *Women in Decision-Making in Trade Unions* (Brussels: ETUC, 1994), reported in C. Cockburn, "Women's Access to European Industrial Relations," *European Journal of Industrial Relations* 1 (July 1995): 184.

90. "European Year Against Racism," *European Industrial Relations Review,* no. 278 (March 1997): 27–30.

91. The European Metalworkers Federation was something of an exception, unusual in having a women's committee and active voices raising gender issues within its secretariat, though from such quarters there are comments about the continuing exclusion of women among affiliated unions. In the food industry, negotiations between the multinational company Danone and the International Union of Foodworkers included gender issues, though more on the initiative of the company management than the union. See Cockburn, "Women's Access to European Industrial Relations."

92. Cockburn argued as recently as 1995 that "men talk to men" at the European level, in "Women's Access to European Industrial Relations," p. 175.

93. H. Kriesi et al., *New Social Movements in Western Europe: A Comparative Analysis* (Minneapolis: University of Minnesota Press, 1995), especially chap. 3.

94. Kriesi et al., *New Social Movements in Western Europe,* p. 68.

95. Greenwood, *Representing Interests in the European Union,* pp. 169, 172.

96. As Leo Flynn and others argue, the central figure in the emergent conception of European citizen is still the working person who is a citizen of a member state—largely excluding migrant workers and therefore many of those who are racially "other." See L. Flynn, "The Internal Market and the European Union: Some Feminist Notes," in *Feminist Perspectives,* ed. Bottomley. Stychin also makes this point in *A Nation by Rights,* pp. 119–126.

97. Stychin, *A Nation by Rights,* pp. 137–138, drawing in part on K. Rose, *Diverse Communities: The Evolution of Lesbian and Gay Politics in Ireland* (Cork, Ireland: Cork University Press, 1994).

Ronald Holzhacker

12   Labor Unions and Sexual Diversity in Germany

The modern struggle within German labor unions for nondiscrimination and equality in the workplace and society began with the efforts of gay and lesbian activists who emerged from the student protest movement during the late 1960s. The earliest activists were members of the Berlin branch of the Union of Public Services and Transport (*Gewerkschaft Öffentliche Dienste, Transport, und Verkehr* or ÖTV). The union's reaction to their appearance on the public stage was swift and harsh, including threats of expulsion if the activists continued to represent themselves as gay and lesbian members of the ÖTV.

Now, two decades later, officially recognized gay and lesbian caucuses or "working groups" exist within a number of unions throughout Germany. A statement by the president of the ÖTV, Herbert Mai, in a foreword to a newsletter prepared by the ÖTV working group in Berlin, illustrates the current support for sexual-minority rights in a number of German labor unions: "For many years, our organization has been involved in the rights of lesbian and gay colleagues. Because social exclusion of the homosexual person is still strong today in the workplace, it harms their work environment and their very employment may be threatened. That is why our union has developed an antidiscrimination program to work against disadvantages faced by lesbians and gays in industry and bureaucracies and to improve the societal acceptance of same-sex relationships."[1]

Mai's statement signals a major shift in ÖTV position, though it is silent on the most powerful vehicle that unions *could* use to pursue their goals—the inclusion of issues of importance to gays and lesbians in the collective bargaining process. This is typical of the strategy generally followed by the unions in Germany: recognition of sexual diversity groups and support for change at the level of "human rights"—but failure of nerve when pressed to include equity issues in collective bargaining.

This chapter discusses the origins, goals, and successes of the union working groups formed by sexual diversity activists in Germany. It deals as well with the constraints placed on them, especially the opposition they have at times aroused within labor organizations. The chapter also examines the influence employers have in either supporting or hindering the efforts of working groups to achieve their goals.

These union working groups, which began forming two decades ago in Germany, are grounded in two broader social movements. The first is the labor movement, which took form in the second half of the nineteenth century and has pursued a wide range of issues designed to improve the living standards of working-class people and to reform society more generally. The second is the homosexual movement, which was founded at the turn of the century, decimated by the rise of the Nazis in the 1930s, and refounded in the early 1970s. This 1970s movement was heavily influenced by the gay and lesbian social movement in the United States, but it was also shaped by the class politics of the 1960s student protest movement and memories of the earlier German homosexual movement.

Germany is a particularly important site of struggle for sexual diversity activists in Europe. With the collapse of the Soviet empire and reunification in 1990, Germany has emerged as the largest, most powerful economic and political force in Europe. As a leader in the European Union (EU), Germany has the potential to help move law and public policy throughout the union toward the progressive stances adopted by the Netherlands, Denmark, and Sweden. The likelihood of this has now increased with the 1998 election victory of the German Social Democratic party (SPD), the political party most closely aligned with labor. With the SPD in power at the federal level, in coalition with the Greens, important gains for sexual minorities may be possible.

Organized Labor in Germany

For a number of reasons, gay and lesbian activists in Germany have seen unions as important players in their struggle for nondiscrimination and equality. First, German labor unions have been powerful actors in relation to employers and to the policy processes of government. Second, the unions have traditionally concerned themselves with the social as well as the purely economic issues facing their members. These two factors suggested to movement activists that they could enlist the unions as allies in their struggle in the 1970s and 1980s.

Historically, working-class movements throughout Western Europe and the rest of the industrialized world have sought to further the interests of workers and their families. In addition to creating political parties designed to reform the state and society, the leaders of these movements formed labor unions to bargain collectively with employers. In Germany as well as in a number of other European countries, these early unions saw themselves as having a much broader mandate than merely to bargain for livable wages, expand benefits, and fight for safer working conditions. They established educational, health, sport, and free-time organizations to enlighten and mobilize working-class people. They were also involved in pressing political institutions for legislative changes important to their members. In Germany, as elsewhere in Europe, labor unions have become powerful institutions, integral to the transformation of society.

Although decimated during the Hitler years, labor unions were among the first organizations to reestablish themselves during the postwar recovery. Four principles guided the reestablishment of labor unions in West Germany.[2] First, the movement organized itself into autonomous units, independent of religious and politically partisan institutions. Second, unions were organized along industrial lines so that all workers in a plant and in a given industry were represented by the same union, increasing union power considerably. Third, unions were usually organized into a federal structure, so that local, district, Land (state), and national offices each exercised some power in decision-making. Finally, German unions relied heavily on the political process for the protection of workers' rights. Issues such as the conditions under which strikes may occur, union membership, and basic social welfare benefits were determined by legislation, and remain so. This means that labor is very dependent on how the government and state agencies interpret and enforce labor legislation and how law is interpreted by the Federal Labor Court (*Bundesarbeitsgericht*). It also means that contract negotiations with industry typically focus on improving the economic conditions of workers, leaving other issues to be carried forward in consultations and negotiations with the federal government.

Most of the unions in Germany are organized into a peak association, the German Trade Union Federation (*Deutscher Gewerkschaftsbund* or DGB). The DGB represents the interests of labor within the policy-making processes of government, while its sixteen individual unions focus on the collective bargaining process. The association unites almost all organized industrial workers, a majority of white-collar employees, and many government employees.[3]

Labor unions and their members are in a position to exercise substantial influence in German society. Approximately 40 percent of German workers are represented by a labor union, and 90 percent of all jobs are covered by collective bargaining agreements.[4] Workers in Germany have additional ways to influence the companies they work for. Employees have a say on the shop floor through work councils (*Betriebsrat*) and have representatives on the supervisory boards of large corporations (similar to the board of directors of U.S. corporations), an institutional arrangement called codetermination (*Mitbestimmung*).

The Gay and Lesbian Movement in Germany

The homosexual rights movement in Europe began in Berlin at the turn of the century. The sentencing in England in 1895 of the playwright Oscar Wilde to two years in prison for his homosexuality sent shock waves through Europe and was the impetus for a new social movement to challenge the criminalization of homosexuality. In 1897, Dr. Magnus Hirschfeld, the Berlin-based sexuality researcher, founded the Scientific-Humanitarian Committee (*Wissenschaflich-humanitaere Komitee* or WhK).[5] This group petitioned the *Reichstag* to eliminate Paragraph 175 of the German penal code, which criminalized homosexual activity between men as "unnatural acts," and began discussions with the Berlin police to discourage police raids on nightclubs.[6] Seeking to build a wider movement, the group fostered the establishment of branches in the Netherlands (1911), England (1913), and for a brief period Austria (1914).[7]

Following World War I, the defeat of Imperial Germany, and the founding of the Weimar Republic, the gay and lesbian scene was able to blossom in the larger cities. This was a time of hope for the movement because of the liberalizing tendencies of the

Social Democratic government led by Friedrich Ebert. The joys of Weimar Berlin are reflected in the novels of Christopher Isherwood, as is the impending tragedy of Nazi Germany.[8] In 1935, two years after the rise of Hitler, Paragraph 175 was strengthened. In the ensuing years, many gays and lesbians were imprisoned, sent to concentration camps, or killed, along with other groups despised by the Nazis.

After World War II, the gay and lesbian movement in West Germany began to rebuild. The climate was one of renewed repression against homosexuals. The strengthened Paragraph 175 from the Nazi period was retained by the Christian Democrats under Chancellor Konrad Adenauer. This was part of an ugly set of decisions taken by the Adenauer government, including the failure to recognize or pay reparations to homo-sexual victims of the concentration camps.[9] International gay and lesbian groups tried to fight the reinstatement of Paragraph 175, but they were unsuccessful. The decades of the 1950s and most of the 1960s were a period in which homosexual groups in Germany remained small, private organizations, and few political gains were made.[10]

The political climate of the late 1960s was very different. Paragraph 175 was at last reformed. Consensual sex between men was no longer punishable, and the age of consent for homosexuals was set at twenty-one. In 1973, gay and lesbian groups were successful at getting the *Bundestag* to lower the age of consent for homosexuals to eighteen, although for heterosexuals it remained fourteen.

A new gay and lesbian rights movement began in the early 1970s, a kind of late child to the student protest movement that swept across the United States and Europe in the late 1960s. Gay and lesbian students in universities were especially successful at form-ing groups that would survive. The first such group was founded in Bochum in 1970, the *Homosexuelle Aktionsgruppe Bochum* (HAB), and in the following year a similar group was founded in Münster, the *Homosexuellen Studentengruppe Münster* (HSM). Another organization with a diverse membership that formed at this time in Hamburg was a branch of a group founded in Scandinavia, the *Internationale Homophile Welt-organisation* (IHWO).

In 1971, a group that became especially important later for its influence on gay and lesbian activists within labor unions was founded, the *Homosexuellen Aktion Westberlin* (HAW). HAW wanted to build a political group that was distinguished from previous gay organizations, in which rebellion and not integration was the goal. HAW was espe-cially effective at bringing about change because of its strategy of dual membership—encouraging members to engage themselves in other organizations and to press within these organizations for change beneficial to gays and lesbians.[11] The group split in 1974, and members of the moderate left joined the *Allgemeinen Homosexuellen Arbeits-gemeinschaft* (AHA), which had formed a few months before from the dissolution of an IHWO branch in Berlin. This group eventually played a pivotal role in moving the struggle for gay and lesbian rights to the German labor unions. Union members who were activists in the AHA established the first gay and lesbian working groups in the ÖTV union in Berlin.

These activist groups of the early 1970s saw themselves as part of the broad left stu-dent protest movement of 1968, raising issues of social justice, peace, women's rights, and environmental protection. Women were beginning to react against patriarchal struc-tures in society and question traditional gender roles. Within the context of a broad reappraisal of society, homosexual groups could also challenge traditional thinking about sexual identity. Their politics were centered around the coming-out process—the first step toward social recognition and acceptance of their sexual identity. However, they viewed their concerns as tied to the broader issues of power and class raised by the 1968 protest movement.[12]

By the mid-1970s, dedication to class struggle had begun to fade, and the broad coalition of groups that had cohered in the protest movement of the late 1960s began to splinter and disintegrate. The gay and lesbian movement became more tightly focused on issues of sexual identity, nondiscrimination, equality, and the celebration of gay and lesbian culture. This brought the German movement more in line with the American movement, which had not been as influenced by notions of class struggle. Not coincidentally, "pride" celebrations in numerous German cities are referred to as Christopher Street Day, named after the Greenwich Village street in New York in which a 1969 protest marked what many take as the origins of the modern-day American gay and lesbian liberation movement.

With the heady days of the student protest movement fading and the desire by some in society for a return to stability came a change in Germany's political leadership. When the Christian Democrats won power again in 1983, further advances for gays and lesbians were stymied by the party's sympathy for "Christian values" in the interpretation of family and gender roles. Neither the women's movement nor the gay and lesbian movement could expect much progress from the federal government during this period.

When the AIDS crisis hit Germany in the 1980s, it brought personal tragedy to many, but it also brought political gains. Media coverage and public awareness of a whole range of gay and lesbian issues rose. The feared rollback in the advances won by the gay and lesbian community did not occur. In terms of national AIDS policy, the approach was one of tolerance and education instead of hate and repression. The crisis also provided a new impetus for gays and lesbians to organize. By the 1990s, the German gay and lesbian movement was capable of mounting the kind of large-scale demonstrations and public coming-out events typical of the United States almost a decade previously.

The situation faced by gays and lesbians in the German Democratic Republic (GDR) in the East was very different from that faced by those in the West. Although homosexuality was no longer a crime in the GDR after Paragraph 175 was struck in 1968, the communist regime's general restrictions on the ability of independent groups to assemble and disseminate information made organization difficult.[13] Thus, even though homosexuality was decriminalized, the establishment of homosexual groups and newspapers remained forbidden. The official reasoning was that sexuality was private and that no right of organization would be given in such circumstances. In fact, the repressive state security apparatus, the *Ministerium für Staatssicherheit* or Stasi, often used information it had about closeted homosexuals to its advantage and in 1982 began a formal program to infiltrate and monitor the activities of the gay and lesbian movement.[14]

An underground gay and lesbian movement took shape in the GDR in the early 1970s; the first organization, *Homosexuelleninitiative Berlin* (HIB), formed in 1973. The group began by meeting in the homes of individuals and in cafes and restaurants.

HIB attempted to present itself as a self-help group and argued that its purpose was the "free development of personality" protected in a socialist society. The group was banned in 1978 as their activities began to draw more and more people.

In the early 1980s, the East German homosexual movement began to organize itself under the protection of the Lutheran church, the main current of Protestantism, which had defined itself as the "church in socialism" and engaged actively in social debate. Many peace, environmental, and women's groups had formed under the protection of the church after the signing of the Helsinki Agreements in 1975, in which all governments in Europe, East and West, guaranteed to protect freedom and civil rights. The church was emboldened in these efforts by the success that the labor union Solidarity was achieving in Poland.

Two of the groups that formed under church auspices were the *Arbeitskreis Homosexualität* (Homosexual Working Group) in Leipzig in 1982 and *Schwule in der Kirche* (Gays in the Church) in East Berlin shortly thereafter. Additional groups formed in other cities, and by 1988, twenty-two church-related gay and lesbian groups had organized.[15] They typically held informational sessions during church meetings and discussed their demands for recognition and equality. By the late 1980s, the gay and lesbian groups were key participants in the broad coalition that had formed under the protection of the church and that began to oppose the communist regime through large-scale demonstrations.

The open discussion of homosexuality in East German society began in earnest with a series of conferences held in the mid-1980s on the "psycho-social aspects of homosexuality," hosted by the medical profession and attended by psychologists, Marxist philosophers, journalists, and gays and lesbians who related their own experiences. Two themes emerged from the conferences: Prejudice had no place in a socialist society, and discrimination against homosexuals was historically connected to ways of maintaining certain political and social orders.[16] Also by this time, another type of gay and lesbian group had formed in the GDR, so-called "state groups." Groups such as the *Sonntags-Club* in Berlin or *Felix Halle* in Weimar declined to work within the church and, instead, attempted a closer degree of cooperation with the state under the motto "Homosexual Emancipation and Integration."[17]

With the GDR's collapse and German reunification in 1990, broad-ranging discussions about the legal and constitutional order of the new Germany began. This examination of contemporary circumstances was ultimately beneficial to gays and lesbians because it provided the political impetus for finally striking the dreaded Paragraph 175, and for a more tolerant climate generally.

Political Changes After Reunification

Reunification brought significant changes to German society, to some extent helping lesbians and gays. Whereas the West's political and economic institutions were transferred to the East, there was a reluctance among Easterners to forfeit certain social programs they enjoyed. They were especially reluctant to give up provisions for child-care services to families and laws granting a woman's right to choose abortion. The East's more progressive laws on homosexuality made the Bonn government's efforts to maintain Paragraph 175 after reunification politically untenable.

The majority of the political parties in Germany became more supportive of the goals of the gay and lesbian movement after reunification. The environmental and activist party, Alliance '90/the Greens (created by a merger of West and East Green parties as well as the activist groups in the GDR-based Alliance '90), adopted the most positive stance and has had openly gay leaders. The Party of Democratic Socialism (PDS), successor to the communist party that had governed the GDR, also became a public proponent of gay and lesbian rights.

The Social Democratic Party (SPD), the main opposition party in Germany after it lost the federal *Bundestag* election in 1983, has been generally supportive of gay and lesbian rights but somewhat restrained in their enthusiasm. Some in the party have been concerned that too much emphasis on "rights issues" might detract from its economic objectives, such as fighting unemployment, which appeal to the party's traditional working-class clientele. Certain elements of the Free Democratic Party (FDP), the small party that emphasizes free-market economic policies and the protection of civil rights, endorse gay and lesbian rights. However, as the traditional junior coalition partner of either the SPD or the CDU, it has only occasionally addressed these issues in government.

The Christian Democratic Union (CDU), uniting conservatives and religious voters (especially Catholics), held power at the federal level from 1983 to 1998 and has been a barrier to most of the legislation desired by the gay and lesbian movement. This is true at the federal level and in the *Länder* (states) where the party holds power. Even so, the CDU has generally avoided homophobic public attacks, unlike segments within, for example, the American Republican Party.[18]

The impetus to finally strike Paragraph 175 is to be found in the negotiations leading to the Reunification Treaty. This treaty between the East and West contained provisions in which certain laws would be maintained in the eastern part of the country after reunification until agreement could be reached in the *Bundestag* to reconcile the discrepancies. Debate was especially heated in two areas: the more liberal laws regarding abortion and the legality of homosexual activity in the East. Alliance '90/the Greens took the lead in pushing for the removal of Paragraph 175 from the German penal code, a position the SPD supported. The FDP, which held the position of justice minister in the cabinet as the junior coalition partner of the CDU, agreed to press for this change as part of the party's historical commitment to civil rights. Thus, the necessary alliance was in place, and Paragraph 175 was expunged from German law. At the same time, sixteen was adopted as a uniform age of consent for both heterosexuals and homosexuals.

Some of the *Länder* in Germany have gone farther than the federal government in assuring equality for gays and lesbians. The constitutions of three *Länder* now explicitly protect gays and lesbians from discrimination. A number of *Länder* also have civil service positions in the bureaucracy designed to serve the lesbian and gay community and investigate incidents of discrimination. Quite a few cities provide funding for gay and lesbian centers that have been established to provide information, education, discussion, counseling, and organization for events and celebrations in the community. Mayors and city councils in numerous German cities now send official greetings during the yearly Christopher Street Day events and international gay and lesbian sporting events like the Euro-Games.

In addition to these legislative changes, recent court decisions have been favorable to gays and lesbians. According to law, employees in Germany generally cannot be fired "at will" (the basis of employment in the United States, for example), but only "for cause." The German Labor Court held specifically in 1994 that homosexuality was not legal grounds for firing an employee. This means that some of the protections available if a nondiscrimination law were enacted by the *Bundestag* are already legally in place (though of course discriminatory treatment short of firing is still possible).

Germany's extensive social welfare state provides a degree of protection for all citizens, including gays and lesbians, not seen in many other countries. Every German is required to have health insurance, either through the social insurance scheme available to all or private insurance, and normally it is provided by one's place of employment. As a result, there is somewhat less pressure for certain types of benefits to be extended to the partners of gays and lesbians or their children than, for example, in the United States. The difficulty of obtaining private health insurance in the United States has provided a strong impetus there for gays and lesbians to press for same-sex partner benefits through the workplace.

The existence of important legal rights and social welfare benefits in Germany may dampen the ability of gay and lesbian groups within the unions and elsewhere to mobilize the support necessary to press for further changes. There are, however, very important rights and benefits currently denied gay and lesbian partners. The right to spousal benefits for partners is important in areas such as pensions, sick leave, vacation time, rental housing, taxation, and inheritance. Their absence interferes with one's ability to receive an income based on a partner's pension, the right to have time off work to visit a sick partner, coordinate vacation schedules, continue to live in an apartment after a partner's death, obtain the income-tax preferences granted to married persons, and inherit property from a partner. Gay and lesbian working groups within the German labor unions hope to make substantial progress in these areas in the next few years, through legislative changes and collective bargaining agreements.

Sexual Diversity Activism and Union Response

The working groups that formed within Germany's unions to promote sexual diversity issues have achieved some of their goals, but not without difficulty.[19] In general, the elimination of Paragraph 175 and other gains have taken their toll on the organized gay and lesbian movement. The annual Christopher Street Day demonstrations held in German cities each summer have become much less pointedly political and more broadly a celebration of the varied and highly differentiated lifestyles within the gay and lesbian community.[20] A degree of political complacency has also been fed by mainstream press stories trumpeting gains made by lesbians and gays.[21] At the same time, gay and lesbian working groups have emerged in a number of West German trade unions to fight for change in their unions, the workplace, and in society. Five working groups will be used here to illustrate: the public employees union (ÖTV) in Berlin and Nuremberg, the teachers union (GEW) in Berlin, the union umbrella organization (DGB) in Freiberg, and the banking and commerce union (HBV) in Berlin. It will become apparent that the public employees' unions and the teachers' union have been the most successful in implementing a gay rights agenda.

The first gay and lesbian working group started in the Berlin branch of the ÖTV union. Activists from the *Allgemeinen Homosexuellen Aktion Westberlin* (AHA) who were also members of the ÖTV began to organize and press for change in the mid-1970s. They raised issues concerning gays and lesbians in the workplace and submitted articles to the union newspaper, arguing that the union should be more involved in protecting the interests of gay and lesbian workers. The union's reaction in 1977 was to threaten them with expulsion from the union. However, after the initial flare-up, activists persuaded the union to begin to study the realities facing gays and lesbians in the workplace, as well as the broader society. In order to document the alleged discrimination, they convinced the union to recognize the working group in 1978, although it was not until 1984 that the group was able to meet officially in the union central offices and take part in official meetings of the ÖTV.

From these early beginnings in Berlin—first in the ÖTV and then in the Union for Education and Science (GEW, the teachers' union) in 1978 and the Commerce, Banking, and Insurance Union (HBV) in 1983—the initiative spread to other German cities. In 1986, an ÖTV gay and lesbian working group formed in Cologne and became an official group the following year, after a vote of the union conference with only a few voicing opposition. In 1988, the ÖTV federal conference passed a resolution establishing working groups in a number of other German cities, including Hamburg, Frankfurt, Essen, and Dusseldorf. Some of them included members from other unions in the German Trade Union Federation (DGB), who helped spread the idea beyond the ÖTV. The pace of change quickened after the late 1980s—groups forming, for example, in the DGB in Saarland and the media union (IG Medien) in Berlin.[22]

Gays and lesbians work together in many of these organizations, a situation that is not always the case in the broader gay and lesbian movement in Germany. The working groups from the various unions now meet regularly at the federal level. They have also established an educational commission that organizes ÖTV and DGB seminars on the situation faced by sexual minorities in the workplace. The Berlin ÖTV working group currently produces the *ÖTV Lesbian and Gay Report* (*ÖTV Report Lesben & Schwule*), a newsletter with an editorial staff drawn from various ÖTV working groups around the country as well as from working groups in other unions.[23]

The objectives of these working groups are captured by the Berlin ÖTV working group's organizational goals: (1) to be available to lesbian and gay employees to discuss any problems arising in their employment environment, (2) to sensitize the union to be constructive in dealing with lesbian and gay concerns, and (3) to seek to identify the union with the broader political and societal struggle for the acceptance of gays and lesbians in society and the provision of equal rights in law. Some groups emphasize educational programming. The DGB working group in Freiberg, for example, specializes in conducting educational programs on gay and lesbian issues for members of other unions. One of their main goals is "consciousness raising" not only within the unions, but also in demographic groups that other lesbian and gay groups find difficulty reaching.

The GEW working group in Berlin has been especially successful in representing the concerns of gays and lesbians as part of the very core mission of the union, not as issues on the periphery. Detlef Mücke, the working group's leader, reminds audiences of the traditional duty of the union to protect workers in questions related to employment and to represent their interests, arguing that this role must be extended to include discrimination against gays and lesbians. He also insists that because the GEW has played a role in political education on other fronts, it should take a stand "that homosexuality is a form of living which is positive and equal with heterosexuality."[24]

The GEW working group has been successful at getting the Berlin Senate—the overseer of school matters—to agree that homosexuality is not grounds for dismissal or reprimand, to grant permission for lesbian and gay groups to hold educational seminars in Berlin schools, and to allow the *Länd* education office to accept films for the lending library that discuss the history of gay oppression and the present circumstances of lesbians and gays. The working group has also lobbied for curricular change, counting as one of its successes that homosexuality is no longer treated in the Berlin curriculum as perverse or a disease. The group is now lobbying the Berlin Senate to include aspects of homosexuality not only in biology classes but also in German, history, social studies, foreign languages, and art classes.

These policy shifts have been accompanied by considerable opposition. Except for a brief SPD/Green coalition government, Berlin was governed from 1982 until 1996 by the Christian Democrats. As Detlef Mücke notes, the CDU "has not been prepared to even discuss our issues. The CDU makes homosexuality a taboo and only responds to public pressure. The only time they acted was in response to an attack by right-wing youths at a gay and lesbian spring festival." According to Mücke, because of public pressure after this violent attack, the Berlin Senate decided to allow lesbian and gay organizations to organize seminars in the schools in order to reduce prejudices against sexual minorities. "Up until that time," Mücke states, "these seminars were not allowed under a rule which prohibited the 'promotion of intimate relationships.'"

Control of the Berlin Senate has since shifted, and its new leaders are more amenable to the issues raised by the GEW working group. Two years ago, the Social Democrat Ingrid Stahmer received the school portfolio in the Berlin government. The GEW working group had met with her in early 1988 to discuss curriculum issues, the success of those talks contributing to the development of an inner-party dialogue that began with the gay and lesbian organization within the SPD, the "*Schwussos*." The 1996 election program of the Berlin SPD contained many anti-discrimination appeals, some of which were suggested by the GEW working group. This cooperation and support between the gay and lesbian working group in the teachers' union and the gay and lesbian organization in the SPD is an example of a whole range of cooperative endeavors now happening within the movement.

Not all of the working groups have been so successful. Charles Mündler, leader of the HBV working group in Berlin, paints a relatively gloomy picture: "When we formed the group in the early 1980s, we wanted to break the taboo surrounding homosexuality in society and the union and to win support for eliminating Paragraph 175. We were able to force a resolution through our unions and the DGB. But the union, after these resolutions passed, never really became politically active on them." Mündler notes that political activism among gays and lesbians within the union has waned.

Working groups have difficulty organizing and achieving success in unions whose members are employed by private businesses. One explanation for this is that individuals working for businesses may have more concerns about being open about their sexual identity in their work environment than those who work for public employers, which provide greater employment security. Even if recent court decisions have offered some protections for gays and lesbians, for example, against arbitrary firing, employees would still have grounds for fearing discriminatory treatment not yet covered by law or concealed behind other rationales.

Overall, across the public as well as the private sectors, working groups have been unsuccessful at getting changes in the collective bargaining agreements in the interests of gays and lesbians. The working groups' long-term goal in the area of collective bargaining is to make equal benefits available to all domestic partnerships, regardless of gender composition. The Berlin ÖTV has attempted to have such issues addressed during collective bargaining but admits that they have not advanced far. Klaus Timm, leader of the ÖTV working group, explains the difficulty: "Collective bargaining issues are not determined at union conventions where resolutions are passed, but at yearly meetings of the tariff commission. They can decide, autonomously, what at the present time should be bargained for. They can decide that the recommendations of the lesbians and gays don't fit into their bargaining scheme, at least not this time." Ingo Busch, leader of the DGB working group in Freiburg, complains of similar problems, explaining that "the situation in collective bargaining is always difficult, and there is hardly room for lesbian and gay demands to play a role, because always 'more important' things seem to take the forefront."

In a greeting in the June 1997 ÖTV *Lesbian and Gay Report,* the president of the DGB, Dieter Schulte, notes that although unions take seriously their efforts to end discrimination faced by sexual minorities in the workplace and in society, "It would be misleading to believe that the time-tested ways of conducting collective bargaining and co-determination are sufficient to come to terms with all problems."[25] This is indicative of the unions' reluctance to use their most powerful tools to press for issues of importance to sexual minorities. Moreover, unions have thus far refused to raise sexual minority issues in the supervisory boards of large corporations in which they hold seats.

Opposition to the goals and activities of the working groups comes from a variety of sources within and outside the union. According to Berlin ÖTV members, some union leaders are anti-gay and may think they can win favor with certain members by taking such positions. However, as group leader Klaus Timm notes, opponents are now more likely to be considered "on the fringe." He adds that with the passage of supportive conference resolutions, union officials can no longer deny responsibility for lesbian and gay workplace concerns. That said, members of the working group must nonetheless "push and make sure that the issue stays ever present" and is not simply forgotten after supportive resolutions are passed.

The leader of the ÖTV working group in Nuremberg, Thomas Huber, echoes these comments: "In general, no one can allow themselves to be seen openly opposing homosexuals. But problems facing lesbians and gays are often shoved aside as long-range problems and their resolutions are delayed through inaction." Huber states that suggestions are ignored at times, "braked by the union bureaucracy with claims that the current resolutions don't allow us to do this or that, or claims that members have protested about a suggested course of action." The Nuremberg ÖTV working group also notes that tensions exist at times between "old functionaries" and "classic members" on the one hand, and newer, more progressive leaders and younger, more tolerant members on the other. This suggests generational differences within the leadership and membership of the unions, which may fade as younger members continue their ascent to leadership positions within the unions.

Opposition to working group goals comes also, of course, from those sitting across from the union at the bargaining table. Employers can influence the issues discussed and benefits offered during collective bargaining through their actions in industry peak associations. They can also take actions on their own in terms of personnel policies and in the individual employer-specific agreements within the general tariff agreement in the industry. Employers have a good deal of say in how agreed contracts are implemented in a given workplace. How an employer responds to incidents such as complaints of sexual harassment or "mobbing" by fellow employees is very important and can be either supportive of the victimized employee or dismissive of the complaint. An employer might allow or prevent employees from attending gay and lesbian educational seminars as part of their bargained-for paid education week, or permit or ban information announcements of a working group in the workplace. Further gains for sexual minority employees in Germany certainly do not depend solely on the positions of the unions, but also on the positions of employers and the government.

Conclusion

Sexual diversity activists in the German labor unions have achieved considerable success over the past two decades. They overcame initial union resistance and established viable and lasting working groups with financial backing from the unions. They convinced their unions to accept that opposition to workplace discrimination based on sexual orientation is a legitimate area of interest and engagement, and many unions approved gay-positive resolutions by wide margins. The working groups have also been able to organize services to support sexual minorities who face discrimination in the workplace. They mobilized union support for the elimination of the federal law that criminalized homosexuality, Paragraph 175 of the penal code.

To some extent, their success may be contributing to a decline in activism. The working groups have become dependent on funding from their unions to enable them to serve their clientele within the organization. This has the advantage to the working group of ensuring that the necessary money is available for seminars, newsletters, and counseling and assistance to lesbians and gays in the coming-out process at work, and for assistance in fighting cases of discrimination. The disadvantage is that the working group leadership may be co-opted to the more cautious and conservative viewpoint of the broader organization.

Working groups have been reluctant to press new demands because the German labor unions are in a weaker position today than they were before reunification. The economic difficulties of reunification and foreign competition have placed pressure on German industry, placing unions in a defensive position in their attempts to retain existing wages and benefits in the West and raise levels in the East to those in the West. Unions have therefore been reluctant to address other issues during collective bargaining, especially those that involve new costs.

Young lesbian and gay activists who are most likely to be pushing the limits of reform are less likely to be union members today. Although a higher percentage of the German population is unionized than in other countries, the trend is nonetheless downward, and many white-collar and service sector jobs are not unionized. In contrast to the early activists who were simultaneously union members and participants in the broader gay and lesbian movement, younger sexual diversity activists are more likely to look to other types of groups than union groups to press their agenda.

Working groups faced an unsympathetic government with the election of the Christian Democrats in 1983. In comparison with other European countries (such as Great Britain under Margaret Thatcher), the CDU government was not actively opposed to homosexual rights, but it certainly did not demonstrate the kind of proactive stance shown by governments in such countries as the Netherlands, Denmark, and Sweden. Germany steered a middle course, being neither overly hostile nor supportive of sexual minority issues. Thus, sexual diversity activists were not energized by the need to fight back against a hostile government, or by feelings of empowerment inspired by a sympathetic government.

Gay and lesbian working groups in German labor unions seem to be expecting their next gains to occur as a result of membership in the European Union and, in particular, through EU law requiring respect and recognition of the policies and laws of other member states. The leader of the ÖTV working group in Nuremberg, Thomas Huber, believes that reluctance to press for change through the bargaining process is to be expected, but he is among many leaders looking optimistically to Europe. "The European Union is in a position of flux right now," Huber notes, and Germany "is not in a leadership role in terms of lesbian and gay politics." According to Huber, however, "one must pay careful attention to both tariff contracts and the legal framework." He notes that several EU countries have already recognized same-sex partnerships. Because of reciprocal rights requirements for all EU citizens in Germany, Huber states, "something must change here." Already the discussion of same-sex marriage has been thrust onto the public agenda in Germany because of statutory change in favor of lesbians and gays in Denmark and Sweden.[26]

The kind of organizing and cooperation that has taken place among the working groups in Germany is continuing on a European and international level. The ÖTV together with union umbrella organizations in the Netherlands and the British union UNISON sponsored a 1998 international conference on "Trade Unions, Homosexuality, and Work" in Amsterdam.[27] With the strengthening of ties between gay and lesbian union groups throughout Europe and the increasing importance of political and legal developments in other EU countries, the international sexual diversity movement will continue to have a major impact on Germany in the years ahead.

Notes

1. *ÖTV Report: Lesben & Schwule,* no. 1, June 1996, p. 2. (Translations in this chapter are by the author.)

2. R. Dalton, *Politics in Germany* (New York: HarperCollins, 1993), p. 239.

3. Dalton, *Politics in Germany,* p. 240.

4. Dalton, *Politics in Germany,* p. 243.

5. For a history of the early homosexual movement in Germany, see J. D. Steakley, *The Homosexual Emancipation Movement in Germany* (New York: Arno Press, 1975). For a comparison of Hirschfeld's group to the second homosexual organization that formed in Germany at this time led by Adolf Brand, the *Gemeinschaft der Eigenen,* see H. Oosterhuis and H. Kennedy, *Homosexuality and Male Bonding in Pre-Nazi Germany* (New York: Harrington Park, 1991). See also excerpts in M. Blasius and S. Phelan, eds., *We Are Everywhere: An Historical Sourcebook in Lesbian and Gay Politics* (New York: Routledge, 1997).

6. For a history of Paragraph 175, see H. Sievert, "Das anomale bestrafen. Homosexualität, Strafrecht, und Schwulenbewegung im Kaiserreich und in der Weimarer Republik," in *Ergebnisse* 24 (1984).

7. M. Herzer, "Anfänge einer Schwulenbewegung im Ausland," in *Goodbye to Berlin? 100 Jahre Schwulenbewegung,* Schwules Museum and the Akademie der Künste (Berlin: Rosa Winkel Verlag, 1997), pp. 76–79.

8. In addition to his novel, *Goodbye to Berlin,* see his autobiography: C. Isherwood, *Christopher and His Kind, 1929–1939* (New York: Farrar, Straus and Giroux, 1976).

9. K.-H. Steinle, "Homophiles Deutschland," in *Goodbye to Berlin?,* p. 196.

10. For a description of the homosexual movement in the 1950s and 1960s, see M. Dannecker, "Der unstillbare Wunsch nach Anerkennung. Homosexuellenpolitik in den fünfziger und sechziger Jahren," in *Was heisst hier Schwul: Politik und Identitäten im Wandel,* ed. D. Grumbach (Hamburg: MaennerschwarmSkript Verlag, 1997), pp. 27–44. See also W. Theis, "Mach Dein Schwulsein Offentlich—Bundesrepublik," in *Goodbye to Berlin?,* p. 280.

11. W. Theis, "Mach Dein Schwulsein Offentlich—Bundesrepublik," in *Goodbye to Berlin?,* p. 284.

12. H.-G. Stümke, "Demokratie ist abendfuellend. Die alte Coming-out-Bewegung ist tot. Wir brauchen eine politische Schwulenbewegung," in *Was heisst hier Schwul,* ed. Grumbach, p. 46.

13. See G. Grau, "Sozialistische Moral und Homosexualität. Die Politik der SED und das Homosexuellenstrafrecht 1945 bis 1989—eine Rückblick," in *Die Linke und das Laster: Schwule Emanzipation und linke Vorurteile,* ed. D. Grumbach (Hamburg: MännerschwarmSkript Verlag, 1995), pp. 85–141.

14. K.-H. Steinle, "DDR und UdSSR," in *Goodbye to Berlin?,* pp. 295–297.

15. Steinle, "DDR und UdSSR," p. 295.

16. D. M. Sweet, "The Church, the Stasi, and Socialist Integration: Three Stages of Lesbian and Gay Emancipation in the Former German Democratic Republic," in *Gay Men and the Sexual History of the Political Left,* ed. G. Hekma, H. Oosterhuis and J. Steakley (New York: Haworth, 1995), p. 360.

17. Sweet, "The Church, the Stasi, and Socialist Integration," p. 296.

18. Germany's Republicans (*Republikaner*) are not represented in the federal parliament because of the party's failure to win 5 percent of the vote. A virulent anti-immigrant, antiforeigner party, the Republicans have been known to unleash anti-gay rhetoric.

19. The information for this section was gained through interviews and questionnaires with leaders of the gay and lesbian working groups in the German labor unions during the fall of 1997.

A personal interview was conducted with an early leader of the movement, Klaus Timm of the Berlin ÖTV working group. Timm referred me to additional leaders around the country, who then provided written answers to a survey questionnaire.

20. Grumbach, *Die Linke und das Laster,* p. 9.

21. For example, the weekly news magazine *Focus* (similar to *Time* magazine in the United States), recently published an article called "Do Gays Live Better?" See also S. Bettermann, "Leben Schwule besser?," *Focus* 12 (1996): 205–214. A recent book that trumpets the many gains achieved by gays and lesbians is W. Hinzpeter, *Schöne schwule Welt. Der Schlussverkauf einer Bewegung* (Berlin: Quer Verlag, 1997). In English, the title would be "Beautiful Gay World."

22. K. Timm, "Historisches zu Lesben, Schwule, und Gewerkschaften," in *Lesben, Schwule, und Gewerkschaften* (Oberursel: Haus der Gewerkschaftsjugend, 1993), pp. 51–54, and personal communication with the author.

23. About 8,000 copies of the June 1997 edition were produced and distributed during Christopher Street Day events, May 1 celebrations, and various other union activities.

24. D. Mücke, "Schwule and Schule. 11 Jahre Initiativen von schwulen Lehrergruppen," in *Schwule Regungen, Schwule Bewegungen,* ed. W. Frieling (Berlin: Rosa Winkel Verlag, 1985), p. 161.

25. *ÖTV Report: Lesben & Schwule,* p. 2.

26. Recent polling suggests that Germans are split in their support for same-sex marriage. A 1996 poll conducted for *Spiegel* magazine found that 49 percent of Germans are in favor of state recognition of same-sex partnerships, 48 percent are opposed, and 3 percent had no response. Public opinion survey conducted for *Spiegel* magazine by Emnid. See R. Wolfert, "Skandinavische Hochzeit," in *Goodbye to Berlin?,* p. 306.

27. For a detailed treatment of UNISON, see the chapter by Fiona Colgan in this volume.

Phil Greasley

13   British Trade Unions and Sexual Diversity: Survey Evidence Since the 1980s

In 1975, only a few years after the surge of gay liberation activism, the National Union of Journalists became the first labor union in Britain, and one of the first in the world, to formally adopt a progressive policy on sexual orientation. This was in a country in which resistance to such measures was very powerfully embedded in the legal and political order, and inside the union movement itself.

As Fiona Colgan shows in her contribution to this volume, parts of the British labor movement have been actively engaged with the concerns of lesbian and gay members for a substantial time. As in a number of other countries, however, progress since the initial steps to embrace diversity has been uneven, a few unions leading the pack by a considerable margin by taking up sexual orientation issues affirmatively and assertively. In the last few years, considerable progress has been made by activists in convincing a relatively broad range of unions to express at least some degree of support for equality—a range that now extends beyond the public sector and those unions with substantial female membership. This chapter chronicles the development of union movement engagement with these issues by drawing on the results of surveys undertaken over the course of the 1980s and 1990s, the most recent a 1997 survey by the author focusing on union policies toward their own paid employees.

Legal and Political Context

It is still not illegal in Britain to discriminate against lesbians and gays in employment, housing, and other areas of life, although the recent incorporation of the European Convention into British law may provide some degree of protection against such discrimination. A substantial number of statutes actively discriminate on the basis of sexual orientation. Discriminatory provisions of the 1956 and 1967 Sexual Offences Acts criminalize activity that would not be considered illegal if committed by heterosexuals.

Lesbians and gays are barred from the armed forces, and their relationships are largely unrecognized in family law.

Protections against workplace discrimination are uneven. An employee fired for discriminatory reasons can make a claim of "unfair dismissal" to an industrial tribunal, which can order reinstatement and compensation.[1] Some tribunals have favored lesbians and gays, but there are cases in which an employer's decision to dismiss employees simply because of their sexuality has been upheld. Beyond cases of individualized discrimination, same-sex relationships are often unrecognized in employer-provided benefits and other conditions of service. Many employees in same-sex relationships, for example, are not given access to compassionate leave or pension entitlement.

Survey evidence from the mid-1980s on indicates that many gays and lesbians have been subjected to discrimination at work. One of the earliest such surveys was undertaken in 1985 by the author, among gays and lesbians.[2] Though many of the respondents worked in the public sector or in other white-collar jobs where equal opportunity policies included sexual orientation, most felt that the majority of the people they worked with were not or would not be supportive of them as gays and lesbians. More than three-quarters indicated that they were not open about their sexual orientation when applying for jobs, though more than 90 percent wanted to be. One early 1990s survey undertaken by the lobbying group Stonewall indicated widespread discrimination, and another of about the same period indicated that about half of sexual-minority respondents experienced discrimination at work, in accommodation, or in access to services.[3]

Early Developments

Sexual diversity activists from the first development of the modern political movement believed that the labor movement was an important part of the struggle for equality and liberation. Bob Cant was one of the activists who took steps to form a nationwide union group in 1974, the political networks so formed being the crucial impetus for early policy change.[4] The first unions to adopt policies on lesbian and gay rights as a result of that work were the National Union of Journalists (NUJ) in 1975 and, in 1976, two large public sector unions—the National and Local Government Officers' Association (NALGO) and the National Association of Teachers in Further and Higher Education (NATFHE).[5] In the late 1970s and early 1980s, following the example of NALGO and NATFHE, a number of other unions adopted anti-discrimination clauses that included sexual orientation. These included the Civil and Public Services Association (CPSA), the National Union of Public Employees (NUPE), the Confederation of Health Service Employees (COHSE), and the Association of First Division Civil Servants (FDA). One 1982 Labour Research Department summary reported that nine unions had passed motions opposing such discrimination.[6]

On the other hand, few gays and lesbians had formal links to policy-making centers of their unions. Also, at this point, few unions had produced any information on sexual orientation issues or had supported lesbian and gay initiatives beyond formal resolutions opposing discrimination. Speaking of the passage of such a resolution by

NATFHE, Bob Cant recalls: "It seemed like a real victory at the time but the union generated no publicity about it and, despite lengthy consultations with the group [Rank and File], it produced no report on the implications of the policy. Nothing changed—the group became very demoralized."[7]

In 1985, the Trades Union Congress (TUC) passed a resolution calling for equal opportunities for lesbians and gays, asserting the importance of labor-union action to combat discrimination and prejudice.[8] This was an important development, and a testament to the work of activists within the movement. In 1986, a survey was undertaken of eighty-nine unions affiliated to the TUC, asking them if they had policies that included lesbians and gays. The survey was a project of Lesbian and Gay Employment Rights (LAGER), an activist group established in 1983 specifically to challenge workplace discrimination. Fourteen unions replied that they had passed motions or had policy statements about sexual orientation discrimination. A few had gone beyond that by producing information on the issues, holding working parties, or supporting lesbian and gay events. In the period from 1984 to 1988, three unions established national groups or committees within formal union structures to take up sexual orientation issues—NALGO, the teachers union NUT, and the Association of Cinematograph, Television, and Allied Technicians (ACTT). Within a couple of years, they had been joined by Manufacturing Science Finance Union (MSF). As from the beginning, the most active unions were generally in the public sector—NALGO, NUT, and the civil service union CPSA being notable examples—and tended to have large female memberships.

LAGER undertook a follow-up survey in 1989.[9] Twenty unions were found to have had specific policies addressing sexual orientation discrimination. An additional five said they did not have specific policies but would not support discrimination. Eight of the unions who responded had a lesbian and gay group at the national level. Few unions representing manual workers in areas of employment traditionally considered "men's work" had policies or equal opportunities or bothered replying at all to the questionnaire.

In 1991, the Labour Research Department conducted a survey about the extent to which unions were taking up lesbian and gay concerns.[10] Twenty-five unions replied, representing 65 percent of the total TUC-affiliated membership. Twenty-one of them had a policy supporting gay and lesbian rights, or a reference to "sexual orientation" included in an equal opportunities statement, and fully twenty had taken action in response to Section 28 of the 1988 Local Government Act (a section prohibiting local government authorities from "promoting" homosexuality). More than half of the twenty-five responding had taken action to counteract anti-gay harassment; more than half had also produced and distributed educational materials on sexual orientation. NALGO was still among those with the most wide-ranging commitment, with a "comprehensive structure" for dealing with sexual orientation issues and gay and lesbian representation. By this time, a few unions were pushing for recognition of same-sex relationships in benefit packages negotiated with management, successfully so in the case of employees at the British Council and the British Library.

Though in general the male-dominated unions had a less favorable record than those with substantial female membership, the National Union of Mineworkers (NUM) had become a vociferous supporter of pro-gay resolutions in TUC and Labor Party conferences, in part because of visible gay and lesbian support during the 1984–1985 strike. In 1989, the Transport and General Workers Union, Britain's largest union at the time, approved a resolution favoring the inclusion of sexual orientation in equal opportunity policies negotiated by the union, calling for the creation of educational materials for negotiators and positive images of lesbians and gays in union publications, and ensuring equal treatment in benefits for union employees and their partners. The union itself characterized this is a major breakthrough, adding, "The TGWU must be one of the few... predominantly male and manual worker unions to adopt such a progressive policy."[11]

1997 Labour Research Department Survey

A 1997 survey conducted for the Labour Research Department by Tessa Wright elicited responses from thirty unions, covering 75 percent of the TUC's total affiliated membership.[12] Of these, twenty-eight had a policy or an equal opportunity statement that included lesbians and gays. The survey also showed an increased level of activity by those unions already working on sexual diversity issues, including the sponsorship of conferences or educational courses. Twenty-one of the responding unions had full-time equality officers, and in all but two of these, the office's remit includes lesbian and gay rights.[13] Nineteen unions reported having educational courses addressing sexual orientation issues. Eighteen unions had some form of committee or support group for lesbian and gay members, ranging from a national committee such as the UNISON National Lesbian and Gay Committee to the informal contact group at the shipping officers' union, NUMAST. (The number of unions with national-level committees had increased from four reported in the 1991 survey to six.) Thirteen unions gave publicity and support to the annual Pride Day festivities.

Of the unions responding to this survey, the following thirteen had a significant range of commitments to such issues:

AUT	Association of University Teachers	*
BIFU	Banking, Insurance, and Finance Union	*
CPSA	Civil and Public Services Association	
CWU	Communication Workers Union	*
EIS	Educational Institute of Scotland	
GMB	General Municipal Boiler Makers Union	
IPMS	Institute of Professionals, Managers, and Specialists	
MSF	Manufacturing Science Finance Union	*
NAPO	National Association of Probation Officers	*
NATFHE	National Union of Teachers in Further and Higher Education	*
NUJ	National Union of Journalists	
NUT	National Union of Teachers	*
UNISON	(amalgamation of NALGO, NUPE, and COHSE)	*

Most of these unions (those marked *) had either a national committee for gay and lesbian issues or sponsored annual national conferences. Only one of these relatively active unions was a blue-collar union (GMB), though a relatively wide range of unions had taken at least some gay-affirmative steps.

1997 Survey on Trade Unions as Employers

One test that can be applied to assess whether a lesbian or gay policy is being operationalized is the extent to which internal employment policies and procedures have been reviewed and revised to ensure that they do not discriminate against employees on the basis of sexual orientation. A survey of TUC-affiliated unions (as employers of staff) conducted by the author in 1997 sought to examine just that issue.[14] Twenty-six usable responses were received (see Appendix 1 for a list of responding unions). These included most of the UK's largest unions, and in total they employed over 5,000 staff.[15]

All twenty-six unions had a national-level general statement committing the union to adhere to an equal opportunity policy. All but one of them had policy statements that included sexual orientation, the same number as included race and sex explicitly. These twenty-five unions represented about 5.5 million members, more than 80 percent of the TUC total affiliates, and a staff total of over 5,000. This is encouraging, since it shows unions are as likely to include sexual orientation as they are to include two other grounds for discrimination given statutory recognition in British law.

The 1989 LAGER survey found that a majority of unions representing male manual workers did not have policies that included lesbians and gays or did not respond. In 1997, the unions with such policies had a total membership that was 60 percent male.[16] Among the unions including sexual orientation in policy statements was the General and Municipal Boiler Makers Union (GMB) and the Amalgamated Engineering and Electrical Union (AEEU), these male-dominated and blue-collar unions representing a significant broadening of union recognition of sexual diversity issues.

Sixteen of the unions went beyond generalized commitments to nondiscrimination by establishing either a specific policy devoted to sexual orientation issues or by including gays and lesbians within general policies intended to back up their equal employment statements. Asked about steps taken to monitor such policies, six unions mentioned such responsibility being lodged in an equal rights or equal opportunities committee or in a lesbian and gay network. Two unions indicated that there were other mechanisms in place to monitor the policies, and an additional two pointed out that the policy in question was very new or in the process of being formulated. Three indicated that there was no monitoring, and the rest did not answer the question.

As for policies specifically relevant to the unions' own employees, the results indicate some unevenness. Seventeen respondents said that their unions had policies or procedures that attempted to ensure that lesbians and gays are not discriminated against in the staff recruitment process. Over half of the twenty-six unions responding to the questionnaire included sexual diversity issues in courses given to staff, although that left a third giving neither information nor training to staff on these issues. Twelve of the responding unions treat discrimination against lesbians and gays as a disciplinary offense, and one additional union said that the disciplinary procedures were under review. Only nine said that conditions of service offered to employees had been reviewed to ensure that they do not discriminate on the basis of sexual orientation. (A further two indicated that conditions were currently under review.)

Significant steps have been taken to recognize the same-sex relationships of lesbian and gay employees. Twenty responding unions reported that they offered equal benefits in relation to both compassionate leave and bereavement leave. Fourteen unions said that their pension schemes allowed for a nominated partner to receive benefits equal to opposite-sex couples, and a further three unions said that pension benefits were currently being negotiated for lesbians and gays. These numbers are especially notable, since only in 1996 did Inland Revenue announce that there were no legal impediments to establishing such provisions. More controversial, however, are questions relating to parenting. Only six unions said that the conditions of service offered lesbian and gay employees included equal benefits in relation to the coparenting of children, with an additional two unions saying that such conditions were under review. (One of the union's responding in the negative did not offer paternity leave to anyone.)

Conclusion

The survey on unions' own employment practices signals major change in the course of the 1990s. In the last years, the profile of unions with affirmative policies related to sexual diversity has broadened substantially from the small core of public sector unions, especially those with substantial female membership, that formed a vanguard on these issues in the 1980s. Now, most of the country's largest unions have policies and procedures that attempt to ensure that sexual minorities are not discriminated against in recruitment and employment inside the unions themselves. Most have policies recognizing same-sex relationships, despite the laggard legal recognition of such relationships in Britain.

That so many labor unions have adopted policies to counter discrimination, with some of them assertively proactive on a number of fronts, is remarkable. Colgan's contribution to this volume highlights the particularly distinctive record of UNISON, but the survey results reported here indicate that there is now a broader base of support for at least the most elementary steps on the road to a more inclusive and egalitarian workplace. Such developments are even more striking given Britain's and the labor movement's long thraldom to traditional views of gender and sexuality.

The surveys summarized here also indicate how much distance is still to be traveled. A significant number of unions with paid staff simply failed to respond to the author's 1997 questionnaire—surely an indication of relatively low commitment to sexual diversity issues. A number of unions with formal policy commitments to equality follow them up with little information and no educational courses on sexual diversity issues. Many unions have still not fully addressed inequalities in procedures and conditions of service for sexual minority employees. Less than half of the unions responding to the survey indicated that discrimination against such employees would be considered a disciplinary offense. Less than a quarter said that lesbians and gays were given equal benefits in relation to the coparenting of children.

The absence of fully equal policies for sexual minorities reinforces structural discrimination in the broader social and political environment. The absence of information and training for union members and employees reduces the likelihood that members and employees will take action to combat individual discrimination. Some unions have led the way as employers and campaigners for equality, but many more have a long way to go before they could be considered models of good employment practice.

Appendix 1:
Trade Unions Responding to the 1997 Survey

AEEU	Amalgamated Engineering and Electrical Union
AUT	Association of University Teachers
BFAWU	Bakers, Food, and Allied Unions
BIFU	Banking, Insurance, and Finance Union
CPSA	Civil and Public Services Association
CSP	Chartered Society of Physiotherapy
CYWU	Community and Youth Workers' Union
EIS	Educational Institute of Scotland
FBA	Fire Brigades Union
FDA	Association of First Division Civil Servants
GMB	General and Municipal Boiler Makers Union
GPMU	Graphical Paper and Media Union
IPMS	Institution of Professionals, Managers, and Specialists
MSF	Manufacturing Science Finance Union
NAPO	National Association of Probation Officers
NATFHE	The University and College Lecturers' Union
NUMAST	National Union of Maritime, Aviation, and Shipping Transport Officers
NUT	National Union of Teachers
PTC	Public Services, Tax, and Commerce Union
RMT	National Union of Rail, Maritime, and Transport Workers
SOR	Society of Radiographers
SUPLO	Scottish Union of Power-Loom Overlookers
TGWU	Transport and General Workers' Union
UCAC	Undeb Cenedlaethol Athrawon Cymru
UniFI	The Union for Barclays Staff

Appendix 2:
Other Unions Cited

ACTT	Association of Cinematograph, Television, and Allied Technicians
COHSE	Confederation of Health Service Employees
CWU	Communication Workers Union
NALGO	National and Local Government Officers' Association
NUM	National Union of Mineworkers
NUPE	National Union of Public Employees

Notes

Acknowledgments: Many thanks to David Taylor, Faculty of Environment and Social Studies, North London University, for providing excellent supervision for this chapter and the research behind it. Thanks also to Tessa Wright of the Labour Research Department for previously published results of the 1997 LRD trade union survey. This distillation of survey results was written with the help of David Rayside (University of Toronto).

1. An industrial tribunal comprises a panel of three—a lay member for the employees, a lay member for the employers, and a chair. To be eligible to initiate such a case, an employee must have worked for two continuous years for the same employer.

2. P. Greasley, *Gay Men at Work: A Report on Discrimination Against Gay Men in Employment in London* (London: Lesbian and Gay Employment Rights, 1986).

3. D. Snape et al., *Discrimination Against Lesbians and Gay Men: A Study of the Nature and Extent of Discrimination Against Homosexual Men and Women in Britain Today* (Social and Community Planning Research, 1995). This research is based on responses from 116 lesbians and gays and 619 heterosexuals. See also Stonewall, *Less Equal Than Others—A Survey of Lesbians and Gay Men at Work* (London: Stonewall, 1993).

4. Reported in "Normal Channels," in *Radical Records: Thirty Years of Lesbian and Gay History,* ed. B. Cant and S. Hemmings (London: Routledge, 1988), p. 213.

5. In the early 1990s, NALGO amalgamated with the National Union of Public Employees (NUPE) and the Confederation of Health Service Employees (COHSE) to form UNISON—now the largest union in the United Kingdom.

6. Labour Research Department, "Gay Rights: Action in the Unions," *Labour Research* (February 1983). No details as to how the information was collected are provided.

7. "Normal Channels," p. 213.

8. Reported in more detail in Greasley, *Gay Men at Work.*

9. Lesbian and Gay Employment Rights, *Trade Union Survey: Equal Opportunities* (Lesbian and Gay Employment Rights, 1989).

10. Reported in "Sexuality: A Trade Union Issue?" *Labour Research* (June 1991): 10–12.

11. "Sexuality," p. 11.

12. Reported in "Taking Pride in the Unions," *Labour Research* (July 1997): 16–18.

13. UNISON had two staff dedicated to lesbian and gay work at the national office, and one staff in each region with lesbian and gay issues as part of her or his remit.

14. A postal questionnaire was sent to all seventy-four unions affiliated to the TUC. It contained a number of closed questions, a number of open questions, and a general invitation to elaborate on any question posed.

15. Some unions provided only estimates of their staff numbers. Several of the unions not responding to the survey would have been small enough to not have paid staff, eliminating the relevance to them of this survey. SUPLO was in that category but completed a questionnaire in any event. That response—the twenty-seventh—has been excluded from the compilation of results. One of the included responses was sent anonymously, precluding certain forms of analysis.

16. Gender breakdowns were known for only twenty-two of the twenty-five unions.

Fiona Colgan

14   Moving Forward in UNISON: Lesbian and Gay Self-Organization in Action

> *I was a NUPE [National Union of Public Employees] member for a cou-
> ple of years, and then 6 months after vesting day, which was 1993, I was
> actually given a booklet on the aims and objectives of UNISON, and it
> actually says in there that I can exist, that lesbians and gays actually exist
> within the union, and that I was allowed to be lesbian or gay and that
> the support would be there for me. . . . I wasn't out as a lesbian at work,
> and this union, i.e., UNISON, was actually saying that not only could I
> exist but that they would support me, that I could actually belong to a
> group of lesbian and gay people.*
>
> (Mary, May 1997)[1]

UNISON is Britain's largest trade union and the largest public service union in Europe. It organizes 1.4 million public service workers in the United Kingdom. During the 1990s, UNISON engaged in one of the most radical attempts in the history of British trade unionism to encourage the participation and representation of *all* sections of its membership, including a specific commitment to lesbian and gay workers and their employment and human rights. Equality was at the heart of UNISON's constitution when it was formed in 1993 from the merger of three public sector unions: the National Association of Local Government Officers (NALGO), the National Union of Public Employees (NUPE), and the Confederation of Health Service Employees (COHSE).[2] The route UNISON followed is a radical departure from traditional, unitarist trade union-ism and, as such, a model worth evaluating.[3]

This chapter undertakes a detailed case study of UNISON as an instructive illustra-tion and assessment of one union's attempt to place sexual diversity issues firmly on its trade union agenda. The chapter first outlines the political and social context within which UNISON developed its innovative approach and then discusses the formation of UNISON, highlighting the goals and objectives the union set for itself in relation to internal democracy and equity issues. Drawing on the views and experiences of twenty-five lesbian and gay UNISON activists, the chapter considers the progress made toward achieving these goals. Additionally, it draws on a research project funded by the Economic and Social Science Research Council that examined union structures and equal opportunity policies and practices within UNISON.[4]

A Changing Political and Social Context

Over the last decade, trade union interest in lesbian and gay issues has increased steadily, as has lesbian and gay participation within trade union structures.[5] One of the major ways these advances have been achieved is by lesbians and gays forming groups inside their own unions to increase visibility, raise sexual diversity issues, and exert pressure for change within the main union structures.[6] This has come during two decades when British trade unions have seen membership figures plummet, leaving a number of them open to reconsidering their approaches to recruitment and organization in order to reverse membership declines.[7] Thus, progress on sexual diversity issues within trade unions has been made despite a fairly hostile political and social context following the election of a Conservative government in 1979.

Under the Conservative government, little support was to be found for legislation on lesbian and gay equality. Rather, the government introduced the repressive Section 28 of the Local Government Act (1988), which makes it illegal for local authorities to "intentionally promote homosexuality." Section 28 was a reaction to the inclusion by Labour local authorities of sexual orientation as an integral part of their commitment to equal opportunity.[8] This move came during a high point in the development of the lesbian and gay movement as it sought to affirm lesbian and gay identity, develop political alliances, and work toward equal opportunity, particularly within Labour-run local authorities and trade unions.[9] Thus, although the national government was hostile to lesbian and gay rights, the 1980s saw considerable progress in the inclusion of sexual orientation within equal opportunities policies in Labour local authorities and other public services where NALGO, NUPE, and COHSE represented much of the workforce.

The British Social Attitudes Survey shows that hostility towards lesbians and gays increased in the 1980s, perhaps linked to an AIDS backlash and the climate created by the Conservative government and Section 28. Surveys by Stonewall and Social and Community Planning Research provide recent evidence of the extent of workplace discrimination and harassment still experienced by lesbians and gays.[10] However, since 1988, British public opinion has shifted. Homophobia is still a problem, but a majority of the British public now supports lesbian and gay equality, including anti-discrimination laws and the recognition of same-sex couples.[11]

Within this changing social and political context, an awareness of equality issues has been developing in the trade union movement. Women and minority groups have increasingly looked to their unions for representation and support in challenging workplace discrimination and harassment.[12] Through their unions, women and black workers have sought and gained equality legislation in the form of the Equal Pay Act (1970), Sex Discrimination Act (1975), and Race Relations Act (1976). The Disability

Discrimination Act (1996), although fundamentally flawed, similarly provides a framework of rights for disabled people.[13]

However, no legislation offers protection from discrimination on the grounds of sexuality. Despite the election of a Labour government in 1996, little has been done by government to address equality issues relating to sexual minorities.[14] Although such legislation would be unlikely to provide a panacea, its absence makes it vitally important for unions to stand up for lesbian and gay workers and make that commitment clear. A 1992 Labour Research Department (LRD) survey of lesbian, gay, and bisexual trade unionists found that workers gave five major reasons for being able to be openly lesbian or gay: their union's commitment to lesbian and gay issues, the presence of other out lesbian or gay workers, their own self-confidence and pride as gay people, their employer's equal opportunities policy, and the degree of open-mindedness among their workmates.[15]

Out in the Union?

Over the last twenty years, British trade unions have been forced to operate in a consistently hostile environment.[16] Economic restructuring has meant the expansion of service sector employment, the introduction of part-time and temporary contract work, and the loss of jobs in the primary and manufacturing sectors—the traditional base of union support.[17] Individual employment rights have come under attack, and the autonomy of union organization has been seriously reduced by state regulations that reshape unions' freedom to represent their members and participate in industrial action.[18] The Conservative government consistently promoted the view in the political arena that trade unions were undemocratic and had abused their power and, thus, needed to be regulated. The Labour government elected in 1996 has indicated its reluctance to reverse much of this legislative change and has signaled its wish to reexamine its links with the trade union movement.[19]

In the face of this onslaught, unions have been forced to argue the case for their continued relevance to employees and employers. This has been a difficult task, as can be seen from the overall decline in union membership since 1979, the difficulty in gaining union recognition rights in new establishments, and the problems created for unions by the "new industrial relations" and privatization programs.[20] In 1979, total union membership was 13.3 million, representing 54 percent of the workforce. By 1995, union density had dropped to approximately 31 percent of the workforce.[21] Trade unions had to appeal to a wider section of the workforce in order to rebuild their membership.

As a result of pressure on the unions from lesbian and gay members, the 1980s saw trade unions starting to oppose discrimination against lesbians and gays and to promote lesbian and gay rights. In 1985, the Trades Union Congress (TUC) called on affiliated trade unions to engage in the following actions:

- campaign for legislation to protect lesbians and gays against all forms of discrimination in all areas of life
- include lesbians and gays in all negotiated equal opportunity clauses and agreements
- raise awareness of the issues within their own organizations

- examine terms and conditions of employment such as pensions, bereavement leave, and caring for children and dependents to ensure that no discrimination exists on the grounds of sexual orientation
- openly support members who are victimized as a result of their sexuality

Following calls to action at TUC conferences in 1985 and 1988 and at a TUC Women's Conference in 1991, the TUC at last called a meeting of trade union equality officers and lesbian and gay activists to discuss how to develop lesbian and gay rights. These discussions were reported to the TUC Equal Rights Committee, which agreed to hold a Lesbian and Gay Rights at Work seminar, the first ever to be held by the TUC on the subject of lesbian and gay rights.[22]

The position on lesbian and gay rights in unions at the time is revealed by a survey by the LRD.[23] It found that twenty-one of the twenty-five unions (representing 65 percent of TUC-affiliated membership) had a policy supporting lesbian and gay rights or included sexual orientation in an equal opportunity policy statement or in their constitution. Since the mid-1980s, many unions had adopted these policies. Two of the UNISON partner-unions led the way. NALGO, described by LRD as a trailblazer on lesbian and gay issues, was the first to adopt policy in this area. At its 1976 conference, NALGO adopted a resolution instructing all NALGO negotiators to attempt to add sexual discrimination to the nondiscrimination clause in all collective agreements. NUPE passed its first resolution on lesbian and gay issues at its 1981 conference, calling for sexuality clauses to be negotiated in equal opportunities agreements.[24]

Unions were beginning to recognize the need for the representation of lesbian and gay members as a constituency within union structures. Lesbian and gay activists argued that separate organization provided a strategy whereby sexual minorities could be recruited and empowered while at the same time continuing to work within "mainstream" traditional union structures.[25] Again NALGO was the trailblazer. Black, women, lesbian, gay, and disabled members of NALGO were all campaigning for improved representation within their union during the 1980s.[26] The campaigns by lesbian and gay activists led to the first NALGO Lesbian and Gay Conferences, held in 1983 and 1984. This pressure to "have a voice" did not let up until the 1986 National Conference, when NALGO finally passed a motion accepting the need to change the culture of the union and supporting lesbian and gay members' self-organization to assist in developing union policy. As a result, NALGO set up a National Steering Committee of lesbians and gays from all of NALGO's regions and began to hold annual National Lesbian and Gay Conferences.[27] By 1992, the Manufacturing Services and Finance Union (MSF) and the Communication Workers Union (CWU) had set up a national-level lesbian and gay committee or group as a formal part of the union's structure. Informal groups existed in a further fourteen unions, including a lesbian and gay group in COHSE.[28]

Some unions made huge steps forward on sexual diversity issues during the 1990s (see Phil Greasley's discussion in this volume); others have no structures or policies to promote equality of sexual minorities.[29] Pushed by proactive unions such as UNISON, MSF, and CWU, the TUC sought to provide leadership. It produced a checklist of relevant workplace issues and encouraged unions to engage with these issues and develop services for sexual minority members.[30] By 1998, the TUC held four annual Lesbian and Gay Pride at Work seminars or conferences, arranged to coincide with the annual National Lesbian and Gay Pride march and festival in London.

In 1996, the TUC undertook a consultation with its affiliates on the future structure of a TUC Lesbian and Gay Conference similar to those already in existence for women and black workers. Only twenty-one of the TUC's seventy-four affiliates responded, and only nineteen sent representatives to the meeting to discuss the way forward. Thus, although delegates at the 1996 and 1997 lesbian and gay seminars strongly pressed to move from the one-day workshop format to an annual policy-making conference, the TUC argued that no consensus had emerged from the consultation.[31] The TUC remained cautious about moving forward, arguing that a large diversity of practice exists within British trade unions and that it was important to structure the conference in such a way as to encourage those unions who had not yet developed work on lesbian and gay issues.[32] However, lesbian and gay delegates argued that a TUC Lesbian and Gay Conference would act as an important catalyst, encouraging unions to take action to develop policy and self-organized structures for lesbian and gay members.

In a great breakthrough at the 1997 TUC conference, despite the opposition of the TUC General Council, a motion was carried to make the annual TUC Lesbian and Gay Conference a policy-making, three-day event organized on the same footing as the TUC Women's and Black Workers Conferences. The first TUC Lesbian and Gay Conference was held in 1998.

The success of this motion proposed by Equity and seconded by UNISON testifies to the networking and caucusing skills of lesbian and gay activists within and across their trade unions, as well as to the more supportive attitude that developed within the trade union movement as a whole over the last decade. The TUC survey of union structures and work for lesbian and gay members and a 1997 LRD survey highlight that a number of British trade unions have become more responsive to sexual diversity issues.[33] One of the unions that stood out as being at the forefront of action for its lesbian and gay members was UNISON. It provides a useful case study of one union's attempt to change its structures and culture to encourage lesbian and gay activists and increase trade union interest in sexual diversity issues as part of a core trade union agenda.

UNISON, Proportionality, and Fair Representation

At its formation, UNISON set itself the task of establishing "new standards for trade unionism" in the United Kingdom and across Europe.[34] When NALGO, NUPE, and COHSE joined in 1993, they thought a merger to form the biggest union in Britain and the largest public service union in Europe would better enable them to represent public service workers in a hostile climate. Central to the merger was the need to meet the concerns for fair representation of the women who make up three-quarters of its members.[35] COHSE organized members across health service occupations, with a particular stronghold among nurses in the mental health sector. In 1992, it had 201,253 members, of whom 79 percent were women. NALGO was a white-collar union that in 1992 had 744,453 members, of whom 55 percent were women. Its membership ranged from clerical workers to professionals such as architects, surveyors, and accountants, and vertically from junior staff to chief officer level. Among the strong traditions of NALGO were the practices of overt political groupings, slates and caucusing, decentralized local-branch control, and a strong emphasis on leadership by lay members. NUPE, traditionally referred to as a manual union, nevertheless organized a wide range of members across the public sector, including refuse collectors, home helps, hospital porters, municipal gardeners, and nurses. At the merger, its membership was 605,000, of whom 74 percent were women. Traditionally officer-led, NUPE had nevertheless developed a strong local shop-steward system in the 1970s. Proportionality and fair representation were important concepts, given the concerns raised during the merger talks about the diversity of UNISON's membership in terms of occupation, class, gender, race, and sexual orientation and the need for all groups to be represented and reflected within its structures.

UNISON committed itself to challenging discrimination on all fronts. The *Rulebook* states, for example, that the union exists "to seek to ensure equality of treatment . . . for all members and to work for the elimination of discrimination on grounds of race, gender, sexuality, disability, age or creed" and "to seek to protect the rights of all members to be treated with dignity and respect irrespective of race, gender, sexuality, disability, age or creed."[36] UNISON aims "to achieve equal access to public services for all and to ensure that all users of public services are treated with dignity and respect, irrespective of race, gender, sexuality, disability, age or creed" (rule B.1.6). These core commitments are set out alongside the more traditional trade union objectives of improving members' pay and conditions and promoting their interests.

Annual reports on the merger to form UNISON were presented to each union's delegate conference, culminating in a vote by the membership on whether to go ahead with a merger. To work out the merger arrangements, a number of working parties made up of members of the three partner unions were established, including one on equal opportunities. The equal opportunity working party proposed that proportionality, low-paid women's seats, and self-organization should be the mechanisms used to ensure women's fair representation, and that self-organization was the way forward for the representation of lesbian and gay, black, and disabled members.[37] The latter approach was modeled on the strategy of self-organized groups (SOGs) that had been established in NALGO during the 1980s.[38] NALGO members sought to maintain these gains within the new UNISON structure; indeed, many would not have supported merger unless self-organization was retained. As one lesbian ex-NALGO activist described the premerger campaigning, "We had been sold the new union on the basis that we wouldn't lose anything we already had, and that is how they courted the lesbian and gay vote, which is fairly substantial" (Ellen, June 1996). Proportionality, fair representation, and self-organization emerged as key concepts to encourage democratic representation and involvement within UNISON.

Proportionality is a strategy to ensure that the representation of women and men is in proportion to the numbers of female and male members composing the electorate.[39] The first elections for the union's National Executive Committee to be based on proportionality took place in 1995. Members stood for "general," "women's," and "low-paid women's" seats in each of thirteen regions, plus designated seats for the seven service groups. As a consequence, the proportion of women on the executive (65 percent) is now more truly representative of UNISON's predominantly female membership (78 percent). Proportionality applies at all levels of representation in UNISON: branch (workplace), regional, and national. It also applies to national, service-group, and SOG conference delegations.

Structures at all levels of UNISON are required to reach proportionality for women by the year 2000. The union recognizes that success depends on support at the grass roots level.[40] In support of their goal, UNISON publishes guidance to members on how to introduce proportionality.[41] Moreover, regions and branches are required to conduct membership audits, set targets, and produce action plans as part of UNISON's Strategic Review.[42] Although progress has been made in moving toward proportionality, difficulties arose in monitoring proportionality at branch and regional levels, in large part because of poor membership records systems and branch-level mergers. However, inevitably, some difficulties stem from apathy and opposition from some quarters within the union.[43]

As with proportionality, the year 2000 is UNISON's target date to achieve fair representation, but "there is no cut-off point to this process." Rather, achieving fair representation is perceived to be a "continuous process which will constantly grow and change." The aim is to ensure "the broad balance of representation of members of the electorate, taking into account such factors as the balance between part-time and full-time workers, manual and nonmanual workers, different occupations, skills, qualifications, responsibilities, race, sexuality and disability."[44] Establishing this concept was very important in the new UNISON, given that its membership is drawn widely from manual, clerical, professional, and managerial occupations across the public services. UNISON sees itself as taking "the lead in the trade union movement in making a commitment to achieve fair representation throughout its structures."[45] It recognizes that change will not be achieved overnight and that success will depend on all members working together toward this goal.

The principle of fair representation is meant to apply to all elections, committees, and the composition of conference delegations within the union. However, the principle is by nature imprecise, and it is proving even harder than proportionality to implement and monitor. Some union activists appear apathetic about its successful implementation.[46] By the first UNISON National Delegate Conference in 1994, activists were already expressing anger and disillusionment at the union's failure to deliver fully on the commitment to equal opportunities. A composite motion approved by conference, while welcoming UNISON's commitment to proportionality and fair representation, noted that "manual workers, health workers and part-time workers were badly underrepresented in UNISON's structures." As a result of the 1994 conference decision, a national joint working group was set up to study the underrepresentation of specific groups within the union. Its report recognized that the fair representation rule constituted an excellent set of principles but was a poor and imprecise guide to practice. The report concluded that although progress was being made in the representation of lesbians and gays, there appeared to be a problem concerning the underrepresentation of manual workers generally, women, and black workers.[47] In 1996, a working group was set up to investigate and report progress on fair representation; as a consequence,

UNISON undertook a consultation exercise throughout the union and drew up guidelines explaining the concept and the need for branch development reviews and action plans.[48]

UNISON realized at its inception that it had to recognize union members as heterogeneous if it wished to deliver democracy to all its members. Thus, it set out to acknowledge the different constituencies with different interests deriving from gender, race and ethnicity, sexuality, and disability in addition to the geographical and sectoral or occupational constituencies more traditionally acknowledged within unions.[49] In order to do this, UNISON utilizes a number of new democratic principles and mechanisms. Cockburn describes proportionality, low-paid women's seats, and fair representation as systems whereby individuals are elected by "mixed" constituencies principally as individuals in a specific category. Thus, for example, proportionality requires that women be elected by men and women to union positions primarily as a member of a "sex category," and low-paid women's seats require that women be elected as a member of a "sex category" as well as a "low wage category." Although this system has an impact on the numbers of women within union structures, it does not guarantee that women's concerns will be better represented, since the women are elected as representatives of a mixed constituency. Cockburn argues that self-organization provides a more genuine route to democracy because it represents "oppressed social groups" such as women and sexual minorities as a legitimate constituency from which individuals are elected specifically to speak for that constituency.[50] The following section describes the structure, aims, and objectives of self-organization in UNISON.

Self-Organization in UNISON: Recognizing the Lesbian and Gay Constituency

Self-organization is a key ingredient in UNISON's strategy to deliver proportionality and fair representation. Four constituencies are recognized by UNISON as having a need and a right to form a self-organized group (SOG) within the framework of the union: lesbians and gays, women, black members, and disabled members. Self-organization (inherited from NALGO) provides UNISON with a radical strategy to redress power imbalances and ensure that groups made invisible by discrimination are given union space, resources, and legitimacy in order to work together and establish their own agenda. Any UNISON member who self-identifies as lesbian or gay may join the lesbian and gay self-organized group. Figure 14.1 provides a diagram of how self-organization fits alongside and links with the other structures of the union. Unitarist UNISON members refer to these structures as the "mainstream"; they aim to primarily represent members from geographical (e.g., branch, region) and occupational/employment sectors (e.g., service groups).[51]

According to UNISON rules, SOGs enable their members to:

- meet to share concerns and aspirations and establish their own priorities
- elect their own representatives to other levels of self-organization and to other appropriate levels of union organization

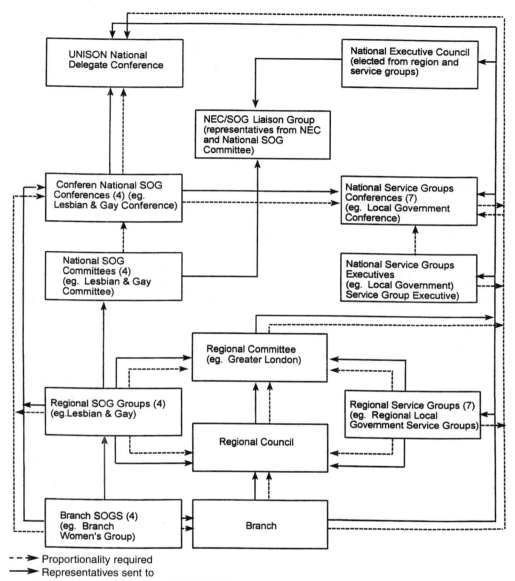

FIGURE 14.1.   Overview of UNISON's structure.

- have adequate and agreed funding and other resources, including education and training access, publicity, and communications
- work within a flexible structure to build confidence, encourage participation, and provide opportunities for a fuller involvement of disadvantaged members
- work within the established policies, rules, and constitutional provision of the union

UNISON's equal opportunities director states that "self-organization is not equated with separatism; it is about empowerment."[52] UNISON's support for lesbian and gay self-organization "adds lesbian and gay talent, skill and creativity to UNISON" that it might otherwise not attract.[53] A number of lesbian and gay activists make clear that this is the case. According to Gill, a member of the Disabled Members Caucus in a regional lesbian and gay group, who was interviewed in March 1997, "If it wasn't for self-organization, I would not be a UNISON activist." Self-organization also encourages workers who may not feel able to be out at work or in their local branch to become active in the union.

Inevitably, there are debates about the purpose of self-organization within the union. Its challenge to the traditional union values of unity and solidarity is very resented by some sections of the union.[54] A minority of lesbian and gay activists are indeed separatist, seeing self-organization as an end in itself and choosing to be active only within its structures (where they are guaranteed confidentiality). The majority of lesbian and gay activists, however, see it as a way of raising lesbian and gay issues within the union, changing the union's culture, and establishing a visible lesbian and gay presence throughout the organization. Notwithstanding these divergent views, there is broad agreement within UNISON that lesbian and gay self-organization is about organizing autonomously within the union structure and that it extends involvement to a section of the membership that previously might not have been active. Also, self-organization may well attract lesbians and gays to join UNISON on the grounds that commitment to their rights is a core part of its trade union agenda.

Self-organization is supported and resourced at all levels in UNISON. However, SOGs do not have reserved seats on UNISON's National Executive Council (NEC), which is composed solely of representatives from the regions and service groups (see Figure 14.1). The lack of SOG representation seems contradictory, given UNISON's commitment to fair representation, and it is a subject for consultation at the current time. Nationally, UNISON has established an Equal Opportunities Department, headed by a director who is assisted by a deputy and by a national officer for each of the SOGs. Thus, the National Lesbian and Gay Committee (NLGC) is serviced by a National Lesbian and Gay Officer. In each of UNISON's thirteen regions, there is a Regional Lesbian and Gay Committee (RLGC). At the grass roots of UNISON's organization, the workplace branch, is a developing network of lesbian and gay groups.

The sections that follow, drawn primarily from interviews with UNISON lesbian and gay activists, describe SOG structures and consider how lesbian and gay self-organization works in practice.

Self-Organization at the National Level

The top tier of lesbian and gay self-organization is the National Lesbian and Gay Committee (NLGC) and the annual Lesbian and Gay Conference. The NLGC's main focus is to promote the interests of lesbians and gays in the union and the workplace and to campaign more broadly for lesbian and gay rights. The NLGC is made up of twenty-six regional representatives (a lesbian and a gay from each of UNISON's thirteen regions) plus six representatives each from the disabled and black lesbian and gay caucuses.

The NLGC organizes the annual national Lesbian and Gay Conference, at which delegates set policies and priorities for lesbian and gay self-organization in the coming year.

The conference has the right to send two motions and two delegates to UNISON's National Delegate Conference (NDC), as well as to each of the seven Service Group Conferences. The NLGC is a "highly visible and organized presence" at the NDC. It arranges fringe meetings on specific topics and daily lesbian and gay caucus meetings. It produces a daily conference news sheet that is funny, friendly, and informative. The NLGC also organizes a stall with UNISON lesbian and gay literature where members can get information and advice and sign up for the lesbian and gay mailing list. These initiatives establish a high-profile presence at the NDC, publicizing the work of the SOG to all UNISON delegates and encouraging lesbian and gay activists to become involved in self-organization.

The UNISON annual Lesbian and Gay Conference is one of the largest events of its kind.[55] It is a policy-making, motion-based conference with time scheduled for service group, disabled, and black members caucuses as well as meetings by regional groups to discuss priorities and motions and to network. A number of UNISON lesbian and gay activists describe their first conference experience as "very liberating," "exciting," and a spur to becoming active within the union. Pauline, interviewed in April 1997, states: "I was really taken with the idea of the lesbian and gay people meeting in that way, and having a say in the union and then getting together and without heterosexual people being there." Pauline admits that the first time she attended the conference, "I was in the bar at five AM and didn't always get up in the morning, but I was really taken with it. As the conferences have gone by, I have taken the nitty gritty of it a lot more seriously, and I got up and spoke at the conference last time." Encouraged by her conference experiences, Pauline is now a coordinator of a regional lesbian and gay group, a branch equalities officer, and a delegate to her regional council and regional women's committee.

NLGC Proportionality and Fair Representation

Lesbian and gay self-organization reflects the diversity of the British lesbian and gay community. Within the NLGC, for example, are lesbian, gay, black, and disabled members caucuses. However, the NLGC has acknowledged that manual workers, part-time, low-paid, young, and retired members remain generally underrepresented in national and regional lesbian and gay structures, and that this needs to be addressed through regional development.[56]

One way the NLGC addresses proportionality and fair representation is by ensuring parity of representation between lesbians and gays (e.g., women in at least 50 percent of all positions, elections, and delegations) and allowing scheduled time within NLGC meetings for the caucuses to meet. On the whole, the NLGC members interviewed agreed that, although there were differences at times, "gay men and lesbians worked well together" (Ellen, June 1996). A training session was arranged in 1997 to clarify areas of strength and difficulty, increase understanding, and improve cooperation among lesbians and gays. Both groups find their separate caucuses "constructive." Bob, a member of the Disabled Members Caucus (DMC) interviewed in March 1997, said that he welcomed "men caucusing because, on a personal level, it's an area that I need to work with, and I have got hurdles to get over with the men on the committee, or they have got hurdles to get over with me."

The DMC and the Black Members Caucus (BMC) hold two annual "network days" for black and disabled members, and they elect six members each to the NLGC. The BMC and DMC are recognized as "an integral part of lesbian and gay self-organization in UNISON, and caucus representatives make an essential contribution to its work, both as the elected, accountable voice for black and disabled lesbians and gay men and as individual committee members."[57]

Recognizing that black lesbians and gays may experience racism in the lesbian and gay community and homophobia in the black community, the BMC developed its work in recent years around the themes of "Black Visibility" and "Layers of Oppression."[58] The caucus seeks to highlight the specific needs and concerns of black lesbians and gays, ensure that all NLGC campaigns involve black lesbians and gays, and provide an effective bridgehead between the NLGC and the National Black Members Committee, on which it has two representatives.[59] Key activities include the network days, submission of motions to the Lesbian and Gay Conference, and work on all of the NLGC subcommittees (particularly publicity and campaigning, education, regional development, and health), the international subcommittees, and the *Out in UNISON* newsletter. Recent priorities include the development of the BMC within the regions, joint work with the DMC to ensure the views of the caucuses are taken on board by the NLGC, and work with the broader anti-racist and sexual diversity movements.[60]

Disabled lesbians and gays also suffer complex forms of oppression and discrimination, including homophobia within the disabled community as well as disableism and a denial of their sexuality within some quarters of the lesbian and gay community.[61] Active across the range of NLGC subcommittees, the DMC sought representation at training events as facilitators, at public meetings such as the TUC, Lesbian and Gay Conference, and National Delegate Conference, and on the conference news sheet team. The DMC promoted disability equality training courses, contributed to *Out in UNISON,* and produced the first issue of *Shout,* a newsletter for disabled lesbians and gays in UNISON.[62] Additionally, the DMC has links with UNISON's National Disabled Members Committee (NDMC) as well as non-UNISON campaigning groups, including the Lesbian and Gay Carers Campaign, ILGA, the Pride Access Working Group, and REGARD—the major national organization of disabled lesbians and gays.[63]

Caucus members say that raising issues of importance to them is still difficult within UNISON's structures, and that they need more resources from the NLGC to develop the regional BMC and DMC. However, they acknowledge that the NLGC is perhaps in the forefront of good practice within the union. According to Freda, a member of the BMC interviewed in June 1997, a number of members on the NLGC are committed to achieving the changes set out in the rulebook, and in the main, it is being "true to its commitment and true to taking on board the issues raised by the caucuses." She concedes that "it may not be perfect at the moment, but we will enlarge on that." Lena, interviewed in March 1997, states that she learned "an awful lot through being on the NLGC, working in an inclusive rather than an exclusive way, particularly in terms of the caucuses." Because of her experiences, Lena says, "I have been able to take a lot of that to the regional and branch level in terms of how we should be working."

The NLGC Working Within UNISON's Structures

The NLGC sets out to be "strategic" and "inclusive" in the way it works. Its approach is well summarized by Sav, a committee member interviewed in October 1996, who said the NLGC is there "to ensure that lesbian and gay issues and the needs of lesbian and gay members are addressed effectively by our trade union." To cover what is potentially a huge workload, much of the work of the NLGC is undertaken by subcommittees that liaise with other UNISON departments. In 1997, there were seven NLGC subcommittees: Conference, Education, Health, International, Publicity and Campaigning, Regional Development, and TUC/Affiliated Political Fund.

To ensure that lesbian and gay self-organization is strategic in setting its priorities and in how it relates to other parts of the union, an overall review of strategy and organization (ROSE) is underway. Through this review, the NLGC aims to build a consensus about the objectives and priorities for lesbian and gay self-organization. One goal is the integration of lesbian and gay issues into all areas of UNISON's work. Thus, the review will establish "targets for the short, medium, and longer term within such areas as liaison with service groups and communications with regional groups or international work."[64]

Members of the NLGC are mindful that lesbian and gay self-organization "can't operate in isolation," Sav states, and that it is therefore important to work with the three other SOGs (for women, blacks, and disabled members). Aside from the formal meetings that take place between SOG representatives at forums such as the NEC SOG Liaison Committee, the four SOG committee chairs maintain informal contacts to exchange information and discuss possible areas of collaboration. According to Sav, at the UNISON National Delegate Conference, the SOGs try to take a common view on motions and make a conscientious effort to support each other's initiatives. In 1995, a joint fringe meeting was held with the other SOGs at UNISON's National Delegate Conference, an initiative repeated in 1996.

The seven UNISON national service groups acknowledge the success of the NLGC in forging links with them and bringing bargaining and policy issues to their attention.[65] This is important because the service groups coordinate policy on pay and service conditions. The NLGC's links with these mainstream structures affect whether or not the NLGC can deliver to its constituents. Cara, a NLGC member interviewed in April 1997, states: "We are not a single issue group; we are about being a trade union." According to Cara, "It's very important that I am visible within the mainstream union; I think that's absolutely key, that we are progressing the agenda." She believes that the NLGC must be seen to advance the union's agenda, "not just one from the SOG perspective." As she points out, "my politics are far wider than lesbian and gay politics."

Thus, the lesbian and gay self-organized group has put motions to the service group conferences since 1996. Kerry, interviewed in July 1996, views this as a very useful step in engaging with the mainstream service-group structures. "I think that moved us on," she states, adding, "not so much what was achieved in policy terms but in the process of the contact it brought us with the service group executives." The NLGC works with service groups in a variety of ways. With the Local Government Service Group, where the relationship is most developed, two formal liaison meetings as well as a number of informal consultations were held in 1997 concerning the implications for the service group of motions from the fourth national Lesbian and Gay Conference. The service group also requested the SOG to comment on service-group policy and the contents of collective agreements negotiated with local government employers (e.g., the Single Status Agreement in Local Government).[66]

This strategic approach has been adopted in all parts of the union. Thus, detailed submissions on a number of key areas have been prepared for discussion by the NLGC, and their hard work and commitment were recognized by a number of UNISON members and officers within regional and national union structures.[67] To some extent, the approach developed out of adversity. Ellen, interviewed in June 1996, states that in the NLGC, "We were always fighting, and that certainly can bring out the best in you; it can make you have to be more political. Like we basically haven't been allowed to rest on our laurels. We had to be fighting the NEC, we had to be putting motions up, we had to be seen to be active and not for a minute let people forget we existed, otherwise we lost things. We lost our voice."

The NLGC strategy is not only to encourage lesbian and gay activists to bring NLGC issues to the attention of the union, but also to build support for its agenda within the union mainstream. As Sav stresses, "part of the underlying agenda is to empower lesbian and gay men, and through that empowerment process they are able then to take up the roles that the branch and regions have." Sav mentions "lay activist posts" throughout the union's structure, for example. "I think one of the reasons we are successful is precisely that is what's happening and we are able to exploit those networks."

Recent NLGC Priorities

Recent SOG priorities for addressing lesbian and gay issues within UNISON and within a broader political context can be identified in two major ways: first, from an examination of the two motions sent annually to the National Lesbian and Gay Conference and to UNISON's National Delegate Conference (NDC), and second, from an examination of the work of NLGC subcommittees.

In 1995, the motions sent to the NDC from the national Lesbian and Gay Conference sought to strengthen the position of self-organization within UNISON, following some threatened cutbacks during a period of financial constraint as the new UNISON put its "house in order."[68] In 1996, the two motions sent to the NDC were more externally focused, seeking to encourage UNISON to develop links with other unions in order to "work with other trade unions on lesbian and gay rights" and address "civil rights and law reform."[69] Both motions were carried. In 1997, the motions focused on terms and conditions and the need to improve the levels of advice and support UNISON provides to lesbian and gay members. Again, both were carried. Motions sent to the NDC in 1998 reflect the SOG's desire to build pressure for change on sexual minority rights in the United Kingdom, Europe, and internationally through the TUC; to seek UNISON's full support at all levels; and to participate in campaigns such as the Stonewall Equality 2000 Campaign.[70]

Developing links outside UNISON to make progress on lesbian and gay civil and employment rights is crucial to the NLGC and its subcommittees. The Publicity and

Campaigning subcommittee has been raising the profile of lesbian and gay self-organization within and outside UNISON. The TUC/Affiliated Political Fund subcommittee played a crucial role in working with other trade unions to push for an annual TUC lesbian and gay policy-making conference. This subcommittee worked with the Scottish TUC (STUC) on issues of concern to lesbian and gay members during the Scottish referendum campaign.[71] Finally, the subcommittee has been trying to use the union's Affiliated Political Fund structures and connections with the Labour Party to raise the issue of lesbian and gay equality legislation.

The NLGC International subcommittee has sought to ensure that lesbian and gay rights are included wherever UNISON or the TUC argues for action on trade union and human rights issues. "Our international work seeks to promote lesbian and gay issues within the trade union movement, and to promote trade union perspectives and UNISON policies within lesbian and gay organizations."[72] To this end, the NLGC International subcommittee has continued to work with the International Lesbian and Gay Association (ILGA), for example, by running workshops at the 1996 European Regional Conference and hosting the 1997 ILGA conference in London, during which the UNISON general secretary, Rodney Bickerstaffe, hosted the first night's reception, and Chris Smith, an out gay cabinet minister, addressed the conference.[73]

The NLGC worked with other trade unions to arrange the first international lesbian and gay trade union conference, held in the Netherlands in 1998. Other important international work to highlight discrimination and oppression against lesbians and gays throughout the world has been done with organizations such as Amnesty International's UK Gay, Lesbian, and Bisexual Network, the National Coalition of Gay and Lesbian Equality in Southern Africa, and War on Want. In conjunction with War on Want, the NLGC prepared a report called *Pride World-Wide,* which in 1996 was submitted to the United Nations Subcommittee on the Prevention of Discrimination and Protection of Minorities.[74] This international work complements and builds on NLGC links with other trade unions and lesbian and gay organizations in Britain. It does much to demonstrate the way the lesbian and gay self-organized group has helped UNISON develop a reputation as a trade union that will fight for lesbian and gay employment and civil rights issues.

All of this work is underpinned by the work the NLGC is doing within UNISON to develop lesbian and gay self-organization and influence internal union policy and strategy. The SOGs do not have reserved seats on UNISON's National Executive Committee but liaise through an NEC subcommittee, the SOG Liaison Group. One SOG, the National Black Members Committee (NBMC), wished to support an election across the union for three reserved NEC seats for black members. The NLGC, however, prefers observer status, with speaking rights, at the NEC. Because it is not currently feasible to identify UNISON's lesbian and gay membership, the NEC representatives cannot be solely elected by lesbian and gay members. A related concern is that lesbian and gay NEC representatives elected by a predominantly heterosexual membership would not be accountable to lesbian and gay members and might in fact hold views counter to the NLGC and Lesbian and Gay Conference. The NLGC provided submissions to the NEC on the representation of the SOGs on the NEC and has been involved in a consultation reviewing how the SOG Liaison Committee works.[75]

The NLGC has prioritized developing effective liaison with the service groups to increase the representation and participation of lesbian and gay members within the service groups and ensure that their issues are addressed in developing pay and conditions policy. It has also been working with the Legal Services Committee to improve legal advice and assistance to lesbian and gay members.[76] The Health subcommittee has been working hard to secure funding for HIV/AIDS work, as well as raising awareness of lesbian health issues and developing a report on black lesbian health issues.[77]

The NLGC Education subcommittee in conjunction with the Education and Training Department set up courses nationally for lesbian and gay trade unionists on race equality and disability awareness and on regional development. They also surveyed regional education officers to build on the existing training available to activists at regional level. The NLGC Regional Development subcommittee prepared a report highlighting examples of good practice in the regions. In 1997, it ran a Regional Convenors Development Day, and it is preparing a regional guidelines handbook. A key priority for the NLGC is developing a vibrant network of regional and branch lesbian and gay groups.

Regional and Branch-Level Self-Organization

The regional lesbian and gay groups are often the first and major point of contact for UNISON members.[78] It is at the grass roots—the region and branch levels—that most members are active. Regional lesbian and gay (and other SOG) groups exist in each of UNISON's thirteen regions, and branches are beginning to establish them too.

Regional Lesbian and Gay Groups

Regional groups exist to promote the active involvement and empowerment of lesbian and gay members at all levels of UNISON. They offer workplace support for lesbian and gay members, including those who are not "out" at work. They can provide information on lesbian and gay issues, support local initiatives, and work with other regional SOGs to support campaigns for anti-discrimination and civil rights.[79] Most arrange quarterly meetings for lesbians and gays in the region. They may provide information to lesbian and gay members through a regular regional mailing list and regional handbook (Northern Region), or they may organize training and network events on topics such as lesbians and gays and the law (South East Region), effective public speaking, and campaigning for change through the political process (Yorkshire and Humberside).[80] They may link with local and national lesbian and gay organizations and work with other trade unions to raise sexual diversity issues in their regions (e.g., Scotland and the STUC). They may provide a forum to support individuals who are being treated in a homophobic way, or simply an opportunity to meet and network with other lesbian and gay members.[81]

Regional groups provide a route for lesbian and gay members to get involved in UNISON through the lesbian and gay SOG and through UNISON's regional mainstream structures. The regional group can raise awareness of the needs and rights of sexual minority members in the union and workplace by campaigning as a group and through the group's elected delegates to policy-making bodies.[82] In each region, the lesbian and gay groups have pushed for the right to have representatives within the regional structures. Regional lesbian and gay groups can now send delegates to their regional councils (with delegates from branches, service groups, and SOGs in the region) and regional committees (which run business between regional council meetings).

Although some lesbian and gay activists feel positive about their region's attitudes to lesbian and gay self-organization, others feel that they are working in an anti-SOG and homophobic climate. While some groups feel well regarded and adequately resourced, others report problems. According to Ellen, "letters don't get sent, minutes don't come out, things get lost; maybe it's disinterest, but it doesn't half feel like deliberate blocking." Meg, interviewed in May 1997, was a delegate from the regional lesbian and gay group to her regional council. She states: "I have spoken but I found it a very difficult experience, and also the attitudes there, there were a lot of anti-SOG people there. But the regional secretary I found pretty encouraging; he's always been fine, and the deputy regional secretary as well."

Ellen says that working within mainstream union structures such as a regional publicity committee can be hard "because you don't know who your allies are," although, "to be fair, nobody's been overtly anything." According to Ellen, "You can't help but feel you're a side issue when you bring things up." For example, if asking for money to support Pride activities, "you'd just feel people were saying yes because they daren't say politically no. You don't feel there's that much active support."

To counter this anti-SOG and anti-equal opportunities climate, the regional SOGs may work together through informal links (Greater London), formal collaborative meetings such as SOG strategy meetings (South West), or network meetings or training days on "Working Together" (South East). They can set priorities, agree on strategies, and support each other's motions at regional meetings. They can also propose and elect candidates to regional positions and committees who are supportive of self-organization and culture change within the union. In more than one region, trade unionists who have become active through self-organization are now being elected to Regional Convenor and Deputy Convenor posts (most senior regional lay-member positions), as well as positions on key regional subcommittees such as education and training, recruitment and organization, finance, and international. Increasingly, these candidates also find support from branches that take a positive view of self-organization and wish to see proportionality and fair representation implemented at regional level.[83]

The regional groups try to strike a balance between getting the work done and offering a friendly and supportive group for new activists to join. Most of the regional groups rotate the location of the meetings around their region to encourage people to participate. "We always have an agenda; we have a lot of business to get through," says Lena, interviewed in March 1997. She notes that "we had two new members last time and we had quite a busy agenda, and although we tried to explain to people what is going on, we need to work harder at making more space for some of the informal stuff as well, a speaker or a workshop or just time for people to say their bit."

This approach to trade union organization aims to encourage lesbians and gays to become active and feel able to raise issues within the union. Deirdre, interviewed in January 1997, was trying to become active in her branch. She states: "I felt empowered in the lesbian and gay SOG but I didn't feel empowered in the general union steward bit, which is quite interesting." The regional lesbian and gay group can be an important place to find out how the union works. Nelarine, interviewed in April 1997, explains that she was able to find out about different structures. "I didn't know anything about the regional council or regional committees, how they function or what role they play. People can't put themselves up for nominations if they don't even know what exists."

The regional groups are tackling the issues of proportionality and fair representation in different ways. Four regions have recognized that lesbians are underrepresented in their regional group. Ruth, interviewed in March 1997, believes that the underrepresentation in her group is because the male regional convenor "doesn't know how to handle situations with women. He has expectations of them to be the way men are and our needs are different, our perspectives are different, our way of working is different, and what he does is, we have a meeting and two new lesbians come, and he tries to get them to be on regional committee or regional council, and they have never been to a union meeting before, and they never come again."

Ruth states that, instead of becoming active on the Regional Lesbian and Gay Committee, lesbians turn to the Regional Women's Committee (RWC), "which is a lovely committee and I have never felt so warmly welcomed, and the meetings are very much based on discussing objectives and ideas." According to Ruth, "you can have time when you can sit and have a chat, and they have a really good AGM, they have speakers, that helps." At the RCW, she says, members "talk about things that matter to women, so it works." To encourage lesbians to become involved in the regional lesbian and gay group, Ruth and the lesbian regional convenor are trying to change the style of the meetings and arrange a "lesbian caucus at regional meetings." However, not all lesbians find RWC meetings such a positive experience. A number report that they did not get involved in women's self-organization because they found some women on the RWC to be homophobic and racist.

The BMC and the DMC are trying to ensure that black and disabled lesbians and gays feel able to get involved in regional lesbian and gay groups. At the 1997 Regional Convenors day, coordinators ran a workshop to talk about the issues regional groups should consider in facilitating caucus development at the regional level. Regional groups are trying to respond to this by selecting accessible venues, using a loop system, reserving seats on lesbian and gay committees, publicizing caucuses, and linking with other SOGs to do this. However, for the DMC and BMC, progress can seem slow. Sue, interviewed in March 1997 and active in the DMC, states that "the issues that affect disabled lesbians don't get given the priority they need." According to Nelarine, who is active in lesbian and gay self-organization, "It is hard sometimes; the chances are I am the only Afro-Caribbean there." BMC and DMC members may be active trying to raise the issues across the SOGs. "I find there are particular issues around confidentiality and homophobia in black members' self-organization," says Sav. "I felt that I had got a particular contribution to make to lesbian and gay activism, and I felt that I would derive some greater benefit from that personally in satisfaction." He believes that "more work needs to be done in terms of raising the profile of the lesbian and gay membership and the needs and expectations of lesbians and gay men in the workplace. Having said that, my personal political agenda is that it is vital that we raise the issues of black lesbians and gay members, or lesbians and gay men within black self-organization."

At regional level, the work the lesbian and gay groups do is crucially important in introducing issues, changing the union culture, and reminding UNISON that lesbian and gay issues need to be a core part of the union agenda. The regions are responding, if at times reluctantly. "I think we irritate them dreadfully," Ruth observes. "I'm always having meetings with my regional secretary at which he tells me I am expecting too much and I say I am expecting my rights, within UNISON, but they do praise us. They say, oh you have done some really good work; you have brought a lot of things to our attention."

Yet some of those active in the SOGs are made to feel by some UNISON members and employers that their activism "is not real trade union work," states Jen, interviewed in March 1997. According to Janet, interviewed in May 1997, some activists who perceive themselves as operating in the mainstream of the union criticize SOG work for not addressing the "bread and butter issues of trade unionism" and being too narrowly focused on "identity politics." A very real problem for trade unionists active in self-organization is time off to attend union meetings in working time. This is a problem affecting all areas of lay-member activity in the union. However, "there are particular difficulties for representatives of SOGs at national and regional level because many employers refuse to recognize such work as trade union duties."[84] If UNISON wants activism to develop in regional and national self-organization, this needs to be addressed. A majority of people interviewed considered getting paid time off for SOG activities a problem. Half of the group interviewed had taken on branch positions as one route to gaining time off for their union activities.

Branch Lesbian and Gay Groups

The primary unit of UNISON is the local branch, where members organize together for negotiations, services, advice, and information. At branch level is a developing network of lesbian and gay groups that meet to discuss local service conditions, build support for members facing problems at work, maintain confidential mailing lists, debate lesbian and gay issues, and help members gain the confidence to get involved in other parts of the union.[85]

The Code of Good Branch Practice sets out the aims of branch self-organization as follows:

- develop the union's policy on equality issues at branch level
- identify the particular service conditions and workplace issues affecting members of the group
- establish the group's priorities within a clearly defined trade union context
- elect representatives to other levels of the union's organization
- increase the group's visibility and participation within the union
- build confidence, encourage participation, and provide opportunities for the fuller involvement of disadvantaged members
- provide a link between the union and the wider community on equality issues[86]

It is up to the branch to facilitate the establishment of branch SOGs, and ensure that the branch committee is composed of stewards from each work group plus representatives from the SOGs. The branch should ensure that members' rights to confidentiality in the lesbian and gay group are respected, that facility time is negotiated for the officers of the SOGs, and that they are involved in determining priorities and service-conditions issues. Branches are expected to provide appropriate levels of funding to the SOGs and to implement proportionality and fair representation by conducting branch audits that consider their branch structures, ways of working, and education and training provision. Branches are encouraged to monitor proportionality and fair representation in the branch on an ongoing basis.[87]

Lesbians and gays have been involved in setting up branch groups for a number of reasons. Bob did so because "I figured there must be a lot of people around out there and I wanted their support. I was coming out at work in a visible way and I wanted to know where my supports were." According to Bob, "It started off as a support, but then very quickly we recognized that there were jobs that needed to be done from the branch." He notes, for example, "looking at some of the local authority policies."

Pauline, a branch equality officer interviewed in April 1997, was trying to ensure the branch took on equality issues as part of the bargaining agenda. Having set up an equal opportunity committee in the branch, she wanted it to draw on the priorities raised by women and minority groups. "I'm organizing meetings for all SOGs separately, and trying to get each group to elect two representatives for the branch committee so that they can then go there and have voting rights. What I want to do is for myself and those representatives of the four SOGs to have regular meetings and try and coordinate our activities a bit." Pauline believes that "we will be a stronger lobby if we stick together."

In some cases, the branch has been quite positive about the establishment of a lesbian and gay group. Gill, interviewed in March 1997, says that her branch is "very supportive about self-organization because they want to be seen to do the right thing." She states that "they have always been incredibly open to all the suggestions I have made, like recruiting leaflets for self-organization in all new members' packs and including it on the stewards training and all that." In other branches, however, the establishment of lesbian and gay self-organized groups has been more of an uphill struggle. "It's not easy and you have to make a big effort to get involved and be active," says Meg, interviewed in May 1997. "When you are trying to get venues that are accessible and things like that, you are made to feel a bit of a pain because you are the equalities person, you are always the one bringing it up. I also worry about being kind of used as a badge, if you are the only lesbian and gay person being asked along."

Not all lesbians and gays are in favor of having a lesbian and gay group in their branch. Lee, interviewed in February 1996, said that although he was happy to be active in the regional lesbian and gay group, a group at branch level would be too "close to home," given that he did not wish to be out at work. Deirdre expressed similar concerns. "I don't know how safe it would be for other people," she noted. "There are a lot of issues that, if that was going to go ahead, I would need to be aware of and sensitive to, because not everybody's at the same stage of being an out stroppy lesbian like me, and I've got to appreciate that."

Certainly, there were reports of how difficult it could be to be out and active in lesbian and gay self-organization in the branch, particularly where branches were very opposed to self-organization. Opposition meant that branches could opt to provide minimal budgets, block information to lesbian and gay representatives, impede raising issues, and make life difficult for lesbian and gay representatives on the branch committees. "The last national lesbian and gay conference I attended, I was funded by the branch," says

Mhinder, interviewed in May 1997, and "therefore I was reporting back to the branch committee about the conference, the issues which took place, the motions and so on, and you could hear the inner fear of people, homophobia, that sort of thing."

Nevertheless, establishing a lesbian and gay group was seen by the majority of those interviewed as an important step in "becoming visible," particularly in branches that were prepared to be constructive. Mary, interviewed in May 1997, said of her branch, "they're very willing to be motivated, but there are issues around that aren't always top of people's agenda, and that allows us to keep them focused and supportive and also at the same time develop new ideas and ways of looking at equalities—for example, dependent care and child care. We can remind them it's not always heterosexual people who have children." Rick, interviewed in November 1997, was grateful to the branch lesbian and gay group for support in the face of harassment and homophobia in the workplace. "If a similar situation happened tomorrow, then I would take it all the way," he states, "because I'm more aware of the system and what my rights are, and that comes from being in UNISON."

Lesbian and gay self-organized groups at the branch level can play a key role in ensuring that bargaining and consultation with employers takes account of the needs of lesbian and gay members. Branches may draw here on guidance and direction from the national service groups as well as SOG resources. For example, in the electricity sector, much of the bargaining takes place at the local level, so the Electricity Service Group has issued guidelines for its negotiators.[88] UNISON aims to ensure, for example, the inclusion of sexuality within all equal opportunity policies and statements, the extension of harassment policies to include the harassment and homophobia experienced by lesbians and gays, an entitlement to carer's leave for lesbians and gays, plus guidelines for branches dealing with a range of issues around HIV/AIDS.[89] Where branches are supportive, lesbian and gay branch groups have direct input into the local bargaining process. In one London local government branch described by Ed, interviewed in May 1998, the branch SOG is able to discuss lesbian and gay issues directly with management. As a result, a lesbian and gay equality strategy statement has been agreed on, and a corporate strategy group on lesbian and gay rights in employment and service delivery has been established.

Despite UNISON's rule-book commitments to proportionality, fair representation, and self-organization, challenging the union's culture is still an ongoing project for lesbian and gay activists. This is clearly the case where members active in branch, regional, and service-group mainstream structures are proving unsupportive and even oppositional. The next section considers the barriers that activists face as the union tries to move forward toward genuine equality for all its members.

Transforming Unions

All of the lesbian and gay activists who were interviewed perceived a lack of support for proportionality, fair representation, and self-organization within the mainstream of the union. This was seen, in part, as inevitable following a merger of three unions with different approaches to equal opportunity. This was particularly the view of ex-NALGO activists. As Ellen reports, "In NALGO, we had reached quite a good level of involvement in the union. UNISON came along and we got the ex-NUPE and COHSE staff people who hadn't heard of self-organization, they certainly hadn't any lesbian and gay self-organization, and it seemed to give those people in ex-NALGO who had big-oted and homophobic ideas a lift rather than the opposite." It was, Ellen says, "a bit of a backlash almost." Even so, most interviewees were optimistic, taking the view that as the transition into UNISON took place and UNISON members became familiar with the rationale for proportionality, fair representation, and self-organization, levels of support across the union would increase.

In his major address to the delegates at the 1996 UNISON National Lesbian and Gay Conference in Manchester, Rodney Bickerstaffe, the UNISON general secretary, made clear his commitment to lesbian and gay equality within society and the trade union movement. He acknowledged that, despite its policies and formal commitments, the union was not free from bigotry and prejudice. He also stressed the need for equality to remain at the heart of UNISON's bargaining and campaign agendas so that fair repre-sentation at work and in society would become a reality for all members.[90] This affir-mation was important, given the politics of his recent election to the position of general secretary. The candidate who came second stood on a platform critical of what he saw as "political correctness gone mad" within the union. In his election address, he argued that self-organization was a "drain on resources." Virulently opposed to lesbian and gay self-organization, he called for all SOGs to be disbanded.[91] Activists were sobered by his popularity. According to Sav, this very conservative candidate was "very successful in securing a high level of votes because of people's perceptions about self-organization, or he exploited people's perceptions." Sav states, "we need to dispel those notions, and one of the main ways of doing that is to show that lesbian and gay members are not merely concerned with lesbian and gay issues, that there are whole areas of work that affect us because we're members of a trade union as well as being lesbians and gay men."

Two surveys of UNISON activists (1995, 1997) revealed evidence to support this strategy. Trade union activists who were critical of proportionality, fair representation, and self-organization tended to deny the need for these measures on the grounds that "all UNISON members are equal." They believed that all members' needs could be met through the mainstream structures and tended to hold a traditional, unitarist view of trade unionism. As one respondent to UNISON's 1995 survey expressed it, "The dic-tionary states that 'union' is a 'joining together; the state of being united.' In my opin-ion, having SOGs is a contradiction of these terms. I am a member of a 'union' and wish to stay that way, not be fragmented by small groups." However, those support-ing self-organization held views more akin to this response to the 1995 survey: "I feel that UNISON still reflects the divisions within society—this includes the gender hierarchy. I do, however, feel that at least UNISON creates the space for groups which are marginalized within society to organize and speak out against their/our oppression."

The majority of respondents recognized a need for the union to adopt special meas-ures to ensure all members were able to participate, raise issues, and feel confident that their views would be represented. It was acknowledged that women and minority groups were constituencies that deserved to be represented and listened to within the union. Table 14.1 presents the survey results, indicating the level of support within UNISON for special measures to assist women to get elected to leadership positions in the union (e.g., through proportionality and self-organization). It also shows the level

TABLE 14-1. UNISON Activist Views on Special Measures to Ensure the Representation of Women, Black, Lesbian and Gay, and Disabled Members, 1995–1997

	Women activists, 1995 survey	Women branch activists, 1997	Men branch activists, 1997
Should be measures to help women get elected to leadership*			
Agree	203 (56%)	83 (58%)	42 (39%)
Disagree	157 (44)	60 (42)	67 (61)
Should be measures to ensure blacks, disabled, lesbians and gays in leadership			
Agree	209 (58%)	88 (62%)	43 (39%)
Disagree	150 (42)	54 (38)	66 (61)
In favor of self-organization in UNISON			
Yes	N/A	76 (53%)	47 (43%)
No	N/A	15 (11)	23 (21)
Don't know	N/A	52 (36)	39 (36)

Source: F. Colgan and S. Ledwith, Survey of UNISON women (1995) and branch activists (1997)
* Question wording:
  (1) "There should be special measures to help women to get elected to leadership positions in the union": agree; disagree.
  (2) "There should be special measures to ensure the representation of black, disabled, lesbian and gay members in leadership positions in the union": agree; disagree.
  (3) "Are you in favor of self-organization in UNISON?" agree; disagree; don't know.

of support for special measures to ensure representation of black, lesbian, and gay members in leadership positions in the union (e.g., through fair representation and self-organization). It is clear that more women respondents are in favor of these measures than their male counterparts.

This gender difference was less dramatic but in the same direction when branch activists were asked their views on self-organization. More than half of the women were in favor, but only 43 percent of the men. A third of male and female branch activists hadn't yet decided if they were in favor of self-organization or not. It is to be hoped that as more branches establish self-organized groups, more grass roots branch activists will have a direct and positive experience of working alongside self-organization. This will assist UNISON in drawing on representatives from across a number of constituencies, thus allowing it to better reflect and represent the interests of *all* its membership through self-organized and mainstream structures.

Employer Impact

UNISON addressed its internal equity issues creatively and with a large measure of success. For a variety of reasons, however, it has been less successful with employers. Given Britain's lack of a legislative framework to outlaw discrimination on the basis of sexuality, employers have shown considerable reluctance to address equality issues for sexual minorities unless pressed to do so by trade unions and other activist groups. At the same time, after the Conservative government changed the bargaining agenda in favor of employers in the 1980s and 1990s, trade unions found it difficult to make any gains for their members.[92] There has been a danger that equality issues would slide down the bargaining agenda as unions were forced to concentrate on minimizing the impact of contracting out, privatization, and job losses.

In spite of this difficult bargaining context, UNISON has sought to keep equity issues alive in its negotiations with employers. It has, for instance, won a number of equal pay cases for its women members and made some progress on sexuality issues.[93] For example, two of UNISON's largest employers, the National Health Service and the Metropolitan Police, now include sexuality in their equal opportunity policies. Gains have also been made with local government employers. Guidelines by the National Joint Councils call on local authorities to include the lesbian and gay press when advertising job vacancies, and those involved in recruitment and selection are required to undertake training in equal opportunities issues, including lesbian and gay equality issues.[94] In addition, the majority of local authorities now include sexual harassment in their overall harassment policies. The London Borough of Hounslow's Harassment Policy includes this definition: "Employees may face harassment because they are lesbian women or gay men. Such harassment includes written, verbal, physical abuse or insults, physical assault, denial of job opportunities or exclusion from certain types of work, comments/jokes that imply that lesbian and gay lifestyles are inferior, abnormal or should not be talked about, and exclusion from social groups which form at work on the basis of their sexuality."[95]

Nevertheless, a number of equality initiatives have been stalled, particularly in the area of same-sex relationship recognition. UNISON is on record supporting equal access to benefits relating to parenting, child care, pensions, and various types of leaves for same-sex couples, but negotiating these provisions with employers has been difficult. Employers argue that reform in the area requires government action via changes in pension law, and UNISON is pressing the Labour government to address this inequity. In fact, this argument has been successfully challenged in the private sector, with the result that a UNISON employer, British Gas, opened its pension scheme to include the same-sex partners of its employees, following a shift in attitude by the Inland Revenue.[96] This outcome represents an important precedent for UNISON in extending these rights with private and public sector employers and when lobbying the Labour government on the issue of equalizing relationship-based benefits.

Conclusion

From its creation in 1993, UNISON aimed to change and democratize its structures to ensure the participation and representation of all sections of its membership, including sexual minorities. The union's approach has been informed by social movements that struggled to develop equal opportunities in employment and service delivery in British public services. Lesbian and gay groups were particularly active in opposing Section 28 of the Local Government Act (1989) and in organizing within and outside trade unions to fight for sexual minority rights as part of a broader progressive coalition in opposition to the monetarist and anti-union agenda of the Conservative government.

Building on the work of its three partner unions, UNISON set itself the task of achieving proportionality and fair representation by the year 2000. Notwithstanding a fairly hostile industrial-relations climate and an unsupportive environment for sexual minority rights, considerable progress has been made. The research shows that lesbian and gay self-organization is alive and working well in UNISON. Self-organization appears to be remarkably effective in bypassing union bureaucracy and the blockages created by bigotry and homophobia; it has been able to release the energy and commitment of lesbians and gays, to educate them, and to empower them. In short, self-organization allows and encourages them to become active trade unionists. Self-organization ensures that lesbians and gays can raise their issues through democratic structures and pursue them through branch, regional, and national mainstream structures in a supported and strategic manner. It allows UNISON to link with other trade unions and sexual minority organizations and sexual diversity campaigns, nationally and internationally, in order to work collectively toward a union agenda within which sexual diversity issues have their rightful place.

The NLGC, regional lesbian and gay groups, and the developing branch groups play an active and visible role within the union. This has had immediate implications in every facet of union organization and policy. This process of change is necessarily developmental. During the early years of UNISON, much of the work had to focus on developing lesbian and gay self-organization and establishing links with other union structures (within UNISON and with other trade unions). Alongside that, lesbian and gay activists have sought to work through SOG and mainstream structures to ensure that all UNISON policies and activities incorporate lesbian and gay concerns. Future work needs to focus on national and local bargaining with employers to ensure that UNISON's policies begin to change the workplace. Other priorities for the coming years include the improvement of time-off rights for those active in lesbian and gay self-organization and the advice, representation, and legal assistance offered to lesbians and gay members at the branch and regional levels. Finally, to continue the progress being made on sexual minority rights through union representation and collective bargaining, the union needs to continue its campaign for legislation on sexual minority rights at the national and European levels.

Unsurprisingly, given the challenges they pose to entrenched structures and power systems, proportionality, fair representation, and self-organization remain contested (and sometimes misunderstood) in some parts of the union. As one NLGC member reflected, "In terms of self-organization, we are not just fighting for our corner; it's the whole notion of self-organization. There is some willingness in terms of the mainstream structures to actually take our issues on board, and there are some people who see self-organization as being quite valuable. My experience of being on the union's strategic review is that there are also other people that think it's a luxury. Well actually they think it's a complete waste of time" (Cara, April 1997).

Inevitably, as the SOGs push for change, opposition will continue from groups that feel they have something to lose from UNISON's ambitious attempt to democratize its structures and incorporate the issues and concerns of *all* its members. Rather than being afraid of provoking a backlash, it is perhaps wise to acknowledge that change usually doesn't come without a fight. Kerry, interviewed in July 1996, states that opposition comes when "you begin to reach the parts where you haven't had the argument yet." In her view, real progress will have occurred in UNISON when the SOGs are seen to be "having a positive contribution to make, to sort of improve things" rather than to be "causing trouble, throwing up obstacles." In some branches, regions, and service groups, this very positive culture change is starting to be achieved.

Notes

Acknowledgments: This chapter would not have been possible without the agreement, cooperation, and assistance of the UNISON National Lesbian and Gay Committee and UNISON Regional Lesbian and Gay Groups. In addition, I would like to thank the many UNISON lay members and officers who took time to talk with me about their experiences within UNISON. I am grateful to Hassan Ortega, Jacky Lewis, Rangit Kaur, Carola Towle, Kursad Kahramonoglu, Andy Stovold, and Gloria Mills for giving me access to UNISON meetings, documents, and information. Finally, my special thanks must go to Jacky Lewis, Rangit Kaur, Pauline Baseley, Sue Ledwith, and Gerald Hunt for their patience and good humor while providing me with comments on an earlier draft.

1. To protect confidentiality, pseudonyms are used to identify the UNISON lesbian and gay trade unionists interviewed.

2. M. Terry, "Negotiating the Government of UNISON: Union Democracy in Theory and Practice," *British Journal of Industrial Relations* 34, no. 1 (1996): 87–110.

3. M. Mann, S. Ledwith, and F. Colgan, "Women's Self-Organizing and Trade Union Democracy—Proportionality and Fair Representation: A Case Study of the UK Public Sector Trade Union UNISON," in *Strife: Sex and Politics in Unions,* ed. B. Pocock (London: Allen and Unwin, 1997), p. 194.

4. F. Colgan and S. Ledwith, "Sisters Organizing—Women and Their Trade Unions," in *Women in Organizations: Challenging Gender Politics,* ed. Ledwith and Colgan (Basingstoke, UK: Macmillan, 1996); Mann, Ledwith, and Colgan, "Women's Self-Organizing"; and F. Colgan and S. Ledwith, *Women in UNISON Report* (1999). The research was carried out by Fiona Colgan (CERB, University of North London) and Sue Ledwith (Oxford Brookes University). It was funded by the Economic and Social Research Council (ESRC) in Britain and is part of a two-year project examining trade union democracy, union structures, and the strategies of women union activists in UNISON and the Graphical Paper and Media Union (GPMU).

5. Labour Research Department, "Taking Pride in the Unions," *Labour Research* (July 1997): 16.

6. Labour Research Department, *Out at Work: Lesbian and Gay Workers Rights* (London: Labour Research Department, 1992), p. 2.

7. H. Bradley, "Divided We Fall: Trade Unions and Their Members in the 1990s," in "Unions on the Brink? The Future of the Movement," *Management Research News* 5, no. 5/6 (1993); Trades Union Congress (TUC), *New Unionism: Organizing for Change* (London: TUC National Seminar, 15 March 1997); *TUC, New Unionism, New World: Organizing Across Frontiers* (London: TUC National Seminar, 1997).

8. M. French, "Love, Sexualities and Marriage: Strategies and Adjustments," in *Modern Homosexualities,* ed. K. Plummer (London: Routledge, 1992), p. 87.

9. T. Barnett, "Profile: Tim Barnett, Executive Director, the Stonewall Group," *Equal Opportunities Review,* no. 39 (September–October 1991): 31; D. Cooper, *Sexing the City: Lesbian and Gay Politics Within the Activist State* (London: Routledge, 1994), p. 19.

10. A. Palmer, *Less Equal Than Others: A Survey of Lesbians and Gay Men at Work* (London: Stonewall, 1993); and Social and Community Planning Research, *Discrimination Against Gay Men and Lesbians* (London: Social and Community Planning Research, 1995).

11. Stonewall, *Stonewall Factsheet: Public Opinion on Lesbian and Gay Rights* (London: Stonewall, 1997).

12. Colgan and Ledwith, "Sisters Organizing"; A. Phizacklea and R. Miles, "The British Trade Union Movement and Racism," in *Racism and Anti-Racism: Inequalities, Opportunities and Policies,* ed. A. Brahmin, A. Rattansi, and R. Skellington (London: Sage, 1992); Trade Union Disability Alliance, *TUDA News* (December 1997); Labour Research Department, "Taking Pride in the Unions."

13. Trades Union Congress, *Civil Rights for Disabled People: A TUC Statement* (London: Trades Union Congress, 1995); D. Brindle, "Shaky Step Forward," *Guardian,* 27 November 1996.

14. D. Northmore, "What Is There Left to Do?" *Pink Paper,* 26 December 1997, pp. 7–8.

15. Labour Research Department, *Out at Work,* p. 7.

16. N. Millward et al., *Workplace Industrial Relations in Transition* (Aldershot, UK: Dartmouth, 1992).

17. J. Jensen, C. Reddy, and E. Hagen, *Feminization of the Labour Force* (Cambridge: Cambridge University Press, 1988).

18. R. Martin et al., "The Legislative Reform of Union Government 1979–1993," in "Unions on the Brink? The Future of the Movement," *Management Research News* 5, no. 5/6 (1993).

19. S. Milne, "Labour Rejects Unions' Hope of Partnership," *Guardian* (30 December 1996).

20. Millward et al., *Workplace Industrial Relations in Transition;* I. Beardwell, ed. *Contemporary Industrial Relations* (Oxford: Oxford University Press, 1997).

21. S. Kessler and E. Bayliss, *Contemporary British Industrial Relations,* 2nd ed. (Basingstoke, UK: Macmillan, 1995), p. 153.

22. Trades Union Congress, *Lesbian and Gay Rights at Work: Report of a TUC Seminar for Trade Unionists* (London: Congress House, 1992).

23. Labour Research Department, *Out at Work.*

24. Labour Research Department, *Out at Work,* p. 17.

25. L. Briskin and P. McDermott, eds., *Women Challenging Unions: Feminism, Democracy, and Militancy* (Toronto: University of Toronto Press, 1993), p. 90; F. Colgan, "Recognizing the Lesbian and Gay Constituency in Trade Unions: Moving Forward in UNISON," *Industrial Relations Journal* (forthcoming December 1999).

26. Mann, Ledwith, and Colgan, "Women's Self-Organizing," p. 198.

27. Trades Union Congress, *Lesbian and Gay Rights at Work,* p. 11.

28. Labour Research Department, *Out at Work,* p. 20.

29. Trades Union Congress, *Unions Working for Lesbian and Gay Members* (London: Trades Union Congress, 1996); Trades Union Congress, *TUC Lesbian and Gay Conference, Pride at Work: Discussion Paper* (London: Trades Union Congress, 1997).

30. Trades Union Congress, *TUC Lesbian and Gay Conference, Pride at Work: Discussion Paper,* 1997, p. 1.

31. Trades Union Congress, *TUC Lesbian and Gay Conference, 1996: Conference Consultation* (London: Trades Union Congress, 1996).

32. Trades Union Congress, *TUC Lesbian and Gay Conference, Pride at Work: Report of Conference* (London: Trades Union Congress, 1997), p. 2.

33. Trades Union Congress, *Unions Working for Lesbian and Gay Members*; and Labour Research Department, "Taking Pride in the Unions."

34. COHSE-NALGO-NUPE, *A Framework for a New Union*, report of the COHSE, NALGO, and NUPE National Executives to the 1991 Annual Conferences (London: 1991), p. 1.

35. Terry, "Negotiating the Government of UNISON"; Mann, Ledwith, and Colgan, "Women's Self-Organizing," p. 199.

36. *UNISON Rulebook* (London: UNISON, 1994), rules B1.2 and B1.3.

37. Terry, "Negotiating the Government of UNISON."

38. Trades Union Congress, *Lesbian and Gay Rights at Work*, pp. 10–12.

39. UNISON, *Getting the Balance Right: Guidelines on Proportionality* (London: UNISON, 1994).

40. Mann, Ledwith, and Colgan, "Women's Self-Organizing," p. 201.

41. UNISON, *Getting the Balance Right*; and UNISON, *Code of Good Branch Practice* (London: UNISON, 1995).

42. UNISON, *Playing Fair: UNISON Guidelines on Fair Representation* (London: UNISON, 1997).

43. Colgan and Ledwith, *Women in UNISON Report*.

44. UNISON, *Strategic Review: Making Local Organization Our Priority* (London: UNISON, 1997), p. 2.

45. UNISON, *Strategic Review*, p. 2.

46. Colgan and Ledwith, *Women in UNISON Report*.

47. UNISON, *Integration and Participation in UNISON: From Vision to Practice*, Report of Joint Working Group (London: UNISON, 1995).

48. UNISON, *Code of Good Branch Practice* and *Playing Fair*.

49. Colgan, "Recognizing the Lesbian and Gay Constituency in Trade Unions."

50. C. Cockburn, *The European Social Dialogues: Strategies for Gender Democracy* (Brussels: Equal Opportunities Union, European Commission, 1995).

51. The seven Service Groups in UNISON coordinate pay and service-conditions policy in the areas where UNISON organizes: local government (857,513 members), health (464,090), higher education (48,254), water (22,892), gas (18,396), electricity (17,024), transport (3,683).

52. Interview with Gloria Mills, 1993.

53. M. Moriarty, *Working in UNISON for Lesbian and Gay Rights* (London: UNISON, Equal Opportunities, 1997), p. 3.

54. Mann, Ledwith, and Colgan, "Women's Self-Organizing," p. 219.

55. Moriarty, *Working in UNISON*, p. 7.

56. UNISON National Lesbian and Gay Conference, *Minutes of the Fourth National Lesbian and Gay Conference*, Manchester, 22–24 November 1996, p. 51.

57. UNISON National Lesbian and Gay Committee, *Annual Report* (London: UNISON, 1996) p. 2.

58. UNISON National Lesbian and Gay Committee, *Annual Report* (London: UNISON, 1997), p. 19.

59. UNISON National Lesbian and Gay Committee, *Annual Report*, 1996 (1997), p. 19.

60. Moriarty, *Working in UNISON*, p. 8.

61. Moriarty, *Working in UNISON*, p. 8.

62. UNISON National Lesbian and Gay Committee, *Annual Report*, 1997, p. 19.

63. UNISON National Lesbian and Gay Committee, *Annual Report*, 1995, 1996, 1997.

64. UNISON National Lesbian and Gay Committee, *Review of Organization and Strategy* (London: UNISON, November 1997), p. 4.

65. Colgan and Ledwith, *Women in UNISON Report*.

66. UNISON National Lesbian and Gay Committee Local Government Liaison Representatives, *Report from Local Government Liaison Representatives* (1997).

67. Colgan, "Recognising the Lesbian and Gay Constituency in Trade Unions."

68. UNISON National Lesbian and Gay Committee, *Annual Report,* 1995.

69. UNISON National Lesbian and Gay Committee, *Annual Report,* 1996.

70. UNISON National Lesbian and Gay Committee, *Annual Report,* 1997, p. 1.

71. UNISON National Lesbian and Gay Committee, *Annual Report,* 1997, p. 17.

72. UNISON National Lesbian and Gay Committee, *Annual Report,* 1996.

73. UNISON National Lesbian and Gay Committee, *Annual Report,* 1997.

74. War on Want/UNISON, *Pride World-Wide: Sexuality, Development, and Human Rights* (London: UNISON, 1996).

75. NEC SOG Liaison Committee, November 1996; NLGC Response to Development and Organization Committee, August 1996.

76. UNISON National Lesbian and Gay Committee, *Supplementary Reports and Further Information for the Fourth National Lesbian and Gay Conference* (London: UNISON, 1996).

77. UNISON National Lesbian and Gay Committee, *Annual Report,* 1997, p. 13.

78. Moriarty, *Working in UNISON.*

79. UNISON South East Lesbian and Gay Group, *Who We Are: Lesbians and Gay Men in UNISON* (Banstead, UK: UNISON South East, 1997), p. 2.

80. UNISON, "Yorkshire and Humberside Regional Lesbian and Gay Group," in *Out in UNISON* (London: UNISON Equal Opportunities, 1997) p. 2.

81. UNISON South East Lesbian and Gay Group, *Who We Are,* p. 2.

82. UNISON South East Lesbian and Gay Group, *Who We Are,* p. 3.

83. Colgan and Ledwith, *Women in UNISON Report.*

84. UNISON National Lesbian and Gay Committee, *Annual Report,* 1997, p. 3.

85. Moriarty, *Working in UNISON.*

86. Quoted in Moriarty, *Working in UNISON.*

87. UNISON National Lesbian and Gay Committee, *Review of Organization and Strategy.*

88. UNISON Electricity Service Group, *Improving the Working Life of Lesbian and Gay Members* (London: UNISON, 1997).

89. UNISON, *HIV and AIDS: A Guide for Branches* (London: UNISON, 1995); UNISON, *Harassment: A UNISON Guide to Policy and Representation* (London: UNISON Equal Opportunities, 1997).

90. UNISON National Lesbian and Gay Conference, *Minutes of the Fourth National Lesbian and Gay Conference,* 1996.

91. UNISON, *Election of General Secretary 1995: Candidates, Election Addresses* (London: UNISON, 1995), p. 3.

92. D. Marsh, *The New Politics of British Trade Unionism: Union Power and the Thatcher Legacy* (Basingstoke, UK: Macmillan, 1992).

93. K. Gilbert and J. Secker, "Generating Equality? Equal Pay, Decentralization and the Electricity Supply Industry," *British Journal of Industrial Relations* 32, no. 2 (1995): 389–411.

94. National Joint Councils, *Equalities: Changes to National Agreement—Equal Opportunities Guide* (London: National Joint Councils, 1995).

95. London Borough of Hounslow, "Harassment at Work Policy" (London: Borough of Hounslow, 1997).

96. J. Welch, "The Invisible Minority," *People Management,* 26 September 1996.

Gerald Hunt

---

15   Laboring for Rights in Global Perspective

The cases presented in this book highlight the real gains and considerable progress made by sexual minorities through alliances with organized labor. Since the 1980s, labor organizations in a growing number of locations around the world have helped to bring about change not only through policy and education initiatives within their own organizations, but also by pressing employers to adopt inclusive collective-agreement provisions and by lobbying governments for expansive reading of anti-discrimination provisions in human rights codes and other legislation. Some labor organizations have committed considerable financial and human resources to assist litigants in challenges before arbitrators, courts, and other tribunals. When large and influential trade unions such as CUPE in Canada, UNISON in the United Kingdom, ÖTV in Germany, and UNITE in the United States have taken up the challenge to fight for equal rights for gays, lesbians, bisexuals, and the transgendered, considerable progress has occurred very quickly, with a direct impact on thousands of people.

Some examples of what has been achieved include the following. Labor unions in Germany worked with community activists to remove from the penal code the notorious "Paragraph 175," which had made homosexual acts unlawful. The persistent work of unions such as the American-based UNITE made inclusive domestic-partner (including same-sex) health care benefits a reality for much of its membership. UNISON, the large and very influential British union, made equality issues, including those of concern to gays and lesbians, a core part of its mission. The Canadian Auto Workers' Union fought successfully for same-sex benefit coverage for its membership, in spite of extremely resistant employers such as Chrysler. In Australia, the political wing of the labor movement was an important ally in the struggle for sexual minority rights at the state and national levels. The American-based Service Employees International Union, grappling with all kinds of diversity issues since the early 1980s, now treats its Lavender Caucus as an important source of advice. In the Netherlands, the Christian Police Union fights for equal opportunities and practices in relation to sexual minorities, in spite of considerable opposition from its own membership.

Several other examples illustrate the important role organized labor can play beyond the boundaries of a given workplace. British unions have supported court and tribunal cases, taking a few to the European courts, thus providing a dramatic example of the financial and legal assistance labor can extend. Some unions have gone even farther, undertaking costly and time-consuming litigation on their own. The Canadian-based CUPE, for example, successfully undertook to challenge—all the way to the Ontario Court of Appeal, and over a four-year period—the exclusively heterosexual definition of "spouse" contained in the Income Tax Act. Many unions have shown a willingness to lobby governments for change in discriminatory policies and legislation, and some have used their leverage to influence political parties in the development of progressive policies and positions on sexual diversity, especially in countries such as Australia and Britain where labor-oriented parties retain official links to the union movement.

There have also been significant developments among many of the world's largest trade union federations. The British Trades Union Congress, the Canadian Labour Congress, FNV in the Netherlands, DGB in Germany, the Australian Council of Trade Unions, and the American Federation of Labor–Congress of Industrial Organizations (AFL-CIO) now have proactive gay and lesbian policies, and many financially support caucuses that help to keep sexual diversity a dynamic issue.

The story is not one of uniform success, however. In many parts of the world, organized labor has been largely unresponsive to sexual orientation issues. Labor movements throughout Africa, India, the South Pacific, South America, Asia, Russia, China, and Eastern Europe appear to be inactive on equality issues related to sexuality; some are openly antagonistic.[1] Clearly, there is a global divide. In North America, Australia, and many parts of Europe, gays and lesbians enjoy a fairly high level of support from organized labor; in the rest of the world, they do not. The impact of this divide is at its starkest when we compare neighboring settings such as Australia and the South Pacific. Australia has an elaborate set of legal and constitutional protections for sexual minorities, and a labor movement that is highly responsive to the needs of gays and lesbians in the workplace and society at large. In contrast, throughout much of the South Pacific islands, homosexual acts remain illegal, often punishable by prison terms, and the labor movement shows little support for change.

In those countries where organized labor has been most active, significant differences in response occur among the unions and sectors. Overall, public sector unions and national, central labor federations have tended to lead the way. As Ostenfeld points out in his chapter on Australia, by 1980, trade unions representing such public sector workers as teachers, social workers, and government workers had all adopted anti-discrimination policies inclusive of their lesbian and gay membership, as had national white-collar union confederations, some of which were also promoting their ideas within the Australian Council of Trade Unions. Similarly, larger public sector unions have been very active on sexual diversity issues for a decade or more in Germany, the Netherlands, Canada, and Britain. In most cases, these unions have worked in tandem with large labor federations, creating a formidable defense against opposition. As Rayside points out, ABVAKABO, the largest public sector union in the Netherlands, along with the Dutch labor federation, FNV, were early and complementary leaders in promoting equity for sexual minorities. The alliance between the British Trades Union Congress and UNISON, the largest public sector union, also illustrates this pattern, as does the partnership between the Canadian Union of Public Employees and the Canadian Labour Congress. A similar pattern is emerging in the United States, where public sector unions such as AFT, SEIU, and AFSCME are among the most assertive on sexual diversity issues and have helped to push the AFL-CIO in this direction. As a result, the AFL-CIO is now more supportive of sexual minority rights than at any other point in its history. As Goldberg-Hiller notes in his chapter, fourteen years after the federation went on record in support of gay and lesbian rights, it finally made Pride at Work an official constituency group in 1997.

In contrast, some unions, mainly in the private sector and in male-dominated crafts and industries, have been silent at best on sexual diversity issues, at worst antagonistic. As Frank points out in her chapter, many American unions neither broach the subject of sexual orientation issues to their members, nor welcome the introduction of such issues into the union discourse. In many of the building trades, lesbian and gay construction workers routinely hide their identities and hesitate to organize gay and lesbian union caucuses. My own research on Canada revealed a number of unions to be fairly hostile to sexual diversity issues. One union in the building trades, for example, reported bargaining for a range of benefits for members that would include current heterosexual partners as well as partners from previous relationships, but drew the line at same-sex coverage. Some unions affiliated with the Dutch Christian labor federation—public and private sector—continue to argue against same-sex relationship recognition, even though the federation itself has pushed for such inclusion in benefit coverage. Nevertheless, some predominately private sector, male-dominated unions such as the Canadian Auto Workers and the miners unions in Britain have been very active on sexual diversity issues and offer commendable and noteworthy exceptions to these trends.

Regional variation within countries emerges as another trend differentiating labor responses to sexual orientation issues. Support is more likely to be found in urban centers—most labor gay and lesbian caucuses are based in major cities, although some have membership from smaller centers—and in areas known to be less politically conservative. In the United States, for instance, there has been much more activism in the large urban centers on the west and east coasts than in other settings. In Canada, the politically conservative province of Alberta has seen less progress on sexual diversity issues generally, and in unions in particular (even in public sector unions), than other parts of the country. The same is true for the politically conservative state of Tasmania in Australia. Similar variations occur in Europe; alliances between sexual minorities and labor have been strong in a number of northwestern countries, but weak or absent in most eastern and southern countries such as Spain and Greece.

The partnerships that have emerged between sexual diversity activists and organized labor have not come about without a struggle. Only after years of persistent activism and a number of failed attempts have American activists begun to achieve stronger and more successful links with labor. Similarly, only after decades of confrontation and many disappointments can Australian gays and lesbians claim to have one of the best relationships with labor found anywhere in the world. Even in settings with a reputation of relative acceptance of sexual diversity, such as the Netherlands, unions have needed some convincing to work alongside gay and lesbian activists. In South Africa, where organized labor played a key role in developing new constitutional arrangements inclusive of gays and lesbians, recent appeals by activists for union support and assistance have proved problematic. As the case studies in this volume attest, however, once they become committed, some unions respond in extraordinary ways, not only at the bargaining table and in political lobbying efforts, but within their own organizational cultures.

Why Progress?

What accounts for the growing number of positive alliances between organized labor and sexual diversity activists in North America, Europe, and Australia? Many of the reasons for these developments can be found in a series of changes that have occurred across the industrialized world since the mid-1970s. These changes include the erosion of the so-called post–World War II settlement, the transformation of union demographics, and the escalation of "new social movement" activism. All of these developments created openings for minorities to raise and successfully pursue their concerns.

The post–World War II period was a major turning point in the history of industrial-relations practices and related government policy.[2] The economic depression of the 1930s, the labor conflicts of the 1920s through the 1940s, and the war itself had all provided sufficient political and economic disruption to act as a catalyst for a massive review and restructuring of social and industrial policy throughout much of the developed world. The postwar settlement—a period marked by a shift to Keynesian macroeconomic policies, the development or expansion of a welfare state, and commitments to such things as full employment—has become the hallmark of industrial and social policy for many industrialized countries. In concert with these policy shifts were legislative initiatives throughout much of the industrialized world designed to contain labor-management conflict. Measures such as the Taft-Hartley Act in the United States were designed to bring peace and order to anarchic and often violent relations between unions and bosses, in part by recognizing in law the right of unions to represent workers and bargain collectively on their behalf. During this period as well, many countries, especially in Europe, moved toward a philosophy of tripartism whereby labor, management, and government were construed as working together to develop social and economic policies.

Although the details of these developments vary throughout Europe, North America, and Australia, in all cases they created a situation in which organized labor acquired significantly more power and stability than it had in the past. From this more solid footing, labor was able to focus on maximizing economic benefits for its members. The relative prosperity of the 1950s and 1960s increased the capacity of trade unions to secure major improvements in the standard of living of their members. It was also at this time that employment-based benefits such as health care packages, pension plans, and various types of leaves were further established and expanded, largely as a result of collective bargaining. These developments were particularly pronounced in countries such as the United States where the social welfare system had been less developed than in Europe, but even in Europe, employment-based benefits were expanded. Also during this period, many countries began to ease restrictions on public sector unionization, resulting in a significant rise in union membership, especially within white-collar occupations and professions.

The postwar settlement began to come apart in the 1970s and early 1980s as part of another massive restructuring of the social, political, and economic landscape in the industrialized world. Several severe economic downturns increased unemployment and led governments to begin accumulating deficits. At the same time, government spending as a tool for improving the economy became more and more discredited, largely due to the rise of right-wing political leaders. These leaders, who espoused a return to free-market economics and vowed to undermine the power of organized labor, were typified by Thatcher in the United Kingdom and Reagan in the United States. These changes were more muted in the countries of Western Europe considered in this volume, but even there, steps have been taken to create a freer, less restrictive market, based on American and British ideas. Tripartite systems of policy-making have also been weakened, in some cases altogether excluding labor from formal political discourse.

By the 1990s, labor movements around the world were in trouble. Union membership was in serious decline in Great Britain, the United States, and most of Europe, and barely remaining stable in settings such as Canada and Australia. The industrial-relations systems that had been won at such cost to labor in the early years had been at least partially deregulated or altered in ways that provided a less constraining environment for employers and a less favorable situation for unions.

Accompanying these developments and partly as a result of them, there came a shift in union demographics. Public sector workers became a broader and more influential union membership, even though their unions, too, were under attack by deficit-cutting governments. This upward shift in membership from the public sector introduced more semiprofessionals, women, and minorities into the labor mosaic. The shift in employment patterns away from industrial work with its traditionally high rate of unionization also meant a shift in membership away from those with traditional working-class or proletarian identities. This created new challenges for labor solidarity and brought issues of gender, race, and diversity to the fore.

This complex juggernaut of economic, political, and demographic changes constituted a crisis for labor movements everywhere. While it forced some unions into a defensive posture, reengaging them with traditional core issues of wage and job security, it pushed other unions toward a recognition and legitimization of new constituencies and the issues they brought with them. Other social changes taking place in the same period intensified the pressure. During the 1970s and 1980s, the rise of social movements generally, and of activism around gender, race, ethnicity, disability, and sexual orientation specifically, helped to increase the visibility and intensity of diversity issues.

The women's movement was a particularly important source of pressure for change on organized labor. Throughout the 1960s and 1970s, more and more women joined forces to pursue the goal of eliminating gender-based discrimination in all facets of society, including the workplace. Within unions, feminists drew attention not only to issues of occupational segregation and salary discrepancies, but also to those of male-dominated union structures and organizational culture. Many of these concerns were relatively new to unions, and deeply challenging to the notion of labor solidarity, since they raised the specter of member-on-member conflict and discrimination. The changed union demographics and growing awareness of women's issues within the broader society eventually forced change. Women unionists established committees and caucuses, often within a less than friendly climate, slowly laying the foundations for radical change. By the mid 1980s, women were beginning to see their issues become part of labor's main agenda in many parts of the developed world.[3]

Feminist activism inside unions was often the critical first ingredient for wider change. Women were the first to raise issues beyond traditional working-class concerns and, in their struggles, opened minds to the fact that fellow workers might be part of the problem. Feminists generated the idea that union structures should be more representative, and they developed the notion of self-organization into caucuses. Thus, space was created for a broader set of equality debates over such things as race and sexual orientation, and a method of organizing around these concerns (caucuses) was developed and made to work. As many of the contributors to this book attest, women's caucuses were often the site where other voices and issues were heard, addressed, and legitimized.

A rise in gay and lesbian visibility in general, combined with an increasingly assertive rights movement, significantly augmented pressure for equity within labor movements. Activists saw the workplace as a site of discrimination, especially in relation to harassment and benefit policies.[4] Ironically, AIDS proved to be an important catalyst in raising gay and lesbian and associated issues. The spread of the epidemic among gays in particular alerted some unions and many of their members to the potential for discrimination. This was and is particularly the case with health care workers, because they provide services that can easily be discriminatory against people with HIV/AIDS, and because they themselves can easily be the subject of discrimination if known to be infected. Ostenfeld makes this point, noting that blue-collar, front-line workers in hospitals in the midst of the HIV/AIDS crisis in South Australia became more and more attuned to the problems of gay and lesbian discrimination, and more and more amenable to union policies designed to fight it.

Union activity in support of sexual orientation issues was further stimulated by anti-gay political activity. Examples include the homophobic Section 28 in the United Kingdom, and the Briggs Initiative in California, which had been designed to exclude gays and lesbians from the teaching profession. Unions were also drawn into campaigns for progressive law reform, such as the elimination of Paragraph 175 in Germany, and the passing of an inclusive constitution in South Africa.

As individual rights became more firmly secured in law during the late 1980s and early 1990s, either through legislative change or court interpretation, new battle lines were drawn around relationship recognition and benefit issues—matters that easily translated into union issues. Statutory protections gave lesbian and gay union members a sense of entitlement as well as confidence, increasing their demands for union support. Changes in the legal landscape have forced many private and public corporations to alter discriminatory policies and practices, and they have been a stimulus for union activity. Fears that employers might get ahead of unions on gay and lesbian rights has sometimes sparked unions to act.

Why Variation?

The interplay of the factors I have laid out here varies from country to country. Together, though, these dynamics have created a window of opportunity for labor and sexual minority-rights activists to work together. As we have seen, some labor organizations and some countries have opened this window wider than others. What accounts for these differences?

An important factor in shaping differences among countries, especially on the issue of same-sex partner benefits, has been the character of national social policies and programs. In much of continental Europe, for example, where there continue to be quite expansive social programs, unions have experienced less pressure to take up benefit-related equity issues. State-provided or state-financed medical and pension benefits are readily available, with equal access regardless of employment status. In contrast, in countries such as the United States, where most people access basic health care benefits through their employer, the issue is much more relevant for workers and their unions. In some other countries, employers offer a range of perks and benefits beyond state programs. Canada, for example, has universal, basic medical coverage for all citizens, but such things as prescription drugs, vision, and dental care are not included in the general plan and must be obtained (if at all) through employer-sponsored insurance schemes. These are highly valued benefits that unions have fought hard to establish and expand through collective bargaining. Traditionally, such insurance schemes have had provisions to cover heterosexual but not homosexual spouses and families, making them among the most visible signs of discrimination, and important sites for activism in a practical and symbolic sense. Benefits offered to employees for such things as bereavement leave, child care provisions, and educational, housing, and travel assistance usually exclude coverage for nontraditional families and same-sex partners. Ending discrimination in the heterosexual bias of these sorts of benefits has become a point of struggle for gays and lesbians and their unions.

Differences in the availability and source of these benefits among countries affect the role of unions in extracting such benefits as part of the employment contract, as well as the relative financial burden these benefits place on employers. In precisely those countries with less developed state social and medical programs, such as the United States, the battle to obtain coverage through the workplace has been the most intense.

The success or failure of sexual minority activists in turning their unions into allies, as well as the pace of these developments, depends in part on the extent of organized opposition to sexual diversity rights in the broader public arena. Largely because of right-wing, religious opposition, progress has been slower in countries such as the United States and totally impaired in the South Pacific region, in relation to lesbian and gay rights generally, and in labor alliances to fight for these rights specifically. Although several of the American cases described in this book are success stories that describe a growing number of labor alliances in spite of highly organized opposition, there remain many geographical areas and occupations sectors where obvious discrimination exists. In most of the United States, new initiatives for equity rights encounter a well-organized, politically well-connected, and highly effective conservative opposition. As Holcomb points out in her chapter about domestic partner coverage in the United States, the religious right is such a political force in some cities and states that it is extremely difficult to achieve nondiscrimination laws and contract language, much less domestic partner benefits. Religion-based intolerance has also been an important factor in Australian developments because a very conservative Catholic Church was integral to the early labor movement. As Ostenfeld points out, religious rhetoric for a long time provided justification for employment discrimination and reasons to block partnerships between labor and gay and lesbian activists. He argues that it was precisely the influence of the Irish-Catholic right that delayed the passage of anti-discrimination initiatives in New South Wales, Queensland, and West Australia. In Canada as well, in the areas of greatest religious conservatism such as Alberta, change has been the slowest and recent battles the most intense.

As the case studies in this volume indicate, there are major variations among sectors and individual unions. Some of this variation reflects differences in demographics and other union characteristics. Public sector unions, where support has been most pronounced, tend to have high female membership and are therefore most likely to be influenced by feminist activism. The public sector also has more occupations associated with higher education levels and professionalism, such as nursing, teaching, and social work, which arguably lead to more tolerant attitudes toward minorities. These are also occupations where the number of gays and lesbians is thought to be disproportionately large, making equity issues of direct concern to many union members. At the same time, occupational categories such as teaching and the health care professions can be particularly vulnerable for gays and lesbians (some of the more blatant discrimination has been directed toward teachers, for example), thus reinforcing the need for formal protection within their unions and in collective agreements. In the public sector, equity issues in general are likely to be a subject of debate and policy-making, which makes issues about sexuality seem less foreign.

Size and strength are other factors that help to explain the differences that occur among unions. Unions vary in membership numbers and dues generated, obviously affecting what they can do. Unions that operate in large organizations and sectors, and especially in relatively high-wage public sectors, are likely to have better financial and human resources than smaller unions or those in low-wage sectors. Larger, more financially secure unions are more likely to have the ability and incentive to go beyond basic survival and wage issues, and to have the head office resources to initiate and support educational programs and caucuses. Clearly, most of the progressive unions mentioned in this book are large and financially secure, many with staff resources such as secretaries, lawyers, and equity officers to provide assistance to minority activists.

Other factors shaping union response are the culture of the union and its leadership. Unions that are male-dominated, representing workers and jobs shaped by a strong masculine ethos, such as those often found in the building trades, are less likely to engage with sexual diversity activists. By contrast, unions with a more democratic and egalitarian culture, such as the Canadian Auto Workers Union, are more likely to be active on a whole range of equity issues. Similarly, unions with leadership supportive of women's issues and minority concerns in general are more likely to support and initiate action on sexual orientation.

Hawai'i demonstrates the relationship between labor's response and the issue being raised. As Goldberg-Hiller points out, unions were much more reluctant to engage when the issue was framed as "the right to marry" versus individual protection from workplace discrimination or equalization of employment benefits. Marriage, it would seem, is a very demanding test of labor's commitment. This suggests that the nature of the issue being raised makes a difference in the willingness of labor to be involved and in the outcomes that are likely to accrue.

Another factor beginning to play a role in the level and pace of union response, and one that will almost certainly increase in significance, is peer pressure. As more and more unions become identified as supportive of lesbian and gay rights, it will become harder and harder for others to remain inactive and silent, let alone antagonistic. My own research highlights this factor quite dramatically. The response of Canadian unions had shifted significantly over the three-year period of my studies, and many of the more recently active unions and provincial federations cited the impact and pressure of the Canadian Labour Congress and other unions as a key reason for their actions. Interunion learning and pressure of this type will probably be a very important catalyst to developments within and between nations in the years to come.

Conclusion

During the 1990s, there has been a significant increase in the number of unions and labor federations around the world prepared to speak out in favor of sexual diversity, and increasing numbers are prepared to take action to back up their words. Some contributors to this volume emerge with less optimism than others about what has been done and what is possible. This is partly a reflection of the different social and political contexts they write about, but also a measure of the different analytical frameworks of the authors themselves.

Those unions that already have a history of support for these issues appear to have deepened their commitment over the past few years, offering a set of role models for others. It is unlikely that this momentum will stop, and it should spread to more and more regions over the coming decade. Some contributors to this volume suggest that the next wave of intense activity may well come from international bodies such the International Labor Organization (ILO) and the Public Service International (PSI). Activists are already seeing developments in these areas. The PSI, for example, appointed a staff person with a specific mandate to foster gay and lesbian equality among its several hundred affiliates around the world. Actions such as this could be of tremendous assistance to activists in locations such as the South Pacific and parts of Africa, where speaking out on sexuality issues can be extremely dangerous.

Much of the progress we see has come after years of hard work by feminists and other activists, as well as from the early recognition of the need for support by at least a few unions. The American, Canadian, European, Australian, and South African chapters all point to the impact of feminist organizing inside unions and the space they created for other minority activists. Noteworthy as well is the important role played by caucuses in initiating discussion about gay and lesbian concerns and bringing these issues to the attention of the union hierarchy, as well as their ongoing role in keeping these issues alive and active within their unions.

So far, the record of organized labor in taking up issues related to sexual orientation has been mixed. Because of stark variations between regions of the world, gays and lesbians in many parts of North America, Europe, and Australia enjoy a high level of support from organized labor, but in most other parts of the world, they receive no support at all. Many factors contribute to the overall experience of being homosexual in different parts of the world, but the level of trade union support for sexual minority rights in a given setting has become a significant factor in shaping this experience. Yet we have seen that labor's voice has been completely silent in some parts of the world and with respect to some controversial issues. The absence of labor support in the Hawai'i marriage cases is one example. Elsewhere, organized labor has shown little engagement with the concerns of the transgendered, despite there being urgent issues of job protection for those who challenge or cross gender boundaries. However, sexual diversity activists are increasingly engaged by these issues, which may emerge more prominently on labor's agenda over the next decade.

The coalitions between activists in the lesbian and gay rights movement and the labor movement offer insight into current debates in social theory. In particular, they illustrate the inadequacy of distinctions that are made between so-called "old" and "new" social movements. The lesbian and gay rights movement has been used to typify newer social movements, ones focused on cultural change, whereas the labor movement is used as the model of older forms of social movements concerned only with "materialistic" goals. The cases in this volume highlight the inflexibility of such distinctions. We find many examples of labor assertively pursuing not only materialistic goals, but social and cultural ones as well. Likewise, we see gay and lesbian activists increasingly focused on workplace issues, including the distribution of social goods and benefits, as well as cultural change. The cases illustrate that old and new social movements do not exist in isolation from one another, and they are capable of coming together in the pursuit of common interests and issues, often involving the same people.

The cases presented here indicate that union participation in the struggle for recognition of sexual diversity rights can make a difference. The accomplishments to date—mostly within the last ten years—are impressive, in spite of some failures and shortcomings. Millions of gays and lesbians now have formal redress within their unions to help combat discrimination, and growing numbers have full access to benefit packages and pension schemes that only a short time ago were beyond their reach. Perhaps even more importantly, organized labor's educational and political action has helped to expose myths and overturn long-standing stereotypes about homosexuality, helping in the process to create a better, less prejudicial world for everyone.

Notes

1. Although some of these countries are not covered in the book, the author attended a trade union and homosexuality conference held in Amsterdam in July 1998 where representatives from some of these countries were in attendance. Based on reports made by people at this conference,

as well as with conversations with labor leaders around the world, the statement would appear to be true. Additional research in parts of the world not covered by this book is needed.

2. For a more elaborated discussion of these events and their impact on labor movements see, for example, S. Lipset, ed., *Unions in Transition: Entering the Second Century* (San Francisco: ICS Press,1986); M. Golden and J. Pontusson, eds., *Bargaining for Change: Union Politics in North America and Europe* (Ithaca: Cornell University Press, 1992); T. Kochan, H. Katz, and R. McKersie, *The Transformation of American Industrial Relations* (Ithaca: Cornell University Press, 1994); M. Dubofsky, *The State and Labor in Modern America* (Chapel Hill: University of North Carolina Press, 1994); W. Carroll, ed., *Organizing Dissent: Contemporary Social Movements in Theory and Practice,* 2nd ed. (Toronto: Garamond Press, 1997); D. Yergin and J. Stanislaw, *The Commanding Heights: The Battle Between Government and the Marketplace That Is Remaking the Modern World* (New York: Simon and Schuster 1998).

3. See L. Briskin and P. McDermott, eds., *Women Challenging Unions: Feminism, Democracy, and Militancy* (Toronto: University of Toronto Press, 1993); D. Cobble, ed., *Women and Unions: Forging a Partnership* (Ithaca: Cornell University Press, 1993); B. Pocock, ed., *Strife: Sex and Politics in Labour Unions* (St. Leonards, Australia: Allen and Unwin,1997).

4. Elaborate accounts of the rise and changing character of gay and lesbian activism are covered in D. Altman, *The Homosexualization of America* (New York: Beacon Press, 1982); M. Cruikshank, *The Gay and Lesbian Liberation Movement* (New York: Routledge, 1992); B. Adam, *The Rise of a Gay and Lesbian Movement,* rev. ed. (New York: Twayne, 1995); U. Vaid, *Virtual Equality: The Mainstreaming of Gay and Lesbian Liberation* (New York: Anchor Books, 1995); D. Rayside, *On the Fringe: Gays and Lesbians in Politics* (Ithaca: Cornell University Press, 1998); C. Stychin, *A Nation by Rights* (Philadelphia: Temple University Press, 1998).

About the Contributors

CHRISTIAN ARTHUR BAIN has published a newsletter and written a column in the *Advocate* (an American national lesbian and gay news magazine) on the work-related issues of sexual minorities. He lives and works in New York City.

FIONA COLGAN is Director of the Centre for Equality Research in Business and a Senior Lecturer in Industrial Relations and Organizational Studies at the University of North London. Her research interests include trade-union democracy and social movements. She recently coedited a book with Sue Ledwith, *Women in Organizations: Challenging Gender Politics* (Macmillan, 1996).

MIRIAM FRANK is Master Teacher of Humanities in the General Studies Program at New York University. She has collected oral histories with labor activists concerned with unions' response to gay and lesbian issues and is writing a book based on this material for Temple University Press.

JONATHAN GOLDBERG-HILLER is an Assistant Professor in the Department of Political Science at the University of Hawai'i. He is presently completing a book on the politics of same-sex marriage entitled *The Limits to Union* (University of Michigan Press, forthcoming).

PHIL GREASLEY is Project Director at the Lesbian and Gay Rights (LAGER) organization based in London, England. He has a long history of work in the social research field.

DESMA HOLCOMB is Research Director at the Union of Needletrades, Industrial, and Textile Employees in New York. She has negotiated domestic partner benefits and is co-author, with Miriam Frank, of the handbook *Pride at Work: Organizing for Gay Rights in Unions, 1990*. She was a founding national co-chair of Pride at Work, now affiliated with the AFL-CIO, and lives in New York City.

RONALD HOLZHACKER is a postdoctoral researcher and lecturer for European Union (EU) politics at the University of Twente, the Netherlands. Previously, he was a lecturer in European politics at the University of Michigan.

GERALD HUNT is an Associate Professor of Organizational Behavior and Industrial Relations at Nipissing University in North Bay, Canada. He is the author of several articles concerned with minority issues in organizations.

MAZIBUKO K. JARA is the National Manager of the National Coalition for Gay and Lesbian Equality, based in Johannesburg. He is an active member of the South African Communist Party and the HIV/AIDS Treatment Action Campaign. He is active in many other political, social development, demilitarization, and human rights struggles in South Africa.

JACQUELINE LECKIE is a Senior Lecturer of Anthropology at the Otago University in Dunedin, New Zealand. Her research interests focus on gender constructs in South Pacific societies.

SHANE OSTENFELD is a lecturer of Industrial Relations at the University of Newcastle in Australia. He recently completed his doctoral thesis on organized labor's response to sexual orientation in Australia.

CYNTHIA PETERSEN is a partner at the law firm of Sack Goldblatt Mitchell in Toronto, where she specializes in union-side labor law, human rights, and constitutional litigation.

DAVID RAYSIDE, Professor of Political Science at the University of Toronto, is the author of *On The Fringe: Gays and Lesbians in Politics* (Cornell University Press, 1998) as well as several articles on lesbian and gay politics in Britain, Canada, and the United States. He has also been an activist working on gay rights and feminist issues.

NAOMI WEBSTER is involved with the Coalition for Gay and Lesbian Equality in Johannesburg, South Africa, and works as a legal researcher for the Tshwaranang Legal Advocacy Center to end violence against women.